D0026756

THE HOMERIC
HYMN TO DEMETER

- read many
  Chodrow
  - excerpt

THE HOMERIC
HYMN TO DEMETER

TRANSLATION, COMMENTARY, AND
INTERPRETIVE ESSAYS

Edited by

Helene P. Foley

WITHDRAWN

PRINCETON UNIVERSITY PRESS

PRINCETON, NEW JERSEY

FLIP

COPYRIGHT © 1994 BY PRINCETON UNIVERSITY PRESS

"POLITICS AND POMEGRANATES" COPYRIGHT © 1977 BY MARILYN A. KATZ

PUBLISHED BY PRINCETON UNIVERSITY PRESS, 41 WILLIAM STREET,

PRINCETON, NEW JERSEY 08540

IN THE UNITED KINGDOM: PRINCETON UNIVERSITY PRESS,

CHICHESTER, WEST SUSSEX

LIBRARY OF CONGRESS CATALOGING-IN-PUBLICATION DATA

THE HOMERIC HYMN TO DEMETER : TRANSLATION, COMMENTARY, AND

INTERPRETIVE ESSAYS / HELENE P. FOLEY.

P. CM.

INCLUDES A TRANSLATION, THE GREEK TEXT, A LITERARY COMMENTARY, A

DISCUSSION OF THE ELEUSINIAN MYSTERIES AND RELATED CULTS OF DEMETER,

AN INTRODUCTORY ESSAY BY H. P. FOLEY, AND 5 PREVIOUSLY PUBLISHED

ARTICLES ON THE POEM AND RELATED ISSUES.

INCLUDES BIBLIOGRAPHICAL REFERENCES AND INDEX.

ISBN 0-691-06843-7 — ISBN 0-691-01479-5

1. HYMN TO DEMETER.   2. HYMNS, GREEK (CLASSICAL)—TRANSLATIONS

INTO ENGLISH.   3. HYMNS, GREEK (CLASSICAL)—HISTORY AND CRITICISM.

4. DEMETER (GREEK MYTHOLOGY) IN LITERATURE.   5. ELEUSINIAN MYSTERIES

IN LITERATURE.   6. DEMETER (GREEK MYTHOLOGY)—POETRY.   I. FOLEY,

HELENE P., 1942– .   II. HYMN TO DEMETER. ENGLISH & GREEK. 1993.

PA4023.H83H66 1993

883'.01—DC20   93-761

THIS BOOK HAS BEEN COMPOSED IN GALLIARD

THE PAPER USED IN THIS PUBLICATION MEETS THE MINIMUM

REQUIREMENTS OF ANSI/NISO Z39.48-1992 (R1997)

(*PERMANENCE OF PAPER*)

THIRD PRINTING, WITH BIBLIOGRAPHICAL ADDENDUM, AND FIRST

PRINTING IN THE MYTHOS SERIES, 1999

HTTP://PUP.PRINCETON.EDU

PRINTED IN THE UNITED STATES OF AMERICA

5   7   9   10   8   6   4

For Nicholas Foley

CONTENTS

ILLUSTRATIONS

PREFACE AND ACKNOWLEDGMENTS

OVER THE DECADE of the 1980s, the traditional Western canon has been subject to ardent defense and criticism. The privileging of the works of upper-class, Western, white males in standard introductory humanities courses across the United States has been at the center of this controversy. In many cases these courses have been adjusted to include a few token works by female, minority, or non-Western authors. Even this minimal gesture is more difficult in the case of Greco-Roman antiquity. Classical works often form a substantial part of the reading list of such courses, but few Greek and Roman authors were nonwhite or female. As a scholar and teacher of courses on women in antiquity, I often found myself consulted about what could be done. This book developed as part of an attempt to reconsider the syllabus of the typical core curriculum in response to the questions that have been raised about it. Western culture courses will continue to be taught (if not necessarily required) for many good reasons: above all to provide an understanding of the strengths and limits of the tradition. In reading Western literature critically, as anthropologists of the tradition, we must ask questions of the texts that the original authors might not have dreamed of asking. At the same time, when we introduce new texts into such courses, they should ideally continue to provoke dialogue of the same depth and complexity as well as to articulate in a provocative fashion with those already included.

Classical literature, far more explicitly than much later Western literature until the nineteenth century, virtually begs us to ask questions about gender. Plato and Aristotle confronted such issues directly. Most Greek comedies and tragedies commonly taught put gender conflict at the heart of the plot and allow their female characters to challenge male authority and assumptions: Aeschylus's *Oresteia*, Sophocles' *Antigone*, Euripides' *Medea* and *Bacchae*, Aristophanes' *Lysistrata*, to name a few. As male-generated texts, these works reflect anxieties and concerns experienced by at least some Greek males about the nature of their society. What is largely missing, however, is a female perspective that could provide a glimpse of what ancient women meant to each other and the concerns that were of greatest significance to them. Although we have very little to go on in this respect, the fragments of the poet Sappho have of late been successfully taught in translation to a broad, general audience. In my view the text that can best supplement Sappho in putting the experience of ancient women and its symbolic importance into some perspective is the Homeric *Hymn to Demeter*, even though the anonymous author (or authors) of the poem was far more likely to have been male. (Sappho herself wrote hymns, but those who recited in the public contexts where the *Hymn to Demeter* was likely to have been performed would have been largely or perhaps exclusively men.)

As will be emphasized in my interpretive essay (Part 2 of this book), the *Hymn* puts the female experience of the goddesses Demeter and Persephone, as well as the disguised Demeter's interactions with the mortal women of Eleusis, at the center of its narrative; it closes with the founding of the Eleusinian Mysteries, which accepted initiates of both sexes. The Demeter/Persephone myth was celebrated in all-female rites of Demeter. Because it was as participants in religious rites from marriages and funerals to festivals that ancient women engaged most directly and significantly in the public life of their culture, a poem that illuminates that experience can give us important insights into the lives of the Greek women of antiquity.

Nevertheless, there are many other reasons for giving this important poem a more central place than it has generally had in courses on Western culture and on classical antiquity. This book is in part an attempt to introduce general readers to the *Hymn to Demeter*, and to provide such readers with the background necessary to read the text in a knowledgeable and sophisticated fashion. In particular, I aim to show how the poem resonates with canonical texts like the Homeric epics, Greek drama, or the New Testament and how a knowledge of this text can correct a number of popular misapprehensions about ancient religion. Composed in the period between Homer and Hesiod and literature of the classical city-state, the *Hymn* offers a basis for discussing the transition between those two important periods and demonstrates the central role that ritual and cult (as opposed to myth) played in ancient religion; the poem also illustrates how the view of divinity offered in mystery cults differs from that represented in Homer and tragedy and permits us to examine a central religious mystery that is based on female experience and especially on the relation of mother to daughter. In addition, a knowledge of ancient mystery cults makes the transition to Christianity easier to locate historically and to understand.

By treating the *Hymn to Demeter* separately from the other Homeric hymns, I want to present the poem as a profound short epic, an outstanding representative of an often underrated literary form, and a brilliant work of literature in its own right. The earliest writers of Greek epic attributed an equal amount of prestige to hymnic poetry, the celebration of the deeds of the gods, and to heroic epic. As Hesiod put it in his famous cosmological poem the *Theogony*, itself an expanded hymn to the god Zeus: "Yet the poet, servant of the Muses, hymns the famous deeds of men of old and the blessed gods who inhabit Olympus." (99–101)[1] Yet hymns, including the Homeric hymns, have been relatively neglected in recent times. For all these reasons,

---

[1] See also *Odyssey* 1. 338. Clay 1989: esp. 4–5 discusses the tradition of the criticism of the Homeric hymns. In ancient Greek tradition, the hymn remained an important literary form and enjoyed renewed popularity in the Hellenistic period.

my interpretive essay aims to provide a broad range of insights into the text itself.

The *Hymn to Demeter* is a central text in Greek mythology courses precisely because it has shown itself to be accessible to analysis from many modern theoretical perspectives: Freudian and Jungian psychoanalysis, structuralism, sociological analysis of myth, myth and ritual theory. The poem and its subject, the myth of Demeter and Persephone, have also been of interest to a wide range of feminists such as sociologists Nancy Chodorow and Carol Gilligan; literary critic Marianne Hirsch, who is interested in representations of the mother/daughter relation; poet Adrienne Rich; and spiritual feminists interested in appropriating pagan myths and cults of goddesses to create a new religion revolving around female deity. In fact, the *Hymn to Demeter* has already found its way into women's studies courses. Although my interpretive essay (Part 2) discusses all critical approaches to the poem, it emphasizes the poem's insights into questions of gender and female experience. The *Hymn* offers a challenging perspective on the relation of male and female subjects to the forms of fantasy and power that shaped ancient Greek social life. The poem's cyclical rather than linear narrative (mother and daughter separate and unite eternally in a seasonal pattern) represents a female quest that differs significantly from the male quests embodied in the myths of Gilgamesh or Odysseus.

My translation of the *Hymn to Demeter* is designed to be literal but readable, while following as closely as possible the original lines of verse; the commentary gives the reader important literary and historical background. Readers interested in poetic translations of the *Hymn* should consult the efforts of Athanassakis (1976), Boer (1970), Hines (1972), and Sargent (1973). Although the *Hymn* represents a myth that had particularly deep associations with the cult whose founding it describes—to the point where participants imitated events in the narrative throughout the rites—I have deliberately chosen to separate the discussion of the content of the Mysteries themselves, along with other closely related cults of Demeter based on this myth, from my examination of the *Hymn* itself. Most of our sources for the Mysteries come from periods later than the *Hymn* and we do not know, even though parts of the cult are founded during its narrative, what form they may have taken at the early date of this poem. More important, scholarly discussion of the content of the Mysteries has tended to distract readers of the *Hymn* from examining the poem on its own terms. The Greek text is reprinted from the Oxford text of N. J. Richardson (1974) unless otherwise noted. It is included for the sake of readers who would like to follow the text and commentary with the original. I have been unable to acknowledge fully my debt to Richardson's magisterial commentary.

The interpretive essay, which represents my own reading of the *Hymn*, is in some respects openly tendentious. It also orients the reader to the collection of essays on the poem reprinted at the back of the book. Each of these essays on the *Hymn* was selected both for its intrinsic excellence and for the important role it has played in the history of criticism of the text. Each also represents a different approach to interpreting the poem. Because the methodologies employed in these essays have proved valuable in the study of Greek poetry generally, they expose readers to techniques that can be used elsewhere. Mary Louise Lord's essay builds on the work done in comparative studies in Mediterranean and Near Eastern mythology and oral epic to show how the same underlying story patterns are at work in the *Iliad*, the *Odyssey*, and the *Hymn to Demeter*. Jean Rudhardt's essay locates the *Hymn* and its narrative in the context of early Greek cosmology. Nancy Rubin's and Harriet Deal's narratological analysis illuminates the connections between the divine story that frames the narrative of the poem and the separate encounter between Demeter and mortals at its center. Marylin Arthur offers a reading of the poem that combines Freudian, feminist, and structuralist perspectives. Also included is an essay on the psychology of the mother/daughter relation by the sociologist Nancy Chodorow, which, together with the Freudian and post-Freudian material in the essay by Marylin Arthur, forms the background for my own interpretation of the mother/daughter relation in the poem.

Readers should begin the book with the translation and commentary, along with the section on the Eleusinian Mysteries and related cults of Demeter, because all the essays assume a knowledge of the text and the historical background of the Mysteries. My own interpretive essay depends on and adds to the arguments presented in the reprinted essays. It has been designed as a continuous argument, but its sections can be read separately. Readers with a theological or narratological bent will find of special interest the sections of the interpretive essay on "The 'Theology' of the Mysteries," "Gender Politics," and the "Psychology of the Mysteries," as well as the essays by Lord, Rubin and Deal, and Rudhardt. Mythology students will profit from the sections on "The 'Theology' of the Mysteries," "Variants of the Myth," "Gender Politics," and "The Mother/Daughter Romance," as well as the essays by Lord, Rudhardt, and Arthur; important extant versions of the myth in Greek and Roman antiquity are listed at the beginning of the commentary. Those concerned with gender studies will want to read both my interpretive essay and the essay by Arthur. The Appendix on "Athens and Eleusis" and "The *Hymn* as a Panhellenic Poem" addresses scholarly controversies tangential to a literary interpretation of the *Hymn to Demeter*. It treats the historical and literary context in which the *Hymn* was probably composed.

Because this book is designed to be accessible to the general reader, footnotes have been kept to a minimum and reference is made wherever possible to works in English. Spellings of a few familiar ancient Greek names (such as Aeschylus) are Latinized, their most familiar form in our culture; all other names, such as Korê, retain the Greek spelling. All abbreviations used in the text are defined in the Bibliography under the name of the relevant author, e.g., Page *GLP*. A reference such as "frag. 63 Nauck" indicates that Nauck is the editor of the volume of fragments referred to. The contributed articles in Part 3, all previously published, have been edited only to conform stylistically with each other and the book as a whole (see individual notes at article beginnings for other minor changes). Jenny Clay's recent literary study of the Homeric hymns, *The Politics of Olympus*, came out after this book was well under way. I hope that this book will whet the appetite of enthusiastic readers to read Clay's study, Richardson's commentary, and the recent essay by Parker (1991), as well as other books and essays cited in the notes and in the bibliography.

I am extremely grateful for the valuable comments I have received on an early draft of the manuscript from the students in my 1990 class on Women in Antiquity. Darice Birge, Erwin Cook, Frederick Griffiths, Marianne Hirsch, Vivian Nyitray, Dirk Obbink, Robert Parker, Nicholas Richardson, Richard Seaford, Karen Van Dyke, and Christian Wolff offered helpful suggestions for revision on an earlier draft. Duncan Foley gave the manuscript a final reading. I also profited from the opportunity to present oral versions of some parts of the interpretive essay at Smith College, Reed College, Emory University, Georgia State University, Oxford University, and a seminar in the Columbia Humanities Program. Deborah Boedeker and the other anonymous referee for Princeton University Press also provided valuable suggestions for revision. Marta Steele served as a careful copy editor for the Press. Revisions of this manuscript were made during the tenure of a Guggenheim Fellowship.

I also wish to thank *Classical Journal* for the permission to reprint the essay by M. L. Lord, to *Quaderni Urbinati di Cultura Classica* for the permission to reprint the essay by N. Felson-Rubin and H. Deal, to The Johns Hopkins University Press and *Arethusa* for the permission to reprint the essay by M. Arthur, to *Museum Helveticum* for permission to reprint a translated version of the essay by J. Rudhardt, to Stanford University Press for the permission to reprint the essay by N. Chodorow, and to Oxford University Press for the permission to reprint N. J. Richardson's Greek text from *The Hymn to Demeter* (1974). I am also grateful for permission to quote from modern poems influenced by the Demeter/Persephone myth. An excerpt from Edgar Lee Master's "Persephone" appears through the permission of Ellen C. Masters. A quotation from Dorothy Wellesley's "Demeter in Sicily" appears courtesy of Withers Solicitors, 20 Essex Street, London WC2R 3AL. New Directions Publishing Corporation and Carcanet Press granted permission to quote from H.D.'s "Demeter," in her *Collected Poems 1912–1944*, copyright 1982 by "The Estate of Hilda Doolittle." Quotations from Kathleen Raine's "Transit of the Gods" appear courtesy of Hamish, Hamilton, 57–59 Long Acre, London WC2 E9JL. Harcourt, Brace, Jovanovich, Inc. granted permission to quote from Robert Lowell's "The Mills of the Kavanaughs," in *The Mills of the Kavanaughs*, copyright 1951 by Robert Lowell and renewed 1979 by Harriet W. Lowell. An extract from "The Return of Persephone" by A. D. Hope from his *Collected Poems* appears courtesy of A. D. Hope and Collins/Angus & Robertson Publishers. Excerpts from *The Book of Persephone* by Robert Kelly (copyright 1978 by Robert Kelly, all rights reserved) are reprinted by permission of the publisher, McPherson and Company, P.O. Box 1126, Kingston, New York 12401. A part of Carolyn Kizer's "Persephone Pauses," from *Mermaids in the Basement*, copyright 1984 by Carolyn Kizer, is reprinted with the permission of Copper Canyon Press, P.O. Box 271, Port Townsend, Washington 98368. Excerpts from Michèle Roberts's "Persephone descends to the underworld" and "Persephone gives birth," published in *The Mirror of the Mother*, are reprinted by permission of Methuen London. Excerpts from Enid Dame's "Persephone" appear courtesy of West End Press, and part of Margaret Atwood's *Double Persephone* is reprinted by permission of Margaret Atwood, (c) 1980. W. W. Norton, Inc., granted permission to quote from Adrienne Rich's *Of Woman Born*.

I am dedicating this book to my son Nicholas Foley, who loves the story told in the *Hymn to Demeter*.

PART ONE

THE TEXT AND TRANSLATION,

COMMENTARY, AND BACKGROUND

THE HOMERIC *HYMN TO DEMETER*

Translated by Helene P. Foley

Demeter I begin to sing,* the fair-tressed awesome goddess,	1

Demeter I begin to sing,* the fair-tressed awesome goddess,   1
herself and her slim-ankled daughter whom Aidoneus**
seized; Zeus, heavy-thundering and mighty-voiced, gave her,
without the consent of Demeter of the bright fruit and golden
    sword,
as she played with the deep-breasted daughters of Ocean,   5
plucking flowers in the lush meadow—roses, crocuses,
and lovely violets, irises and hyacinth and the narcissus,
which Earth grew as a snare for the flower-faced maiden
in order to gratify by Zeus's design the Host-to-Many,**
a flower wondrous and bright, awesome for all to see,   10
for the immortals above and for mortals below.
From its root a hundredfold bloom sprang up and smelled
so sweet that the whole vast heaven above
and the whole earth laughed, and the salty swell of the sea.
The girl marveled and stretched out both hands at once   15
to take the lovely toy. The earth with its wide ways yawned
over the Nysian plain; the lord Host-to-Many rose up on her
with his immortal horses, the celebrated son of Kronos;
he snatched the unwilling maid into his golden chariot
and led her off lamenting. She screamed with a shrill voice,   20
calling on her father, the son of Kronos highest and best.
Not one of the immortals or of humankind
heard her voice, nor the olives bright with fruit,
except the daughter of Persaios; tender of heart
she heard it from her cave, Hekate of the delicate veil.   25
And lord Helios, brilliant son of Hyperion, heard
the maid calling her father the son of Kronos. But he sat apart
from the gods, aloof in a temple ringing with prayers,
and received choice offerings from humankind.

---

* The following divine genealogy will assist the reader in following the text. Gaia (Earth) and Ouranos (Sky) are the parents of Rheia and Kronos, who are in turn parents of Zeus, Hades, and Demeter. Zeus and Hades are thus both sons of Kronos. Demeter and Zeus are the parents of Korê/Persephone.
    ** Hades

ΥΜΝΟΣ ΕΙΣ ΔΗΜΗΤΡΑ

Δήμητρ' ἠΰκομον σεμνὴν θεὸν ἄρχομ' ἀείδειν,　　　　　1
αὐτήν ἠδὲ θύγατρα τανίσφυρον ἣν Ἀϊδωνεὺς
ἥρπαξεν, δῶκεν δὲ βαρύκτυπος εὐρύοπα Ζεύς,
νόσφιν Δήμητρος χρυσαόρου ἀγλαοκάρπου
παίζουσαν κούρῃσι σὺν Ὠκεανοῦ βαθυκόλποις,　　　　5
ἄνθεά τ' αἰνυμένην ῥόδα καὶ κρόκον ἠδ' ἴα καλὰ
λειμῶν' ἂμ μαλακὸν καὶ ἀγαλλίδας ἠδ' ὑάκινθον
νάρκισσόν θ', ὃν φῦσε δόλον καλυκώπιδι κούρῃ
Γαῖα Διὸς βουλῇσι χαριζομένη πολυδέκτῃ
θαυμαστὸν γανόωντα, σέβας τό γε πᾶσιν ἰδέσθαι　　10
ἀθανάτοις τε θεοῖς ἠδὲ θνητοῖς ἀνθρώποις·
τοῦ καὶ ἀπὸ ῥίζης ἑκατὸν κάρα ἐξεπεφύκει,
†κῶδιστ' ὀδμῆ† πᾶς δ' οὐρανὸς εὐρὺς ὕπερθε
γαῖά τε πᾶσ' ἐγέλασσε καὶ ἁλμυρὸν οἶδμα θαλάσσης.
ἡ δ' ἄρα θαμβήσασ' ὠρέξατο χερσὶν ἂμ' ἄμφω　　　15
καλὸν ἄθυρμα λαβεῖν· χάνε δὲ χθὼν εὐρυάγυια
Νύσιον ἂμ πεδίον τῇ ὄρουσεν ἄναξ πολυδέγμων
ἵπποις ἀθανάτοισι Κρόνου πολυώνυμος υἱός.
ἁρπάξας δ' ἀέκουσαν ἐπὶ χρυσέοισιν ὄχοισιν
ἧγ' ὀλοφυρομένην· ἰάχησε δ' ἄρ' ὄρθια φωνῇ　　　20
κεκλομένη πατέρα Κρονίδην ὕπατον καὶ ἄριστον.
οὐδέ τις ἀθανάτων οὐδὲ θνητῶν ἀνθρώπων
ἤκουσεν φωνῆς, οὐδ' ἀγλαόκαρποι ἐλαῖαι,
εἰ μὴ Περσαίου θυγάτηρ ἀταλὰ φρονέουσα
ἄϊεν ἐξ ἄντρου Ἑκάτη λιπαροκρήδεμνος,　　　　　25
Ἥλιός τε ἄναξ Ὑπερίονος ἀγλαὸς υἱός,
κούρης κεκλομένης πατέρα Κρονίδην· ὁ δὲ νόσφιν
ἧστο θεῶν ἀπάνευθε πολυλλίστῳ ἐνὶ νηῷ
δέγμενος ἱερὰ καλὰ παρὰ θνητῶν ἀνθρώπων.

Against her will Hades took her by the design of Zeus   30
with his immortal horses—her father's brother,
Commander- and Host-to-Many, the many-named son of Kronos.
So long as the goddess gazed on earth and starry heaven,
on the sea flowing strong and full of fish,
and on the beams of the sun, she still hoped   35
to see her dear mother and the race of immortal gods.
For so long hope charmed her strong mind despite her distress.
The mountain peaks and the depths of the sea echoed
in response to her divine voice, and her goddess mother heard.
Sharp grief seized her heart, and she tore the veil   40
on her ambrosial hair with her own hands.
She cast a dark cloak on her shoulders
and sped like a bird over dry land and sea,
searching. No one was willing to tell her the truth,
not one of the gods or mortals;   45
no bird of omen came to her as truthful messenger.
Then for nine days divine Deo*** roamed over the earth,
holding torches ablaze in her hands;
in her grief she did not once taste ambrosia
or nectar sweet-to-drink, nor bathed her skin.   50
But when the tenth Dawn came shining on her,
Hekate met her, holding a torch in her hands,
to give her a message. She spoke as follows:
"Divine Demeter, giver of seasons and glorious gifts,
who of the immortals or mortal men   55
seized Persephone and grieved your heart?
For I heard a voice but did not see with my eyes
who he was. To you I tell at once the whole truth."
Thus Hekate spoke. The daughter of fair-tressed Rheia***
said not a word, but rushed off at her side   60
holding torches ablaze in her hands.
They came to Helios, observer of gods and mortals,
and stood before his horses. The most august goddess*** spoke:
"Helios, respect me as a god does a goddess, if ever
with word or deed I pleased your heart and spirit.   65
The daughter I bore, a sweet offshoot noble in form—
I heard her voice throbbing through the barren air

    *** Demeter

τὴν δ᾽ ἀεκαζομένην ἦγεν Διὸς ἐννεσίῃσι   30
πατροκασίγνητος πολυσημάντωρ πολυδέγμων
ἵπποις ἀθανάτοισι Κρόνου πολυώνυμος υἱός.
ὄφρα μὲν οὖν γαῖάν τε καὶ οὐρανὸν ἀστερόεντα
λεῦσσε θεὰ καὶ πόντον ἀγάρροον ἰχθυόεντα
αὐγάς τ᾽ ἠελίου, ἔτι δ᾽ ἤλπετο μητέρα κεδνὴν   35
ὄψεσθαι καὶ φῦλα θεῶν αἰειγενετάων,
τόφρα οἱ ἐλπὶς ἔθελγε μέγαν νόον ἀχνυμένης περ.
ἤχησαν δ᾽ ὀρέων κορυφαὶ καὶ βένθεα πόντου
φωνῇ ὑπ᾽ ἀθανάτῃ, τῆς ἔκλυε πότνια μήτηρ.
ὀξὺ δέ μιν κραδίην ἄχος ἔλλαβεν, ἀμφὶ δὲ χαίταις   40
ἀμβροσίαις κρήδεμνα δαΐζετο χερσὶ φίλῃσι,
κυάνεον δὲ κάλυμμα κατ᾽ ἀμφοτέρων βάλετ᾽ ὤμων,
σεύατο δ᾽ ὥς τ᾽ οἰωνὸς ἐπὶ τραφερήν τε καὶ ὑγρὴν
μαιομένη· τῇ δ᾽ οὔ τις ἐτήτυμα μυθήσασθαι
ἤθελεν οὔτε θεῶν οὔτε θνητῶν ἀνθρώπων,   45
οὔτ᾽ οἰωνῶν τις τῇ ἐτήτυμος ἄγγελος ἦλθεν.
ἐννῆμαρ μὲν ἔπειτα κατὰ χθόνα πότνια Δηὼ
στρωφᾶτ᾽ αἰθομένας δαΐδας μετὰ χερσὶν ἔχουσα,
οὐδέ ποτ᾽ ἀμβροσίης καὶ νέκταρος ἡδυπότοιο
πάσσατ᾽ ἀκηχεμένη, οὐδὲ χρόα βάλλετο λουτροῖς.   50
ἀλλ᾽ ὅτε δὴ δεκάτη οἱ ἐπήλυθε φαινόλις Ἠώς,
ἤντετό οἱ Ἑκάτη σέλας ἐν χείρεσσιν ἔχουσα,
καί ῥά οἱ ἀγγελέουσα ἔπος φάτο φώνησέν τε·
Πότνια Δημήτηρ ὡρηφόρε ἀγλαόδωρε
τίς θεῶν οὐρανίων ἠὲ θνητῶν ἀνθρώπων   55
ἥρπασε Περσεφόνην καὶ σὸν φίλον ἤκαχε θυμόν;
φωνῆς γὰρ ἤκουσ᾽, ἀτὰρ οὐκ ἴδον ὀφθαλμοῖσιν
ὅς τις ἔην· σοὶ δ᾽ ὦκα λέγω νημερτέα πάντα.
Ὣς ἄρ᾽ ἔφη Ἑκάτη· τὴν δ᾽ οὐκ ἠμείβετο μύθῳ
Ῥείης ἠυκόμου θυγάτηρ, ἀλλ᾽ ὦκα σὺν αὐτῇ   60
ἤϊξ᾽ αἰθομένας δαΐδας μετὰ χερσὶν ἔχουσα.
Ἥλιον δ᾽ ἵκοντο θεῶν σκοπὸν ἠδὲ καὶ ἀνδρῶν,
στὰν δ᾽ ἵππων προπάροιθε καὶ εἴρετο δῖα θεάων·
Ἠέλι᾽ αἴδεσσαί με θεὰν θεός, εἴ ποτε δή σευ
ἢ ἔπει ἢ ἔργῳ κραδίην καὶ θυμὸν ἴηνα.   65
κούρην τὴν ἔτεκον γλυκερὸν θάλος εἴδεϊ κυδρὴν
τῆς ἀδινὴν ὄπ᾽ ἄκουσα δι᾽ αἰθέρος ἀτρυγέτοιο

as if she were suffering violence. But I did not see her with my eyes.
With your rays you look down through the bright air
on the whole of the earth and the sea.   70
Tell me the truth about my child. Have you somewhere
seen who of gods or mortal men took her
by force from me against her will and went away?"
Thus she spoke and the son of Hyperion replied:
"Daughter of fair-tressed Rheia, mighty Demeter,   75
you will know the truth. For I greatly revere and pity you
grieving for your slim-ankled daughter. No other
of the gods was to blame but cloud-gathering Zeus,
who gave her to Hades his brother to be called
his fertile wife. With his horses Hades   80
snatched her screaming into the misty gloom.
But, Goddess, give up for good your great lamentation.
You must not nurse in vain insatiable anger.
Among the gods Aidoneus is not an unsuitable bridegroom,
Commander-to-Many and Zeus's own brother of the same stock.   85
As for honor, he got his third at the world's first division
and dwells with those whose rule has fallen to his lot."
He spoke and called to his horses. At his rebuke
they bore the swift chariot lightly, like long-winged birds.
A more terrible and brutal grief seized the heart   90
of Demeter, angry now at the son of Kronos with his dark clouds.
Withdrawing from the assembly of the gods and high Olympus,
she went among the cities and fertile fields of men,
disguising her beauty for a long time. No one of men
nor deep-girt women recognized her when they looked,   95
until she came to the house of skillful Keleos,
the man then ruler of fragrant Eleusis.
There she sat near the road, grief in her heart,
where citizens drew water from the Maiden's Well
in the shade—an olive bush had grown overhead—   100
like a very old woman cut off from childbearing
and the gifts of garland-loving Aphrodite.
Such are the nurses to children of law-giving kings
and the keepers of stores in their echoing halls.
The daughters of Keleos, son of Eleusis, saw her   105
as they came to fetch water easy-to-draw and bring it
in bronze vessels to their dear father's halls.

ὥς τε βιαζομένης, ἀτὰρ οὐκ ἴδον ὀφθαλμοῖσιν.
ἀλλὰ σὺ γὰρ δὴ πᾶσαν ἐπὶ χθόνα καὶ κατὰ πόντον
αἰθέρος ἐκ δίης καταδέρκεαι ἀκτίνεσσι,   70
νημερτέως μοι ἔνισπε φίλον τέκος εἴ που ὄπωπας
ὅς τις νόσφιν ἐμεῖο λαβὼν ἀέκουσαν ἀνάγκη
οἴχεται ἠὲ θεῶν ἢ καὶ θνητῶν ἀνθρώπων.

    Ὣς φάτο, τὴν δ᾽ Ὑπεριονίδης ἠμείβετο μύθῳ·
Ῥείης ἠϋκόμου θυγάτηρ Δήμητερ ἄνασσα   75
εἰδήσεις· δὴ γὰρ μέγα ἅζομαι ἠδ᾽ ἐλεαίρω
ἀχνυμένην περὶ παιδὶ τανισφύρῳ· οὐδέ τις ἄλλος
αἴτιος ἀθανάτων εἰ μὴ νεφεληγερέτα Ζεύς,
ὅς μιν ἔδωκ᾽ Ἀίδη θαλερὴν κεκλῆσθαι ἄκοιτιν
αὐτοκασιγνήτῳ· ὁ δ᾽ ὑπὸ ζόφον ἠερόεντα   80
ἁρπάξας ἵπποισιν ἄγεν μεγάλα ἰάχουσαν.
ἀλλὰ θεὰ κατάπαυε μέγαν γόον· οὐδέ τί σε χρὴ
μὰψ αὕτως ἄπλητον ἔχειν χόλον· οὔ τοι ἀεικὴς
γαμβρὸς ἐν ἀθανάτοις πολυσημάντωρ Ἀϊδωνεὺς
αὐτοκασίγνητος καὶ ὁμόσπορος· ἀμφὶ δὲ τιμὴν   85
ἔλλαχεν ὡς τὰ πρῶτα διάτριχα δασμὸς ἐτύχθη·
τοῖς μεταναιετάει τῶν ἔλλαχε κοίρανος εἶναι.

    Ὣς εἰπὼν ἵπποισιν ἐκέκλετο, τοὶ δ᾽ ὑπ᾽ ὁμοκλῆς
ῥίμφα φέρον θοὸν ἅρμα τανύπτεροι ὥς τ᾽ οἰωνοί·
τὴν δ᾽ ἄχος αἰνότερον καὶ κύντερον ἵκετο θυμόν.   90
χωσαμένη δἤπειτα κελαινεφέϊ Κρονίωνι
νοσφισθεῖσα θεῶν ἀγορὴν καὶ μακρὸν Ὄλυμπον
ᾤχετ᾽ ἐπ᾽ ἀνθρώπων πόλιας καὶ πίονα ἔργα
εἶδος ἀμαλδύνουσα πολὺν χρόνον· οὐδέ τις ἀνδρῶν
εἰσορόων γίνωσκε βαθυζώνων τε γυναικῶν,   95
πρίν γ᾽ ὅτε δὴ Κελεοῖο δαΐφρονος ἵκετο δῶμα,
ὃς τότ᾽ Ἐλευσῖνος θυοέσσης κοίρανος ἦεν.
ἕζετο δ᾽ ἐγγὺς ὁδοῖο φίλον τετιημένη ἦτορ
Παρθενίῳ φρέατι ὅθεν ὑδρεύοντο πολῖται
ἐν σκιῇ, αὐτὰρ ὕπερθε πεφύκει θάμνος ἐλαίης,   100
γρηῒ παλαιγενέϊ ἐναλίγκιος, ἥ τε τόκοιο
εἴργηται δώρων τε φιλοστεφάνου Ἀφροδίτης,
οἷαί τε τροφοί εἰσι θεμιστοπόλων βασιλήων
παίδων καὶ ταμίαι κατὰ δώματα ἠχήεντα.
τὴν δὲ ἴδον Κελεοῖο Ἐλευσινίδαο θύγατρες   105
ἐρχόμεναι μεθ᾽ ὕδωρ εὐήρυτον ὄφρα φέροιεν
κάλπισι χαλκείῃσι φίλα πρὸς δώματα πατρός,

Like four goddesses they were in the flower of youth,
Kallidikê, Kleisidikê, fair Demo, and Kallithoê,
who was the eldest of them all.   110
They did not know her—gods are hard for mortals to recognize.
Standing near her, they spoke winged words.
"Who are you, old woman, of those born long ago?
From where? Why have you left the city and do not
draw near its homes? Women are there in the shadowy halls,   115
of your age as well as others born younger,
who would care for you both in word and in deed."
They spoke, and the most august goddess replied:
"Dear children, whoever of womankind you are,
greetings. I will tell you my tale. For it is not wrong   120
to tell you the truth now you ask.
Doso's my name, which my honored mother gave me.
On the broad back of the sea I have come now from Crete,
by no wish of my own. By force and necessity pirate men
led me off against my desire. Then they   125
put into Thorikos in their swift ship, where
the women stepped all together onto the mainland,
and the men made a meal by the stern of the ship.
My heart did not crave a heartwarming dinner,
but racing in secret across the dark mainland   130
I escaped from my arrogant masters, lest
they should sell me, as yet unbought, for a price overseas.
Then wandering I came here and know not at all
what land this is and who lives here.
But may all the gods who dwell on Olympus   135
give you husbands to marry and children to bear,
such as parents wish for. Now pity me, maidens,
and tell me, dear children, with eager goodwill,
whose house I might come to, a man's
or a woman's, there to do for them gladly
such tasks as are done by an elderly woman.   140
I could nurse well a newborn child, embracing it
in my arms, or watch over a house. I could
spread out the master's bed in a recess
of the well-built chamber and teach women their work."
So spoke the goddess. To her replied at once Kallidikê,   145
a maiden unwed, in beauty the best of Keleos' daughters.

τέσσαρες ὥς τε θεαὶ κουρήϊον ἄνθος ἔχουσαι,
Καλλιδίκη καὶ Κλεισιδίκη Δημώ τ' ἐρόεσσα
Καλλιθόη θ', ἣ τῶν προγενεστάτη ἦεν ἁπασῶν·   110
οὐδ' ἔγνων· χαλεποὶ δὲ θεοὶ θνητοῖσιν ὁρᾶσθαι.
ἀγχοῦ δ' ἱστάμεναι ἔπεα πτερόεντα προσηύδων·

   Τίς πόθεν ἐσσὶ γρηῢ παλαιγενέων ἀνθρώπων;
τίπτε δὲ νόσφι πόληος ἀπέστιχες οὐδὲ δόμοισι
πίλνασαι, ἔνθα γυναῖκες ἀνὰ μέγαρα σκιόεντα   115
τηλίκαι ὡς σύ περ ὧδε καὶ ὁπλότεραι γεγάασιν,
αἵ κέ σε φίλωνται ἠμὲν ἔπει ἠδὲ καὶ ἔργῳ;

   Ὣς ἔφαθ', ἡ δ' ἐπέεσσιν ἀμείβετο πότνα θεάων·
τέκνα φίλ' αἵ τινές ἐστε γυναικῶν θηλυτεράων
χαίρετ', ἐγὼ δ' ὑμῖν μυθήσομαι· οὔ τοι ἀεικὲς   120
ὑμῖν εἰρομένῃσιν ἀληθέα μυθήσασθαι.
Δωσὼ ἐμοί γ' ὄνομ' ἐστί· τὸ γὰρ θέτο πότνια μήτηρ·
νῦν αὖτε Κρήτηθεν ἐπ' εὐρέα νῶτα θαλάσσης
ἤλυθον οὐκ ἐθέλουσα, βίῃ δ' ἀέκουσαν ἀνάγκῃ
ἄνδρες ληϊστῆρες ἀπήγαγον. οἱ μὲν ἔπειτα   125
νηῒ θοῇ Θορικὸν δὲ κατέσχεθον, ἔνθα γυναῖκες
ἠπείρου ἐπέβησαν ἀολλέες ἠδὲ καὶ αὐτοὶ
δεῖπνον ἐπηρτύνοντο παρὰ πρυμνήσια νηός·
ἀλλ' ἐμοὶ οὐ δόρποιο μελίφρονος ἤρατο θυμός,
λάθρῃ δ' ὁρμηθεῖσα δι' ἠπείροιο μελαίνης   130
φεῦγον ὑπερφιάλους σημάντορας, ὄφρα κε μή με
ἀπριάτην περάσαντες ἐμῆς ἀποναίατο τιμῆς.
οὕτω δεῦρ' ἱκόμην ἀλαλημένη, οὐδέ τι οἶδα
ἥ τις δὴ γαῖ' ἐστὶ καὶ οἵ τινες ἐγγεγάασιν.
ἀλλ' ὑμῖν μὲν πάντες Ὀλύμπια δώματ' ἔχοντες   135
δοῖεν κουριδίους ἄνδρας καὶ τέκνα τεκέσθαι
ὡς ἐθέλουσι τοκῆς· ἐμὲ δ' αὖτ' οἰκτίρατε κοῦραι

προφρονέως φίλα τέκνα τέων πρὸς δώμαθ' ἵκωμαι
ἀνέρος ἠδὲ γυναικός, ἵνα σφίσιν ἐργάζωμαι
πρόφρων οἷα γυναικὸς ἀφήλικος ἔργα τέτυκται·   140
καί κεν παῖδα νεογνὸν ἐν ἀγκοίνῃσιν ἔχουσα
καλὰ τιθηνοίμην καὶ δώματα τηρήσαιμι
καί κε λέχος στορέσαιμι μυχῷ θαλάμων ἐϋπήκτων
δεσπόσυνον καί κ' ἔργα διδασκήσαιμι γυναῖκας.

   Φῆ ῥα θεά· τὴν δ' αὐτίκ' ἀμείβετο παρθένος ἀδμὴς   145
Καλλιδίκη Κελεοῖο θυγατρῶν εἶδος ἀρίστη·

"Good mother, we mortals are forced, though it hurt us,
to bear the gifts of the gods; for they are far stronger.
To you I shall explain these things clearly and name
the men to whom great power and honor belong here,   150
who are first of the people and protect with their counsels
and straight judgments the high walls of the city.
There is Triptolemos subtle in mind and Dioklos,
Polyxenos and Eumolpos the blameless,
Dolichos and our own lordly father.   155
And all these have wives to manage their households.
Of these not one at first sight would scorn
your appearance and turn you away from their homes.
They will receive you, for you are indeed godlike.
But if you wish, wait here, until we come to the house   160
of our father and tell Metaneira our deep-girt mother
all these things straight through, in case she might bid
you come to our house and not search after others'.
For her only son is now nursed in our well-built hall,
a late-born child, much prayed for and cherished.   165
If you might raise him to the threshold of youth,
any woman who saw you would feel envy at once,
such rewards for his rearing our mother will give you."
Thus they spoke and she nodded her head. The girls
carried proudly bright jars filled with water and   170
swiftly they reached the great house of their father.
At once to their mother they told what they saw and heard.
She bade them go quickly to offer a boundless wage.
Just as hinds or heifers in the season of spring
bound through the meadow sated with fodder,   175
so they, lifting the folds of their shimmering robes,
darted down the hollow wagon-track, and their hair
danced on their shoulders like a crocus blossom.
They found the famed goddess near the road
just where they had left her. Then to the house   180
of their father they led her. She, grieved in her heart,
walked behind with veiled head. And her dark robe
swirled round the slender feet of the goddess.
They soon reached the house of god-cherished Keleos,
and went through the portico to the place where   185
their regal mother sat by the pillar of the close-fitted roof,

Μαῖα θεῶν μὲν δῶρα καὶ ἀχνύμενοί περ ἀνάγκῃ
τέτλαμεν ἄνθρωποι· δὴ γὰρ πολὺ φέρτεροί εἰσιν.
ταῦτα δέ τοι σαφέως ὑποθήσομαι ἠδ᾽ ὀνομήνω
ἀνέρας οἷσιν ἔπεστι μέγα κράτος ἐνθάδε τιμῆς,   150
δήμου τε προὔχουσιν, ἰδὲ κρήδεμνα πόληος
εἰρύαται βουλῇσι καὶ ἰθείῃσι δίκῃσιν.
ἠμὲν Τριπτολέμου πυκιμήδεος ἠδὲ Διόκλου
ἠδὲ Πολυξείνου καὶ ἀμύμονος Εὐμόλποιο
καὶ Δολίχου καὶ πατρὸς ἀγήνορος ἡμετέροιο   155
τῶν πάντων ἄλοχοι κατὰ δώματα πορσαίνουσι·
τάων οὐκ ἄν τίς σε κατὰ πρώτιστον ὀπωπὴν
εἶδος ἀτιμήσασα δόμων ἀπονοσφίσσειεν,
ἀλλά σε δέξονται· δὴ γὰρ θεοείκελός ἐσσι.
εἰ δ᾽ ἐθέλεις, ἐπίμεινον, ἵνα πρὸς δώματα πατρὸς   160
ἔλθωμεν καὶ μητρὶ βαθυζώνῳ Μετανείρῃ
εἴπωμεν τάδε πάντα διαμπερές, αἴ κέ σ᾽ ἀνώγῃ
ἡμέτερον δ᾽ ἰέναι μηδ᾽ ἄλλων δώματ᾽ ἐρευνᾶν.
τηλύγετος δέ οἱ υἱὸς ἐνὶ μεγάρῳ ἐϋπήκτῳ
ὀψίγονος τρέφεται, πολυεύχετος ἀσπάσιός τε.   165
εἰ τόν γ᾽ ἐκθρέψαιο καὶ ἥβης μέτρον ἵκοιτο
ῥεῖά κέ τίς σε ἰδοῦσα γυναικῶν θηλυτεράων
ζηλώσαι· τόσα κέν τοι ἀπὸ θρεπτήρια δοίη.
  Ὣς ἔφαθ᾽· ἡ δ᾽ ἐπένευσε καρήατι, ταὶ δὲ φαεινὰ
πλησάμεναι ὕδατος φέρον ἄγγεα κυδιάουσαι.   170
ῥίμφα δὲ πατρὸς ἵκοντο μέγαν δόμον, ὦκα δὲ μητρὶ
ἔννεπον ὡς εἶδόν τε καὶ ἔκλυον. ἡ δὲ μάλ᾽ ὦκα
ἐλθούσας ἐκέλευε καλεῖν ἐπ᾽ ἀπείρονι μισθῷ.
αἱ δ᾽ ὥς τ᾽ ἢ ἔλαφοι ἢ πόρτιες ἤαρος ὥρῃ
ἄλλοντ᾽ ἂν λειμῶνα κορεσσάμεναι φρένα φορβῇ,   175
ὣς αἱ ἐπισχόμεναι ἑανῶν πτύχας ἱμεροέντων
ἤϊξαν κοίλην κατ᾽ ἀμαξιτόν, ἀμφὶ δὲ χαῖται
ὤμοις ἀΐσσοντο κροκηΐῳ ἄνθει ὁμοῖαι.
τέτμον δ᾽ ἐγγὺς ὁδοῦ κυδρὴν θεὸν ἔνθα πάρος περ
κάλλιπον· αὐτὰρ ἔπειτα φίλα πρὸς δώματα πατρὸς   180
ἡγεῦνθ᾽, ἡ δ᾽ ἄρ᾽ ὄπισθε φίλον τετιημένη ἦτορ
στεῖχε κατὰ κρῆθεν κεκαλυμμένη, ἀμφὶ δὲ πέπλος
κυάνεος ῥαδινοῖσι θεᾶς ἐλελίζετο ποσσίν.
αἶψα δὲ δώμαθ᾽ ἵκοντο διοτρεφέος Κελεοῖο,
βὰν δὲ δι᾽ αἰθούσης ἔνθα σφίσι πότνια μήτηρ   185
ἧστο παρὰ σταθμὸν τέγεος πύκα ποιητοῖο

holding on her lap the child, her young offshoot. To her
they raced. But the goddess stepped on the threshold. Her head
reached the roof and she filled the doorway with divine light.
Reverence, awe, and pale fear seized Metaneira. 190
She gave up her chair and bade the goddess sit down.
But Demeter, bringer of seasons and giver of rich gifts,
did not wish to be seated on the shining seat.
She waited resistant, her lovely eyes cast down,
until knowing Iambe set out a well-built stool 195
for her and cast over it a silvery fleece.
Seated there, the goddess drew the veil before her face.
For a long time she sat voiceless with grief on the stool
and responded to no one with word or gesture.
Unsmiling, tasting neither food nor drink, 200
she sat wasting with desire for her deep-girt daughter,
until knowing Iambe jested with her and
mocking with many a joke moved the holy goddess
to smile and laugh and keep a gracious heart—
Iambe, who later pleased her moods as well. 205
Metaneira offered a cup filled with honey-sweet wine,
but Demeter refused it. It was not right, she said,
for her to drink red wine; then she bid them mix barley
and water with soft mint and give her to drink.
Metaneira made and gave the drink to the goddess as she bid. 210
Almighty Deo received it for the sake of the rite.
Well-girt Metaneira spoke first among them:
"Hail, lady, for I suppose your parents are not lowborn,
but noble. Your eyes are marked by modesty
and grace, even as those of justice-dealing kings. 215
We mortals are forced, though it may hurt us, to bear
the gifts of the gods. For the yoke lies on our necks.
But now you have come here, all that's mine will be yours.
Raise this child for me, whom the gods provided
late-born and unexpected, much-prayed for by me. 220
If you raise him and he comes to the threshold of youth,
any woman who saw you would feel envy at once,
such rewards for his rearing would I give you."
Rich-crowned Demeter addressed her in turn:
"Hail also to you, lady, may the gods give you blessings. 225
Gladly will I embrace the child as you bid me.

παῖδ' ὑπὸ κόλπῳ ἔχουσα νέον θάλος· αἱ δὲ παρ' αὐτὴν
ἔδραμον, ἡ δ' ἄρ' ἐπ' οὐδὸν ἔβη ποσὶ καί ῥα μελάθρου
κῦρε κάρη, πλῆσεν δὲ θύρας σέλαος θείοιο.
τὴν δ' αἰδώς τε σέβας τε ἰδὲ χλωρὸν δέος εἷλεν·   190
εἶξε δέ οἱ κλισμοῖο καὶ ἑδριάασθαι ἄνωγεν.
ἀλλ' οὐ Δημήτηρ ὡρηφόρος ἀγλαόδωρος
ἤθελεν ἑδριάασθαι ἐπὶ κλισμοῖο φαεινοῦ,
ἀλλ' ἀκέουσα ἔμιμνε κατ' ὄμματα καλὰ βαλοῦσα,
πρίν γ' ὅτε δή οἱ ἔθηκεν Ἰάμβη κέδν' εἰδυῖα   195
πηκτὸν ἕδος, καθύπερθε δ' ἐπ' ἀργύφεον βάλε κῶας.
ἔνθα καθεζομένη προκατέσχετο χερσὶ καλύπτρην·
δηρὸν δ' ἄφθογγος τετιημένη ἧστ' ἐπὶ δίφρου,
οὐδέ τιν' οὔτ' ἔπεϊ προσπτύσσετο οὔτε τι ἔργῳ,
ἀλλ' ἀγέλαστος ἄπαστος ἐδητύος ἠδὲ ποτῆτος   200
ἧστο πόθῳ μινύθουσα βαθυζώνοιο θυγατρός,
πρίν γ' ὅτε δὴ χλεύῃς μιν Ἰάμβη κέδν' εἰδυῖα
πολλὰ παρὰ σκώπτουσ' ἐτρέψατο πότνιαν ἁγνὴν
μειδῆσαι γελάσαι τε καὶ ἵλαον σχεῖν θυμόν·
ἡ δή οἱ καὶ ἔπειτα μεθύστερον εὔαδεν ὀργαῖς.   205
τῇ δὲ δέπας Μετάνειρα δίδου μελιηδέος οἴνου
πλήσασ', ἡ δ' ἀνένευσ'· οὐ γὰρ θεμιτόν οἱ ἔφασκε
πίνειν οἶνον ἐρυθρόν, ἄνωγε δ' ἄρ' ἄλφι καὶ ὕδωρ
δοῦναι μίξασαν πιέμεν γληχῶνι τερείνῃ.
ἡ δὲ κυκεῶ τεύξασα θεᾷ πόρεν ὡς ἐκέλευε·   210
δεξαμένη δ' ὁσίης ἕνεκεν πολυπότνια Δηὼ
τῇσι δὲ μύθων ἦρχεν ἐΰζωνος Μετάνειρα·
    Χαῖρε γύναι, ἐπεὶ οὔ σε κακῶν ἄπ' ἔολπα τοκήων
ἔμμεναι ἀλλ' ἀγαθῶν· ἐπί τοι πρέπει ὄμμασιν αἰδὼς
καὶ χάρις, ὡς εἴ πέρ τε θεμιστοπόλων βασιλήων.   215
ἀλλὰ θεῶν μὲν δῶρα καὶ ἀχνύμενοί περ ἀνάγκη
τέτλαμεν ἄνθρωποι· ἐπὶ γὰρ ζυγὸς αὐχένι κεῖται.
νῦν δ' ἐπεὶ ἵκεο δεῦρο, παρέσσεται ὅσσα τ' ἐμοί περ.
παῖδα δέ μοι τρέφε τόνδε, τὸν ὀψίγονον καὶ ἄελπτον
ὤπασαν ἀθάνατοι, πολυάρητος δέ μοί ἐστιν.   220
εἰ τόν γ' ἐκθρέψαιο καὶ ἥβης μέτρον ἵκοιτο
ἦ ῥά κέ τίς σε ἰδοῦσα γυναικῶν θηλυτεράων
ζηλώσαι· τόσα κέν τοι ἀπὸ θρεπτήρια δοίην.
    Τὴν δ' αὖτε προσέειπεν ἐϋστέφανος Δημήτηρ·
καὶ σὺ γύναι μάλα χαῖρε, θεοὶ δέ τοι ἐσθλὰ πόροιεν.   225
παῖδα δέ τοι πρόφρων ὑποδέξομαι ὥς με κελεύεις·

I will raise him, nor do I expect a spell or the Undercutter
to harm him through the negligence of his nurse.
For I know a charm more cutting than the Woodcutter;
I know a strong safeguard against baneful bewitching." 230
So speaking, she took the child to her fragrant breast
with her divine hands. And his mother was glad at heart.
Thus the splendid son of skillful Keleos, Demophoön,
whom well-girt Metaneira bore, she nursed
in the great halls. And he grew like a divinity, 235
eating no food nor sucking [at a mother's breast];
[For daily well-crowned divine] Demeter anointed
him with ambrosia like one born from a god
and breathed sweetly on him, held close to her breast.
At night, she would bury him like a brand in the fire's might,
unknown to his own parents. And great was their wonder 240
as he grew miraculously fast; he was like the gods.
She would have made him ageless and immortal,
if well-girt Metaneira had not in her folly
kept watch at night from her fragrant chamber
and spied. But she shrieked and struck both thighs 245
in fear for her child, much misled in her mind,
and in her grief she spoke winged words.
"Demophoön, my child, the stranger buries you
deep in the fire, causing me woe and bitter cares."
Thus she spoke lamenting. The great goddess heard her. 250
In anger at her, bright-crowned Demeter snatched
from the flames with immortal hands the dear child
Metaneira had borne beyond hope in the halls and,
raging terribly at heart, cast him away from herself to the ground.
At the same time she addressed well-girt Metaneira: 255
"Mortals are ignorant and foolish, unable to foresee
destiny, the good and the bad coming on them.
You are incurably misled by your folly.
Let the god's oath, the implacable water of Styx, be witness,
I would have made your child immortal and ageless 260
forever; I would have given him unfailing honor.
But now he cannot escape death and the death spirits.
Yet unfailing honor will forever be his, because
he lay on my knees and slept in my arms.

θρέψω, κού μιν ἔολπα κακοφραδίῃσι τιθήνης
οὔτ' ἄρ' ἐπηλυσίη δηλήσεται οὔθ' ὑποταμνόν·
οἶδα γὰρ ἀντίτομον μέγα φέρτερον ὑλοτόμοιο,
οἶδα δ' ἐπηλυσίης πολυπήμονος ἐσθλὸν ἐρυσμόν.   230
   Ὣς ἄρα φωνήσασα θυώδεϊ δέξατο κόλπῳ
χερσίν τ' ἀθανάτῃσι· γεγήθει δὲ φρένα μήτηρ.
ὣς ἡ μὲν Κελεοῖο δαΐφρονος ἀγλαὸν υἱὸν
Δημοφόωνθ', ὃν ἔτικτεν ἐΰζωνος Μετάνειρα,
ἔτρεφεν ἐν μεγάροις· ὁ δ' ἀέξετο δαίμονι ἶσος   235
οὔτ' οὖν σῖτον ἔδων, οὐ θησάμενος
                              Δημήτηρ
χρίεσκ' ἀμβροσίῃ ὡς εἰ θεοῦ ἐκγεγαῶτα,
ἡδὺ καταπνείουσα καὶ ἐν κόλποισιν ἔχουσα·
νύκτας δὲ κρύπτεσκε πυρὸς μένει ἠΰτε δαλὸν
λάθρα φίλων γονέων· τοῖς δὲ μέγα θαῦμ' ἐτέτυκτο   240
ὡς προθαλὴς τελέθεσκε, θεοῖσι δὲ ἄντα ἐῴκει.
καί κέν μιν ποίησεν ἀγήρων τ' ἀθάνατόν τε
εἰ μὴ ἄρ' ἀφραδίῃσιν ἐΰζωνος Μετάνειρα
νύκτ' ἐπιτηρήσασα θυώδεος ἐκ θαλάμοιο
σκέψατο· κώκυσεν δὲ καὶ ἄμφω πλήξατο μηρὼ   245
δείσασ' ᾧ περὶ παιδὶ καὶ ἀάσθη μέγα θυμῷ,
καί ῥ' ὀλοφυρομένη ἔπεα πτερόεντα προσηύδα·
   Τέκνον Δημοφόων ξείνη σε πυρὶ ἔνι πολλῷ
κρύπτει, ἐμοὶ δὲ γόον καὶ κήδεα λυγρὰ τίθησιν.
   Ὣς φάτ' ὀδυρομένη· τῆς δ' ἄϊε δῖα θεάων.   250
τῇ δὲ χολωσαμένη καλλιστέφανος Δημήτηρ
παῖδα φίλον, τὸν ἄελπτον ἐνὶ μεγάροισιν ἔτικτε,
χείρεσσ' ἀθανάτῃσιν ἀπὸ ἕο θῆκε πέδον δὲ
ἐξανελοῦσα πυρὸς θυμῷ κοτέσασα μάλ' αἰνῶς,
καί ῥ' ἄμυδις προσέειπεν ἐΰζωνον Μετάνειραν·   255
   Νήϊδες ἄνθρωποι καὶ ἀφράδμονες οὔτ' ἀγαθοῖο
αἶσαν ἐπερχομένου προγνώμεναι οὔτε κακοῖο·
καὶ σὺ γὰρ ἀφραδίῃσι τεῇς νήκεστον ἀάσθης.
ἴστω γὰρ θεῶν ὅρκος ἀμείλικτον Στυγὸς ὕδωρ
ἀθάνατόν κέν τοι καὶ ἀγήραον ἤματα πάντα   260
παῖδα φίλον ποίησα καὶ ἄφθιτον ὤπασα τιμήν·
νῦν δ' οὐκ ἔσθ' ὥς κεν θάνατον καὶ κῆρας ἀλύξαι.
τιμὴ δ' ἄφθιτος αἰὲν ἐπέσσεται οὕνεκα γούνων
ἡμετέρων ἐπέβη καὶ ἐν ἀγκοίνῃσιν ἴαυσεν.

In due time as the years come round for him,   265
the sons of Eleusis will continue year after year
to wage war and dread combat against each other.
For I am honored Demeter, the greatest
source of help and joy to mortals and immortals.
But now let all the people build me a great temple   270
with an altar beneath, under the sheer wall
of the city on the rising hill above Kallichoron.
I myself will lay down the rites so that hereafter
performing due rites you may propitiate my spirit."
Thus speaking, the goddess changed her size and appearance,   275
thrusting off old age. Beauty breathed about her and
from her sweet robes a delicious fragrance spread;
a light beamed far out from the goddess's immortal skin,
and her golden hair flowed over her shoulders.
The well-built house flooded with radiance like lightning.   280
She left the halls. At once Metaneira's knees buckled.
For a long time she remained voiceless, forgetting
to pick up her dear only son from the floor.
But his sisters heard his pitiful voice and
leapt from their well-spread beds. Then one took   285
the child in her arms and laid him to her breast.
Another lit the fire; a third rushed on delicate feet
to rouse her mother from her fragrant chamber.
Gathering about the gasping child, they bathed and
embraced him lovingly. Yet his heart was not comforted,   290
for lesser nurses and handmaids held him now.
All night they tried to appease the dread goddess,
shaking with fear. But when dawn appeared,
they explained to wide-ruling Keleos exactly
what the bright-crowned goddess Demeter commanded.   295
Then he called to assembly his innumerable people
and bid them build for fair-tressed Demeter
a rich temple and an altar on the rising hill.
Attentive to his speech, they obeyed at once and did
as he prescribed. It grew as the goddess decreed.   300
But once they finished and ceased their toil,
each went off home. Then golden-haired Demeter
remained sitting apart from all the immortals,
wasting with desire for her deep-girt daughter.

ὤρῃσιν δ᾽ ἄρα τῷ γε περιπλομένων ἐνιαυτῶν   265
παῖδες Ἐλευσινίων πόλεμον καὶ φύλοπιν αἰνὴν
αἰὲν ἐν ἀλλήλοισι συνάξουσ᾽ ἤματα πάντα.
εἰμὶ δὲ Δημήτηρ τιμάοχος, ἥ τε μέγιστον
ἀθανάτοις θνητοῖσί τ᾽ ὄνεαρ καὶ χάρμα τέτυκται.
ἀλλ᾽ ἄγε μοι νηόν τε μέγαν καὶ βωμὸν ὑπ᾽ αὐτῷ   270
τευχόντων πᾶς δῆμος ὑπαὶ πόλιν αἰπύ τε τεῖχος
Καλλιχόρου καθύπερθεν ἐπὶ προὔχοντι κολωνῷ·
ὄργια δ᾽ αὐτὴ ἐγὼν ὑποθήσομαι ὡς ἂν ἔπειτα
εὐαγέως ἔρδοντες ἐμὸν νόον ἱλάσκοισθε.

  Ὣς εἰποῦσα θεὰ μέγεθος καὶ εἶδος ἄμειψε   275
γῆρας ἀπωσαμένη, περί τ᾽ ἀμφί τε κάλλος ἄητο·
ὀδμὴ δ᾽ ἱμερόεσσα θυηέντων ἀπὸ πέπλων
σκίδνατο, τῆλε δὲ φέγγος ἀπὸ χροὸς ἀθανάτοιο
λάμπε θεᾶς, ξανθαὶ δὲ κόμαι κατενήνοθεν ὤμους,
αὐγῆς δ᾽ ἐπλήσθη πυκινὸς δόμος ἀστεροπῆς ὥς.   280
βῆ δὲ διὲκ μεγάρων, τῆς δ᾽ αὐτίκα γούνατ᾽ ἔλυντο,
δηρὸν δ᾽ ἄφθογγος γένετο χρόνον, οὐδέ τι παιδὸς
μνήσατο τηλυγέτοιο ἀπὸ δαπέδου ἀνελέσθαι.
τοῦ δὲ κασίγνηται φωνὴν ἐσάκουσαν ἐλεινήν,
κὰδ δ᾽ ἄρ᾽ ἀπ᾽ εὐστρώτων λεχέων θόρον· ἡ μὲν ἔπειτα 285
παῖδ᾽ ἀνὰ χερσὶν ἑλοῦσα ἑῷ ἐγκάτθετο κόλπῳ,
ἡ δ᾽ ἄρα πῦρ ἀνέκαι᾽, ἡ δ᾽ ἔσσυτο πόσσ᾽ ἁπαλοῖσι
μητέρ᾽ ἀναστήσουσα θυώδεος ἐκ θαλάμοιο.
ἀγρόμεναι δέ μιν ἀμφὶς ἐλούεον ἀσπαίροντα
ἀμφαγαπαζόμεναι· τοῦ δ᾽ οὐ μειλίσσετο θυμός·   290
χειρότεραι γὰρ δή μιν ἔχον τροφοὶ ἠδὲ τιθῆναι.
  Αἱ μὲν παννύχιαι κυδρὴν θεὸν ἱλάσκοντο
δείματι παλλόμεναι· ἅμα δ᾽ ἠοῖ φαινομένηφιν
εὐρυβίῃ Κελεῷ νημερτέα μυθήσαντο,
ὡς ἐπέτελλε θεὰ καλλιστέφανος Δημήτηρ.   295
αὐτὰρ ὅ γ᾽ εἰς ἀγορὴν καλέσας πολυπείρονα λαὸν
ἤνωγ᾽ ἠΰκόμῳ Δημήτερι πίονα νηὸν
ποιῆσαι καὶ βωμὸν ἐπὶ προὔχοντι κολωνῷ.
οἱ δὲ μάλ᾽ αἶψ᾽ ἐπίθοντο καὶ ἔκλυον αὐδήσαντος,
τεῦχον δ᾽ ὡς ἐπέτελλ᾽· ὁ δ᾽ ἀέξετο δαίμονος αἴσῃ.   300
αὐτὰρ ἐπεὶ τέλεσαν καὶ ἐρώησαν καμάτοιο,
βάν ῥ᾽ ἴμεν οἴκαδ᾽ ἕκαστος· ἀτὰρ ξανθὴ Δημήτηρ
ἔνθα καθεζομένη μακάρων ἀπὸ νόσφιν ἁπάντων
μίμνε πόθῳ μινύθουσα βαθυζώνοιο θυγατρός.

For mortals she ordained a terrible and brutal year   305
on the deeply fertile earth. The ground released
no seed, for bright-crowned Demeter kept it buried.
In vain the oxen dragged many curved plows down
the furrows. In vain much white barley fell on the earth.
She would have destroyed the whole mortal race   310
by cruel famine and stolen the glorious honor of gifts
and sacrifices from those having homes on Olympus,
if Zeus had not seen and pondered their plight in his heart.
First he roused golden-winged Iris to summon
fair-tressed Demeter, so lovely in form.   315
Zeus spoke and Iris obeying the dark-clouded
son of Kronos, raced swiftly between heaven and earth.
She came to the citadel of fragrant Eleusis
and found in her temple dark-robed Demeter.
Addressing her, she spoke winged words: 320
"Demeter, Zeus, the father, with his unfailing knowledge
bids you rejoin the tribes of immortal gods.
Go and let Zeus's word not remain unfulfilled."
Thus she implored, but Demeter's heart was unmoved.
Then the father sent in turn all the blessed immortals;   325
one by one they kept coming and pleading
and offered her many glorious gifts and whatever
honors she might choose among the immortal gods.
Yet not one could bend the mind and thought
of the raging goddess, who harshly spurned their pleas.   330
Never, she said, would she mount up to fragrant
Olympus nor release the seed from the earth,
until she saw with her eyes her own fair-faced child.
When Zeus, heavy-thundering and mighty-voiced,
heard this, he sent down the Slayer of Argos**** to Erebos   335
with his golden staff to wheedle Hades with soft words
and lead back holy Persephone from the misty gloom
into the light to join the gods so that her mother
might see her with her eyes and desist from anger.
Hermes did not disobey. At once he left Olympus's height   340
and plunged swiftly into the depths of the earth.
He met lord Hades inside his dwelling,

**** Hermes

αἰνότατον δ' ἐνιαυτὸν ἐπὶ χθόνα πουλυβότειραν 305
ποίης' ἀνθρώποις καὶ κύντατον, οὐδέ τι γαῖα
σπέρμ' ἀνίει· κρύπτεν γὰρ ἐϋστέφανος Δημήτηρ.
πολλὰ δὲ καμπύλ' ἄροτρα μάτην βόες εἷλκον ἀρούραις,
πολλὸν δὲ κρῖ λευκὸν ἐτώσιον ἔμπεσε γαίῃ.
καί νύ κε πάμπαν ὄλεσσε γένος μερόπων ἀνθρώπων 310
λιμοῦ ὑπ' ἀργαλέης, γεράων τ' ἐρικυδέα τιμὴν
καὶ θυσιῶν ἤμερσεν Ὀλύμπια δώματ' ἔχοντας,
εἰ μὴ Ζεὺς ἐνόησεν ἑῷ τ' ἐφράσσατο θυμῷ.
Ἶριν δὲ πρῶτον χρυσόπτερον ὦρσε καλέσσαι
Δήμητρ' ἠΰκομον πολυήρατον εἶδος ἔχουσαν. 315
ὣς ἔφαθ'· ἡ δὲ Ζηνὶ κελαινεφέϊ Κρονίωνι
πείθετο καὶ μεσσηγὺ διέδραμεν ὦκα πόδεσσιν.
ἵκετο δὲ πτολίεθρον Ἐλευσῖνος θυοέσσης,
εὗρεν δ' ἐν νηῷ Δημήτερα κυανόπεπλον,
καί μιν φωνήσασ' ἔπεα πτερόεντα προσηύδα· 320
    Δήμητερ καλέει σε πατὴρ Ζεὺς ἄφθιτα εἰδὼς
ἐλθέμεναι μετὰ φῦλα θεῶν αἰειγενετάων.
ἀλλ' ἴθι, μηδ' ἀτέλεστον ἐμὸν ἔπος ἐκ Διὸς ἔστω.
    Ὣς φάτο λισσομένη· τῆς δ' οὐκ ἐπεπείθετο θυμός.
αὖτις ἔπειτα ⟨πατὴρ⟩ μάκαρας θεοὺς αἰὲν ἐόντας 325
πάντας ἐπιπροΐαλλεν· ἀμοιβηδὶς δὲ κιόντες
κίκλησκον καὶ πολλὰ δίδον περικαλλέα δῶρα,
τιμάς θ' ἅς κεν ἕλοιτο μετ' ἀθανάτοισι θεοῖσιν·
ἀλλ' οὔ τις πεῖσαι δύνατο φρένας οὐδὲ νόημα
θυμῷ χωομένης, στερεῶς δ' ἠναίνετο μύθους. 330
οὐ μὲν γάρ ποτ' ἔφασκε θυώδεος Οὐλύμποιο
πρίν γ' ἐπιβήσεσθαι, οὐ πρὶν γῆς καρπὸν ἀνήσειν,
πρὶν ἴδοι ὀφθαλμοῖσιν ἑὴν εὐώπιδα κούρην.
    Αὐτὰρ ἐπεὶ τό γ' ἄκουσε βαρύκτυπος εὐρύοπα Ζεύς,
εἰς Ἔρεβος πέμψε χρυσόρραπιν Ἀργειφόντην, 335
ὄφρ' Ἀΐδην μαλακοῖσι παραιφάμενος ἐπέεσσιν
ἁγνὴν Περσεφόνειαν ἀπὸ ζόφου ἠερόεντος
ἐς φάος ἐξαγάγοι μετὰ δαίμονας, ὄφρα ἑ μήτηρ
ὀφθαλμοῖσιν ἰδοῦσα μεταλλήξειε χόλοιο.
Ἑρμῆς δ' οὐκ ἀπίθησεν, ἄφαρ δ' ὑπὸ κεύθεα γαίης 340
ἐσσυμένως κατόρουσε λιπὼν ἕδος Οὐλύμποιο.
τέτμε δὲ τόν γε ἄνακτα δόμων ἔντοσθεν ἐόντα

reclining on a bed with his shy spouse, strongly reluctant
through desire for her mother. [Still she, Demeter,
was brooding on revenge for the deeds of the blessed gods].   345
The strong Slayer of Argos stood near and spoke:
"Dark-haired Hades, ruler of the dead, Father Zeus
bids me lead noble Persephone up from Erebos
to join us, so that her mother might see her with her eyes
and cease from anger and dread wrath against the gods.   350
For she is devising a great scheme to destroy
the helpless race of mortals born on earth,
burying the seed beneath the ground and obliterating
divine honors. Her anger is terrible, nor does she go
among the gods but sits aloof in her fragrant temple,   355
keeping to the rocky citadel of Eleusis."
Thus he spoke and Aidoneus, lord of the dead, smiled
with his brows, nor disobeyed king Zeus's commands.
At once he urged thoughtful Persephone:
"Go, Persephone, to the side of your dark-robed mother,   360
keeping the spirit and temper in your breast benign.
Do not be so sad and angry beyond the rest;
in no way among immortals will I be an unsuitable spouse,
myself a brother of father Zeus. And when you are there,
you will have power over all that lives and moves,   365
and you will possess the greatest honors among the gods.
There will be punishment forevermore for those wrongdoers
who fail to appease your power with sacrifices,
performing proper rites and making due offerings."
Thus he spoke and thoughtful Persephone rejoiced.   370
Eagerly she leapt up for joy. But he gave her to eat
a honey-sweet pomegranate seed, stealthily passing it
around her, lest she once more stay forever
by the side of revered Demeter of the dark robe.
Then Aidoneus commander-to-many yoked   375
his divine horses before the golden chariot.
She mounted the chariot and at her side the strong
Slayer of Argos took the reins and whip in his hands
and dashed from the halls. The horses flew eagerly;
swiftly they completed the long journey; not sea nor   380
river waters, not grassy glens nor mountain peaks
slowed the speed of the immortal horses,

ἥμενον ἐν λεχέεσσι σὺν αἰδοίῃ παρακοίτι
πόλλ᾽ ἀεκαζομένη μητρὸς πόθῳ † ἠδ᾽ ἐπ᾽ ἀτλήτων
ἔργοις θεῶν μακάρων μητίσετο βουλῇ†   345
ἀγχοῦ δ᾽ ἱστάμενος προσέφη κρατὺς Ἀργειφόντης·
   Ἅιδη κυανοχαῖτα καταφθιμένοισιν ἀνάσσων
Ζεύς με πατὴρ ἤνωγεν ἀγαυὴν Περσεφόνειαν
ἐξαγαγεῖν Ἐρέβευσφι μετὰ σφέας, ὄφρα ἑ μήτηρ
ὀφθαλμοῖσιν ἰδοῦσα χόλου καὶ μήνιος αἰνῆς   350
ἀθανάτοις παύσειεν· ἐπεὶ μέγα μήδεται ἔργον
φθῖσαι φῦλ᾽ ἀμενηνὰ χαμαιγενέων ἀνθρώπων
σπέρμ᾽ ὑπὸ γῆς κρύπτουσα, καταφθινύθουσα δὲ τιμὰς
ἀθανάτων. ἡ δ᾽ αἰνὸν ἔχει χόλον, οὐδὲ θεοῖσι
μίσγεται, ἀλλ᾽ ἀπάνευθε θυώδεος ἔνδοθι νηοῦ   355
ἧσται, Ἐλευσῖνος κραναὸν πτολίεθρον ἔχουσα.
   Ὣς φάτο· μείδησεν δὲ ἄναξ ἐνέρων Ἀϊδωνεὺς
ὀφρύσιν, οὐδ᾽ ἀπίθησε Διὸς βασιλῆος ἐφετμῆς.
ἐσσυμένως δ᾽ ἐκέλευσε δαΐφρονι Περσεφονείῃ·
ἔρχεο Περσεφόνη παρὰ μητέρα κυανόπεπλον   360
ἤπιον ἐν στήθεσσι μένος καὶ θυμὸν ἔχουσα,
μηδέ τι δυσθύμαινε λίην περιώσιον ἄλλων.
οὔ τοι ἐν ἀθανάτοισιν ἀεικὴς ἔσσομ᾽ ἀκοίτης
αὐτοκασίγνητος πατρὸς Διός· ἔνθα δ᾽ ἐοῦσα
δεσπόσσεις πάντων ὁπόσα ζώει τε καὶ ἕρπει,   365
τιμὰς δὲ σχήσησθα μετ᾽ ἀθανάτοισι μεγίστας,
τῶν δ᾽ ἀδικησάντων τίσις ἔσσεται ἤματα πάντα
οἵ κεν μὴ θυσίαισι τεὸν μένος ἱλάσκωνται
εὐαγέως ἔρδοντες ἐναίσιμα δῶρα τελοῦντες.
   Ὣς φάτο· γήθησεν δὲ περίφρων Περσεφόνεια,   370
καρπαλίμως δ᾽ ἀνόρουσ᾽ ὑπὸ χάρματος· αὐτὰρ ὅ γ᾽ αὐτὸς
ῥοιῆς κόκκον ἔδωκε φαγεῖν μελιηδέα λάθρῃ
ἀμφὶ ἓ νωμήσας, ἵνα μὴ μένοι ἤματα πάντα
αὖθι παρ᾽ αἰδοίῃ Δημήτερι κυανοπέπλῳ.
ἵππους δὲ προπάροιθεν ὑπὸ χρυσέοισιν ὄχεσφιν   375
ἔντυεν ἀθανάτους πολυσημάντωρ Ἀϊδωνεύς.
ἡ δ᾽ ὀχέων ἐπέβη, παρὰ δὲ κρατὺς Ἀργειφόντης
ἡνία καὶ μάστιγα λαβὼν μετὰ χερσὶ φίλῃσι
σεῦε διὲκ μεγάρων· τὼ δ᾽ οὐκ ἄκοντε πετέσθην.
ῥίμφα δὲ μακρὰ κέλευθα διήνυσαν, οὐδὲ θάλασσα   380
οὔθ᾽ ὕδωρ ποταμῶν οὔτ᾽ ἄγκεα ποιήεντα
ἵππων ἀθανάτων οὔτ᾽ ἄκριες ἔσχεθον ὁρμήν,

slicing the deep air as they flew above these places.
He brought them to a halt where rich-crowned Demeter
waited before the fragrant temple. With one look she darted   385
like a maenad down a mountain shaded with woods.
On her side Persephone, [seeing] her mother's [radiant face],
[left chariot and horses,] and leapt down to run
[and fall on her neck in passionate embrace].
[While holding her dear child in her arms], her [heart   390
suddenly sensed a trick. Fearful, she] drew back
from [her embrace and at once inquired:]
"My child, tell me, you [did not taste] food [while below?]
Speak out [and hide nothing, so we both may know.]
[For if not], ascending [from miserable Hades],   395
you will dwell with me and your father, the
dark-clouded [son of Kronos], honored by all the gods.
But if [you tasted food], returning beneath [the earth,]
you will stay a third part of the seasons [each year],
but two parts with myself and the other immortals.   400
When the earth blooms in spring with all kinds
of sweet flowers, then from the misty dark you will
rise again, a great marvel to gods and mortal men.
By what guile did the mighty Host-to-Many deceive you?"
Then radiant Persephone replied to her in turn: 405
"I will tell you the whole truth exactly, Mother.
The Slayer of Argos came to bring fortunate news
from my father, the son of Kronos, and the other gods
and lead me from Erebos so that seeing me with your eyes
you would desist from your anger and dread wrath   410
at the gods. Then I leapt up for joy, but he stealthily
put in my mouth a food honey-sweet, a pomegranate seed,
and compelled me against my will and by force to taste it.
For the rest—how seizing me by the shrewd plan of my father,
Kronos's son, he carried me off into the earth's depths—   415
I shall tell and elaborate all that you ask.
We were all in the beautiful meadow—
Leukippê; Phaino; Elektra; and Ianthê;
Melitê; Iachê; Rhodeia; and Kallirhoê;
Melibosis; Tychê; and flower-faced Okyrhoê;   420
Khryseis; Ianeira; Akastê; Admetê;
Rhodopê; Plouto; and lovely Kalypso;

ἀλλ' ὑπὲρ αὐτάων βαθὺν ἠέρα τέμνον ἰόντες.
στῆσε δ' ἄγων ὅθι μίμνεν ἐϋστέφανος Δημήτηρ
νηοῖο προπάροιθε θυώδεος· ἡ δὲ ἰδοῦσα   385
ἤϊξ' ἠΰτε μαινὰς ὄρος κάτα δάσκιον ὕλη.

Περσεφόνη δ' ἑτέρ[ωθεν ἐπεὶ ἴδεν ὄμματα καλὰ]
μητρὸς ἑῆς κατ' [ἄρ' ἥ γ' ὄχεα προλιποῦσα καὶ ἵππους]
ἆλτο θέει[ν, δειρῇ δέ οἱ ἔμπεσεν ἀμφιχυθεῖσα·]
τῇ δὲ [φίλην ἔτι παῖδα ἑῆς μετὰ χερσὶν ἐχούσῃ]   390
α[ἶψα δόλον θυμός τιν' ὀίσατο, τρέσσε δ' ἄρ' αἰνῶς]
πα[υ]ομ[ένη φιλότητος, ἄφαρ δ' ἐρεείνετο μύθῳ·]
   Τέκνον μή ῥά τί μοι σ[ύ γε πάσσαο νέρθεν ἐοῦσα]
βρώμης; ἐξαύδα, [μὴ κεῦθ', ἵνα εἴδομεν ἄμφω·]
ὡς μὲν γάρ κ' ἀνιοῦσα π[αρὰ στυγεροῦ Ἀίδαο]   395
καὶ παρ' ἐμοὶ καὶ πατρὶ κελ[αινεφέϊ Κρονίωνι]
ναιετάοις πάντεσσι τετιμ[ένη ἀθανάτοι]σιν.
εἰ δέ, πτᾶσα πάλιν ⟨σύ γ'⟩ ἰοῦσ' ὑπ[ὸ κεύθεσι γαίης]
οἰκήσεις ὡρέων τρίτατον μέρ[ος εἰς ἐνιαυτόν,]
τὰς δὲ δύω παρ' ἐμοί τε καὶ [ἄλλοις ἀθανά]τοισιν.   400
ὁππότε δ' ἄνθεσι γαῖ' εὐώδε[σιν] ἠαρινο[ῖσι]
παντοδαποῖς θάλλει, τότ' ἀπὸ ζόφου ἠερόεντος
αὖτις ἄνει μέγα θαῦμα θεοῖς θνητοῖς τ' ἀνθρώποις.
καὶ τίνι σ' ἐξαπάτησε δόλῳ κρατερ[ὸς πολυδ]έγμων;
   Τὴν δ' αὖ Περσεφόνη περικαλλὴς ἀντίον ηὔδα·   405
τοιγὰρ ἐγώ τοι μῆτερ ἐρέω νημερτέα πάντα·
εὖτέ μοι ἄγγελος ἦλθ' ἐριούνιος Ἀργειφόντης
πὰρ πατέρος Κρονίδαο καὶ ἄλλων οὐρανιώνων
ἐλθεῖν ἐξ Ἐρέβευς, ἵνα μ' ὀφθαλμοῖσιν ἰδοῦσα
λήξαις ἀθανάτοισι χόλου καὶ μήνιος αἰνῆς,   410
αὐτὰρ ἐγὼν ἀνόρουσ' ὑπὸ χάρματος, αὐτὰρ ὁ λάθρῃ
ἔμβαλέ μοι ῥοιῆς κόκκον, μελιηδέ' ἐδωδήν,
ἄκουσαν δὲ βίῃ με προσηνάγκασσε πάσασθαι.
ὡς δέ μ' ἀναρπάξας Κρονίδεω πυκινὴν διὰ μῆτιν
ᾤχετο πατρὸς ἐμοῖο φέρων ὑπὸ κεύθεα γαίης   415
ἐξερέω καὶ πάντα διίξομαι ὡς ἐρεείνεις.
ἡμεῖς μὲν μάλα πᾶσαι ἀν' ἱμερτὸν λειμῶνα,
Λευκίππη Φαινώ τε καὶ Ἠλέκτρη καὶ Ἰάνθη
καὶ Μελίτη Ἰάχη τε Ῥόδειά τε Καλλιρόη τε
Μηλόβοσίς τε Τύχη τε καὶ Ὠκυρόη καλυκῶπις   420
Χρυσηίς τ' Ἰάνειρά τ' Ἀκάστη τ' Ἀδμήτη τε
καὶ Ῥοδόπη Πλουτώ τε καὶ ἱμερόεσσα Καλυψὼ

Styx; Ourania; and fair Galaxaura; Pallas,
rouser of battles; and Artemis, sender of arrows—
playing and picking lovely flowers with our hands,   425
soft crocus mixed with irises and hyacinth,
rosebuds and lilies, a marvel to see, and the
narcissus that wide earth bore like a crocus.
As I joyously plucked it, the ground gaped from beneath,
and the mighty lord, Host-to-Many, rose from it   430
and carried me off beneath the earth in his golden chariot
much against my will. And I cried out at the top of my voice.
I speak the whole truth, though I grieve to tell it."
Then all day long, their minds at one, they soothed
each other's heart and soul in many ways,   435
embracing fondly, and their spirits abandoned grief,
as they gave and received joy between them.
Hekate of the delicate veil drew near them
and often caressed the daughter of holy Demeter;
from that time this lady served her as chief attendant.   440
To them Zeus, heavy-thundering and mighty-voiced,
sent as mediator fair-tressed Rheia to summon
dark-robed Demeter to the tribes of gods; he promised
to give her what honors she might choose among the gods.
He agreed his daughter would spend one-third   445
of the revolving year in the misty dark and two-thirds
with her mother and the other immortals.
So he spoke and the goddess did not disobey his commands.
She darted swiftly down the peaks of Olympus
and arrived where the Rarian plain, once life-giving   450
udder of earth, now giving no life at all, stretched idle
and utterly leafless. For the white barley was hidden
by the designs of lovely-ankled Demeter. Yet as spring came on,
the fields would soon ripple with long ears of grain;
and the rich furrows would grow heavy on the ground   455
with grain to be tied with bands into sheaves.
There she first alighted from the barren air.
Mother and daughter were glad to see each other
and rejoiced at heart. Rheia of the delicate veil then said:
"Come, child, Zeus, heavy-thundering and mighty-voiced,   460
summons you to rejoin the tribes of the gods;
he has offered to give what honors you choose among them.

καὶ Στὺξ Οὐρανίη τε Γαλαξαύρη τ' ἐρατεινὴ
Παλλάς τ' ἐγρεμάχη καὶ Ἄρτεμις ἰοχέαιρα
παίζομεν ἠδ' ἄνθεα δρέπομεν χείρεσσ' ἐρόεντα,   425
μίγδα κρόκον τ' ἀγανὸν καὶ ἀγαλλίδας ἠδ' ὑάκινθον
καὶ ῥοδέας κάλυκας καὶ λείρια, θαῦμα ἰδέσθαι,
νάρκισσόν θ' ὃν ἔφυσ' ὥς περ κρόκον εὐρεῖα χθών.
αὐτὰρ ἐγὼ δρεπόμην περὶ χάρματι, γαῖα δ' ἔνερθε
χώρησεν, τῇ δ' ἔκθορ' ἄναξ κρατερὸς πολυδέγμων.   430
βῆ δὲ φέρων ὑπὸ γαῖαν ἐν ἅρμασι χρυσείοισι
πόλλ' ἀεκαζομένην, ἐβόησα δ' ἄρ' ὄρθια φωνῇ.
ταῦτά τοι ἀχνυμένη περ ἀληθέα πάντ' ἀγορεύω.

   Ὣς τότε μὲν πρόπαν ἦμαρ ὁμόφρονα θυμὸν ἔχουσαι
πολλὰ μάλ' ἀλλήλων κραδίην καὶ θυμὸν ἴαινον   435
ἀμφαγαπαζόμεναι, ἀχέων δ' ἀπεπαύετο θυμός.
γηθοσύνας δὲ δέχοντο παρ' ἀλλήλων ἔδιδ[όν τε.]
τῇσιν δ' ἐγγύθεν ἦλθ' Ἑκάτη λιπαροκρήδεμνος,
πολλὰ δ' ἄρ' ἀμφαγάπησε κόρην Δήμητρος ἁγνῆς·
ἐκ τοῦ οἱ πρόπολος καὶ ὀπάων ἔπλετ' ἄνασσα.   440
ταῖς δὲ μετάγγελον ἧκε βαρύκτυπος εὐρύοπα Ζεὺς
Ῥείην ἠΰκομον Δημήτερα κυανόπεπλον
ἀξέμεναι μετὰ φῦλα θεῶν, ὑπέδεκτο δὲ τιμὰς
δωσέμεν, ἅς κεν ἕλοιτο μετ' ἀθανάτοισι θεοῖσι·
νεῦσε δέ οἱ κούρην ἔτεος περιτελλομένοιο   445
τὴν τριτάτην μὲν μοῖραν ὑπὸ ζόφον ἠερόεντα,
τὰς δὲ δύω παρὰ μητρὶ καὶ ἄλλοις ἀθανάτοισιν.
ὣς ἔφατ', οὐδ' ἀπίθησε θεὰ Διὸς ἀγγελιάων.
ἐσσυμένως δ' ἤϊξε κατ' Οὐλύμποιο καρήνων,
εἰς δ' ἄρα Ῥάριον ἷξε, φερέσβιον οὖθαρ ἀρούρης   450
τὸ πρίν, ἀτὰρ τότε γ' οὔ τι φερέσβιον, ἀλλὰ ἔκηλον
εἱστήκει πανάφυλλον· ἔκευθε δ' ἄρα κρῖ λευκὸν
μήδεσι Δήμητρος καλλισφύρου· αὐτὰρ ἔπειτα
μέλλεν ἄφαρ ταναοῖσι κομήσειν ἀσταχύεσσιν
ἦρος ἀεξομένοιο, πέδῳ δ' ἄρα πίονες ὄγμοι   455
βρισέμεν ἀσταχύων, τὰ δ' ἐν ἐλλεδανοῖσι δεδέσθαι.
ἔνθ' ἐπέβη πρώτιστον ἀπ' αἰθέρος ἀτρυγέτοιο·
ἀσπασίως δ' ἴδον ἀλλήλας, κεχάρηντο δὲ θυμῷ.
τὴν δ' ὧδε προσέειπε Ῥέη λιπαροκρήδεμνος·

   Δεῦρο τέκος, καλέει σε βαρύκτυπος εὐρύοπα Ζεὺς   460
ἐλθέμεναι μετὰ φῦλα θεῶν, ὑπέδεκτο δὲ τιμὰς
[δωσέμεν, ἅς κεν ἕλοιο] μετ' ἀθανάτοισι θεοῖσι.

He agreed that his daughter would spend one-third
of the revolving year in the misty dark, and two-thirds
with her mother and the other immortals. 465
He guaranteed it would be so with a nod of his head.
So come, my child, obey me; do not rage overmuch
and forever at the dark-clouded son of Kronos.
Now make the grain grow fertile for humankind."
So Rheia spoke, and rich-crowned Demeter did not disobey. 470
At once she sent forth fruit from the fertile fields
and the whole wide earth burgeoned with leaves
and flowers. She went to the kings who administer law,
Triptolemos and Diokles, driver of horses, mighty
Eumolpos and Keleos, leader of the people, and revealed 475
the conduct of her rites and taught her Mysteries to all of them,
holy rites that are not to be transgressed, nor pried into, 478
nor divulged. For a great awe of the gods stops the voice.
Blessed is the mortal on earth who has seen these rites, 480
but the uninitiate who has no share in them never
has the same lot once dead in the dreary darkness.
When the great goddess had founded all her rites,
the goddesses left for Olympus and the assembly of the other gods.
There they dwell by Zeus delighting-in-thunder, inspiring 485
awe and reverence. Highly blessed is the mortal
on earth whom they graciously favor with love.
For soon they will send to the hearth of his great house
Ploutos, the god giving abundance to mortals.
But come, you goddesses, dwelling in the town of 490
fragrant Eleusis, and seagirt Paros, and rocky Antron,
revered Deo, mighty giver of seasons and glorious gifts,
you and your very fair daughter Persephone,
for my song grant gladly a living that warms the heart.
And I shall remember you and a new song as well. 495

[νεῦσε δέ σοι κούρην ἔτεος π]εριτελλομένοιο
[τὴν τριτάτην μὲν μοῖραν ὑπὸ ζόφον ἠ]ερόεντα,
[τὰς δὲ δύω παρὰ σοί τε καὶ ἄλλοις] ἀθανάτοισιν.   465
            ]εσθαι· ἑῷ δ᾽ ἐπένευσε κάρητι.
[ἀλλ᾽ ἴθι τέκνον] ἐμὸν καὶ πείθεο, μηδέ τι λίην
ἀ[ζηχὲς μεν]έαινε κελαινεφέϊ Κρονίωνι·
α[ἶψα δὲ κα]ρπὸν ἄεξε φερέσβιον ἀνθρώποισιν.
    Ὣ[ς ἔφατ᾽, οὐ]δ᾽ ἀπίθησεν ἐϋστέφανος Δημήτηρ,   470
αἶψα δὲ καρπὸν ἀνῆκεν ἀρουράων ἐριβώλων.
πᾶσα δὲ φύλλοισίν τε καὶ ἄνθεσιν εὐρεῖα χθὼν
ἔβρισ᾽· ἡ δὲ κιοῦσα θεμιστοπόλοις βασιλεῦσι
δ[εῖξε,] Τριπτολέμῳ τε Διοκλεῖ τε πληξίππῳ,
Εὐμόλπου τε βίη Κελεῷ θ᾽ ἡγήτορι λαῶν,   475
δρησμοσύνην θ᾽ ἱερῶν καὶ ἐπέφραδεν ὄργια πᾶσι,
σεμνά, τά γ᾽ οὔ πως ἔστι παρεξ[ίμ]εν οὔ[τε] πυθέσθαι,   478
οὔτ᾽ ἀχέειν· μέγα γάρ τι θεῶν σέβας ἰσχάνει αὐδήν.
ὄλβιος ὃς τάδ᾽ ὄπωπεν ἐπιχθονίων ἀνθρώπων·   480
ὃς δ᾽ ἀτελὴς ἱερῶν, ὅς τ᾽ ἄμμορος, οὔ ποθ᾽ ὁμοίων
αἶσαν ἔχει φθίμενός περ ὑπὸ ζόφῳ εὐρώεντι.
    Αὐτὰρ ἐπεὶ δὴ πάνθ᾽ ὑπεθήκατο δῖα θεάων,
βάν ῥ᾽ ἴμεν Οὔλυμπον δὲ θεῶν μεθ᾽ ὁμήγυριν ἄλλων.
ἔνθα δὲ ναιετάουσι παραὶ Διὶ τερπικεραύνῳ   485
σεμναί τ᾽ αἰδοῖαί τε· μέγ᾽ ὄλβιος ὅν τιν᾽ ἐκεῖναι
προφρονέως φίλωνται ἐπιχθονίων ἀνθρώπων·
αἶψα δέ οἱ πέμπουσιν ἐφέστιον ἐς μέγα δῶμα
Πλοῦτον, ὃς ἀνθρώποις ἄφενος θνητοῖσι δίδωσιν.
    Ἀλλ᾽ ἄγ᾽ Ἐλευσῖνος Θυοέσσης δῆμον ἔχουσαι   490
καὶ Πάρον ἀμφιρύτην Ἄντρωνά τε πετρήεντα,
πότνια ἀγλαόδωρ᾽ ὡρηφόρε Δηοῖ ἄνασσα
αὐτὴ καὶ κούρη περικαλλὴς Περσεφόνεια
πρόφρονες ἀντ᾽ ᾠδῆς βίοτον θυμῆρε᾽ ὀπάζειν.
αὐτὰρ ἐγὼ καὶ σεῖο καὶ ἄλλης μνήσομ᾽ ἀοιδῆς.   495

COMMENTARY ON THE HOMERIC
HYMN TO DEMETER

Helene P. Foley

THE HOMERIC HYMNS were songs composed to honor and praise deities and apparently served as preludes (*prooimia*) to the recitation of other epic poetry.[1, 2] Although we know nothing certain about their audience and the circumstances of their performance, they were probably composed for recitation at feasts, at poetic contests, and at seasonally recurring festivals (the last two would often occur in combination). In a tradition where oral recitation is the primary mode of poetic communication, the context of performance (here uncertain) is probably the determining feature of a poetic "genre". Yet the Homeric hymns are a body of poems with some shared characteristics. (The *Hymn to Demeter* includes all the features described below unless otherwise noted.) To the degree that they represent a genre from a formal perspective, the hymns describe the acquisition of distinctive powers and honors (including major cults and sanctuaries) by gods or goddesses. They tend to begin and close with an address to the deity or deities celebrated and a description of or an allusion to their special prerogatives, haunts, and activities. Both the openings and closings of the poems mark characteristics of the deity with traditional epithets. The closing often brings events up to the present time and includes a farewell and the promise of another song.

The hymns are sung prayers: the elements mentioned above secure the attention and favor of the divinity to the singer and his community. The poet's closing plea to the god generally follows a statement of credentials that justifies the god's granting of the present request on the basis of past favors (sacrifices and gifts to the god or prayers previously answered by the god) or the god's special powers (e.g., the growth of grain is your specialty,

---

[1] This commentary owes greater debts to Richardson 1974 than are accounted for in these notes. I have noted his contributions above all on points of interpretation.

[2] The Homeric hymns are formally preludes to another song. The poets repeatedly close their poems (or sometimes sections of their poems) by saying that they will go on to another song. The *prooimion* described by Thucydides (3.104.3–4) was a version of the Homeric *Hymn to Apollo*. Yet the Homeric hymns may have developed to a length that contradicts their function as preludes. See Nagy 1990b: 353–60.

and therefore you should grant this prayer).[3] A hymn may include an account of the god's birth (absent in the *Hymn to Demeter*), a conflict or challenge faced by the deity, his or her acquisition of honors, a divine epiphany, an ascent to and/or scene on Olympus. The longer hymns like the *Hymn to Demeter* all include a substantial mythological narrative—a sacred narrative reflecting on the origin of things—that also contains recurring motifs. As Jenny Clay has pointed out, these hymns deal with the events that occur after Zeus has consolidated his reign over the universe, but before the world familiar to humankind has taken shape.[4] The audience hears about events that fulfill what it wants fulfilled. In the *Hymn to Demeter*, Rheia finally persuades Demeter to make the crops grow after Persephone's return (469), and Demeter establishes the Mysteries (473–82).[5]

The *Hymn*, composed in dactylic hexameter verse (the same meter that is used in the Homeric epics), follows the tradition of oral epic in its diction, style, and narrative technique. Hence its style is repetitive, if not as repetitive (for example, in the exact repetition of speeches) as Homer. Individual lines are composed in large part by combining in a creative fashion traditional word and phrase patterns (or sometimes whole lines are repeated verbatim), which the poet has learned from the repertory of the oral tradition. Many of its scenes also adapt a predictable narrative pattern (the elements in these type-scenes are noted later in this commentary). I have tried to preserve in my translation much of the repetition of epithets (adjectives) used to describe the major characters (e.g., "fair-tressed Demeter," "Zeus heavy-thundering and mighty-voiced") as well as other important repeated words, lines, and phrases, but eliminated some of the connectives, which are awkward in English style. I have also tried to capture some of the Greek word order wherever it is possible and effective to do so in English. The Appendix to the interpretive essay discusses other features of the *Hymn* that place it within the tradition of Panhellenic poetry (poetry such as the Homeric epics or Hesiod's *Theogony* that was composed for audiences in any Greek city-state, rather than for a local audience in one community).

The author or authors of the poem are unknown, but scholars argue for a date between 650–550 B.C.E. on stylistic and historical grounds. I have been careful not to make assumptions in my interpretation about the authorship of the poem—in any case, the poet (or poets) who composed this text are working in a tradition where individual contributions are impossible to distinguish. Richard Janko has argued that its language assimilates the *Hymn* more closely to the Boeotian tradition of Hesiod, and that its dialectical idiosyncracies are most easily explained by an Attic origin. He

[3] Bremer 1981:193–97 and Graf 1991:esp. 189.

[4] Clay 1989: esp. 15–16. See also Rudhardt 1978, this volume.

[5] On the genre of the hymns, see further Friedländer 1966, Minton 1970, Lenz 1975, Janko 1981, Bremer 1981, Race 1982, and Miller 1985.

prefers a late-seventh- or early-sixth-century date. If the temple of Demeter to which the *Hymn* refers is the early-sixth-century building constructed at the time of the Attic statesman Solon, a date on the later side might be preferable.[6] The section on "Athens and Eleusis" in the Appendix to the interpretive essay discusses the controversial issue of the poem's relation to the historical context in which it was probably composed.[7]

This commentary refers frequently both to the Eleusinian Mysteries that are founded by the goddess Demeter at the conclusion of the poem and to other Greco-Roman versions of the Demeter/Persephone myth. The separate section on the Mysteries gives what information we have about these rites, the final phases of which have remained largely a well-kept secret. These Mysteries, the most important of the mystery cults of antiquity, eventually attracted initiates from the entire Greco-Roman world; in the classical period (480–323 B.C.E.—we are uncertain about who could participate at the time the *Hymn* was composed) most Athenians (including women and slaves) and many other Greeks were initiated into them. They promised initiates happiness in this life and a different lot in the afterlife. A list of other important Greco-Roman versions of the myth is given here.[8]

Hesiod, *Theogony* 913–14
Pamphos, *Hymn to Demeter* (Pausanias 1.38.3, 8.37.9, 9.31.9. See also 1.39.1)
Orphic fragments (esp. 49–52 Kern)[9]
Orphic *Argonautika* 1191–96
Orphic hymns 18, 29, 41, 43
Euripides, *Helen* 1301–68
Isokrates, *Panegyrikos* 28–29
Kallimachos, *Hymn* 6
Nikander, *Theriaka* 483–87 (with scholia) and *Alexipharmaka* 129–32
Philikos, choriambic *Hymn to Demeter* (Page *GLP* 90)[10]
Hellenistic *Hymn to Demeter* (Page *GLP* 91)
Apollodoros, *Library (Bibliotheca)* 1.5.1–3
Hyginus, *Fabulae* 146, 147

[6] Burkert 1977:442–43, review of Richardson 1974.

[7] See further Richardson 1974:5–12 and Janko 1982:181–83.

[8] For additional minor references, some too fragmentary to follow (e.g., Philetas Kous, frags. 673–675D in Lloyd-Jones and Parsons 1983:318–320), see Richardson 1974:74–86. See also Förster 1874. I have included some brief references to the myth in this list because they contain an important version of key elements.

[9] As far as I know, these Orphic fragments are not available as a group in English translation, although individual fragments have been translated (frags. 50 and 52 are from Clement's *Protreptikos* [2.17.1 and 2.20.1–21.1] and frag. 51 = Pausanias 1.14.3). The Orphic hymns are available in a translation by Athanassakis 1977. The Orphic *Argonautika* is translated into French. (Budé edition by Vian 1987)

[10] Lloyd-Jones and Parsons's later version of the text (1983:321–27) does not include a translation.

Diodorus Siculus *Bibliotheca historica* 5.3–5 (see also 5.68–69.1–3)
Cicero, *Against Verres* 2.4. 106–8
Vergil, *Georgics* 1.39 (with the commentary by Servius)
Lucan, *Civil Wars* 6.698–700 and 739–42
Ovid, *Metamorphoses* 5.385–661 and *Fasti* 4.417–620
Lactantius Placidus on Statius *Thebaid* 5.347[11]
Claudian, *On the Rape of Proserpina* (*De raptu Proserpinae*)
Nonnos, *Dionysiaka* 6.1–168
Second Vatican Mythographer 94–100[12]

The text of the *Hymn to Demeter* derives from a single mutilated manuscript of the early fifteenth century C.E., discovered in a stable in Moscow in 1777, supplemented by papyrus fragments. The Greek text is that of N. J. Richardson 1974, with the exception of conjectures added at lines 398–404 (see further ad loc). I have used brackets [] in the translation where the text is so damaged that reliable conjecture is impossible.

1–14 The opening is typical of the hymn form, which invokes the deity to be celebrated. As is often the case in the hymns, the first word of the poem gives its subject, Demeter. Using a framing device standard in early Greek poetry, ring composition, the poem begins and ends with Demeter (492) and her daughter. Also typical of Homeric poetry is the use of compound adjectives or epithets in the opening lines to characterize the subject(s) of the poem. The term *semnê* (1), "awesome" or "sacred," which occurs here in epic for the first time, is also especially characteristic of these two goddesses.

The first eleven lines of the poem form one extended sentence, which emphasizes the shock that the violent abduction produces in the innocent and unnamed daughter and her mother, Demeter; the devious plans of Zeus; and the wondrous effect of the narcissus. The structure of the sentence links and then separates the divine mother and daughter. Such elaborate openings also occur at the beginning of the two Homeric epics. Stylistically, the surprise and brutality of the event is expressed by the delay of the word *hêrpaksen*, "seized," until line 3, by the emphatic positioning of the word at the beginning of this line, and by its juxtaposition with *dôken*, "gave" (in my translation I have had to delay the word until the end of the line).[13] Although marriage by abduction had a place in Greek tradition and marriages may often have taken place without the consent of the bride and her mother,[14] it could be argued that the word order in line 3 creates a sharp

---

[11] Not available in translation.

[12] Bode 1834: vol. I, pp. 94–95. Not available in translation.

[13] Clay 1989: 209.

[14] See Scarpi 1976: 109–30 with further bibliography and the discussion under "Marriage" in my interpretive essay.

contrast between Zeus's giving of Persephone, as in a marriage, and Hades' violent act. The word *nosphin* at the opening of line 4 can imply both that the abduction took place without the knowledge and consent of Demeter and that Persephone was at a physical distance from her mother when it occurred. It is difficult to find an appropriate English word to translate Hades' act of violent abduction. (See Fig. 1). In modern usage the word *rape* emphasizes sexual consummation, which is uncertain in this case. On line 3, for example, I have translated the verb (*hêrpaksen*) as "seized" and at line 19 (*harpaksas*) as "snatched"; later Demeter uses for Persephone's experience a word with even stronger connotations of overpowering force, which I translated as "suffering violence" (*biazomenês*, 68).

Zeus's authorizing of the abduction occurs first in Hesiod (*Theogony* 913–14) and is often emphasized in later versions influenced by the *Hymn*. The language in both versions suggests that Hesiod and the *Hymn* follow a similar tradition. By contrast, in Claudian's *De Raptu Proserpinae*, Jupiter (the Roman Zeus) bows to the demands of fate and Pluto (Hades). In Ovid's *Metamorphoses* Venus (Aphrodite) sets the story in motion by having Cupid (Eros) shoot a love dart into Pluto. A concerned patriarch, Ovid's Jupiter responds at once to Ceres' (Demeter's) appeal, although he sees the advantage of the match. The section on "Marriage" in the interpretive essay discusses in detail the *Hymn*'s treatment of Hades' abduction/marriage and Zeus's role in it.

Zeus's giving of Persephone in Demeter's absence and without her consent inaugurates a series of displacements in the poem, in which gods shift into spheres where they were not present before, or stand apart from each other (This is emphasized by the repetition of Greek words meaning "apart from"; see *nosphin* at 4, 27, 72, 114, and 303 and *apaneuthe*, 355; see also 92 and 158).[15] Demeter's withdrawal first from Olympus and then into her temple during her famine structurally parallels her daughter's removal into the world below.[16] The fact that mother and daughter are separated at the time of the abduction suggests that Persephone is moving toward maturity and independence from her mother. Again in contrast to some later versions but in keeping with Homeric conventions, Zeus remains remote throughout the poem. Here (27–29) he sits apart in his temple on earth, receiving sacrifices from mortals—the very gifts of which Demeter will later deprive him with her famine. It may be significant that Zeus also played at best a marginal role in the Eleusinian Mysteries themselves.[17]

2 Aidoneus is another name for Hades, the god of many names and "Host-to-Many" (9).

---

[15] See Segal 1981:132ff. on the theme of apartness in the poem.
[16] See Van Nortwick:58.
[17] Nilsson 1935:126.

3 The epithet for Zeus I translate as "mighty-voiced" may also mean "far-seeing."

4 Demeter is not generally associated with a golden sword (or sickle?); the meaning and cult association of this epithet is obscure. The chief deities of cities often served as protectors of that city, and the sword may signify such a role for Demeter.[18]

5–14 The Okeanidai, or daughters of Okeanos, are water deities (as is Korê in some contexts) who, like all nymphs, protect and nourish the young as *kourotrophoi*. In other versions of the myth, and in Persephone's later version of the story in this poem (417–24), the powerful virgin goddesses Pallas (Athena) and Artemis are also present at the abduction (see also Orphic fragment 49.40ff.; Euripides' *Helen* 1314ff., where Aphrodite is also present; the Epidaurian Hymn; Diodorus Siculus, *Bibliotheca* 5.3.4; Hyginus 146; Claudian, etc. The vase in Fig. 1 follows this version). In these later versions, they often try but (bowing to Zeus's intervention with a thunderbolt) fail to protect Persephone from being abducted. Given our knowledge of later tradition, the absence at this point in the poem of the powerful eternal virgins Athena and Artemis, goddessses who reject marriage for themselves, could (unless 417–24 are interpolated) be significant in several respects. First, by leaving Persephone without potential defenders, the text highlights her helplessness. (On the failure of the Okeanidai to serve even as witnesses to the abduction, see further on line 17 below.) Second, later versions of the myth use the goddesses' presence to suggest that Persephone was on the verge of joining Artemis and Athena in permanent virginity (Diodorus Siculus *Bibliotheca* 5.3.4, Ovid, *Metamorphoses* 5. 375–77), whereas the *Hymn* hints at her readiness for marriage. In Ovid's *Metamorphoses* the nymph Cyane tries to block Proserpina's abduction as illegitimate (5.411–20). Pluto is acting without Ceres' knowledge, she argues; he should woo Proserpina, not abduct her. When Hades later resorts to using persuasion to make the unwilling Persephone content with being his wife, the *Hymn* makes a similar point.

Girls in myth are traditionally carried off, often from a chorus of maidens, while gathering flowers in a meadow (or by water). Flower-gathering festivals in which girls (often girls on the verge of marriage) participated occurred throughout Greece. Europa and Oreithyia are among the mythical virgins abducted while picking flowers. Nausikäa and her maidens face a potential male threat of this kind when Odysseus emerges from the bushes on the beach at Scheria (*Odyssey* 6. 135ff.). Meadows in Greek myth are liminal sites, associated not only with a transition to sexuality and fertility

---

[18] See Cassolà 1975:ad loc.

but with the underworld and with Elysion and the Isles of the Blest. The motif of abduction from a meadow and a group of maidens suggests the girl's readiness for marriage. Here Persephone is described as fertile or blooming (*thalerên*, 79) and accompanied by mature companions (the deep-breasted Okeanidai).[19] In Claudian's version of the story, Persephone has already had several suitors (1.133–37; see also Nonnos *Dionysiaka* 6.1–7). Persephone's flowerlike face (line 8) links her with the plants she picks. Through her identification with plants and the growth of plants in a seasonal cycle, Persephone is also, mythically speaking, an appropriate spouse for an underworld god, for the seed with which she is identified in later myth and cult disappears and reappears from beneath the ground.

Of the flowers picked by Persephone, roses are associated with eros, and the narcissus, like many other flowers that grow from bulbs and produce fruits, was thought to be an aphrodisiac.[20] Most of these flowers are known at least at a later date to have developed underworld associations.[21] The hyacinth, the narcissus, the violet, and the crocus (as well as the pomegranate) are all associated in later myth with young heroes (Hyakinthos, Narkissos, Attis, and Krokos) who fell victim to untimely death at an earlier age. The narcissus seems to have been associated with the Great Goddesses, Demeter and Persephone (Sophocles *Oedipous at Kolonos* 683), and sacred to the underworld deities, the Eumenides. The flower was thought to have soporific qualities (the root *nark-* in *narkissos* suggests torpor and death). It has been suggested that the picking of flowers (often by women and in a ritual context), especially flowers that grow from bulbs, should be associated with gathering and pre-cereal cultures; if so, the choice of flowers derives from an alternative version of the myth in which the abduction takes place before humans have agriculture (here it is already established).[22] Not all of these flowers are spring flowers, and hence the moment at which Persephone is abducted cannot be definitely linked with spring.[23] The poem's vagueness about the season at which the abduction occurred perhaps suggests a world in which the cycle of seasons is not yet fully established.

The gathering of flowers may have played a part in the rites at Eleusis, although garlands were banned as hateful to the goddesses at Demeter's festival at the Thesmophoria.

[19] Lincoln 1979:224; on the use of *bathukolpos*, or "deep-breasted," as an epithet for Trojan women in the *Iliad*, see Richardson 1974:ad loc.

[20] See Scarpi 1976:49.

[21] See Piccaluga 1966:esp. 241–42 for a detailed discussion of this issue.

[22] Chirassi 1968:91–124, Chirassi-Columbo 1975:199, and Piccaluga 1966: esp. 233. On these alternative versions of the myth, see the section on "Variants of the Myth" in the interpretive essay.

[23] Richardson 1974:142. In the Sicilian version of the myth, flowers are said to bloom all year on the plain of Enna (Diodorus Siculus 5.4.3; Ovid *Metamorphoses* 5.391).

9 Gaia or Earth plays a similar role in facilitating the plans and in arbitrating the succession of her male descendants in Hesiod's cosmology, the *Theogony*.[24] There she first encourages Kronos to castrate his father Ouranos and then helps her daughter Rheia save Zeus from being swallowed by his father Kronos by wrapping a stone in swaddling clothes. Her cooperation with Zeus may prefigure the ultimate compromise between the sexes that concludes the poem. Earth's narcissus produces wonder in the realms of heaven, earth, and the sea (see also 33–35. Nature frequently responds to important divine events in early Greek poetry). The poem's events also occur in heaven, earth, and the underworld, and in the end these three spheres of the cosmos are drawn into a new relation to each other.

This is the first of three important deceptions/acts of secrecy in the poem (Demeter deceives Metaneira by hiding Demophoön in the fire, and Hades deceives Persephone with the pomegranate seed). Secrecy was an important theme in the Mysteries as well.

11 The translation at line 11 (literally, "for the immortal gods and for mortal humans") has been adjusted to capture the elegant parallelism in the line.

15–32 These lines emphasize the august importance of the bridegroom Hades, whose description is augmented, especially in 31, with elaborate compound adjectives; the unwillingness of Persephone (at 19 and 30—this motif frames the passage), who pathetically calls out for the help of her father, the source of her difficulties;[25] the suddenness and violence of the transition to the world below; and the motifs of hearing and seeing so important in the rites of the Mysteries as well (see further below).

The text stylistically anticipates Helios's defense of Hades' abduction by closely juxtaposing in 30–31 the unwillingness of the bride and the august attributes of her powerful uncle. Because the poet does not use multiple epithets indiscriminately (only Zeus, Demeter, and Hades receive them), line 31 stands out (in lines 31–32 three of Hades' epithets also begin with *poly-* or "many" and the alliteration of *p* in these lines emphasizes the repetition).[26] The word *polysêmantôr*, "commander," means "giver of signs to many"; at 131 the pirates who abduct Demeter in her lying tale are called *sêmantoras*. The word *polyonymos* can mean "much-praised" or "many-named." Hades is probably said to have had many names in part because Greeks, especially in cult, often feared to name him or wished to propitiate him; in reality Hades had few epithets and was rarely worshiped in cult on

[24] Clay 1989:213–14.
[25] Ibid.:214n.47.
[26] Segal 1981:112.

his own.[27] Both Hades and Zeus are sons of Kronos; the repetition of this epithet for both gods, in a fashion typical of epic but confusing to the modern reader, also serves to emphasize Hades' close relation to Zeus and thus his suitability as a bridegroom. Marriage to a paternal uncle was not uncommon in Greek culture.

17 The Nysian plain has associations with the wine god Dionysos, who later played a role in the Mysteries, probably under the name Iakchos. In contrast to other versions of the myth, the setting here is vague and mythical; it may, as in the Orphic version (frag. 43 Kern), suggest a location in the region of Okeanos (his descendants the Okeanids are present), that is, the ends of the earth. The abduction occurs in later versions of the myth at about thirteen different sites, and there was clearly no fixed version at the time of the poem or later. In the well-known Sicilian version of the myth, for example, Persephone is abducted into a cave at Enna. At Eleusis, of course, the abduction was later said to have occurred locally.[28] The vague and remote setting in the *Hymn* permits the poet to avoid the presence of informative witnesses, especially the human witnesses to the abduction common in many other versions. (This alternate version receives a covert reference in line 45. Lines 54–56 reappear in a later Orphic version; there Demeter addresses Eleusinians, not Hekate.) The fact that the Okeanidai are present but perform no function in the narrative beyond creating a context for the abduction, either by attempting to save Persephone or to act as witnesses to her abduction, suggests that the *Hymn* is deliberately choosing to ignore this aspect of its tradition. Even Hekate (25, 57), like Demeter herself (68), only *hears* the cry, from her cave, a place between the bright world above and the dark world below, which closes off her vision.

20–21 The cry for help is a call for witnesses standard in primitive justice.[29] *Deuteronomy* 22.24–27 makes it clear that a woman who is raped is not held responsible if she cries out in protest (Potiphar's wife incriminates Joseph by crying out at *Genesis* 39). Euripides' *Ion* 893 and *Trojan Women* 998–1000 suggest that the same implications could be present here.

22 The phrase "of the immortal gods or of humankind" (literally, "mortal humans") is repeated a number of times throughout this section of the poem. It underlines the thematic emphasis on the relation between these two worlds throughout the poem.

---

[27] Cassolà 1975: ad loc.
[28] For Attic and Eleusinian myths that situated the rape locally, see Richardson 1974:150.
[29] Ibid.:ad loc.

23 The olives and Demeter share the same epithet, which I have translated as "of the bright fruit" or "bright with fruit." The olives are also expected to be able to hear Persephone. This may express a special symbiosis between Demeter and the vegetable world and above all with cultivated plants because they mediate between nature and culture. Olives were witnesses of the Athenian ephebic oath for young men about to embark on military service,[30] and personified landscapes appear in later tragedy when characters lack other witnesses to their sufferings.

33–50 Like the Egyptian goddess Isis in mourning for Osiris, Demeter takes on signs of human mourning: change of clothing, the tearing of the veil, the refusal to eat and bathe. (At 82, Helios asks Demeter to cease her *goos*, or ritual lament for the dead, for Persephone.) In *Iliad* 22.405–72, after hearing of the death of Hektor, first his mother Hekabe and then his wife Andromache tear their veils; in the second case the mourning gesture symbolizes the termination of her status as a married woman. In imitation of the liminal status of the typical mourner, Demeter is cut off from gods and humans. Dark clothing was not exclusively associated with mourning the dead. Furies or Erinyes wore it (in Arcadian myth Demeter Erinys or Black Demeter was associated with these goddesses), as did ephebes, who adopted it as a sign of their marginal status. The darkness of Demeter's clothing may thus suggest vengeful wrath as well.

35–36 The lines may also mean, "she still hoped her dear mother and the race of the immortal gods would see her."

38–39 Persephone's abrupt disappearance—only the echo of her voice remains—emphasizes the inaccessibility of the realms below.

47 The exact significance of the nine-day period in which Demeter (Deo is another name for Demeter) wanders in a space between gods and humans is unknown. In rites of transition, the initiate often undergoes a specific period of withdrawal from society. The Trojans mourned Hektor for nine days (*Iliad* 24. 664; see also 610), and other significant transitional periods can also take nine days in epic.[31] Nine days is also about one-third of a lunar cycle.[32] As a moon goddess (see further on 51–89), Hekate would have been absent during the day when the rape occurred.[33] There is a wordplay on *dekatê* (tenth) and Hekate at 51–52.

[30] Tod 1933–48:II, 204.20. See Jameson 1976:445 n.6.
[31] Richardson 1974:ad loc. and Clay 1989:217.
[32] Nilsson 1951–52:I.46ff.
[33] Szepes 1975:31–32.

The word *potnia* applied here to Demeter, and elsewhere in the poem to goddesses and mortal women, elevates the authority of the female figure to whom it is applied. I have found it impossible to translate consistently.

48 The carrying of the torches by the goddesses and initiates is a standard motif on vase paintings associated with the rites at Eleusis, and a chief official of the rites was named the *Daidouchos*, or torch bearer (see Fig. 2). Torches certainly played a role in the Iakchos procession and the *pannychis* (see the section on the Mysteries). Initiates imitated the experiences of Demeter in the rites at Eleusis, probably including a search (possibly exclusive to women) for Korê/Persephone by torchlight (see Clement *Protreptikos* 2.12.2, Lactantius *Epitome divinarum institutionum* 18 [23].7). Torches may have been tossed at the conclusion of the rites to celebrate Persephone's return. The torches may be associated with purification, the bringing of fertility (the mother of the bride carries them in the bridal procession), or the emergence of light and thus mystic illumination in darkness: all three associations are possible here. Ovid *Fasti* 4.494 makes an explicit connection between Demeter's torch and the rite.

51–89 The text emphasizes the isolation of Demeter and Hekate from the rest of the universe. An anomalous witness, Hekate knows no more than Demeter does, although she does suggest to Demeter that her daughter has been abducted (56).[34] In offering support to the goddess and in arriving with a torch, she assimilates herself to Demeter, here called daughter of Rheia (60), and provides a female witness who only *hears* (see 57, 67–68) to balance the male Helios, who *sees* and serves as an apologist for Zeus.[35] This passage emphasizes the important theme of seeing and hearing in the poem. The narcissus is wonderful to *see* (10, 427). Hekate and Demeter alone of gods or mortals *hear* the cry (22–23, 39); Persephone retains hope while she can still *see* the upper air (34) or her mother and the other gods (35–36). Demeter wishes to *hear* the truth from Helios about what he *saw* (70–71). Mortals can *see* gods in disguise but not recognize them (94–95, 111; see also 256–57). The daughters tell what they *saw* and *heard* at the well to their mother (172). Demeter later makes *seeing* her daughter with her eyes a condition for stopping her famine (333, 339, 349–51, 409–10. See further on 333). Metaneira *spies on* Demeter's secret rites with Demophoön (see further below on lines 243–45). Her daughters do not *see* but *hear* the cry of the abandoned Demophoön (284). Zeus *notices* Demeter's famine (313) and *hears* of her ultimatum (334). Demeter is happy to *see* Persephone

[34] Arthur 1977 (this volume) sees this as yet another sign of the helplessness of the female divinities in the first part of the poem.
[35] Ibid., and Scarpi 1976:12ff.

(385), as are Rheia and Demeter to *see* each other (458). The *Hymn* privileges seeing, and especially seeing with understanding and pleasure, over hearing, and the highest level of initiation in the Mysteries is *epopteia*, or seeing (see 480, *opôpen*, of the happiness won by those who have *seen* the Mysteries).[36] Both Demeter and mortals progress toward sight/insight in the course of the poem. The amazing image of a beautiful plant like the narcissus may have played a role in the Mysteries (the display of an ear of corn).

Hekate's traditional association with the moon again serves to contrast her as a bearer of light with the sun god, Helios (although her link with the moon in extant sources is late, her departure from a cave suggests that such associations may be present even at this early date).[37] This assimilation of Demeter and Hekate prepares for the resolution of the poem, where Hekate will become a loving attendant to Persephone. The incident also anticipates the second intervention in Demeter's mourning by the women of Eleusis. Although we know little about Hekate's role in the cult at Eleusis, she was important in Eleusinian iconography.[38] For further associations between Hekate, Demeter, and Persephone, see the section on "The Mother/ Daughter Romance" in the interpretive essay.

56 This is the only time before she becomes a bride (337, 348, 360, 370, 387, 405, 493) that Persephone is so named; elsewhere she is Korê (maiden) or daughter (in the final lines at 493 she is both *kourê* and Persephone). She is unnamed as well in Euripides' and the tragic poet Karkinos's versions of the myth (Euripides *Helen* 1307 and frag. 63 Nauck; Diodorus Siculus *Bibliotheca* 5.5.1 quotes from Karkinos). Some scholars have suggested that historically the goddess was an amalgamation of two goddesses, Persephone the goddess of the underworld and Korê the maiden daughter of Demeter.[39] Bruce Lincoln interprets the nearly exclusive appearance of the name Persephone in the latter part of the poem as an initiatory motif, because initiates often receive adult names in the course of initiation rituals into adulthood.[40] The poem may be marking a change of identity or Korê's acquisition of new powers as goddess of the underworld by using the name Persephone.

[36] Scarpi 1976:7 and 9–46.

[37] Richardson 1974:156 argues that Hekate's associations with chthonic cults may explain the cave and the torches.

[38] Parker 1991:15–16n.22 and 16n.28 and Richardson 1974:155. At Eleusis she may also have been linked with Artemis.

[39] Zuntz 1971:75–83.

[40] Lincoln 1979:229. For a distinction between different kinds of initiation rituals, see my interpretive essay (in this volume) on "The 'Theology' of the Mysteries."

59–60 Demeter's silence in the encounter with Hekate suggests shock and grief;[41] but in the Mysteries such silence may have served a ritual function.

62 The sun, who sees with his own rays (70), serves as a witness and guardian of right in Near Eastern mythology and folktale as well as in Greek epic.

64–65 Demeter's appeal to precedent is typical in epic formulas of entreaty.

66 Demeter calls Persephone a *thalos* or shoot; the same word is used of Demophoön at 187. The word links the two figures and may (although the same or a comparable image is used of children at *Iliad* 22.87 and 18.56, and *Odyssey* 6.157) here reinforce the association of Persephone with the plant world.

83ff. Helios portrays Hades simply as a desirable bridegroom. Elsewhere in the Greek literary and visual tradition he is a more sinister figure.

86 The tripartite division of the heavens, the sea, and the world below among the brothers Zeus, Poseidon, and Hades is first mentioned at *Iliad* 15.187–93.

89 The strongly dactylic meter of this line emphasizes the swift passage of the sun's horses.

90–97 In the *Hymn*, Demeter's motive for wandering on earth and withdrawing from the gods is *anger at Zeus* (*chôsamenê*, 91. At 90, her grief [*achos*] is *kynteron*, more brutal, shameless, or bestial; at 306 mortals experience a *kyntaton* year, due to Demeter's famine.) In other versions she comes to earth to search for her daughter. The wanderings of disguised deities on earth and the difficulty of recognizing them are standard motifs in Greek myth.[42] Often these deities aim to test the piety or hospitality of mortals, and mortals who fail to recognize or who mistreat the gods are punished. Although the Eleusinians are admirably hospitable, Demeter is not aiming explicitly to test them; nor do they as individuals receive rewards or punishments in a fashion directly related to their treatment of the goddess. (By contrast Pausanias 2.35.3 reports an Argive legend in which one family was punished for rejecting Demeter, while another was rewarded for receiving

---

[41] Clay 1989:219n.64.

[42] Stories of hospitality to deities were often used to explain family cults. Richardson 1974:177–79.

her.) Metaneira interferes with Demeter's plans from human ignorance, not from failure of hospitality or piety. Lines 94–96 prepare for Demeter's ultimate recognition, after several failures, by the members of the house of Keleos.

96–97 In the *Hymn*, Keleos appears to be the chief prince among several peers at Eleusis. He is called *koiranos* (97; the same word is used for Hades at 87), whereas the other leaders are called *basileis*. Yet at 103, 215, and 473 Keleos is a *basileus* as well, and at 150 we are told that he is among the men who have power (*kratos*) at Eleusis. He acts in cooperation with the other leaders. (See further on 153ff.) Although Keleos and his wife and daughters were later worshiped in cult at Eleusis, he generally maintained a significant role after the *Hymn* only in the mythical tradition, where in some versions he himself played host to Demeter.

98–112 A goddess of fertility here disguises herself as a postmenopausal old woman, suppliant to mortals.[43] Her "barrenness" (ironic in a goddess who has power over the growth of crops) resonates with the famine that she will soon inflict on mortals. The first figures to encounter her on earth are four young maidens. The comparison of the girls to flowers and goddesses deliberately recalls Persephone and emphasizes the role reversal (from divine to human) undertaken by Demeter. The name used for one daughter here, Demo, was used elsewhere of Demeter herself (see also Demophoön). Pausanias (1.38.3) tells us that the daughters (who in his text have different names) later performed sacred rites with Eumolpos ("Beautiful Singer"), the first Priest of the Mysteries. They received honors after death and perhaps served as prototypes for the priestesses at Eleusis.[44]

Meetings between mortals and gods in disguise and meetings beside water are common in Greek myth. (In the *Odyssey*, Odysseus and Athena meet on Ithaka near a cave of the nymphs with a stream and an olive; the goddess-like Nausikäa encounters Odysseus by the sea.) Fetching water was a typical domestic task for women, here stylized by myth, and Demeter presumably knows that she will encounter women at the well. Springs and rivers are associated with virginity, initiation, marriage, and the cult of the two goddesses. Wells were potentially dangerous; women could be seduced, abducted, or molested there. Water for weddings was drawn from special springs and wells. The name Parthenion or "Maiden's Well" has these very connotations and thus further links the daughters with Persephone. Drawing water from a well and the carrying of water in urns (see 107) also played a role in the cults of Demeter and Persephone. All these associations may

---

[43] Clay 1989:227–28 and Richardson 1974:180.
[44] See further Richardson 1974:183–84.

help to explain why the virgin daughters come to fetch water but are surprised to find an old woman alone there.

In later versions of the myth, Demeter sat beside the well Kallichoron or by the Agelastos Petra ("the rock without laughter"; Demeter is without laughter, *agelastos*, at 200). A sacred olive (see 100) probably also stood by the well Kallichoron (the well Parthenion has not been discovered but may be the same well).[45] Pausanias 1.38.6 tells us that women first danced and came to Demeter at the well Kallichoron.

99 Citizens (*politai*) are said to draw water at the well Parthenion. The word for citizens, *politai* (the singular is not used), appears in Homer and the hymns three times in this context (see also *Odyssey* 7.131 and 17.206); in its other two appearances (*Iliad* 15.558 [*politas*] and 22.429), the word describes the citizens of Troy as victims of war or as mourners of Hektor. In contrast to classical Athens, the Homeric poems rarely emphasize civic identity in this fashion. Wells were communal spots, and here the women are defined as citizens of their community, whereas in the classical context the degree to which women were *politai* is a matter of controversy. For further discussion of women as members of the community of Eleusis and the *Hymn*'s emphasis on civic identity, see my interpretive essay on "The *Hymn to Demeter* and the Polis."

113–44 The tradition of Cretan tales—lies like the truth—is also common in the *Odyssey*, where Odysseus (as well as his patroness, Athena) tells several of them. Demeter calls herself Doso ("Giver"),[46] a name that plays on Demeter's own function of giving. The disguised Demeter, twice called Daughter of Rheia in this poem (60, 75), says she was given this name by her mother, thus emphasizing the maternal (even matrilineal) links among the three generations of females that Zeus and Hades disrupt. The tale displaces some of Persephone's experiences on her mother; both daughter and mother were abducted by violence and against their will as valuable goods, although Doso escapes her captors (who are called not simply pirates, but pirate *men*).[47] As in reality, in the tale Demeter's heart did not crave food (129). Bacchylides frag. 47 Snell=Scholiast on Hesiod *Theogony* 914 makes Crete, the site of Demeter's abduction, the site of Persephone's rape. In one myth Demeter herself was a victim of rape by Poseidon during her search for her daughter (see my interpretive essay [Part 2, this volume] on "The Mother/Daughter Romance" for further discussion).

[45] Richardson 1974:Appendix I argues for the identity of the two wells.
[46] Or, depending on how the manuscript is emended, Dos.
[47] Clay 1989:228.

125ff. The route Demeter takes from Thorikos on the northeast coast of Attika to Eleusis may parallel for some of its way the Sacred Way from Athens to Eleusis. This may be a coincidence, as we have no evidence that the procession from Athens to Eleusis existed at this early date.

131–32 These lines are as hard to follow in the Greek as they are in English.

135ff. The wish for prosperity and request for pity and help are standard in epic scenes of meeting. Interestingly, as a disguised mortal Demeter wishes husbands and children for the maidens (135–37), even though she herself is resisting marriage for her daughter. Odysseus does the same to Nausikäa at *Odyssey* 6.180–85, so this may be a typical element in meetings between strangers and maidens. Lines 136–37 stress the importance of reproduction by using three words derived from a root meaning to give birth (*tekna, tekesthai, tokês*).[48]

137. There is probably a missing line after 137 that supplies a verb asking for information.

140–44 Demeter suggests a number of tasks she could perform in a household (140–44). The role of nurse is appropriate for a woman past childbearing (101–4). Demeter's role here may anticipate her role in the Mysteries, where the goddesses adopted initiates and served as nurses to them.

145–68 The daughters pass the implicit test of hospitality (there is always a threat of failure in such scenes) to the disguised deity (see commentary on 94–97, above) and even note her godlike appearance. In a state of human ignorance, Kallidikê ironically consoles the goddess as if she were a mortal. (She is said to be the most beautiful of the daughters; beauty and readiness for marriage are linked in early Greek "Maiden Songs" [Alkman, frags. 1 and 3].) For similar consolations, see the plea for resignation by Helios earlier in this poem (75–87) and Achilleus's story of the urns at *Iliad* 24, 527ff., which stresses that humans receive either exclusively bad things or a mixture of good and bad from Zeus. Demeter, in a covert hint at her divinity, twice refuses this consolation.

151 At Eleusis men are protectors, not abductors, of women. The word *high walls, krêdemna*, can mean both veils or city battlements; both protect

---

48 Janssens 1962:50.

women from external harm. The *Iliad* deliberately links the fall of Hektor, the fall of Andromache's veil, and the fall of Troy.[49]

153ff. Triptolemos and Eumolpos play more important roles in later versions of the story. Eumolpos became the first Hierophant, or priest of Demeter, and Triptolemos, sometimes said to be a son of Keleos and Metaneira (Apollodoros *Bibliotheca* 1.5.2), received the gift of agriculture from Demeter and disseminated these gifts to humankind in a winged chariot. Important at Eleusis from at least the sixth century, he later replaced Demophoön as the major nursling of Demeter at Eleusis. Although all these leaders were known to be objects of later cults at Eleusis, the other three mentioned here are obscure; two of them disappear when Demeter instructs the Eleusinian princes in her rites at the end of the poem (473–75). The name of one, Polyxeinos, is also an epithet of Hades.[50]

169–89 These lines contrast the joyful youth of the girls with Demeter's sorrow. The imagery of flowers again links the daughters with Persephone. The freely flowing hair and robes and the festal clothing may recall the rites at Eleusis; women's hair was usually veiled outdoors, but at Eleusis it may have been worn unbound. The images of fawns or foals were often used for unmarried girls. The dactylic rhythm of 171 emphasizes the speed and lightness of the girls, and at 183 the striking description of the goddess's walk hints at her true identity. The verb "swirled round," *elelizeto*, at 183 is often used in Homer of rapid movements in battle or the shaking of Olympus.[51]

189–90 The partial epiphany of the goddess at the threshold prepares for her full epiphany later and perhaps hints, along with the further references to seeing and hearing at 172, at different degrees of initiation into mystic truth. Even in sorrow Demeter does not totally obscure her divine nature.[52] The contrast between mortal and immortal is augmented by a doubly emphasized difference in height; not only is Demeter taller than mortals, but Metaneira is seated on a chair. By accepting a stool, Demeter will come down to a mortal level. (For the motif of sitting in the poem, largely associated with Demeter, see also 28, 98, 193, 197, 198, 201, 303–4, 343, 356.) Demeter's epiphany here is unusual in that it is not made to reveal fully to mortals the goddess's divinity.[53] Here, as elsewhere in myth (e.g., Homeric *Hymn to Aphrodite* 91–110), mortals fail to interpret correctly their intu-

---

[49] Nagler 1974:44ff.
[50] See Cassolà 1975: ad loc.
[51] Segal 1981:123.
[52] Thalmann 1984:94.
[53] Clay 1989:232.

ition of divine presence, although Iambe seems more aware of how to handle Demeter than the rest. The fear felt by Metaneira (190) hints at the dangers typical in a visit by a disguised deity. If mortals fail to recognize a divinity and to treat her well, punishment or disaster can follow.

190–211 We have here a typical scene in epic poetry: a journey ends in arrival. The visitor stands in the doorway; the host reacts, rises, leads the visitor in; offers a seat, food, and drink; and then speaks to the stranger. In the *Hymn* all these gestures are atypically refused. Giver of gifts and the seasons (192) and receiver of sacrifices, Demeter here accepts no gifts. In the *Iliad* the consumption of food and drink by the mourning Achilleus signals a preliminary acceptance (in the form of a return to normal behavior) of the loss of Patroklos.[54] (Note the importance of eating and drinking as a theme in the *Hymn* as a whole [see also 236, 372, 393, 412].) When Demeter finally accepts the hospitality offered, are we meant to understand a partial and temporary resignation to the loss of her daughter? We hear no more about her grief for Persephone until after the plan with Demophoön fails. Or are we here seeing the influence of the rite on the narrative? For this scene makes explicit reference (see 211) to stages in the rites at Eleusis: veiling, silence, sitting on a ram's fleece (shown under an initiand's feet on the Lovatelli urn and on the Torre Nova sarcophagus. For the latter, see Fig. 3) spread on a stool or chair,[55] fasting and abstention from wine broken by the drinking of the *kykeôn* (meaning a drink that is mixed), and *aischrologia*, or shameful language.

202–4 Line 204 uses a progressive pattern (a "tricolon crescendo") and an unusual rhythm to underline the effect of Demeter's reluctant move to laughter. The text does not tell us why Iambe makes Demeter laugh. It represents her as knowing wise things, perhaps things associated with the future secrets of the Mysteries. Her name, which links her with an iambic poetic tradition associated at this period with ritual obscenity and/or insult (see Aristotle *Poetics* 1448b31–32 on iambic meter), hints at the probable nature of her communications (see *Etymologicum Magnum*, under the entry Iambe; Diodorus Siculus *Bibliotheca* 5.4.7). The words for joking or jesting (*chleuêis* and *paraskôptousa*, 202–3) used of Iambe here suggest insults directed at someone.[56] Such *aischrologia* (shameful language) was common in

---

[54] See Nagler 1974:174–77 and Burkert 1979:43–45 on the acceptance of seat, food, drink, and consolation as a sign of the return by a mourner to participation in the life cycle.

[55] Museo Nazionale delle Terme, Rome; Palazzo Borghese, Rome. The spreading of a fleece on a stool is also a standard epic gesture of hospitality.

[56] See Clay 1989:234–35 for further speculations on this passage. She argues that Demeter's posture on the stool resembles a woman on a birthing stool, about to give birth. Iambe then jokes at the incongruity of an old woman giving birth.

the cults of Demeter (and Dionysos), although its purpose is by no means certain. Jesting is common in funereal contexts worldwide (the laughter presumably has cathartic effects on the mourner), as are links between rites of mourning and fertility. During the procession to Eleusis, the *gephyristai* (see further, the section on the Mysteries [Part 2 of this volume]) sitting on a bridge over the Kephisos River made insulting jokes at the passers-by. Women sitting in carriages may also have made such jokes during the procession (scholiast on Aristophanes *Ploutos* 1014). The chorus of mystery initiates at Aristophanes' *Frogs* 396ff., using iambic rhythm, make scurrilous remarks and political jokes in their procession. Such *aischrologia* (along with explicit sexuality) was typical of Old Comedy. In the rites at Eleusis, the female initiates culminate their procession with all-night dancing (a torchlit search for Persephone may have been a part of these proceedings). *Aischrologia* may have occurred among the women at this point.

In other versions of the myth (Philikos fragment [Page *GLP* 402–7], Nikander *Alexipharmaka* 131–32, Apollodoros *Bibliotheca* 1.5.1) Iambe is a talkative old rustic woman. Sometimes (Philochoros, *Die Fragmente der Griechischen Historiker* [Fragments from Greek Historians] [Jacoby] 328, fr. 103), as a daughter of Echo and Pan, she both speaks and gesticulates. Her jesting is said by Apollodoros (*Bibliotheca* 1.5.1.) to be the *aition* (causal explanation) for the obscene jesting of the women at the Thesmophoria (see the section on "Women's Rites for Demeter" in the essay following this commentary). The euphemism of Iambe's language in the *Hymn* may be due, as some have argued, to the fact that Panhellenic traditions were more discreet than local ones (the Homeric hymns were very probably composed for a Panhellenic audience; see Appendix to the interpretive essay, "The *Hymn* as a Panhellenic Poem"). In any case, the sophisticated and allusive version of this moment in the *Hymn* contrasts markedly with other rustic and veristic Attic/Eleusinian versions.

In still other versions of the story (Clement *Protreptikos* 2.20.1–21.2 = Orphic frag. 52 Kern, Arnobius *Adversus nationes* 5.25–26, Eusebios *Praeparatio evangelica* 2.3.31–35), Demeter is received by Baubo and Dysaules. After failing to cheer Demeter verbally, Baubo displayed her genitals together with the laughing baby Iakchos, who has his hand under her breast. (In the Suda, Iakchos is defined as "Dionysos at the breast.") Or Baubo displays depilated genitals. By agitating them with her hand, she makes them resemble a child. The goddess laughs. In Egyptian myth the goddess Hathor made her father laugh and resume his work in court by exposing her genitals. Baubo's name may mean "vulva," and statues thought to represent Baubo show the figure of a woman with a large head directly on top of a pair of legs, with genitals below the mouth.[57] A representation of the vulva may have been among the objects displayed at the Mysteries.

---

[57] For full discussion and references on Baubo, see Scarpi 1976:151ff. and Olender 1989.

210 In Homer the *kykeôn*, a "mixed drink" that contains the grain sacred to Demeter, is used to refresh Nestor and the wounded Machaon after battle (*Iliad* 11); in *Odyssey* 10, Kirke prepares a drugged *kykeôn* for Odysseus and his companions. In the *Hymn* (in contrast to Homer) the drink is neither wine (wineless offerings were standard in the cult of the goddesses and in chthonic cults, and this passage offers an *aition* for the practice), the most civilized mortal drink, nor nectar, the immortal drink. In the Eleusinian *kykeôn*, the grain is not baked[58] and is partially, not fully, pounded. The pennyroyal (I translated the word as "mint") added to the drink has medicinal qualities. It was most often used as a medicine by women; it could be used as a contraceptive and abortifacient and in birthing and nursing the newborn (a function Demeter is about to undertake); it was linked in Old Comedy to female sexuality and "digestive problems" (see Aristophanes *Lysistrata* 89 and *Peace* 712, where a *kykeôn* with pennyroyal is offered as a cure for too much intercourse/fruit).[59] Iambe's ministrations and Demeter's choice of a drink may thus both be associated with issues relating to female problems and female sexuality. The theory that the barley grains were fermented, and thus the drink had an hallucinatory effect, is unlikely to be correct.[60] Indeed, the mild and medicinal quality of the drink may explain its suitability for breaking a fast. In drinking the *kykeôn*, the initiates partake of food sacred to the goddess and thus perhaps begin to share in the prosperity promised by the Mysteries. (For its role in the rites at Eleusis, see the essay on the Mysteries following this commentary.) This drink, the laughter, and the nursing of Demophoön all serve to mark a partial assimilation of Demeter into the world of mortals.[61]

A story in Plutarch (*Moralia* 511c) reports a suggestive use of the *kykeôn* in a political context. The citizens of Ephesus reportedly wanted Herakleitos' opinion on the subject of political concord. Herakleitos went to the speaker's stand, mixed and drank the Eleusinian drink, and left the stand in silence. Plutarch comments that this was a lesson in keeping peace and concord through what was at hand rather than expensive things (peace was generally cemented with libations of wine). The notoriously enigmatic and elliptical Herakleitos, although apparently elsewhere critical of the Mysteries, may also be commenting on the concord produced by this simple drink among the disparate (normally unmixable) initiates in the Mysteries.

In Alexandrian and later myth, Askalabos angered Demeter by laughing at her as she thirstily drank the *kykeôn*. She poured the dregs over him and he became a gecko (Nikander frag. 56, Scholiast on Nikander *Theriaka* 483,

---

[58] Delatte 1955:23.

[59] Scarborough 1991:144–45.

[60] See especially Kerényi 1967a:177–80, who thinks that the drink was fermented like beer, and Wasson, Hoffmann, and Ruck 1978, who think the drink contained ergot, with the review of Jameson 1979:197–98 and Burkert 1987:108.

[61] See Scarpi 1976:147.

Ovid *Metamorphoses* 5.446ff., Lactantius Placidus *Fabulae* 5.7). In other versions Demeter's test of mortal piety and hospitality plays an explicit role in the story, and mortals are rewarded and punished according to their treatment of the goddess. The *Hymn* leaves this motif largely implicit. (See my interpretive essay for further discussion.)

After 211, two lines may be lost.

212–30. At 216–17 Metaneira nearly repeats the words of her daughters (147–48) and reemphasizes the ambivalent gifts of the gods, the partial recognition by mortals of the goddess, and the hopeless distance between gods and humans. She ironically promises boundless gifts to the goddess known for giving. This inaugurates a series of exchanges of gifts and honors (the primary archaic mode of establishing relations) in the *Hymn*: Demeter's honors to Demophoön, the Eleusinians' temple to Demeter, Demeter's witholding of the gods' sacrifices, Demeter's and Persephone's acquisition of new honors among the gods, and Demeter's gift of the Mysteries to humanity. Demeter the healing goddess (in Ovid *Fasti* 4 the child is ill) ironically promises a charm (in fact immortality) against children's ills stronger than that of a mortal nurse, capable by nature of error. (It is presumably no accident that the worship of the healing god Asklepios was inserted into proceedings of the early days of the Mysteries in the classical period.) Lines 228–30 have an incantatory quality, marked by strong anaphora.[62] The reference to the undercutter or woodcutter here cannot be clearly interpreted; the cutting of herbs for magical purposes seems to be involved. The undercutter has been thought to be a "toothworm" or a poison.[63]

231–55 The baby Demophoön now becomes a candidate for immortality and perhaps a symbolic first initiate.[64] Demeter's use of fire, the immortal food ambrosia, and her divine breath produce a miraculous growth (underlined by the alliteration of *k* in 238, *hêdu katapneiousa kai en kolpoisin echousa*) like that of baby divinities in other myths. Thetis fails to immortalize the infant Achilleus by a similar process (Apollodoros *Bibliotheca* 3.13.6; Apollonios Rhodios *Argonautika* 4, 869–79), and he also, as does Demophoön in some versions (see below on 253), dies young and glorious. Here she is interrupted by the father Peleus, as Demeter is by the child's father in Hyginus (*Fabulae* 147). The Demophoön episode sets the stage for the Mysteries, in that Demeter has failed to immortalize a mortal and can only mitigate death by another route. The poem pointedly does not tell us why Demeter is trying to immortalize the child. For a discussion, see my interpretive essay (Part 2 of this volume) under "Gender Politics."

---

[62] Ibid.:165–70 and 179–80.

[63] See Allen, Halliday and Sikes 1936, Humbert 1936, and Cassolà 1975: ad loc.

[64] See especially Bianchi 1964, Sabbatucci 1965:163ff., Richardson 1974:233–36, and Clay 1989:243–44.

It is not clear how we should interpret the relation between Demophoön and the mystery initiate. The motif of seeing (Metaneira spies on Demeter's fire ritual) suggests access to a secret mystery. Demeter's secret rites are experienced by both Demophoön and the initiates in a state of ignorance. Neither the initiates nor Demophoön get immortality and become gods; both receive instead privilege in death. Yet Demophoön gets honor and a hero cult,[65] whereas the initiates get through the Mysteries a different existence in the world below; and unlike later participants in the Mysteries, Demophoön does not actively pursue initiation.[66]

Demophoön remains a concern of Demeter's because he was nursed in her bosom. Demeter and Persephone nursed and adopted initiates in the classical period (at Sophocles' *Oedipous at Kolonos* 1050–51, the goddesses "nurse the rites" at Eleusis). The order of the initial events at Eleusis, mourning followed by divine nursing, may hint at the transition of the initiate from death to an existence presided over by the goddesses in the world beyond. The initiate would acquire after death the nursing from which Demophoön was so unfortunately cut off. If the Mysteries, like the later Orphic gold leaves, did make promises of immortality (Orphic frag. 32c Kern), fame (Hipponion Gold Leaf),[67] and nursing in the goddess' bosom to initiates, the correspondence between Demophoön and the initiate would appear far closer.

The use of fire is equally ambiguous. Fire can purge away mortality in myth (the dying Herakles becomes immortal on a pyre on Mt. Oeta) or purify, and it was also used to cremate the body, thus preparing for a transition to the world below. Fire turned the grain into a more permanent substance; the child and the grain are partially linked in the poem by the motif of hiding; Demeter hides Demophoön in the fire and the seed in the earth (307, 353).[68] Frazer argued that children were passed across fire to protect them from the dangers of infancy.[69] Fire also played a central role in the final stages of the Mysteries.

Demophoön, an obscure figure "who never appeared in Eleusinian inscriptions or art,"[70] is but one of such nurslings of the goddesses at Eleusis and not necessarily to be identified with any of them. A hero called Threptos, "nursling," received offerings at Eleusis;[71] a child from the hearth (*pais aph'hestias myêtheis*) was initiated on behalf of the community in the cult; and the Mysteries are said in a late gnostic source to have culminated

[65] Richardson 1974:24.

[66] Sabbatucci 1965:163ff.

[67] See Foti and Pugliese Carratelli 1974 and West 1975. The leaf may (many wish to emend Carratelli's text) contain the word *kleinoi*, or "famous," to describe the inititates.

[68] See Segal 1981:155.

[69] Frazer 1967.

[70] Richardson 1974:237.

[71] Sokolowski 1962:No. 10.69–70. Reference is to *IG*²1357.

with the birth of a divine male child amid much fire (see Hippolytos, *Refutatio Omnium Haeresium* 5.8.40), probably a child of one of the goddesses. The *Hymn* emphasizes not the birth of a divine child but the tragic results of Demeter's failure to immortalize the child. Yet despite the lack of precise correspondence between Demophoön, later nurslings of the goddesses at Eleusis (especially Triptolemos or Iakchos/Dionysos), and the initiate, I think that initiates would have felt an important connection between themselves and the child, because Demeter provides both child and initiate with a mitigation of death and nurses both; fire and the motif of seeing and hearing seem to have played a role in both contexts.[72]

236 A line indicating that Demeter gave the child ambrosia by day must be added to the manuscript here in order to complete the sense of the passage.

239 I have translated the word *krypteske* as "bury," instead of the more neutral "hide" to bring out potential connections between cremation and the fire ritual. (A papyrus fragment perhaps significantly has the word *purêi*, "pyre," instead of the word *fire* at 248.)

243–45 Although the poet stresses Demeter's anger at being interrupted, "the original point" of concealing her actions with the child "was probably that magic could only be worked in secret."[73] Metaneira's spying on Demeter's secret ritual with Demophoön should probably be interpreted in relation to the seeing of prohibited sights in related myths such as those of Orpheus and Eurydike, Amor (Eros) and Psyche, Pentheus and Dionysos, Tiresias, or Askalaphos (Ovid *Metamorphoses* 5. 538–50. For Askalaphos, see below on 371–73).[74] It may be significant that Metaneira is not, in contrast to these other myths, punished as an individual for her transgression; instead humankind is temporarily threatened with extinction by the famine.

253–54 Demeter's gesture of taking the child from the hearth fire, and placing him on the ground to be taken up by the mortal nurses surrounding him, has been read by some as a reference to the ritual of the Amphidromia. The Amphidromia (a rite of "walking or running around") symbolically incorporated the newborn child (five or seven days old) into the family and its hearth cults. Sources indicate that it may have been carried, possibly at a

---

[72] Furley 1981 argues that we should see the Demophoön story as related to the preliminaries of the Mysteries and links the burning of the child with the sacrifice of the initiate's pig. This interpretation has no basis in the text; it underestimates the central role played by the Demophoön episode in the whole poem and the way it functions to prepare for the Mysteries.

[73] Richardson 1974:241.

[74] Scarpi 1976:24ff. and Richardson 1974:241.

run, around the hearth by midwives or by masculine runners (including its father?) who may have stripped for the ceremony; or it may have been laid on the ground by the hearth and ringed by the tramping feet of family members and the midwife (who first purified her hands). This rite was followed by sacrifice, feasting, and at some point the naming of the child. Plato says that the rite was designed to test the child to see if it was fit to raise (*Theaetetus* 160E).[75] If a child who was not to be reared was thrown to the ground (Herodotos 5.92 may refer to the Amphidromia),[76] Demeter's gesture may be significant. In this case contact with the earth certainly implies irrevocable mortality for Demophoön.[77] Some have read the whole fire ritual in relation to the Amphidromia, but Demeter's attempt to immortalize a child *in* the hearth who is already a named member of a human household (he is first named at 234) does not fit the scenario. Instead, we could argue that Demophoön is symbolically reincorporated into the world of mortals by a gesture and scenario reminiscent of the Amphidromia, rather than completing an initiation into immortality. He is placed on the ground and then surrounded by the daughters, who pick him up, wash him, and accept him back into their family. Perhaps there is some connection between this episode and the role of the child initiated into the Mysteries from the hearth (mentioned earlier; see on lines 231–55). Initiates in general appear to have been symbolically adopted by the goddesses, and fire (torches) could play an important part in the initial rites of purification (as in the case of Herakles in the Lesser Mysteries).

253 Demeter presumably stands by her promise to raise Demophoön to the threshold of youth (*hêbês metron*, 166, 221). In other versions of the story, the child dies in the fire (e.g., Apollodoros *Bibliotheca* 1.5.1 and Orphic frag. 49, 100ff.). The *Hymn* apparently hints at this more dire version. Demophoön is thrown to the ground (253) and left gasping there, a word suggesting "near death" (*aspaironta*, 289, is used elsewhere of dying heroes).[78] As elsewhere in the *Hymn*, the poet raises the possibility that mortals will be injured by the visit of the disguised divinity, but the consequences turn out to be less severe than the audience might have expected from their knowledge of other versions and similar stories.

256–74 Demeter's address here emphasizes the unbreachable distance between gods and humans. Like the typical hero, Demophoön is to receive honor in compensation for his loss of immortality.

---

[75] For a recent discussion with full citation of sources, see Hamilton 1984. He argues that the first stage of the ceremony was probably an all-female affair.

[76] Ibid.:247.

[77] Scarpi 1976:37–38.

[78] Clay 1989:243. It is also possible that in later myth Demphoön dies to make way for Triptolemos as the chief nursling of Demeter (Allen, Halliday, and Sikes 1936:157).

265–67 The prophecy of future battles to result from the Demophoön episode appears, like many divine predictions, ominous to the mortals who hear it but cannot understand it. Although his name, Demo-phaon, probably means "giver of light or illumination to the people" (*dêmos*), it might also be thought in popular etymology to mean "destroyer of the people";[79] the name also links him with Demeter. It is thought that the prophecy refers to a mock battle, the *ballêtys*, which will be celebrated at Eleusis for Demophoön. The battle, which probably involved the throwing of stones, was said to have originated in a stoning during civil war.[80] The rite thus marks containment of violent dissension. Games and hero cults were often founded in honor of dead children (see on 253 for versions of the myth in which Demophoön died young), and this mock battle probably took place at the Eleusinian games.

270–72 Demeter's sanctuaries in Athens (the temple at Agrai, where the Lesser Mysteries were celebrated, and the Eleusinion, at the foot of the Akropolis) are also just outside the city or city center. Initiatory rites often occur on the geographical boundaries of society, because they involve a period of exclusion from ordinary life.

273–80 Demeter, after performing a typical divine epiphany in which the deity appears as larger than life and with renewed youth and beauty, delays explaining the nature of her rites to the Eleusinians until the end of the poem. At this point the rites are simply defined as propitiatory to the goddess (273; the same word *orgia* is used both here and later at 476; the Mysteries retained a propitiatory element). In calling herself the greatest help and cause of joy to gods and mortal men (268–69), Demeter hints at both her roles: providing grain to mortals and sacrifices to gods and her future offer of a better afterlife in the Mysteries; at the same time, she makes this assertion just at the point when she has condemned humankind to mortality and is about to institute her famine. Like the narrative, the Mysteries also involved a movement from fear to joy.

281–83 Metaneira's reaction to the divine epiphany—speechlessness, fear, and awe—were said to be reproduced in the initiate in the course of the Mysteries. Like Demophoön, Metaneira thus becomes a surrogate initiate.[81] Her speechlessness[82] parallels the initial speechlessness of the mourning Demeter after she entered the house (198).

---

[79] Kerényi 1967a:126. *Demo-phontês* is not attested, but this does not mean that a contemporary hearer would not make the aural connection.

[80] See Richardson 1974:246 and Cassolà 1975 ad loc. for further discussion.

[81] Richardson 1974:208–9.

[82] Richardson 1974:254 also notes that speechlessness is a characteristic reaction to speeches in epic generally.

285–91 The text, by showing the effects of her absence on Demophoön, emphasizes Demeter's supreme value as a nurse, a role she was to adopt toward the initiates. The unusual assonance at 289–90 (*agromenai de min amphis eloueon aspaironta/amphagapazomenai*) underlines the struggle of Demophoön's sisters to soothe the unhappy child.

292–304 The women wait *all night* before approaching the men, to whom they must explain what has happened and what they have seen (for further discussion, see the interpretive essay [Part II of this book] on "The Psychology of the Mysteries.") At Eleusis, perhaps by sheer coincidence, the women celebrated all-night dances by themselves before the final secret rites of initiation in the Telesterion. The daughters, like Hekate earlier and in contrast to Metaneira, only *hear* the results of the goddess's actions. The text may hint here at different levels of initiation into Demeter's Mysteries.

The poem now shifts from the world of women, secret rites, and the household to the public world.[83] Keleos holds an assembly in the agora and engages the entire city (*polupeirona laon*, 296) in the building of the temple. Demeter is once more preoccupied with the loss of her daughter and, though no longer disguised as a human, she remains on earth in her temple rather than returning to her own world of Olympus. Temples were a site for the exchange of communications and offerings between gods and humans. Demeter blocks this exchange by preventing communication in either direction[84] and then perverts her own function as a goddess of fertility by preventing the seeds from growing.

300 Some have taken the growth that occurs in the second part of the line to refer to the shrine and some to the child. My translation preserves the uncertainty of the referent. It is unclear what it would mean for the temple, the more likely referent, to "grow by the dispensation or decree of divinity."

305–33 In the *Hymn* the famine motif is long delayed and is linked to Demeter's loss of Persephone, which results in infertility on a grand scale.[85] Isolated now from both gods and mortals, to whom she was drawn initially in her grief, Demeter is willing to turn her wrath on both parties. The famine works because it is, unlike the attempt to immortalize Demophoön, an extension of her traditional powers and exploits the weakness of mortals, thereby confirming their natural distance from the gods. (Note that whereas Gaia earlier grew the narcissus as a trap for Persephone at Zeus's behest [8–9], Demeter now prevents the earth (*gaia*) from sending up the seed [306–7].) Similar withdrawals and famines occur in other earlier Near

[83] Clay 1989:245.
[84] Ibid.:246.
[85] Van Nortwick:60.

Eastern myths, and historical famines may have motivated the theme as well. See the section on "The 'Theology' of the Mysteries" in the interpretive essay (Part 2 of this book).

321 Zeus normally has unfailing knowledge (*aphthita eidôs*, "knowing immortal things"). The formula *aphthita mêdea eidôs* is used in Hesiod's *Theogony* during Zeus's contest of wits with the Titan Prometheus (545, 550, 561; see also Homeric *Hymn to Aphrodite* 167 and *aphthita eidôs* at *Iliad* 24.88); there it indicates Zeus's omniscience, whereas here, perhaps ironically, it catches Zeus at a moment of loss.

333 Demeter repeatedly expresses the wish to see her daughter with her eyes. At a climactic moment of the Mysteries, initiates may have "seen" Persephone.

334–74 See the interpretive essay (Part 2) and Lord's essay (Part 3) in this volume for a discussion of the story pattern of wrath, withdrawal, and return underlying the myth.

335ff. Hermes, here also called the Slayer of Argos (the beast Hera sent to watch over Io), was a messenger god and traditionally conducted souls to the world below. He also presided in art over Persephone's annual rising from the earth. (See Fig. 4) As Rudhardt points out (Part 3 in this volume), up to the time of this story no one could enter and depart from the underworld except Hermes. Even Hades only leaves his sphere because Zeus has given him permission to take Persephone. In the *Hymn* Iris serves as Zeus's messenger in the world above (see below on Rheia), and Hermes is called upon only for the message to Hades.

337 The word *hagnên* here, which I have translated "holy," is also used to describe Demeter at 203 and 439 and to describe both goddesses elsewhere. The word links the two goddesses and emphasizes their awesome divinity.

Lines 344–45 are corrupt and untranslatable (the Greek does not make sense, and hence the manuscript does not preserve the original reading). The lines, which may have referred originally to Persephone throughout, were perhaps contaminated by the reference to Demeter's plans at 350.

357–58 Hades only "smiles with his brows." This cryptic phrase may suggest his inability to produce civilized mirth, or an intent to deceive/ engage in secret matters. At Pindar *Pythian* 9.38 the Centaur Cheiron laughs with a benign brow at Apollo, who has been less than straightforward in pretending ignorance over matters of love (his intent to sleep with the maiden Kyrene). Claudian (*De Raptu Proserpinae* 2.326–72) elaborates at length on the remarkable effect Persephone's arrival has on the grim god and his territory. For Hades' conciliatory behavior in 357–69, see my interpretive essay (Part 2 of this volume) under "Marriage."

359 Here Persephone is called *daiphrôn*, "wise," a typical epithet of male leaders and warriors in Homer, and used of Keleos in this poem (96, 233).

364–69 The acquisition of new honors by a deity is typical in the Homeric hymns. Hades promises three things to Persephone: rule over all living things on earth, honors among the gods, and vengeance against those who wrong her or fail to propitiate her with sacrifices and gifts. Here he seems to anticipate the full range of Persephone's later powers, for she will have honors on earth (365), heaven (366), and in the world below (367–69). Because she has honors in three spheres, she will be able to mediate, as no other deity can, between them and make possible the Mysteries and a new relation among these spheres. (See Rudhardt, Part 3 of this volume, and my interpretive essay, Part 2 of this volume, for further discussion.)

The text at 367 appears to refer to eternal punishment (*êmata panta*). Thus, although Hades is being careful not to say directly that Persephone will become queen of the dead, he is apparently hinting at her future powers in the world below. Once the Mysteries are established at the end of the poem, Persephone's authority over those who are initiated or uninitiated into the Mysteries allows her to distinguish in the underworld between those who have or have not honored her. If, as seems likely, the Mysteries promised a different lot in the world below to initiates than to noninitiates (see on 486–89), this deviates from what we are told in other archaic epic.[86] Archaic epic in general is very vague on the punishment of wrongdoers in the world below, although punishment certainly exists, and Orphic notions about rewards and punishments after death were apparently systematized at a later date.[87] A Homeric hero usually expects nothing after death but a good burial, a tomb, and fame. Tityos, Tantalos, and Sisyphos are punished for crimes against the gods in the underworld of the *Odyssey*, but we hear of no other punishments (or rewards, unless Menelaos's Elysion at *Odyssey* 4.563–59 is understood to be located in the world below). In the *Iliad* human beings are punished in Hades for swearing false oaths (3.278–79), and at *Iliad* 9.453–57 the Erinyes or Furies hear the curses of a parent. In the classical period (480–323 B.C.E.), initiation into the Mysteries was prohibited to those polluted by murder, and Aristophanes' *Frogs* asserts that

---

[86] Boyancé 1962:475–76 argues that the menacing litotes (a figure of speech in which an assertion is made by the negation of its opposite) in 481–82 indicates that rewards to the initiates and punishments to the uninitiates lie behind the *Hymn*'s statement.

[87] See Graf 1974:79–150 on Orphic notions of punishment after death.

initiates are holy to strangers (457–59). Pausanias describes a picture by Polygnotos in which both the uninitiated and those who held the Mysteries of no account are depicted carrying broken jars of water in the world below (10.31.9 and 10.31.11). There may have been little distinction between ethical and ritual violations in the cult at Eleusis. Plato, on the other hand, complains at *Republic* 363a–366b that people used mystic rites to buy freedom from punishment after death (he may have been criticizing Orphics, not the rites at Eleusis), and Diogenes the Cynic refused to be initiated, complaining that a thief or a nonentity who was initiated was guaranteed a better life after death than was a virtuous but uninitiated man (Plutarch *Moralia* 21ff., Diogenes Laertios *Vitae Philosophorum* 6.39).

371–73 The translation of these lines is difficult. The Greek verb *nomaô* (373) can imply intellectual perception and self-consciousness, handling, or distribution (especially of food and drink), and it is unclear whether the object of the verb, the Greek word *hê*, refers to the seed or to himself or Persephone. I chose to adopt the possibility that Hades is performing a magical rite to bind Persephone to himself by passing the seed around her or consecrating it in some special magical way.[88] The phrase might also mean, among many possibilities, "handing over or distributing the seed (to her)," "turning it over in his mind," or "peering (furtively) about himself."[89]

The eating of the pomegranate seed is the last of the important episodes involving eating in the poem. As Korê breaks her fast and thus symbolically accepts Hades' hospitality, humans are starving in the world above.[90] In the *Hymn* Persephone is tricked or forced (413) into eating. In Ovid (*Metamorphoses* 5. 534ff.), Persephone picks and eats the seven pomegranate seeds for herself; at Ovid *Fasti* 4. 607–8 she eats three seeds. In later versions Askalaphos is punished for spying and informing on Persephone for eating pomegranate seeds (Nikander frag. 56 and *Theriaka* 483–87 with scholia on 484, Apollodoros *Bibliotheca* 1.5.3, Ovid *Metamorphoses* 5.538–50). In many folktales, eating the food of the dead prevents a return to the world above (see also the similar motifs in the *Odyssey*, where the food of the Lotus Eaters or Kirke's drink that turns men into swine will prevent return home). When a bride eats food in her husband's house, she accepts her transition to a new life under her husband's authority (see my interpretive essay on "Marriage," this volume). Pomegranates were associated with blood, death, fertility, and marriage and may have served, at least symbolically, as an aphrodisiac.[91] The Mystai were forbidden to eat them. The fruit's double

---

[88] See Myres 1938, Bonner 1939, and Faraone 1990:236.

[89] See Richardson 1974 and Cassolà 1976 ad loc.

[90] See Scarpi 1976:100 and Brelich 1972:465–66.

[91] Richardson 1974:276, Chirassi 1968:73–90. See Burkert 1983:285 on the association between blood and the juice of the pomegranate.

association with sexuality and death (deriving from its blood-red color and its multiple seeds) is perfect for this narrative. Persephone has eaten her husband's food among the dead. She may have consummated her marriage—we find her in Hades' bed, an unwilling partner (343–44) who is still longing for her mother (and hence emotionally if not physically uncommitted to sexuality). The eating of the pomegranate seed may for the reasons given above suggest sexual seduction. If so, Persephone becomes, by eating it, symbolically committed both socially and sexually to her future husband.

370–71 Persephone is here called for the first time *periphrôn*: "thought-ful," "circumspect," or "intelligent";[92] perhaps this indicates an acquisition of maturity. At this point it remains ambiguous whether Persephone leaps up joyfully because she is leaving to see her mother, because Hades has promised honors to her, or both. At line 411, Persephone affirms the first motive (she does not mention the honors).

374 Demeter still wears her dark robe (*kyanopeplôi*; see also 42 and 319) during the reunion and even at her return to Olympus (442), a visual reminder both of her past mourning and her future role as the mother who will aways lose her daughter on a yearly basis.

375–404 After a typical epic journey (yoking horses to a chariot, mount-ing the chariot, crossing from one location to another, arrival and greet-ing),[93] Persephone and her mother are reunited. Persephone descends to the world below and ascends from it in a chariot drawn by Hades' horses (this prepares for the ring composition discussed at lines 405–40). Deme-ter's strong emotion is displayed by the comparison in 386 of the goddess to a maenad on the mountains, that is, an ecstatic follower of the god Di-onysos; the description recalls her distraught state as she began to search for her lost daughter. The comparison to a maenad, like the earlier tearing of veils, is suggestive of the removal of women from their proper role and sphere.[94] Andromache at *Iliad* 22.460 is also compared to a maenad as she rushes out of the house distraught over fears for Hektor.

From 387–404 parts of the text are missing due to a tear in the manu-script. Richardson prints the manuscript. The conjectures added from 387–99 are taken from Allen's 1912 Oxford edition of the Homeric hymns, where he adopts Goodwin's conjectures. (I have used brackets in the transla-tion to show reconstructions of the missing text.)

[92] Clay 1989:164.
[93] Arend 1933:86ff.
[94] Seaford 1988 and 1990.

385–87, if the restored text is correct,[95] emphasize eye contact between the two goddesses. Normally in Greek poetry, such language is suggestive of erotic motifs; for the Greeks love begins with the eyes. Although this language might seem out of place for mother and daughter, both the intensity of the goddesses' interaction and the language, especially at 344 (the use of *pothos* or desire; see also 201 and 304) and 434–47, is suggestive of such powerful emotional encounters. The reunion of Demeter and Persephone may have been represented or enacted in some fashion in the cult (Lactantius *Epitome divinarum institutionum* 18(23).7), where the initiates shared in the joy of the goddesses' reunion.

399–400 Post-Alexandrian versions of the myth have Persephone spend half the year in each realm. Three seasons are normal in Homer and Hesiod, but older myths probably divided the year into summer and winter. Yet divine figures do not always inhabit different spheres in accordance with seasonal change. Adonis (Apollodoros *Bibliotheca* 3.14.4), an object of contention between Aphrodite and Persephone, is given one-third of the year with each goddess and one-third for himself. He makes over his third to Aphrodite. The one-third/two-thirds division in the *Hymn* may also reflect Hades' one-third share in the universe and reinforces the linking of the three spheres of earth, heaven, and Hades completed by the end of the poem.[96] Burkert suggests that the two-thirds/one-third division in the *Hymn* may relate to the ritual calendar, not the seasons.[97]

401–3 In the *Hymn* Persephone's return does not explicitly cause the spring but precedes it (at 470 Demeter obeys Rheia's request from Zeus to make the crops grow). The narrative, although it may confirm the regularity of the agricultural cycle, does not establish it (Demeter is the "bringer of seasons" from the first to the last lines [492]).[98] In the *Hymn* Demeter specifies that Persephone will return each year with the spring flowers, but the season when the abduction took place is uncertain (see on lines 5–14. In Ovid *Metamorphoses* 5.554 the abduction specifically occurred while Proserpina was picking spring flowers, whereas in Orphic hymn 29 Persephone was abducted in the fall and appears in the spring shoots). One might expect that Demeter's unexplained prophetic knowledge should derive in part from her knowledge of the natural cycle as "bringer of seasons" in the *Hymn*, but

---

[95] I.e., Goodwin has supplied a text to fill the gap in the manuscipt.

[96] See Richardson 1974:ad loc.

[97] 1983:261.

[98] Rudhardt (this volume), Alderink 1982:6 and 11, and Scarpi 1976:93 argue that the events of the myth imprint a cyclical pattern on an agricultural world that was previously acyclical.

it is not clear how Persephone's coming and going relates to the seasons. (Fig. 4 illustrates a version of this annual return.)

The ritual calendar placed the Mysteries in the fall, close to (and perhaps originally coinciding with) the fall plowing (Diodorus Siculus *Bibliotheca historica* 5.4.7 certainly understands the festival to occur at the time of the sowing of grain). Demeter's festivals generally emphasize the season of ploughing and sowing, rather than the spring growth. Later sources, sometimes said to be Stoic-influenced, interpret earlier myth as indicating that Persephone is associated with the planted seed and thus absent while it is in the ground (contrary to later interpretation, but it is not clear that these sources use Persephone's appearances and disappearances explicitly to explain the seasons).[99] In Greece the grain continues to grow after being sown in the fall, if slowly, throughout the winter season; growth then quickens in the spring.[100] The winter is thus a time of less food but slow growth. Cornford and Nilsson associated the descent of Persephone with the storing of the seed in underground *pithoi* (jars) after the harvest. Her absence then coincided with the dry months of summer (one-third of the year), and she returned in time for the fall plowing (and the fertile two-thirds of the year).[101] Lack of growth coincides in this case with abundance, because the proceeds of the spring harvest are ready at hand. This version corresponds better with the actual growing season in Greece; yet the *Hymn*, by linking Persephone's return to the spring flowers, appears to deny it.

There may be no possibility, or necessity, of consistency here. Insofar as Persephone is linked with the spring flowers (rather than the grain), she reappears in spring; as the daughter of the grain goddess Demeter, she spends two-thirds of the year above ground and one-third below; and as Hades' wife, she is always below. As a prototype of the virgin bride on the verge of the transition to maturity, her story has metaphorical links with the seasons.

405–40 Here the long narrative brings the beginning and the end of the poem together in the ring composition typical of early Greek poetry. The poem begins with Demeter and Persephone and a catalogue of Persephone's

---

[99] See Cornutus 28, Cicero *De natura deorum* 2.66, Scholia on Hesiod *Theogony* 912, Tzetzes on Hesiod *Opera et Dies (Works and Days)* 32, Cleanthes fr. 547 cited in Plutarch *Moralia* 377d, Varro cited in Augustine *De civitate Dei* 7.20, Scholia on Aristophanes *Wasps* 1429. I am grateful to my colleague Dirk Obbink for calling my attention to the difficulties in interpreting these sources. Janssens 1962:44–45 and 54 argues that by keeping Persephone (the seed) underground Hades is violating the cosmic order. Hence Demeter's famine only completes the destruction that Hades had initiated.

[100] Jameson, 1976:443, speculates that the Lesser Mysteries replaced an earlier spring festival of Demeter which stressed this phase of the myth.

[101] Cornford 1913:153ff. and Nilsson 1951–52:576ff. Richardson 1974 and others reject this view, but Burkert 1983:261–62 and Cassolà 1975:25 are still sympathetic to it.

companions. Here the catalogue concludes with the two goddesses. Yet
Persephone's version of the abduction (in a fashion contrary to the typical
exact repetitions characteristic of earlier oral epic) differs from the earlier
one. The *Hymn* generally avoids the exact repetitions found in epic, but the
naming of the companions makes Persephone's version of the experience
appear subjective: for her the companions are individuals and the narcissus
becomes just one of many flowers (she does not seem aware of its pivotal
role in her downfall).[102] At 413 Persephone tells her mother that Hades
forced her to eat the pomegranate seed. No violence is mentioned in the
impersonal narration of this event at 371–72, only secrecy. Does she, as
Richardson argues, here protest too much for the benefit of her mother?
Does she lift the veil from Hades' secrecy and expose the violence that she
experienced beneath it? Is the act violent only in the eyes of Persephone?
Persephone's story emphasizes the combination of trickery and violence
(*dolos* and *biê*) that Hades employs, and the force-feeding of the pomegranate seed is linguistically associated with the abduction itself (see my interpretive essay, Part 2 of this volume, under "Marriage.") Persephone's narrative thus differs in two significant ways from the poet's impersonal narrative.
Demeter herself does not at first share Zeus's and Helios's perspective on the
marriage to Hades. The *Hymn* thus seems to emphasize the disparity in
point of view between the goddesses and others in the poem, without
explicitly questioning the "truth" of either view. In this passage Persephone
acquires an articulate voice (beyond a cry for help) in the narrative for the
first time; this may affirm that she has acquired an adult role and a partial
independence from both Hades and her mother.

428 The narcissus is probably like a crocus because of its similar fragrance
and yellow color, and because it proliferates easily.[103]

434–37 In later versions of the myth (Servius on Virgil *Georgics* 1.39;
Lucan *Civil Wars* 6.698ff. and 739ff.), Persephone falls in love with Hades
or is won over to the point that she does not want to return to her mother.
Here (even if eating the pomegranate seed is a form of sexual seduction; see
my interpretive essay on "Marriage," this volume), Persephone apparently
remains emotionally invested in her mother only. Notice the use of strong
word *amphagapazomenai* ("embracing fondly") for their mutual embraces at
436 (underlined by alliteration) and 439; at 290 the word is used to describe the consoling, nurturant embraces of Demophoön's sisters. The word
homophrona, "like-minded," used at 434 of the state of mind (*thymon*) that
the two goddesses share, is used in the *Odyssey* (6.181, *homophrosynên*; and

---

[102] Segal 1981:130 and Scarpi 1976:49–50. Richardson 1974:ad loc. discusses the meaning of the names of Persephone's companions.
[103] Richardson 1974 and Cassolà 1975:ad loc.

6.183, *homophroneonte*) to describe the ideal relation between husband and wife. There may be aetiological elements here. Festivities celebrated at the conclusion of the Mysteries emphasized the restoration of happiness to both goddesses and initiates.[104]

438–40 Hekate now moves to acquire her own role and prerogatives at Eleusis.[105] In a vase painting she is shown leading Persephone up from Hades. (See Fig. 4). As in the beginning of the poem, she plays a mediating role, and her movement among spheres may be linked to her role as moon goddess (see earlier on lines 51–89), as chthonic goddess, and as in Hesiod, a goddess with powers in more than one realm.

439 It may be significant that Persephone is here called Korê once more, now that she is reunited with her mother and has partially regained her premarital identity.

440 Hekate promises to become an attendant to Persephone (Philodemos [*De pietate. Herculaneum Papyrus* 1088:fr. 6.12–16] took the ambiguous pronoun *hoi* (her) in this line to refer to Demeter, but this seems less likely). The two words for "attendant" in this line (*prospolos* and *opaôn*) suggest that Hekate goes before and after Persephone. Later visual representations (see Fig. 4) depict Hekate leading the way on Persephone's return from the world below. If this event occurred annually, Hekate may be thought to attend Persephone when she is separated from Demeter in the world below. A goddess who later developed underworld associations, Hekate in one version of the myth was sent to Hades to search for Persephone (Kallimachos fragment 466, after the scholiast on Theokritos 2.12).

441–69 Although Hermes or Iris normally play the role of divine messenger in archaic epic, Rheia, Demeter's mother, becomes the agent of reconciliation here. Cult poetry typically repeats verses important to the cult. At 460–66 Rheia repeats the terms of reconciliation between Zeus and Demeter for the third time (see 443–47 and 399–403)[106] and makes the request on which the outcome rests—she asks Demeter to make the crops grow. For a discussion of Rheia's role here, and her links with her daughter both within the poem and in cult, see my interpretive essay, Part 2 of this volume, under "The Mother/Daughter Romance."

450–56 The mention of the Rarian plain, where later myth situated Triptolemos's first plowing of grain, and the mention of the stages in the growth

104 Richardson 1974:ad loc.
105 Clay 1989:257.
106 Richardson 1974:ad loc.

and cultivation of grain, perhaps deliberately hint at the alternate version of the story, that Demeter introduced agriculture to humanity; here the plain is the place where fertility returns to earth.[107]

461 We are not told what honors Demeter chose[108]—probably the Mysteries themselves, because she institutes them immediately after this scene.[109] She already presides over agriculture.

The manuscript is damaged from 462–78, but as the text is more easily reconstructed, I have not used brackets in my translation.

470–95 Agriculture is now restored, the Mysteries founded, and Demeter and her daughter return to their rightful place with Zeus on Olympus (See Fig. 5). The text closely juxtaposes the restoration of agriculture and the founding of the Mysteries, suggesting a connection between them made explicit in other versions of the myth.

476 The text here, if it is genuine, refers to acts of doing (the term *drêsmosynê* suggests actions in a ritual context) and showing; 480 refers to seeing the rites (see also lines **44–46** for further discussion of the motif of sight in the poem). Later sources tell us that the final stages of the Mysteries included things done, shown, and said.[110] Unlike Olympian cult, the Mysteries emphasized experience, epiphany, and revelation. On the content of the secret parts of the Mysteries, see my essay on the Mysteries, following this commentary.

477 Richardson has removed this line from the Greek text due to redundancies; the missing line makes Triptolemos and Diokles once again recipients of the Mysteries.

478–79 Secrecy was very important in the Mysteries. It kept the initiands ignorant and permitted them to experience the transition from terror to bliss described by Plutarch (see my essay on the Mysteries, following this commentary). It may have been due not so much to the actual content of the rites, as to the need to preserve their efficacy by preventing borrowing, imitation, or parody. Known mysteries are transportable, and Eleusis very likely wished to control dissemination of the rites. In the fifth century B.C.E., Alkibiades was prosecuted for defaming the Mysteries (Thucydides 6.27ff., Plutarch *Alkibiades* 19–22) and Andokides barely escaped being condemned to death for revealing the Mysteries (Andokides 1 and [Lysias]

---

[107] Ibid.:297–98 and Clay 1989:259.
[108] Richardson 1974:296.
[109] Clay 1989:261.
[110] See Richardson 1974:302–8.

6); Pausanias, writing in the second century C.E., was prevented by a dream even from describing public sights at the sanctuary (Pausanias 1.38.7 and 1.14.3. See also Ovid *Ars Amatoria* 2.601–4).

486–89 The emphasis on the happiness achieved through initiation is standard in ancient descriptions of the rites. It can include worldly success (the term *olbios*, "blessed," 486, often implies material happiness or success in early Greek poetry) as well as a different relation to the afterlife. The poem does not specify the benefits to the initiate in the world below; instead it tells us that the uninitiated will not have the same lot in the world below as the initiate has. See the section on the Mysteries (Part 2 of this volume) for the problems in interpreting later ancient sources on the benefits provided by the Mysteries. In the *Hymn* the initiate also acquires the love of the goddesses (*prophroneôs philôntai*, "they graciously favor with love," 487; at 117 the daughters use *philôntai* to describe the care that women give to each other at Eleusis).

The sending of Ploutos (sometimes associated with Iakchos, who also played an important role at Eleusis) from heaven to the mortal hearth propitiously reverses the Demophoön story.[111] Ploutos was said to be the child of Demeter and Iasion (*Odyssey* 5. 125–28, Hesiod *Theogony* 969–74), conceived in Crete in the thrice-plowed furrow. His coming suggests a promise of agricultural plenty to the initiate and thus reminds the audience of Demeter's gift of agriculture as well as the Mysteries. The birth of a divine child Brimos is said by one late source to have concluded the Mysteries; if the reference to Ploutos hints at the birth of a divine child, it is by no means explicit.

At 483–89 the poem shifts from historical narrative to the present, signaling the permanence of the new order. This shift is typical in hymns.[112] At 486 and 492–93, the goddesses are addressed by their cult titles, *semnai* and *aidoioi*, "holy and revered"; *potnia*, "female figure of authority"; and *kourê*, "maiden." The places mentioned—Eleusis, Paros, and Antron—include fertile plains, an island on the sea, and mountains—the whole range of the earth's geography.[113] Paros is the site of another important Demeter cult not otherwise featured in the poem. The poem thus emphasizes its claim, typical in Panhellenic epic, to be more than a local poem.

Ending with a prayer and a promise of another celebration in song by the poet is also typical of the Homeric hymns. In hymns and prayers, the request to a divinity is generally made on the basis of past favors given by the divinity to the person praying, as well as offerings (here a song) made to the

---

[111] Clay 1989:264–65.
[112] Ibid.:264, Janko 1981:14.
[113] Clay 1989:264.

divinity. The poet's wish for a "living that warms the heart" (*bioton thumêre'*) at 494 may hint that he has already been initiated in the Mysteries and hopes that the better life that they promise will become his own. The goddesses will send Ploutos to earth as a guest in the houses of those they love, to give them *aphenos* (489), presumably "agricultural abundance." Demeter and Persephone love initiates *prophroneôs* (graciously, 487), and the poet asks here that they be *prophrones* (494) to himself. (The word *prophrôn* is used elsewhere at 140 and 226 of Demeter's proposal to serve the household of Keleos assiduously, and of the daughters' concern to take care of the disguised Demeter at 138.) The identical request for a "living that warms the heart" is made at the close of the later Homeric *Hymn to Earth* (30) and a similar request is made at the close of the *Hymn to Helios* (31). Nevertheless, I would suggest that in the context of the *Hymn to Demeter* the poet is deliberately choosing a particular closing request and using a traditional closing to special effect. Hence he claims like other initiates a living (*bioton*) from Demeter because he is an initiate.

BACKGROUND: THE ELEUSINIAN MYSTERIES AND WOMEN'S RITES FOR DEMETER

Helene P. Foley

The Eleusinian Mysteries

THE ELEUSINIAN MYSTERIES were the most important of the widespread Greek mystery cults of antiquity. Our sources for the Mysteries include the archaeological evidence of the sanctuary buildings, inscriptions, representations on reliefs and vases, and references in literary sources. Eleusis was situated on a trade route where the roads from Attika, Boeotia, and the Peloponnesos meet and approximately fourteen miles west of Athens. Archaeological evidence for a possible cult at the site of the later Mysteries begins in the Mycenaean period (fifteenth century B.C.E.).[1] Substantial remains begin in the late Geometric Age (eighth century B.C.E.); the Goths probably destroyed the sanctuary around 395 C.E.[2] The first hall of initiation or Telesterion was built at the time of the Attic tyrant Peisistratos in the mid-sixth century B.C.E. on the site of a temple dating from the late-seventh or early-sixth century.[3]

For a thousand years from our earliest written testimony, the Homeric *Hymn to Demeter*, the Mysteries brought happiness and solace to initiates from the Greek world and later from the whole Roman Empire. The *Hymn* itself refers in detail only to the mythical origins of preliminary rites at Eleusis that could be revealed to outsiders and culminates with the founding of the cult and veiled references to the promises it offered to the initiate. References to the Demeter/Persephone myth apparently played a role at every stage of the rites, however, and it seems likely that the *Hymn* might illuminate some aspects of the Mysteries and their meaning for the initiate even if it reveals no details about the most secret proceedings.

---

[1] Mylonas 1972 and others may be overly optimistic about the Mycenaean evidence. See Darcque 1981 and Parker 1988: 102n.31 for citation of recent views, including as yet unpublished papers. Graf 1974:274–77, however, argues that the wide diffusion of the cult in Ionia indicates that it antedates the Ionian migration in the late Bronze Age.

[2] On these controversial archaeological points, see esp. Mylonas 1972. Imperial decrees of 390–91 C.E. also prohibited the celebration of pagan cults and thus helped to assure the demise of the cult of Demeter and Persephone.

[3] Mylonas 1972:ch. 3.

At least by the classical period (480–323 B.C.E.), the Mysteries were open to all persons who spoke Greek and had not committed murder: male or female, slave or free, Greek or Greek-speaking foreigner. Only the expense of initiation (fifteen drachmas or the equivalent of about ten days' wages by the fourth century B.C.E.) could have precluded initiation for those qualified. A great civic festival, the Mysteries nevertheless effected no change in the civic status of the individual, such as creating citizens or initiating them into adult roles. The rites were conducted by priests descended from two families.[4] The Eumolpidai provided the chief priest, or Hierophant ("he who shows holy things" or "makes them visible"), assisted by two priestesses; and the Kerykes provided the torchbearer or *daidouchos* (assisted by a priestess) and the sacred herald or *hierokêryx*. The chief priestess of Demeter lived at the sanctuary; several other women, the Panageis or Melissai, may have helped to carry sacred objects from Eleusis to Athens and back.

All initiates, at least from the fifth century B.C.E. on, had to undergo a preliminary stage of initiation at the Lesser Mysteries at Agrai near the banks of the Ilissos River in Athens before undertaking the final initiation at Eleusis. The Lesser Mysteries, which took place in the spring at the Metroön sacred to the Mother of the Gods (Rheia), involved preparation and purification for the Greater Mysteries, and, one source reports, "an imitation of the story of Dionysos."[5] Several ancient sources state that the Lesser Mysteries were celebrated in honor of Persephone.[6] Some of the preliminary rites shown on the two reliefs representing Herakles discussed below may have occurred at the Lesser Mysteries, at least from the fifth century on. The Lesser Mysteries were said to be founded in order to permit Herakles to be initiated into the Mysteries.[7]

At Eleusis there were two stages of initiation. The first stage of initiation was called *myêsis*; a *mystês* (pl. *mystai*) is one who closes his eyes and/or keeps his mouth shut. The final stage is described as *epopteia*; the *epoptês* is one who sees. The initiands, those who were being initiated for the first time, were individually sponsored and directed by initiates called mystagogoi, or leaders of the mystai. One could and did attend the festival more than once, as initiand, as a would-be epoptês, as a mystagogos, and again thereafter. The Mysteries, then, were apparently an experience worth repeating.

The Festival of the Greater Mysteries lasted a week or more. It occurred in the autumn month Boedromion (September/October) shortly before the

---

[4] For later evidence on Eleusinian sacred officials, see Clinton 1974.

[5] Stephanus of Byzantium under the entry *Agra*. See further Parker 1989.

[6] Scholia on Aristophanes *Ploutos* 1013; Athenaios *Deipnosophistae* 6.253D; Hippolytos *Refutatio omnium haeresium* 5.8.

[7] Herakles was purified of the killing of the Centaurs. Because the ordinary initiate had to be "pure in hands," his/her purification at the Lesser Mysteries must have been different. See further Parker 1983:284–85 and Roussel 1930.

fall plowing.[8] On the thirteenth of the month, the ephebes, young men of military age, left Athens for Eleusis to escort holy objects (*hiera*) on the following day to the Eleusinion at Athens. These objects were carried in boxes tied with ribbons by Eleusinian priestesses. On the fifteenth, the first official day of the Mysteries, the mystai, or initiands, gathered at the Stoa Poikilê in the Agora for the *prorrhêsis*, the proclamation made by the hierokeryx that "those impure in hands or incomprehensible in speech" (that is, murderers or barbarians who did not speak Greek) should not participate. On the sixteenth, the mystai marched to the sea in the bay of Phaleron to purify themselves by bathing and washed a piglet that each would sacrifice immediately after returning to the city "on behalf of him or herself."[9] On the seventeenth there may have been a sacrifice to the two goddesses and on the eighteenth the mystai stayed indoors for the Epidauria, a festival for the god of healing Asklepios. Fasting may have occurred at this time.

On the nineteenth, the mystai and their mystagogoi left for Eleusis in procession on the Sacred Way from Athens to Eleusis. The procession included the sacred objects in closed chests, as well as a statue of Iakchos, a minor deity associated with Dionysos, whose name derived from a ritual cry at the procession. Branches called *bakchoi* (myrtle tied with wool) were swung to rhythm. The day's march to Eleusis included stops for sacrifice, prayer, singing, and dancing. On a bridge over the Kephisos River at the boundary between Eleusis and Athens, veiled or masked figures, a man or men and/or a prostitute (perhaps a man disguised as a woman), offered insults and obscene gestures to the mystai. Probably at this point, the descendants of the legendary king Krokos bound the right hand and left leg of each mystes with yellow woolen thread. Another ritual bath occurred at the salt streams on the Eleusinian side of the bridge. The mystai were welcomed at Eleusis and broke their fast. *Kernoi*, circular earthware dishes with tiny cups holding grain, peas, and beans, may have been carried in honor of the goddesses at this time. On this night the women apparently engaged in a *pannychis*, a night of song and dance that included *aischrologia* ("obscene" language).

The Telesterion, or hall where the Mysteries took place, could hold several thousand persons at a time (see the map of Eleusis, Fig. 6). The building was fundamentally different from the standard Greek temple. Almost at the center was the so-called Anaktoron, a rectangular stone construction with a door at the end of one of its longer sides.[10] The throne of the Hierophant stood there, and no one but he could pass into the Anaktoron. A fire burned

---

[8] For discussion of the Mysteries with full citation of sources, see Mylonas 1972, Kerényi 1967b, and Burkert 1983:248–98, 1985:285–89, and 1987.

[9] Scholia on Aristophanes *Acharnians* 747.

[10] The name is associated with the Greek word for "lord" or "ruler," *anax*, or "divine mistress," *anassa*. See Cassolà 1975:25. For further speculations, see Burkert 1983:276, n. 8.

on its top through an opening in the roof. There was no room for elaborate machinery in this dark and crowded hall; the lack of windows, the Anaktoron, and the numerous pillars that held up the building impeded visibility.

The preliminary stages of the Mysteries from the thirteenth to nineteenth Boedromion purified the mystai and put them in the proper mental and ritual state to participate in the final secret rites. The *Hymn* alludes to certain of these preliminaries: fasting, washing, purification by torches, sacrifice, and the wearing of special clothing (and amulets). On the Lovatelli urn and the Torre Nova sarcophagus we see illustrated the veiled initiate (Herakles) sitting on a ram's fleece (see Fig. 3).[11] At some stage a boy initiated "from the hearth" (the only child among adults) said and did certain things on behalf of all initiands.[12]

We cannot reconstruct the well-kept secret of the actual initiation, or *teletê*. The majority of our specific knowledge comes from hostile witnesses who often received their information secondhand: the early Christian fathers. Clement of Alexandria gives the password, or *synthêma*, of the Mysteries: "I fasted, I drank the *kykeôn* (a drink of barley, water, and herbs), I have taken from the chest (*kistê*), I worked, and deposited in the basket (*kalathos*) and from the basket into the chest" (*Protreptikos* 2.21.2) This password may demonstrate that the initiate has performed proper preliminaries, but we do not know what objects are moved from chest to basket and back. Clement hints that they were objects of an obscene nature, perhaps representations of genitalia, but they may also have been tools, perhaps a mortar and pestle for grinding the barley for the *kykeôn*.[13] The rites took place in darkness until a great light shone when the Anaktoron was opened and the Hierophant appeared (Plutarch *Moralia* 81e, *IG* II² 3811, Hippolytos *Refutatio omnium haeresium* 5.8.40, *IG* II–III² 3811).

Aside from the display of sacred objects and sights, spoken words and sounds certainly played some role in the ceremony as well. Initiates seem to have experienced in some form the sufferings and reunion of the goddesses. Late sources tell us of a mystic drama in which the abduction of Persephone and the wandering and mourning of Demeter were re-enacted (Clement *Protreptikos* 2.12.2).[14] Active participation in or elaborate representation of such a drama, however, would have been inhibited by the organization of space in the Telesterion. The mystai may have "seen" Korê (Papyrus d. R.,

---

[11] See the Commentary on lines 33–50, 48, 190–211, and 210 for further detail on these preliminaries. Some commentators attribute certain of these preliminaries to the Lesser Mysteries. See nn. 6 and 7 above. The *Hymn* suggests that at least at this early period they were a part of the rites at Eleusis. See the parody of some of these preliminaries at Aristophanes *Clouds* 254–68.

[12] At a later stage, girls may have been eligible. See Mylonas 1972:236–37.

[13] For discussion see esp. Burkert 1983:275.

[14] See further Richardson 1974:24–25.

University of Milan [1937] #20:176–77), called up by the gong of the Hierophant (Apollodoros *Die Fragmente der Griechischen Historiker* 244 F110). Torches may have been tossed at the conclusion of the rites to celebrate her recovery (Lactantius *Epitome divinarum institutionum.* 18 (23).7). Perhaps a sacred marriage between Hierophant and priestess occurred (Asterios *Homiliae* 10). The Hierophant was said to announce the birth of a divine child: "The Mistress has born a sacred son, Brimo the Brimos, the strong to the strong" (Hippolytos *Refutatio omnium haeresium* 5.8.40. See also Euripides *Suppliant Women* 54).[15] The child may have been identified with Iakchos/Dionysos (son of Persephone); Ploutos (Wealth), son of Demeter; or the child of another goddess. The gnostic Hippolytos tells us that the climax of the Mysteries was the silent display of a cut ear of wheat (*Refutatio omnium haeresium* 5.8.39). Indeed, Varro interpreted the Eleusinian Mysteries entirely in relation to grain (Augustine *De Civitate Dei* 7.20). The child (or Persephone) may have been identified with the ear of wheat and the light, for both myth and cult seem to have associated the Mysteries with Demeter's powers over agriculture. Similarly, the hope of the seed, buried in the ground, may have been linked with the promise of the Mysteries. A fragment of Euripides' lost *Hypsipyle* (Fr. 757N) may illuminate this climactic moment of display. "One buries children, one gains new children, one dies oneself; and this men take heavily, carrying earth to earth. But it is necessary to harvest life like a fruit-bearing ear of grain, and that one be, the other not."[16]

These rites were followed by dancing and sacrifice. Ephebes were said to prove their strength by lifting sacrificial bulls. Two special vessels were filled and poured out, one to the east, one to the west. Looking to the sky, the participants cried, "Rain!" looking to the earth, they cried, "conceive!" (Hippolytos *Refutatio* 5.7.34, Proklos *In Platonis Timaeum commentaria* III 176.28, *IG* II–III² 4876.) The garments of initiates were later used as swaddling clothes for newborn babies (Scholiast on Aristophanes *Ploutos* 845).

Aristotle emphasized that the initiate does not learn (*mathein*) something but is made to experience (*pathein*) the Mysteries and change his or her state of mind (fr. 15 = Synesius Dion 10 p.48a).[17] A rhetorician offers the following description of the experience at Eleusis: "I came out of the mystery hall feeling like a stranger to myself." (Sopatros *Rhetores Graeci* VIII:114–15)

---

[15] Hippolytos quotes a gnostic source; it is possible that a Christianizing influence is at work here, and hence it may not be reliable.

[16] All translations from ancient sources concerning the significance of the Mysteries are taken from Burkert 1987.

[17] Using additional ancient evidence from Aristotle and elsewhere, Boyancé 1962:462ff. suggests that the experience of the initiate involved visual contemplation of divinities and divine symbols.

Terror, anxiety, and bewilderment turned to wonder and clarification (Plutarch *Moralia* 47a); darkness turned to light. Aelius Aristides ("Eleusinios," *Orations* 19.2) describes Eleusis as "the most frightening and the most resplendent of all that is divine for humankind." As Plutarch (frag. 168 Sandbach = Stobaeus *Anthologium* 4.52.49), drawing on the Mysteries, describes the soul at the moment of death:

> The soul suffers an experience similar to those who celebrate great initiations
> . . . Wandering astray in the beginning, tiresome walkings in circles, some
> frightening paths in darkness that lead nowhere; then immediately before the
> end all the terrible things, panic and shivering and sweat, and amazement. And
> then some wonderful light comes to meet you, pure regions and meadows are
> there to greet you, with sounds and dances and solemn, sacred words and holy
> views; and there the intitiate, perfect by now, set free and loose from all
> bondage, walks about, crowned with a wreath, celebrating the festival together
> with the other sacred and pure people, and he looks down on the uninitiated,
> unpurified crowd in this world in mud and fog beneath his feet.[18]

Similarly, the Hipponion gold leaf depicts mystai and Bakchoi in the underworld proceeding on a sacred way to eternal bliss,[19] and in Aristophanes' *Frogs* the chorus of mystai are shown engaged in joyous song, dance, and festival in the world below (448–55). Plato's Seventh Letter (334b7) stresses "the kinship of souls and bodies" produced by participation in mystery rites. It seems clear then, that the secret rites did not pass on any secret doctrine or worldview or inculcate beliefs, but that its blessings came from experiencing and viewing signs, symbols, stories, or dramas and bonding with fellow initiates.

Reliable ancient testimony tells us that the Mysteries guaranteed a better life and a different and probably better fate after death. The *Hymn* asserts that initiates are fortunate (*olbioi*) but that noninitiates do not have the same lot after death (480–82); Ploutos (agricultural abundance) visits the house of those the goddesses love (486–89). For Isokrates (*Panegyrikos* 4.28), the mystai "have better hopes for the end of life and for all eternity." Pindar (fr. 137a) tells us that "blessed is he who has seen this and thus goes beneath the earth; he knows the end of life, he knows the beginning given by Zeus." A fragment of Sophocles (frag. 837 Radt) closely echoes the *Hymn*: "Thrice blessed are those mortals who have seen these rites and enter into Hades: for them alone there is life, for all others is misery." For Cicero the initiate at

---

[18] Trans. Burkert 1987:91–92. See also the passage inspired by the Mysteries at Plato *Phaedrus* 250bc.

[19] The gold leaves, generally found in grave mounds, apparently instructed the dead initiate in Bacchic/Orphic rituals (probably related or similar to the rites at Eleusis) about what to do and say as he or she entered the world below. On the Hipponion gold leaf, see G. Foti and G. Pugliese Carratelli 1974 and West 1975.

Eleusis learns "how to live in joy, and how to die with better hopes"; he adds that the Mysteries were Athens' greatest gift to humanity (*De Legibus* 2.14.36). The funeral inscription of a Hierophant of the Imperial Age announces that he had shown the mystai "that death is not an evil but something good." (*IG* II/III² 3661.5–6=Peck *Griechische Vers-Inschriften* 879)

These sources make it clear that the initiate received benefits from the Mysteries while he or she was alive (probably in the form of better crops). It is also clear that the Mysteries helped the initiate to face death. As for the afterlife, a number of passages suggest that the initiate and the noninitiate did not have the same fate after death (the *Hymn* itself; Aristophanes *Frogs*, where the initiates are separate from those being punished; Plutarch frag. 168; and Plato *Republic* 363a–366b).[20] Diogenes Laertios *Vitae philosophorum* 6.39 suggests that the uninitiated dwell in the mire, while initiates will receive a special privilege (*prohedria*, a front seat at public events) and live in the Isles of the Blest. Pausanias (*Graeciae descriptio* 10.31.9) describes a painting by Polygnotos where the uninitiated are pictured as women carrying water in broken pots. Aristophanes' *Frogs* pictures the existence of initiates in the world below as a happy chorus at a festival. The *Frogs*, which is echoed by the passage from Plutarch quoted above, is perhaps as close as we can come to a concrete image of the Eleusinian afterlife, although it is no doubt adapted for its role in the comedy.[21] It appears, then, that the destiny awaiting initiates was collective; and in the case of mass initiations of this kind, any differentiation of individual fates seems highly unlikely. Further guesses can only come from what we know of texts from related Orphic cults.[22]

Women's Rites for Demeter

All important rites of Demeter in Attika seem to have been linked (at least loosely) to stages of the agricultural year (Proerosia, Thesmophoria, Haloa, Chloaia, the Lesser Mysteries, harvest festivals, Skira, and finally the Greater Mysteries).[23] In many of these, women played an important or exclusive role. One of the purposes of this book is to consider the special significance of the Demeter/Persephone myth in the religious lives of ancient women. Examining related Demeter cults in which a version of this myth played an

[20] See further, the Commentary on lines 365–69.

[21] See also Plutarch *Non posse* 1105b on people's hopes for an afterlife involving dancing, playing, and light in the world below.

[22] For an extensive discussion of the happiness promised by the cult, which does not necessarily agree with what is said here, see Deichgräber 1950.

[23] Brumfield 1981.

important part in the proceedings may also help to illuminate those aspects of the *Hymn* that occur in a female world. Because the Thesmophoria in particular is generally thought to be a very early Greek ritual, its proceedings and its related myths could have influenced Eleusinian rites and myths and explain in part the prominent role of women in both. Before considering the significance of these rites, I will summarize briefly two representative rites of Demeter, the Thesmophoria and the Haloa, in which women played the central or exclusive role.[24]

Of these rites for Demeter, the most important was the Thesmophoria. This ancient rite was celebrated in different ways throughout Greece. In Attika the rite lasted for five days from the ninth to the thirteenth of the month Pyanopsion, at the time of the fall plowing. On the ninth at a festival called the Stenia, the women celebrated the return of Demeter with an all-night ceremony that included ribald jesting. On the tenth there was a local celebration at Halimous. Women performed a sacrifice to Demeter and danced on the shore at nearby Kolias. The first day of the Thesmophoria proper was called the *anodos* (way up) or sometimes the *kathodos* (way down). The name *anodos* was said to refer to a procession up to the Thesmophorion, which was probably located on the hillside of the Pnyx in Athens (this was near the site of the popular assembly, a juxtaposition that was not lost on ancient comedians like Aristophanes, who in his *Thesmophoriazusae* [*Women at the Thesmophoria*] jestingly imagines the women instituting their own assembly); but it was also a term used to describe the ascents of the two goddesses from one sphere of the universe to another. The festival seems to have been dominated by citizen wives but may have included concubines and unmarried women (though probably not slaves).[25] Two prominent women were elected to preside over the rites. Women remained chaste during the period of the festival (the priestesses at the Thesmophoria were also unmarried). They did not wear crowns, because Persephone was captured while gathering flowers, and they could not eat pomegranate seeds that had fallen to the ground. They encamped in huts on the hillside. The second day was called the Nesteia, "fast," or the Mesê, "middle day." The women fasted seated on the ground on beds made from withies and other anaphrodisiac plants; they imitated "the ancient way of life" before the discovery of civilization and mourned, probably in imitation of Demeter, for Persephone.[26] Men were excluded, and no public business

[24] I shall not discuss women's rites at the Proerosia, Kalamaia, or Skira. For useful discussions and interpretations of the Thesmophoria and the Haloa, see Burkert 1985, Parke 1977, Brumfield 1981, Zeitlin 1982, Detienne 1989 (1979) and Winkler 1990:188–209. Brumfield 1981 has full citation of the sources.

[25] See Menander *Epitrepontes* 749, Lucian *Dialogues of Courtesans* 2.1 with the comments of Brumfield 1981:86–87, and Winkler 1990:236n.13.

[26] See Diodorus Siculus *Bibliotheca* 5.4.7 and Plutarch *Moralia* 378E.

or sacrifices were done in the city. Prisoners were released during the Thesmophoria. The final day was called the Kalligeneia, a day celebrating fair offspring. Probably the feast known to have occurred at the festival took place on this day.

Our best ancient source (a scholion to Lucian's "Dialogue of the Courtesans") tells us that the festival was celebrated in accordance with the Demeter/Persephone myth.[27] When the earth opened for Korê, a swineherd named Eubouleus was swallowed with his swine in the same chasm. In honor of Eubouleus, piglets were thrown into the chasms of Demeter and Korê along with wheat cakes in the shape of snakes and phalli as well as the cones of the prolific pine tree. The rotted remains of the piglets are drawn from underground *megara* (probably pits) by women called Bailers (*antlêtriai*) who had purified themselves for three days. They clapped and shouted as they descended to scare away snakes who were said to live in the chasms. The remains were mixed with the seed about to be planted in order to produce a good harvest.

Piglets are symbols of the fertility of animals and humans and of an agricultural rather than nomadic life-style;[28] they were also associated with female genitalia. This mixture of offerings raw and cooked are a thank offering to Demeter because she civilized humankind with her gift of grain. There are no good explanations of the role or time of some other rites in the proceedings. At one point women beat each other with a woven bark scourge called a *morotton*; a sacrifice called "the penalty" was performed, and a ceremony called "the Chalcidian pursuit" was held.[29] *Aischrologia*—ritual abuse, jesting, and "obscene" language (language improper for use at other times)—played a role in this and all other exclusively female festivals for Demeter, as well as in the rites at Eleusis.[30] We are told that this custom derived from Demeter's laughter at coarse jokes when she was grieving for Korê. A Christian source says that the women also worshiped a model of the female pudenda.[31]

The festival contains many elements typical of seasonal fertility rites cross-culturally: mortification (fasting, mourning, sexual abstinence), purgation (the penalty sacrifice?), invigoration (the rite with the piglets, *aischrologia*, and beating with the *morotton* may have been designed to drive out deathlike forces and make room for fertile ones), and jubilation (feasting).[32] As the Lucian scholion states explicitly, the rites both link and promote the repro-

[27] Rabe 1971 (1906):275–76

[28] The scholion states explicitly that pigs, pinecones, and cakes were all fertility symbols.

[29] See Hesychius on *morotton*, *zêmia*, and *diôgma* and the Suda on *chalkidikon diôgma*.

[30] See Diodorus Siculus *Bibliotheça historica* 5.4.7, Cleomedes *De motu circulari corporum caelestium* 2.1, and Apollodoros *Bibliotheca* 1.5.1.

[31] Theodoretos of Kyrrhos, *Graecarum affectionum curatio* 3.84.

[32] See Brumfield 1981:88–95.

duction of humankind and agriculture. The exclusion of men from the festival apparently led to myths of bizarre punishments inflicted on males who spied on the rites, as well as comedies (especially Aristophanes' *Thesmophoriazusae*) about the nature of this separate society of women.[33]

The Haloa was a festival of Demeter and Korê (Dionysos seems to have been included here as well) held at Eleusis in midwinter during the month Posideon (December/January). It was apparently a fertility festival celebrated for the sake of planted land at a time when the growth of the new shoots were slowed or arrested by cold weather. The rite was said to have originated in a mythical incident where wine was introduced into Attika. Dionysos gave wine to Ikarios, who was killed by shepherds maddened by the effects of the unknown drink. Punished by a permanent "state of shame," they consulted the oracle at Delphi, which instructed them to make and dedicate clay sexual organs. The festival was founded in memory of this incident. In the view of some scholars, this aetiological myth was a late addition to a rite of Demeter, designed to explain certain features of the rite. In this festival women again performed *aischrologia* and held up and probably ate representations of male and female organs. The priestess whispered something secret concerning *klepsigamia* (adultery) into the ears of the women. The male archons, or leaders, furnished tables inside the sanctuary for the women loaded with wine and with food of all kinds—though certain foods including pomegranates were prohibited. While the women feasted, the men remained outside expounding stories of the introduction of Demeter's agriculture into Athens.[34] Other sacrifices to the gods were performed at this festival, some by the priestess of Demeter/Korê; and judging from the amount of wood ordered for the festival, a bonfire may have taken place.

Apparently Greek society thought women had closer connections than men had both to the hidden wellsprings of fertility and to death; the festivals of Demeter exploit this connection. Indeed, as Sherry Ortner has argued, human culture generally tends to associate women with nature and the supernatural.[35] The growth of both human child and the seed occur out of sight; women are thus associated with the hidden sources of the fertility they produce. Women also played an important and intimate role in rites for the dead and in mediating between this world and the next. In addition, festivals of Demeter offered women a time to join other women in celebrating myths concerning social transitions from childhood to marriage and motherhood. They were permitted an exceptional autonomy—to act, speak, eat, and drink in ways not permitted to them in ordinary life. They left home and family for rites they themselves presided over; they had their

[33] Aelian, frag. 44 Hercher, the Suda on *Thesmophoros* and *Sphaktriai*, Pausanias *Graeciae descriptio* 4.17.1. See Detienne 1989:129–47.

[34] Our main source for this rite is again a scholion to Lucian (Rabe 1971 [1906]:279–81).

[35] 1974:67–88.

own control over blood sacrifices (normally sacrifice, a rite with an intimate connection to social and political authority, was controlled by men—even at the Thesmophoria, a male slaughtered the beasts for the women before making a quick departure).[36] Husbands felt obligated to finance their women's participation in these important rites. Aeschylus's Danaid trilogy may have revealed an important aspect of these rites if, as some argue, it closed with the founding of the rites of the Thesmophoria in Greece by the Egyptian Danaids, slaughterers of their husbands who were now to accept patriarchal marriage in Greece. The ritual seems to compensate women for marriage. Just as Demeter used her powers over agriculture to bring back her daughter from marriage and the world below, Greek women celebrating the divine mother and daughter were permitted to reunite and ignore for the moment the marriages that had divided them from each other, and to exercise authority and control civic spaces in an unusual fashion.[37]

[36] See Detienne 1989:133 and 143.
[37] Lucian *Dialogues of the Courtesans* 2.1 makes clear that mothers and daughters participated in the rites together.

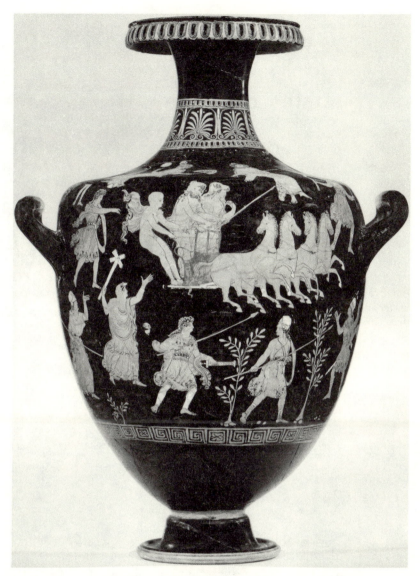

Figure 1. Hades' abduction of Persephone. Apulian red-figure hydria of the fourth century B.C.E.

Figure 2. Marble relief of
Demeter and Korê (or Hekate?)
with torches. Ca. 460 B.C.E.

Figure 3. The Torre Nova Sarcophagus. Palazzo Borghese, Rome.

Figure 4. The Return of Persephone: Persephone rising from the earth in the presence of Hermes, Hekate, and Demeter. Attic red-figure bell-krater, attributed to the Persephone painter. Ca. 440 B.C.E.

Figure 5. Demeter's Return to Olympus. Attic black-figure hydria. Ca. 520 B.C.E.

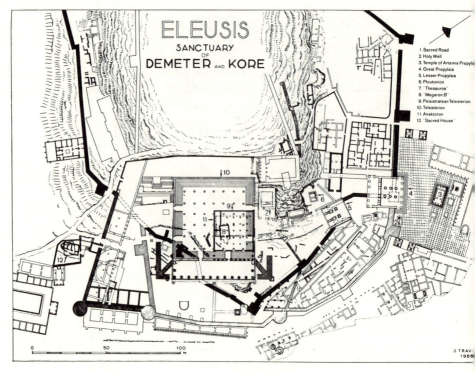

ELEUSIS
SANCTUARY
OF
DEMETER AND KORE

1. Sacred Road
2. Holy Well
3. Temple of Artemis Propylaia
4. Great Propylaia
5. Lesser Propylaia
6. Ploutonion
7. "Thesauros"
8. "Megaron B"
9. Peisistratean Telesterion
10. Telesterion
11. Anaktoron
12. "Sacred House"

J. TRAV.
1966

Figure 6. General Plan of the Sanctuary at Eleusis, by John N. Travlos.

Figure 7. Attic clay stand from
Eleusis depicting Demeter
enthroned with a polos and
garland, Korê wearing a polos
and holding a branch, and a
procession of worshipers.
Ca. 500 B.C.E.

PART TWO

INTERPRETIVE ESSAY ON THE

HOMERIC

HYMN TO DEMETER

HELENE P. FOLEY

The loss of the daughter to the mother, the mother to the daughter, is the essential female tragedy. We acknowledge Lear (father-daughter split), Hamlet (son and mother) and Oedipus (son and mother) as great embodiments of the human tragedy: but there is no presently enduring recognition of the mother-daughter passion and rapture.

There was such a recognition, but we lost it. It was expressed in the religious mystery of Eleusis, which constituted the spiritual foundation of Greek life for two thousand years. . . . The separation of Demeter and Kore is an unwilling one; it is neither a question of the daughter's rebellion against the mother, nor the mother's rejection of the daughter. . . . Each daughter, even in the millennia before Christ, must have longed for a mother whose love for her and whose power were so great as to undo rape and bring her back from death. And every mother must have longed for the power of Demeter, the efficacy of her anger, the reconciliation with her lost self.

Adrienne Rich, *Of Woman Born*

T HE HOMERIC *Hymn to Demeter* brilliantly records "the mother-daughter passion and rapture" whose loss Adrienne Rich laments.[1] Probably composed between 650–550 B.C.E. by an unknown bard (or bards),[2] the *Hymn* honors the Greek goddess of grain Demeter and her daughter Korê ("maiden"), or Persephone. The poem tells the story of the abduction of Korê/Persephone by Hades, god of the underworld, and the struggle of her mother Demeter to win her daughter back along with the idyllic happiness they had enjoyed before their violent separation by the plan of the father Zeus for his daughter's marriage. After a sojourn among mortals at Eleusis during which, disguised, Demeter attempts and fails to immortalize a human child, the goddess uses her power over grain to create a famine on earth. The gods, disturbed over their loss of sacrifices from humankind, capitulate. Yet Persephone has eaten a pomegranate seed in the world below and is thus at least partially committed to the realm of Hades. She can join her mother in Olympus for two-thirds of the year, but for one-third of the year she must become the powerful queen of the underworld at the side of her husband. The poem closes with Demeter's founding of the Eleusinian Mysteries. The *Hymn* thus offers a mythical explanation for the

[1] 1976:237–40.

[2] See the discussion of the date and the authorship of the *Hymn* and its relation to the tradition of oral poetry at the beginning of the commentary.

founding of what later became the most famous of the mystery cults of antiquity (see Diodorus Siculus *Bibliotheca* 5.77.3); the pride of the city of Athens, the Mysteries at Eleusis survived until the site was destroyed, probably by Alaric the Goth in 395 C.E.[3] As Pausanias, writing in the second century C.E., said of the Mysteries (*Graeciae descriptio* 10. 31.11), "Earlier Greeks considered the Eleusinian rite as being as much more to be honored than all other religious rituals as gods are honored above heroes." As a whole, the *Hymn* offers a female version of the heroic quest that plays a central role in Mediterranean and Near Eastern epic from as early as the Sumerian epic *Gilgamesh*.

The myth told in this hymn was profoundly significant in antiquity, both to all initiates in the Mysteries and in particular to ancient women. Initiands of both sexes eventually came from all over the Mediterranean world to acquire the better lot promised by the cult both in this life and in the afterlife.[4] In addition, the myth of Demeter and Persephone played an equally central role in cults of Demeter exclusive to women, above all in the ritual of the Thesmophoria, which was celebrated for three or more days each year in many Greek cities.

Furthermore, in contrast to the Homeric epics, the *Hymn* puts female experience at the center of the narrative by giving the privileged place to the point of view of the divine mother and daughter on their shared catastrophe. The (nevertheless critical) actions of the gods Zeus, Helios, and Hades occur at the periphery of the narrative and receive relatively little attention or sympathy. The mortal men of Eleusis play a central role in founding Demeter's temple and in being the first initiates into her cult. Yet the women of Eleusis are the first witnesses to the miracles of Demeter and host the disguised goddess during her stay on earth.

On the divine level, the *Hymn* represents first a resistance, by the bride and her mother, to an arranged marriage and then stresses the goddesses' reluctant acceptance of this painful transition.[5] Demeter directly challenges the patriarchal reign of Zeus and comes within a hair of entire success. The poem closes with a reaffirmation of female bonds between Demeter, Persephone, Hekate, and Demeter's mother Rheia. By contrast, despite their concern with the adulteries of Helen and Klytemnestra, the major Homeric epics tend to idealize marriage. A young girl like Nausikäa in *Odyssey* 6 looks forward eagerly to marriage, although she has some role in her choice of

[3] Eunapios *Vitae Sophistarum* VII3 reports on a prophecy predicting the destruction of Eleusis. For further discussion of the gradual decline of the site and possible additional destruction by early Christians, see Mylonas 1972:8 and 186.

[4] For a discussion of the content of these promises, see the essay "The Eleusinian Mysteries," which precedes this essay, and the commentary on lines 486–89.

[5] In problematizing Persephone's marriage, the *Hymn to Demeter* reflects later Attic tragedy more closely than Homeric epic. See further below.

husband and is not facing the possibility of leaving home. In the *Iliad*, Achilleus's concubine Briseis or Hektor's wife Andromache love their partners although they did not choose these men. The *Odyssey* celebrates in the union of Penelope and Odysseus the kind of marriage that a genuine likemindedness between husband and wife can achieve. Mortal women of the *Hymn* also accept marriage without question, and Demeter wishes for good marriages for the daughters of Keleos, even as she is resisting her own daughter's union with Hades.

The abduction of Persephone also became linked in Greek art and poetry with the experience of the Greek bride.[6] At Lokri, a Greek colony in Southern Italy, Hades and Persephone served as a paradigm for the married couple and received dedications from girls about to marry.[7] Girls who died before marriage were called "brides of Hades." Ancient poets often exploited the similarity of the rituals of marriage and death as rites of transition from one phase of human existence to another[8] and sometimes used Persephone's

[6] For the visual material, see Jenkyns 1983. He suggests important links between Attic representations of scenes of abduction and scenes of marriage, and above all, between representations of marriage and representations of two mythical scenes: Thetis's resistance to capture by her future husband Peleus (an important literary paradigm in wedding songs) and Hades' abduction of Persephone. The resistance of Persephone's female attendants in some versions of the abduction and the reported resistance of the bride's companions in wedding songs and rites (see note 8 below) offer another potential link between the two. See the section on "Marriage," below, for further discussion.

[7] See Sourvinou-Inwood 1991:147–88 with further bibliography. This cult was unique to this location, but the use of the myth as a literary paradigm for marriage in Attic tragedy (see below) indicates that the analogy was not confined to Greek Italy. Persephone symbolically "dies" by entering the world of Hades. Yet she is also immortal and returns yearly to life and the generation of fertility in the world above. Thus, although the association between the bride and Persephone is by no means a standard wedding theme, the goddess is not necessarily the negative example for a bride she might appear to be.

[8] Marriages and funerals shared common features (garlands, ritual ablutions, the cutting and dedication of hair, songs, a feast, the emphasis on the passage from house to grave or from parents' house to new home, and so forth). It has also long been argued that there were correspondances between the Mysteries and marriage rites, but the precise relation between the two, as Richardson 1978:188 points out in his review of Scarpi 1976, is unclear. For further discussion of the intertwining of marriage and death or sacrifice, see Redfield 1982, Jenkyns 1983, Foley 1985:35–40 and 65–105, and Seaford 1987. Elements in the ancient Greek marriage rite suggest the resistance of the bride to marriage: the doorkeeper who "roars at the women trying to rescue the bride" (Pollux *Onomastikon* 3.42), the burning of the axle of the wagon that carries the bride to her house in Boeotia, etc. The lifting of the bride into the wedding chariot or wagon and the grasping of her wrist by the groom (a gesture that also appears in abduction scenes) also introduce a mock-abduction motif into the wedding ceremony. Wedding songs include the bride's resistance to marriage and her reluctance to lose her virginity or to leave her mother. Catullus 62, which probably goes back to Greek originals, stresses the bride's reluctance to leave her mother, to marry, and to lose her virginity (21–22, 24, 39–48, 59). Euripides' *Medea* 230–251 makes clear why the transition to marriage and life with a stranger could be humiliating and difficult for the bride. All this explains why marriage

story to evoke the connection. Greek girls were often married in their mid-teens to husbands chosen by their fathers; if the husband did not reside near the bride's family, the bride might not see her family often (or at all) after marriage. Thus, like Persephone, a young girl could be thought to undergo in her initiation into marriage a symbolic "death" before emerging into a new life and fertility with a (generally) unknown husband in a strange household. Euripides, for example, exploits the thematic connection between Persephone's abduction and the symbolic remarriage of his heroines Alkestis and Helen.[9] The profound effects of the separation of the youthful bride from family and friends at marriage are also reflected in the fragmentary lyric poetry of Greek women, above all in the work of Sappho and Erinna.

In human culture, women are circulated among men in order to link one household, tribe, or city with another. Persephone's role in what has been called the "traffic in women" creates a new relation between earth, Olympus (heaven), and Hades (the world of the dead below) by linking them for the first time in her own person.[10] As wife of Hades and daughter of Demeter, Persephone thus makes possible the promises offered to the initiates in the Mysteries and indirectly affirms the role of mortal wife.

Finally, we shall see that the representation of the relationship of mother and daughter in this poem—the powerful effects of their separation and reunion and the creative anger of the mother—resonates remarkably with contemporary psychological studies of the dynamics of the mother/daughter bond. Thus Adrienne Rich correctly sees the important role that this myth plays in early Western literature. Greek tragedy has its share of mother/daughter duos from Hekabe and Polyxene (Euripides' *Hekabe*) to the notoriously problematic relation between Elektra and Klytemnestra represented in plays by Aeschylus, Sophocles, and Euripides. But it was not until Mme. de Lafayette's seventeenth-century novel *The Princess of Cleves*, in which the admonitions of the mother play throughout a dominant role in the daughter's struggles with her desire for a man not her husband, that the mother/daughter relation began to win the central literary position it has acquired in recent twentieth-century literature.[11] Unlike de Lafayette's

---

and the abduction of Persephone could be symbolically linked. Furthermore, Danforth 1982 and Alexiou and Dronke 1971 show that modern Greek death ritual, funeral laments, and wedding songs in rural Mediterranean culture can be very similar, and that the bride's departure can be treated as a symbolic death (and her death as a symbolic wedding), even when the bride is simply going to live in another household in the same village.

[9] See the discussion of marriage and the Persephone myth in Euripides' *Alkestis* and *Helen* in Foley 1992.

[10] See Rudhardt 1978, this volume. For the standard feminist discussion of the "traffic in women," a conception developed by Claude Lévi-Strauss, see Rubin 1975.

[11] There are of course other important, if less influential, literary studies of the mother/daughter relation in the intervening period. Tale 10 in the *Heptaméron* of Margaret de Navarre

novel or some later versions of the Demeter/Persephone myth, however, the *Hymn* concentrates on the mother's story rather than the daughter's. Again unlike the novel, the *Hymn* does not conceal the dynamics of this central female relationship in the dark corners of a domestic world but makes it the center of a religious experience of major public importance. Demeter teaches her Mysteries to the male leaders of Eleusis and the experience of the male child Demophoön has many parallels with that of later initiates.[12] The mysterious appeal of this female experience to initiates of both sexes and all classes remains an important question for exploration.

Interpreting the *Hymn to Demeter*

The *Hymn* narrates events that occur in two separate spheres: divine and human. The poem is framed at the beginning and end by the divine story. In the framing story, Persephone is abducted, her mother searches for her, withdraws from the divine sphere, and stages a famine on earth that makes Zeus capitulate and permit the partial return of Persephone to her mother. At the close of the poem, both goddesses return to Olympus and receive new honors. The long central episode of the poem occurs on earth and involves an encounter between the disguised Demeter and certain women of Eleusis. After the goddess's initial plan to immortalize the mortal child Demophoön fails, the men of Eleusis are instructed to build a temple in her honor. Demeter remains in this temple until her famine succeeds in its purpose. The poem brings gods and mortals together once more at the close with Demeter's climactic gift of the Mysteries to humankind. The structure of the poem thus emphasizes the primacy of the framing divine story, the intersection between divine and mortal experience in the central episode, and the final result of that intersection, the Mysteries.[13]

Homeric hymns are short poems in epic style and meter that may have been originally designed as preludes to the recitation of epic poems such as those of Homer.[14] We can best understand the structure and content of the

---

(sixteenth century), for example, prefigures the plot of *The Princess of Cleves*. For a study of Western literature that focusses on the mother/daughter relation, see especially Hirsch 1989, with further bibliography.

[12] See the Commentary at 231–55 for detailed discussion relating Demophoön to the initiates.

[13] For discussions of the structure of the poem, see esp. Rubin and Deal 1980, this volume; Alderink 1982; Scarpi 1976; and Clay 1989. This kind of geometric structure is common in archaic epic (e.g., see the analysis of the structure of the *Iliad* in Whitman 1958), and hence it is clear that an interpreter should take account of the connections between the framing and central story.

[14] See the introduction to the Commentary, this volume, for discussion of this controversial issue.

Hymn to Demeter against the background of the earlier Homeric epics, as well as the other long Homeric hymns to Apollo, Aphrodite, and Hermes. As we shall see below, the *Hymn* adopts themes and story patterns found in earlier epic and in the other hymns—and to some extent in early Greek lyric as well. It is typical in its insertion of one story or mythical digression within another, and in its effort to praise the powers of the deity or deities it celebrates. What is special to this hymn, however, is not so much the juxtaposition of divine and human narratives—for the separation of divine and mortal existence is central to early epic—as the prolonged and intimate encounter between divinity and humankind and the emphasis on the cosmic importance of encounters between female figures, both divine and mortal.

The *Hymn*, like many of the hymns, is an aetiological poem; that is, it explains how Demeter and Persephone came to have the honors that they have in the universe and how the Mysteries were founded. My interpretation of the *Hymn* revolves around the obvious, but often underrated, assumption that the entire *Hymn* is ingeniously structured to prepare for the founding of the Mysteries (closely accompanied by the return of fertility to the earth). I shall emphasize the multiple ways in which the Mysteries are the result of a unique and complex intersection between mortals and immortals and examine the role that female experience plays in modifying forever the relations between divinity and humankind. My interpretation stresses the ways that the *Hymn* itself illuminates for its audience, in explaining how the cult began, what the Mysteries mean for those who were fortunate enough to be initiated into them.[15]

The "Theology" of the Mysteries

Greek religion had no formal theology, no priestly class of interpreters of an authoritative divine scripture. Greeks experienced religion through ritual and myth, and the myths (and, though sometimes more slowly, the rituals) were endlessly changed and reimagined for every generation by its artists and poets. The *Hymn to Demeter* closes with a promise to initiates in the Mysteries that they will experience a different lot in life and death. If we knew more of what happened in the Mysteries, we would still be left with the problem of interpreting the meaning of the rites performed, because such exegesis almost certainly played little role in these as in other Greek rituals. Similarly, myths such as that told in the *Hymn to Demeter* derived their meaning from the narrative itself, from their relation to ritual, and from their similarity to closely related myths. The reader or hearer of the

---

[15] For other interpretations that are optimistic about what the *Hymn* can reveal about the significance of the cult, see esp. Alderink 1982:esp. 6, and Parker 1991.

narrative is left to fill in what we experience as the gaps and to explain the religious significance of the story in the context of his/her knowledge of other and sometimes conflicting narratives about gods, humans, and the relation between the two. This does not mean that we cannot understand to some degree what kind of contribution the *Hymn*, its myth, and the Mysteries made to the experience of Greek worshipers. But we have to approach the problem from a different direction than we would in the case of Christianity, Judaism, or Islam, religions that grew to have a powerful exegetical tradition.[16] Hence I shall begin by trying to locate the *Hymn* and its unique representation of the relation of life and death through a series of comparisons between the *Hymn* and other early Greek and Near Eastern narratives that share similar themes and story patterns. If this approach is sometimes frustrating to the reader unfamiliar with these other texts, it is necessary, because the ancient hearer of the *Hymn* would be responding to the poem out of a rich experience of other poetry on which the *Hymn*'s composer(s) relied in creating its narrative.

Early Greek views of death as expressed in poetry varied according to genre, class, and context. In the Homeric epics and in much of early Greek lyric, poetry that seems frequently to have been composed at least initially for aristocratic patrons, the soul becomes after death a flitting shade in a dark and gloomy world below with neither the strength nor the consciousness of the living person. Faced with this miserable experience after death, the Homeric warrior or the Pindaric aristocrat[17] strives to make the best of his time in the world of light; he attempts to counter death by the production of brilliant children and the celebration of his immortal deeds in epic or lyric poetry. Yet even this fame can offer but a fragile consolation to the shade in the world below. The shade of Achilleus, the greatest hero of the Trojan War, confesses to Odysseus in Book 11 (489–91) of the *Odyssey* that he would rather be a lowly itinerant laborer in the world above than a famous king among the dead. Only those few lucky heroes, like Menelaos in *Odyssey 4* (563–69), who escape Hades for Elysion or the Isles of the Blest, acquire anything like a satisfactory lot in the world beyond. In Elysion Menelaos, who has acquired his fortunate afterlife through his marriage to Zeus's daughter Helen, will encounter the easiest existence possible for mortals: no snow, no rain, and the cooling breeze of the West Wind.

In most of early Greek poetry, the gifts of the gods to humankind are at best mixed. In *Iliad* 24 (525–33), we are told that Zeus bestows gifts to humankind from two jars; the lucky mortals receive a mixture of goods and bads, and the unlucky ones receive an unmitigated portion of disaster. As

---

[16] To some extent, Greek myths themselves could be said to constitute an exegetical tradition, in so far as they attempt to explain religious beliefs and practices and their origins.

[17] Pindar's poems also contain passages that use language and imagery borrowed from the Mysteries.

both the daughters and wife of Keleos make clear to the disguised Demeter in the *Hymn* (147–48, 216–17), humans cannot refuse the divine gifts that often prove to be deceptive and destructive to them; their only choice is to endure them. In the early Greek cosmological poetry of Hesiod, men are condemned to mortality by the acceptance of the most treacherous and enticing of all gifts: woman. Similarly, the human sacrificial portion, bestowed on mortals by the god Prometheus, permits them to eat all the best parts of the sacrificial animal but condemns them to mortality, because they no longer share food with the gods.[18] Gods may favor mortals, but their favor can be lost by a failure to recognize or honor the gods and their will in a proper fashion. Jealous and often fickle, the gods allow humans moments of glory and even of contact with the divine but then withdraw with equal speed and unpredictability from those who are fated to err or die. Despite their seeming resemblance to humankind, the Greek gods exist in a world apart, living forever and free to violate most of the limits of human existence. The Greek view of divinity was built on this fundamental separation of humans and gods, on mortals' constant wish to be godlike and their tragic failure to achieve this dangerous goal.

The Eleusinian Mysteries—like other Greek mystery cults—inaugurated for humankind a different lot and experience of divinity than what we find in Homeric epic.[19] The irrevocable separation between the world of immortals and mortals still holds, and the *Hymn* does not make clear how or to what degree the goddesses will modify human life and afterlife. The pessimism of the somber central episode, in which Demophoön loses immortality, is balanced by the joyful reunion between the goddesses and the new role created for Persephone in the order of the universe. Certainly the happiness that Demeter and Persephone promised to initiates in the Mysteries is a uniquely straightforward and reliable divine gift.[20] Initiates can count on the experience of the beneficent divinities with whom they are united in secret rites and can afford to ignore the struggle for "immortality in song" so central to Homer and archaic lyric; nor do they need to be aristocrats to mitigate their lots in life and death. Every initiate—and at least by the classical period (480–323 B.C.E.) initiation was open to all who spoke Greek and whose hands were pure of human blood, including women and slaves—could expect a better afterlife than that offered to the uninitiated. Later evidence suggests that initiates won the opportunity to taste many of the joys of a blessed afterlife that were once confined to those fortunate aristocrats who reached Elysion.[21]

---

[18] Vernant 1980:45–77.

[19] The alternate view of the afterlife offered by various mystery cults probably goes back to a very early date. What is significant about the *Hymn* is that it attempts to incorporate into epic tradition religious views that may originally have been alien to it.

[20] Although even in this case the gift confirms human mortality (see Scarpi 1976:96–97).

[21] See the essay on "The Eleusinian Mysteries," this volume, for ancient testimony on the

In Homer the Olympian gods sometimes feel pity for mortals, but they generally have no wish to share their earthly experience beyond a brief encounter. The Homeric *Hymn to Aphrodite* stresses the humiliation that gods may undergo even in their fleeting sexual passions for mortals. Gods— particularly the gods who appear in tragedy, like Artemis in the closing scene of Euripides' *Hippolytos* or Apollo at the opening of Euripides' *Alkestis*—normally refuse close encounters with mortal suffering and death. Even those divinities who become more extensively embroiled in mortal existence are often powerless to transform it. Despite her suffering and all her efforts to intervene for him, the goddess Thetis is helpless to change the fate of her beloved son Achilleus in the *Iliad*. Apollo rewards Admetos with an escape from death in return for his hospitable treatment during the time he was forced by Zeus to serve Admetos as a shepherd: but only if Admetos can find another to die for him (the story is told in Euripides' *Alkestis*). Often, as when Apollo and Poseidon build the walls of Troy, the entrance of divinity into the mortal sphere ultimately has ambivalent results for humanity. Among those divinities who become deeply engaged in human existence, Demeter and Persephone have an unusually sustained encounter with mortality that leads them to establish a permanent and beneficial modification of the relation between divinity and humankind.[22]

In Hesiod's seventh-century B.C.E. cosmological poem the *Theogony*, the gods—like God in the Old Testament when he drives Adam and Eve from the Garden of Eden—create marriage, sacrifice, and agriculture as a barrier between humans and gods and a mark of the human fall into mortality.[23] The gods of Homer and Hesiod are not limited by these mortal institutions. They can mate and create children without marriage and can commit incest; they eat the immortal foods nectar and ambrosia, not the meat that humans sacrifice to the gods; they have no need to work the land in order to live. In the Demeter/Persephone myth, by contrast, divinity becomes embroiled in a struggle over the very human issues of marriage, sacrifice, agriculture, and death. Demeter, initially trapped in a painful ignorance and powerlessness characteristic of the human condition, disguises herself as an aged and mourning woman, laments, and refuses to eat, just as Achilleus laments and refuses to eat when mourning Patroklos in the *Iliad*. Persephone, too, longs

---

benefits that they offered. For more pessimistic readings of what the Mysteries promise in the *Hymn* (rather than at later periods), see Chirassi-Columbo 1975 and Parker 1991. The Orphic fragments promise to initiates consciousness—a drink from the stream of Mnemosyne (Memory)—and a place among heroes (see Zuntz 1971:335–40). If the Mysteries did indeed make comparable promises (see Diogenes Laertios *Vitae philosophorum* 6.39 for the suggestion that the initiates lived in the Isles of the Blest), the parallel between the Eleusinian afterlife and the afterlife of privileged epic heroes would be even closer.

[22] Dionysos is another god who has extended encounters with mortals and mitigates mortal existence with his gifts.

[23] See Vernant 1980:130–67.

for her mother and does not eat in the underworld. When Demeter and Persephone finally eat, the daughter eats a pomegranate seed, the mother drinks a *kykeôn*, a drink of grain, water, and herbs—mortal rather than immortal food. Persephone's eating of the seed that appears to bleed symbolizes her commitment to her marriage and the world below. Demeter's *kykeôn* also links her with the life of bread eaters on earth. The drink is associated with a primitive stage of human life, for the grain is uncooked and mixed with water rather than wine, the drink of civilized human (if not divine) existence.

When Demeter becomes a nurse to the mortal child Demophoön at Eleusis, the poem links the love of the mortal mother Metaneira for her only son with that of the goddess for her only daughter. Similarly, the language of the poem associates the daughters of Keleos and Demeter's response to them with the goddess' relation to her own daughter Persephone.[24] Demeter even laughs at human jokes and develops a fondness for the mortal maid Iambe, who is able to share them with her. A goddess, she ironically receives (although she does not accept) from mortals advice on how to endure the lot given by the gods. The *Hymn* is unique in archaic Greek poetry for the degree of humanization its gods experience, and precisely this humanization results in the establishment of the Mysteries at the end of the poem. Demeter's role of nurse to a mortal seems, for example, to have been renewed in the adoption of the initiates by the goddesses, and initiates imitated the experience of Demeter in the course of the rites.

Gods cannot die and normally do not experience the limitations imposed by mortal marriage.[25] But Persephone's marriage with Hades, who lives in a world inaccessible to mortals and immortals alike, forces Demeter and her daughter to encounter and even be permanently marked by the sufferings and limits imposed on humankind. Once linked in an uninterrupted companionship, the goddesses are forced to separate for one-third of each year when Persephone descends to the gloomy realm of her spouse.

Let me expand on this last point. As Rudhardt (this volume) has made clear, Demeter cannot, as in some later versions, descend to Hades to bring back her daughter,[26] because in the *Hymn* Hades' realm is initially inaccessible to anyone, god or mortal, except the god Hermes, who conducts souls

---

[24] See the Commentary on lines 98–112, 145–68, and 169–89 for details.

[25] Rudhardt 1978, this volume. See further the section on "Marriage" below.

[26] See *Orphic Hymn* 41.5ff., where Demeter is called Antaia; Hyginus *Fabulae* 251, Scholiast P. on *Odyssey* 6.160a, Olympiodoros in Plato *Phaedo* 67c8–9 (= frag. 211 Kern), Scholia on Aristophanes *Ploutos* 431, Barcelona Papyrus Inventory No. 158–61. 62–65, and Servius on Vergil *Georgics* 1.39 (in this case, as perhaps in Philikos's version, Demeter descends because Persephone does not wish to return). At Ovid *Fasti* 4.611ff., Ceres asks to descend to the underworld once she learns that Proserpina has eaten the pomegranate seeds and cannot return. See also Claudian *De Raptu Proserpinae* 3.107ff. See further Harrison and Obbink 1986.

and messages to the lower world. The loss of Persephone is the closest that a divinity can come to experiencing the suffering of mortals when a loved one dies; though Persephone is immortal, she is as lost to her mother as any of the pitiful dead below. Demeter, like other divinities who lose their mortal children, is thus able to comprehend the pain suffered by humans who lose a child to death;[27] she moves from grief and a female helplessness in the face of necessities enforced by powerful male deities to joyous reunion and honor and power from Zeus and Hades. The Mysteries are a ritual reenactment of this experience. At the conclusion of the *Hymn*, Demeter gives her Mysteries to humanity on earth and Persephone opens a new path to the world below through her annual descent and ascent. Mortals now have an ear in the underworld, and the universe has a link between heaven, earth, and the world below. Hades becomes for the first time accessible to mortal prayers; we know in fact that the god received cult offerings almost exclusively as the husband of Persephone.[28] Similarly, Demeter, as a goddess of grain, is also ideally placed to mediate among the spheres of the universe; for the seeds over which she presides grow from and return to the darkness beneath the earth.[29]

The *Hymn to Demeter* is typical of Greek cosmological poetry, in that its outcome is predicated on the development of a new set of relations among divinities; yet its tone contrasts with that of the other hymns and even to some degree with that of the major Homeric epics, to underline the unique encounter of the goddesses with mortality. Jenny Clay points out that the major Homeric hymns begin at a time somewhere after the establishment of the universe and the reign of Zeus, but before the present order of the divine world has taken its final form, and end with the establishment of new honors for a divinity (or divinities) and thus a change in mortal (and immortal) experience of the universe.[30] Demeter at first tries and fails to challenge the traditional boundaries between humans and gods by attempting to immortalize the Eleusinian prince Demophoön. She ends by winning new honors (443–44, 461–62; the honors are presumably the Mysteries, though the poem does not specify this) in addition to her role as goddess of grain, and Persephone establishes for the first time a significant role for herself among the gods above and below. As in other hymns, the goddesses win a place for themselves—a more substantial position than before—by challenging the existing order.

Yet if the myth of Demeter and Persephone has fundamental similarities

[27] See Méautis 1959:56.

[28] Pausanias *Graeciae descriptio* 6.25.2 says that Hades' sole cult of his own was in Elis. See further Rudhardt 1978, this volume, and Saintillan 1986.

[29] Scarpi 1976:100 argues that Persephone mediates between Olympus and Hades, and Demeter between gods and mortals.

[30] Clay 1989. See also Rudhardt 1978 (this volume) on the cosmological bent of the poem.

to the other hymns in its cosmological emphasis, it also differs significantly. The hymns generally treat the divine incidents that they narrate with a light and often witty touch. In the Homeric *Hymn to Hermes*, the precocious baby god Hermes wins his prerogatives by mischievous and infectious trickery; the baby god Apollo miraculously slays a dragon at Delphi in the *Hymn to Apollo*; in the *Hymn to Aphrodite*, Zeus turns the goddess's own powers against her, by making her desire a mortal. Aphrodite's delicious seduction of the mortal Anchises follows almost immediately. Even in the Homeric epics, the battle among the gods in *Iliad* 21 makes a comic contrast with the bloody struggle on the earth below; and the quarrel among the gods in *Iliad* 1 is resolved in laughter, unlike the disastrous quarrel between Agamemnon and Achilleus in the same book. The more serious treatment of the gods in the *Odyssey* seems to reflect the constant divine engagement in the mortal affairs of this poem. In Homer the gods may occcasionally pity the deaths of mortals who are their children or their favorites. Yet on Olympus itself, there is no really serious issue but power, and all power struggles are ultimately resolved by Zeus's continuing supremacy.

In the *Hymn to Demeter*, however, we encounter gods who (like Thetis in the *Iliad*) themselves come as close to the human tragedy as divinities can. When Demeter questions Helios about the whereabouts of her daughter, the god expresses pity for the sufferings of the goddess (76). Later, the disguised Demeter asks for pity from the daughters of Keleos (137). Pity is, as Aristotle saw, one of the two emotional reactions produced by the tragic plot, and it is the result of human powerlessness and ignorance. Helios's gesture of pity could not define more clearly the unlikely position in which Demeter as a divinity finds herself in the *Hymn*.

The affinities between mortal and immortal experience in the poem are deepened as well by the many structural parallels created in the narrative between the divine story and Demeter's experience on earth; mortal life even serves as a paradigm for the divine, and the worlds of gods and humans are brought closer together in a promise of reliable exchange between them. As Rubin and Deal (this volume) point out, in both the divine story and in the incident at Eleusis on earth a divinity tries to appropriate a child from its ignorant mother. Zeus gives Persephone to Hades, and Demeter tries to immortalize Demophoön. Demeter and Metaneira do not accept the child's change of status. Each god finally fails to accomplish his or her aim, but the child remains partially in the sphere of the abductor. Each child receives new honors; each can find happiness only in unity with Demeter. Demophoön's bliss in the arms of the goddess perhaps prefigures the happiness of the initiate in the Mysteries; in any case he remains linked with the goddess through the cult she establishes in his honor. Persephone is seemingly appeased by the honors she receives from Hades below, but joyful only during the time she shares with her mother on earth and Olympus.

In a fashion typical of Homeric epic, the poem does not say what, if anything, Demeter learned by attempting and failing to subject ignorant mortals to an experience in certain respects comparable to what she has just undergone herself. Although Homeric gods are capable of feeling pity for mortals, the poem does not tell us whether she pities the child she nursed for his loss of immortality, although we know that she will establish honors for him because he has been nursed in her arms. The motives of Demeter, as a divinity, remain suitably mysterious. What we do know is that an act of extraordinary divine beneficence results from her experience. Initially angry at mortals for their foolish ignorance, Demeter turns after the recovery of Persephone to a nurturing relation to humans and offers them for the first time a different lot in life and death. Happiness in this world (dependent on Demeter's powers over the fertility of the earth and its grain) is linked to a different fate in the world beyond, and activities in the two modes of existence are associated in a new and complex way.

Thus, although the text never explicitly states that the Mysteries are a result of Demeter's encounter with mortals and mortality, the narrative structure and the parallels established between mortal and immortal existence in the language and narrative detail of the poem make this event the most plausible explanation of their foundation. This assumption explains the delay in bestowing the Mysteries until the final moments of the poem, which makes them appear to be the result of its events as a whole. From this perspective the return of Persephone is a mitigation of suffering and symbolic death on the divine level that is then matched by the same event on the mortal level; just as Demeter bestows honors on Demophoön because of the child's intimate connection with herself, the Mysteries are offered to mortals because of her stay in their realm.[31]

Furthermore, as the essay by Lord in this volume shows, the story of the wrath of Demeter and her journey to recover her daughter has remarkable similarities to the wrath of Achilleus in the *Iliad* and the homeward journey of Odysseus in the *Odyssey*.[32] From the historical point of view, the godlike

[31] The Mysteries are presumably also the honors that Zeus awards to Demeter when she returns to Olympus; but this does not preclude additional explanations for the particular nature of these honors.

[32] Lord's argument, which originated in a suggestion of Albert Lord's (1960:97, 121, 186–97), has since been enriched and supplemented by that of Sowa 1984. My own discussion borrows from all three and adds new elements. For Sowa, a number of important mythological story patterns intersect in the narrative of the *Hymn*: the marriage of the fertility goddess, withdrawal and return, the journey, rape, and divine epiphany. The withdrawal and return pattern (see esp. 95–96) includes withdrawal (often motivated by abduction) with destruction and possible revenge (98), visits by embassies, reconciliation, and the death of a substitute. The rape story pattern (122) overlaps. A young person is abducted from a parent; the parent grieves and searches for the child; the parent is informed of the truth and ultimately settles with the abductor.

Achilleus may have borrowed his story from his goddess mother Thetis,[33] for both Greek and Near Eastern parallels suggest an origin in myths about divinity for this particular story pattern. Yet in the case of both the *Iliad* and the *Hymn to Demeter*, the plot pattern of wrath, withdrawal (including destruction), and return (often including revenge) once again serves, like the structure of the *Hymn* itself, to bring the world of gods and humans for a brief time closer together.[34] The wrath (*mênis*) and grief (*achos*) of both hero and goddess derive initially from the abduction of a woman (Briseis, Persephone) who becomes the wife or spear bride of the abductor (Agamemnon, Hades).[35] The withdrawal of hero and goddess then results in immense losses for the Greeks or a destructive famine on earth; in Demeter's case there are two withdrawals, one from heaven to Eleusis, the second to her temple at Eleusis.[36] Both initially refuse embassies that try to persuade them to abandon their wrath. Each finally agrees to return to play an appropriate and beneficial role in his or her community and wins new honors and gifts. The return of each to the role of warrior or goddess is represented as an uncanny revelation of extraordinary power and beauty.

Achilleus's wrath extends finally to both Greeks and Trojans; but at the conclusion he is capable of pity even for Priam, the father of his greatest enemy. Similarly, Demeter's wrath against Zeus is expanded to an anger against the foolish mortals who blocked her plan to immortalize Demophoön; she will destroy humanity with her famine. Yet after the return of Persephone, she founds the Mysteries for the benefit of humankind, for whom she will now feel the bond of *philia* (love or friendship). Both goddess and mortal suffer the permanent or partial loss of one dearest to themselves (Patroklos, Persephone).[37] This loss, which does not seem to be an inevitable aspect of the story pattern in the case of divinity, may serve to underline Demeter's partial assimilation into a mortal context in the *Hymn*. Similarly, Achilleus's wrath brings him both semantically and in action closer to godhead; but ultimately, once he has chosen to reenter the battle to avenge Patroklos, he wins fame only at the price of sealing his mortal doom. *Mênis*,

[33] For a discussion of the wrath of Thetis, see Slatkin 1986 and 1991.

[34] This comparison is not meant to conceal the complex variations in every version of a story pattern. As Nagler 1974:ch. 5, stresses (see also Lord 1970:186–97), Achilleus complicates the story pattern in the *Iliad*. In contrast to Demeter, who must reject the embassy from Zeus because she has not won Persephone's return (324–33), Achilleus has less decisive reasons for rejecting Agamemnon's embassy in *Iliad* 9. His return is delayed when Patroklos takes his place; when he does reenter the battle, he is motivated by a second wrath toward Hektor, against whom he wishes to take revenge for the killing of Patroklos.

[35] Nagy 1979:80–83 points out the semantic links between Demeter's cult title Achaia and the name Achilleus, which both derive from *achos*.

[36] For the double withdrawal, see Sowa 1984:101.

[37] The sequence and causation of events make this particular parallel much looser. Achilleus loses Patroklos in part because he withdrew, and Demeter withdraws because she has lost Persephone. Demeter also partially recovers her daughter.

the Greek word for Achilleus's wrath, is generally used for divine wrath such as that of Demeter (350, 410);[38] after Achilleus returns to battle against the Trojans, his powers in battle become so nearly godlike that he actually becomes embroiled in a battle with the river god Skamander. Demeter's wrath brings her closer to mortality, but finally, with the famine, she uses her divine powers to rescue her daughter at least partially from the world of the dead. By bringing divinity closer to mortal suffering and mortals closer to divine power, the story pattern of wrath, withdrawal, and return as it is enacted in both the *Iliad* and the *Hymn* mixes worlds that the entire Greek cosmos is designed to keep apart. When the world is reconstructed at the return, it can never be quite the same.

Similarly, both the hero Odysseus in the *Odyssey* and Demeter undertake a journey that brings them face-to-face with the world of death and with parts of the universe to which they are strangers;[39] in other versions of the myth, Demeter actually descends to Hades. The absence of both figures from their proper sphere causes disruption and near-disaster. In the image that the disguised Odysseus offers to Penelope in Book 19 (107–114), the rule of the just king brings not only order but fertility to his land; Ithaka is paralyzed without Odysseus. Earth ultimately withers at the withdrawal of Demeter and recovers its fertility and seasonal predictability after Persephone's return. The motifs of recognition and revenge (or in Demeter's case, threat of revenge) play an important role in both poems.[40] Odysseus and Demeter each emerge from disguises as an old and powerless person and tell lying Cretan tales (tales that nevertheless contain a good deal of truth); both punish those who are inhospitable[41] and reward those who instinctively treat them in accordance with their true identity. Indeed, the role that Odysseus plays, of testing hospitality while in disguise, is a feature far more typical of Greek myths about divinity.[42]

Both succeed in their goals and win new honors, but ultimately must

[38] Watkins 1977. Orphic frag. 48 adapted the first line of the *Iliad* to Demeter's story: "Sing, Goddess, the wrath of Demeter . . ."

[39] Here I am adapting Sowa's 1984 model of the journey motif (212–13). In her model the protagonist loses or lacks something and undertakes a search. The search often involves a sea journey and a visit to the underworld. The protagonist encounters two helpers on the journey—one female, one male (like Hekate and Helios in the *Hymn*). The protagonist's absence during the journey has devastating results and a substitute "dies" for the protagonist. Here the pattern overlaps with that of withdrawal and return. In Sowa's view this is fundamentally a human story pattern, involving a confrontation with mortality.

[40] For the element of revenge in the journey motif, see Rose 1967 on the journey of Telemachos in the *Odyssey*.

[41] In other versions of the myth, this aspect of Demeter's story receives greater emphasis (see the Commentary on lines 90–97, 210, 253, and 371–73 for examples). In the *Hymn* Metaneira's spying and her interruption of Demeter's attempt to immortalize Demophoön provoke the goddess's wrath against the Eleusinians.

[42] See Sowa 1984:esp. 252 for examples from the *Odyssey*.

accommodate to new limitations. Demeter must accept her inability to immortalize humans and the partial loss of her daughter but expands her powers on earth by the establishment of the Mysteries. Odysseus, who loses both his mother and all of his men during his journey, makes his choice to return home to Ithaka on the basis of a knowledge of life and death inaccessible to the average mortal. He deliberately rejects immortality on Kalypso's island even though he has observed the miserable existence (or nonexistence) suffered by his companions at Troy in the world below. At the same time, he wins immortal fame not just for his role at Troy, but for his heroic journey and homecoming.

As is the case with the pattern of wrath, withdrawal, and return, the story pattern of the epic journey may have begun as a story about divinity. The first pattern naturally belongs to a deity with powers over fertility; the withdrawal of the Hittite storm god Telepinu is an earlier non-Greek example.[43] The second pattern, as is probable in the case of the *Iliad*, may have been transferred in Sumerian epic from the divine Ishtar/Inanna to the semi-divine hero Gilgamesh. The *Hymn to Demeter*, due to the later date of its composition, is apparently shaped by the two older Homeric epics[44] yet in other ways may represent an earlier stratum of myth. The *Iliad* and the *Odyssey* are thus logically colored by the associations of their underlying story patterns with an immortal story, just as the *Hymn to Demeter* assimilates aspects of famous mortal stories that preceded it.[45] The epic journey, for both mortal and immortal protagonist, is then about coming to terms with death, the pain of loss, and mortal limits. When a divine figure like Demeter undertakes an epic journey or an angry withdrawal, she is drawn into the sphere of human tragedy by all the forceful associations that this narrative has already acquired through its enactment by mortal heroes in the Greek epic tradition.

Comparison of the *Hymn to Demeter* with similar myths in other Mediterranean and Near Eastern cultures again reveals the special character of the confrontation with the world of death experienced by the *Hymn's* divinities. The Sumerian goddess Inanna mentioned above descended into the underworld and returned to earth after "dying" in the world below. Dumuzi fails to prostrate himself before the returning goddess; he is seized by underworld monsters and dragged into the underworld, apparently as a substitute

[43] For discussion of the Near-Eastern parallels (see further below) with sources, see esp. Richardson 1974:258–59: Burkert 1979: ch. 6; and Sowa 1984:46ff.

[44] We do not know in what form the Homeric epics were transmitted or available to the composer(s) of this hymn at this date, but the *Hymn* reflects an awareness of the traditions out of which the two epics as we have them finally emerged.

[45] Epic often defines the brilliance of its heroes by associating them with divinity. My point here is simply that a story pattern shared by gods and humans is particularly likely to bring such associations with it.

for the goddess.[46] The Egyptian goddess Isis lamented and sought her murdered husband Osiris in the world below. She finds Osiris and temporarily revives him to beget his avenger Horus; Horus destroys Seth, Osiris's killer. In an Ugaritic poem, Ba'al is killed by Mot. His sister Anath, a warrior goddess, kills Mot, grinds him up, and sows him in a field. Ba'al is returned to life. In the Akkadian myth of Nergal and Ereshkigal, the goddess of the underworld Ereshkigal tries to lure Nergal into the world of death.[47] Although Nergal is warned not to sleep with Ereshkigal nor to partake of food and drink in the world below, he does. Escaping once more to earth, he is finally forced to return and accept a role as ruler among the dead and consort of Ereshkigal.

The Christian story, too, tells of a divine son who lived, suffered, and died in mortal guise, thereby profoundly altering the relation of the worshiper to God the father. Unique among these similar stories, the Eleusinian cult bases its divine promises of a better life and afterlife to the worshiper on the sufferings and encounter with "mortal" experience of a divine *mother and daughter*.[48] In contrast to the Christian celebration of father and son, the initiates' path from fear and confusion to enlightenment was built on an encounter with the female experience of the two goddesses, and the happiness promised by the cult derives from a nurturing adoption by these divinities. It may not be accidental that Christianity's focus on the male was ultimately modified by the development of Mary's mediating role as suffering mother and by an emphasis in the high Middle Ages on the symbolic motherhood of Christ himself.[49]

Finally, both the *Hymn* and the Mysteries link mortal and immortal experience by exploiting initiatory patterns that traditionally mark stages of human experience. As van Gennep, Turner, and others have shown,[50] rites of initiation, including rites of initiation into religious mysteries, tend to take a similar form in many cultures. Initiates become temporarily detached from their regular environment and enter into a "liminal" experience in which the normal categories and hierarchies by which they define their world are sometimes terrifyingly blurred, transformed, or inverted. Finally, changed or renewed by this detachment from their cultural environment, they are reincorporated into it. The process is often described and experi-

[46] For translations of the texts of most of these myths, see Dalley 1989 and Pritchard 1969. For discussion, see Burkert 1983:263–64 and Sowa 1984:48. Burkert (264) cites Native American parallels.

[47] For a useful discussion of this myth in relation to the *Hymn* and the *Odyssey*, see Crane 1988:61–86.

[48] See Berg 1974.

[49] Bynum 1986 and 1991.

[50] van Gennep 1960 (1909) and Turner 1969. Among the many discussions of initiatory rites by classicists, see Brelich 1969, Sourvinou-Inwood 1988, or Dowden 1989.

enced as a symbolic death and rebirth. We can distinguish here between initiation rituals that involve biological transitions in the life of individuals (transitions to adulthood such as that of Persephone, or from life to death in burial) and those not specifically linked to biological transitions, like the Mysteries (although they help to prepare the initiate for death).[51] Myths such as that told in the *Hymn* often conflate the two kinds of rites, but they are experienced separately by participants.

To some extent, the structure of the *Hymn* itself is shaped by initiatory patterns in which the Eleusinian initiates shared to the degree that they imitated the experiences of the goddesses. As noted earlier, Persephone's experience of abduction, symbolic death, and rebirth into the upper world could be associated with the transition or initiation of women into marriage.[52] The myth's enforced separation of mother and daughter followed by reunion was celebrated in ancient cults special to women and seems to reflect, on the psychological level, the pattern of maturation common to mothers and daughters cross-culturally.

Demeter's withdrawal and return also resonate with initiatory patterns. Once she has recognized the loss of her daughter to the world of death, Demeter adopts a disguise and leaves the world of Olympus for the world of mortals. Her descent threatens to blur the division between the world of mortals and that of immortals. After readopting her divine form, she remains in the liminal space of her temple on earth, using her powers to destroy rather than renew fertility. Finally, she is reunited with her daughter, reincorporated into Olympus, and accepts new powers for herself and her daughter. Throughout the *Hymn*, however, Demeter never more than temporarily abandons her divinity, which shines through her mortal disguise, nor her role as nurse and mother; and it is this latter role that she preserves in taking the initiate under her divine protection in the Mysteries.

The Mysteries themselves are also colored by initiatory patterns. The rites involved a partial detachment from the central civic spaces and values of Greek culture and the deities who presided over them. They took the initiate into a territory not bounded by the hierarchical access to divine blessings generally encountered in household or in civic cults.[53] In civic cults (as well as in many other rites of initiation), the participants' status as male or female, slave or free, citizen or resident alien played a central role; such cults (or rites) firmly embedded the participants in particular social roles. The rites at Eleusis, unlike many other rites of initiation, were tied to no stage of the life

---

[51] See further Richardson 1974:17.

[52] Lincoln 1979 revives the theory of Jeanmaire 1939:69–79 and 98–305 that the Persephone myth reflects a scenario of female initiation. Scarpi 1976:109–38 discusses the myth in terms of traditions about rape-marriage.

[53] Osborne 1985:171, 176, 178, 187. Even the Eleusinian priests were largely not members of the local community by the classical period.

cycle (although initiates were with one exception adults) or aspect of civic life. As the initiates embarked on the procession from Athens to Eleusis, they entered a space that brought them closer to divine experience and to the endless world after death; they moved from fear and disorientation to joy and confidence. They were united by a common religious experience, not by locality or citizenship. Citizens prominent in ordinary life were mocked by a masked figure or figures en route. Women left their homes and put off at times their ordinary modesty of speech. The sacrifices presented to the other Olympian gods were made at temples open to the light where every aspect of the rite was clearly and visibly defined. In all-night dances and in the darkness of the Telesterion (the Hall of Initiation), the mystery initiates moved out of the time and the visual parameters by which they normally defined their world. To the degree that the initiates imitated the experiences of the goddesses, they shared in the reintegration of the divinities into the divine pantheon that closed the myth. In so doing the initiates developed a permanent relation to a more than human experience, not a reentry into the life of the city-state.[54] After initiation, initiates as a group were distinguished from noninitiates by a different lot in life.

Variants of the Myth and the Importance of the Version in the *Hymn to Demeter*

The *Hymn to Demeter* represents the earliest extant version of a myth that appears with many variants in later Greek and Roman literature and art. As was stressed in the last section, even on religious issues of the utmost importance there were no stable versions of a Greek or Roman myth. The poets who composed the Homeric hymns, as representatives of a long tradition of oral poetry, reshaped myths to suit various occasions and audiences; the same was true of later artists in a literate tradition. As we shall see, all versions of the Demeter/Persephone myth explain the origins of various human institutions and of a modified relation between gods and humans, and between heaven, earth, and the underworld. Some later versions apparently motivate the cycle of nature itself: Persephone is associated with the planted seed and absent while it is in the ground.[55] Precisely because poetry

[54] The polis of course supported the Mysteries, but unlike rites of initiation into adulthood, such as those for girls at Brauron, the Mysteries did not aim to incorporate the initiand into a specific social role or social group.

[55] For these views, which are often thought to be Stoic influenced, see Cornutus 28, Cicero *De natura deorum* 2.66, the scholiast on Hesiod *Theogony* 912, Tzetzes on Hesiod, *Works and Days* 32, Cleanthes fr. 547 cited in Plutarch *Moralia* 377d, Varro cited in Augustine *City of God* 7.20, and the scholiast on Aristophanes *Wasps* 1429. For this controversial issue, see the Commentary on lines 401–3.

played such a central religious and cultural role in early Greek society, ancient poets could assume their audience's knowledge of mythical variants and played on this awareness in shaping their own interpretations. We would misread any ancient poem if we did not bring this knowledge to bear on our own analysis of it. The composer or composers of our hymn almost certainly knew important variations on the myth and chose to emphasize or suppress certain aspects of the story to create a particular interpretation.[56] This will be my assumption.

Yet we must go further than simply attempting to distinguish on the basis of later variants the tradition that lies behind the *Hymn to Demeter*. Virtually all interpreters of the *Hymn* have used their knowledge of these variants in interpreting the *Hymn* and in defining its unusual achievement. Knowing something of these alternate versions helps considerably to illuminate aspects of the narrative that are not explicitly motivated and have thus puzzled interpreters of the poem. Let me give a series of examples of what I mean by puzzling features of the text that can be better understood in the light of the later tradition.[57] I shall offer examples first, then possible explanations.

1) In contrast to the expectations of many modern readers, the narrative pattern of the *Hymn* does not link Persephone's descent and ascent explicitly with the cycle of the agricultural year or use the myth to explain the origin of the seasons. Demeter plays the famine as her last card in her conflict with Zeus, and she is from the first moment of the poem already the "bringer of seasons."[58] In the *Hymn* Persephone's return precedes the coming of spring, rather than explicitly causing it or coinciding with it. Demeter predicts that Persephone will in the future reappear annually with the spring flowers. This may indicate a promise of regularity in the seasonal cycle; yet we are not told when Persephone will depart each year for the world below.[59] Seasonal motifs thus serve in the *Hymn* to enhance other more important themes, rather than acquiring a central importance. Yet the *Hymn*'s own promise of a better life on earth must depend on Demeter's powers over agriculture, and

[56] The case for this assumption has been well made in different ways by Richardson 1974:9, 17, 85, and notes on 450ff. and 470ff.; Clay 1989:205–6, 224–25, 231, and 259; and Parker 1991:5. Richardson stresses the *Hymn*'s probable awareness of the alternative version in which agriculture is founded by Demeter and its compromise between local tradition and epic. Detailed examples can be found in the Commentary on lines 5–14 and 450–56.

[57] On these puzzling features of the text, see esp. Richardson 1974 and Clay 1989 passim and Cassolà 1975:33–35. In the nineteenth century, a number of scholars felt that these problematic aspects of the narrative were the result of interpolation.

[58] Burkert 1983:262 argues, in part due to the difficulty of linking myth and cult with the seasonal cycle, that this element of the myth may have been a later and secondary accretion (the famine is apparently missing from Orphic accounts). Clay 1989:255, on the other hand, sees the seasonal motif as one of the oldest elements in the myth. I believe (with Richardson 1974:15) that the two motifs are inextricable (although they can be deployed in various ways) and that priority cannot be established.

[59] See Rudhardt 1978 (this volume).

the poem deploys and alludes to seasonal motifs.[60] The restoration of fertility is closely linked with the bestowal of the Mysteries and the coming of Ploutos to the homes of the initiated. Precisely because the eschatology of the Mysteries and the agricultural motif remain inextricable, the narrative seems to raise rather than resolve the question of their interrelation.

It makes sense to assume, then, that the *Hymn* deliberately deemphasizes but relies on its audience's familiarity with versions of the myth in which seasonal and agricultural motifs play a more central role. Although explaining the founding of the Mysteries is always a major point, many versions of the myth other than the *Hymn*, including Attic/Eleusinian ones, do in fact describe the origins of agriculture. In the *Hymn* agriculture already exists on earth, and humans are living in established cities with all the major features of human culture in place: agriculture, sacrifice, and marriage.[61] Yet when the alternative version begins, mortals have not yet learned from the goddess of grain Demeter to cultivate the land. They live at the mercy of nature, foraging for roots, acorns, and berries. After Demeter loses Persephone, she learns of her daughter's whereabouts not as in the *Hymn* from the gods Helios and Hekate, but from mortals, who are then rewarded with agriculture and/or Mysteries. Many regions in Greece and Italy claimed in their local versions of the myth to have aided Demeter in her search and to have been rewarded for their good deeds; both Athens and Sicily claimed to be the first place to have received agriculture from the goddess.

The Attic/Eleusinian version of this myth is preserved for us in fragmentary form in Orphic versions of the myth.[62] As the orator Isokrates says (*Panegyrikos* 28), Demeter founded the Mysteries "in gratitude for benefits only initiates may hear." In this version, certain (usually rustic) inhabitants of Eleusis witness the rape;[63] Demeter rewards them for their information and their hospitality. She teaches the Eleusinian Triptolemos the miraculous

[60] See the Commentary on lines 5–14, 23, 66, 98–112, 153ff. and 401–3 for further examples.

[61] The leaders (*basileis*) at Eleusis are described as "administering the law" (*themistopoloi*, 473). Rudhardt 1978 (this volume) argues that there may as yet be no seasons on earth.

[62] On the eclectic collection of works attributed to Orpheus, Mousaios, and Eumolpos, see Malten 1909, Graf 1974, West 1983, and Richardson 1974:77–86. Orphic versions of the myth probably reflect early Eleusinian tradition (Richardson 1974:85) in a more concrete fashion (e.g., more details pertain to local ritual) than in the epicizing *Hymn*, although the *Hymn* itself was probably included at one time in this corpus. For a summary of major features of the Orphic myth, see the section on "The Influence of the *Hymn to Demeter* and Its Myth." Malten proposed to date an "Orphic" version of the myth to the mid-sixth century when a circle of "Orphic" poets may have gathered at the court of Peisistratos. Graf 1974:151–81 more cautiously argues for dating an Orphic poem that included the mission of Triptolemos (to distribute Demeter's gift of agriculture) to 469–405 B.C.E. The visual evidence cited below makes clear, however, that the myth would in this case have been well known in Athens before the Orphic poems were.

[63] Keleos, whose name means "woodpecker," would have fit into such a scenario. In the rustic versions like Orphic Frag. 52, Triptolemos is a cowherd, Eumolpos a shepherd, and

gift of agriculture, and Triptolemos, who was often envisioned in art as flying through the world on the goddess's chariot, teaches agriculture to the rest of humankind. He plows the earth for the first time on the Rarian plain near Eleusis. Thus Athens and Eleusis could claim to be the source of two of the greatest benefits of the gods to humankind: agriculture and the Mysteries. Not surprisingly, Athens exploited this myth to make claims to leadership among the Greeks—in particular, a claim to be the Mother City of the Ionians. This Attic/Eleusinian variant on the myth—particularly the role of Triptolemos—could have been developed in the mid-sixth century, after the probable date of the composition of the *Hymn*. It is at this time that we can document the growth of Athenian interest in the Mysteries and the first artistic representations of Triptolemos.[64] Yet the many variations on these aspects of the story would seem to confirm their importance in the mythic tradition from an early date. Moreover, the motif of hospitality, which plays a pivotal role in all other versions of the Demeter story and is, as discussed earlier, a central and expected part of epic journeys and returns, plays a surprisingly minimal role in the encounter with the Eleusinians in the *Hymn*.[65] If the composer(s) of the *Hymn* knew this important and common Eleusinian version of the myth, then, the choice to ignore it and present an alternative version is significant.

2) In other versions Demeter gives mortals the Mysteries (and/or agriculture) at once as a reward for their information, their hospitality, or both. In the *Hymn* Demeter does not, as she promised (273), instruct the Eleusinians in her rites until well after the founding of her temple (476). In fact, Demeter's cult at Eleusis seems at first (despite hints to the contrary) to have been founded only to propitiate the angry goddess, not to open new opportunities for humankind.[66]

3) Whereas in most other versions of the story, Demeter descends to earth explicitly to search for her daughter, the *Hymn* makes the witnesses of the

---

Eubouleus a swineherd. The inhabitants of Eleusis, who also include Baubo and Dysaules, are said to be autochthonous (earthborn). For other versions of the myth where the witnesses are mortals, see Richardson 1974 on lines 75ff. and 96.

[64] See Shapiro 1989:67–83. Artistic representations of Triptolemos date from ca. 540. There are hints in the sources that in some locations the Thesmophoria, one of the oldest and most widespread rituals of Demeter in Greece, staged a version of the myth in which agriculture was not yet established (the women camped out in primitive tents, "imitated the ancient way of life" [Diodorus Siculus *Bibliotheca* 5.4.7], and at least at Eretria, they cured their meat in the sun rather than roasting it [Plutarch, *Moralia* 298b–c]). If so, Demeter's gift of agriculture was likely to have been an early element in the myth.

[65] See the Commentary on lines 90–97, 210, 253, 371–73 for discussion of this motif in the poem and examples of incidents relating to hospitality in other versions. Because the Mysteries are not represented in this poem as the direct result of human hospitality, the motif naturally becomes less explicit.

[66] See Richardson 1974:81 and 174.

rape divine rather than human. Because Demeter knows from Helios where Persephone is and has no way of reaching her, she is left without a stated motive for her journey to earth. Instead, we are told that Demeter is angry at Zeus (91), although the poem never makes explicit how the journey to earth articulates that anger.

4) Demeter's precise motive for nursing and attempting to immortalize the baby Demophoön is similarly left unstated. In many later versions of the myth, Demeter never loses sight for a moment of her goal of rescuing Persephone. Yet in the *Hymn* Demeter, during her time on earth, is temporarily distracted from her pursuit of Persephone by the Demophoön incident.

One might argue that myths and traditional oral narratives consistently have what modern readers would perceive to be gaps in motivation. Oral narratives are often more interested in results than motives: that is, Demeter goes to earth simply because her cult is there and the poem aims to explain its origin.[67] In addition, ellipses in this particular narrative may be motivated in part by the secrecy and the nature of the rites at Eleusis—that is, the *Hymn* may revolve around a series of enacted symbolic moments. The story pattern of wrath, withdrawal, and return that underlines the poem itself generates such powerful expectations for the act of withdrawal to another realm or for revenge (a possible motive for the Demophoön episode discussed below) that no explanation may be needed. At the same time, the probable existence of other versions of the myth that did offer a clearly motivated transition at these points in the story (the Orphic versions may reflect a tradition earlier than the *Hymn*) could shape audience reaction and expectation even in the case of a traditional oral narrative.[68] Furthermore, the initiates' search for Persephone at Eleusis was, at least at a later date, so fundamental a part of the Mysteries that the virtual disappearance of the human dimension to that effort in the *Hymn* might be surprising to any audience that included initiates.

Why would the *Hymn* ignore or suppress important Attic/Eleusinian versions of the story, presuming they were already part of the tradition, in favor of its own interpretation? Why are some parts of its story apparently unmotivated? There are three possible lines of explanation deriving from the historical context in which the *Hymn* may have been composed, from the traditions of Panhellenic poetry (poetry composed, like the Homeric hymns and the Homeric epics, for a broad Greek audience, rather than a

---

[67] On this point, see Parker 1991:11.

[68] For example, in Orphic frag. 49:101ff. Demeter asks who raped Persephone for the first time at the end of the Demophoön episode. In this version there is no need to account for her apparent loss of interest in Persephone, because she only now discovers the truth. See the section on "The Influence of the *Hymn to Demeter*" for a partial reconstruction of an Orphic version of the myth.

local one), and from thematic considerations. The first two lines of explanation are developed in the Appendix to this essay because they involve material not directly related to a literary interpretation of the *Hymn* as well as complex scholarly controversy.

Thematic reasons for selection of the *Hymn* from among available traditions and/or change of the myth have already been suggested in the previous section. The *Hymn* makes the Mysteries not merely the result of favors granted by human witnesses to the goddess, but of the entire set of experiences of the two goddesses and of the final compromise that reordered the universe and made the Mysteries possible.[69] Humans do not earn the Mysteries in the *Hymn*'s version; they are foolish and ignorant, though well-meaning in their treatment of strangers, guests, and suppliants. The Mysteries are founded because deities shared for a time a version of the mortal lot and Demeter was reunited with Persephone—hence the delay in establishing the Mysteries until that reunion has taken place and its ramifications are made clear.[70] The *Hymn* cannot tell us what happens in the secret rites; but it can make its audience understand why the Mysteries offer the particular benefits that they do. The poem, above all by its structure, suggests that, although mortals will never understand divinity, and divinity can never be more than partially and temporarily humanized, it was the profound and unique convergence of the two worlds that produced the Mysteries.

The *Hymn*, then, ignores the origin of agriculture and downplays the theme of hospitality and the origin or regularizing of the seasons to concentrate on the founding of the Mysteries; and it may tell us a good deal more about the fundamental meaning of the Mysteries than our ignorance of the final secret rites may lead us to think. The convergence in the narrative of Persephone's return, the renewed fertility of the earth, and the bestowal of the Mysteries hints at some connection between the blessings of the rites and the earth's cycle.[71] Yet because the famine motif is not closely linked to the disappearance and appearance of Persephone, the *Hymn* can emphasize a psychological interpretation of the origin of the Mysteries—the Mysteries are a product of divine suffering and of the convergence of divine and human experience. The gap between Demeter's initial and final establishment of her rites may also serve a related purpose. At first she inspires awe and terror; finally, she offers happiness. This takes the Eleusinians through two phases of initiation into the rites that may parallel the transition from *mystês* to *epoptês*.[72]

---

[69] Clinton 1986:48 sees the closing reference to the founding of the Mysteries as tacked on to the narrative, whereas I argue that the entire poem aims at this climax.

[70] See Rudhardt 1978 (this volume), Clay 1989:243, and Parker 1991:13.

[71] Parker 1991:12–13.

[72] Ibid.:13. See in addition the treatment of the theme of sight and hearing discussed in the Commentary on lines 17, 51–89, 281–83, and 292–304.

Furthermore, by placing the Demophoön episode before the famine, the poem sets the stage for the Mysteries by demonstrating the impossibility of immortalizing humans and of breaking down the fundamental barriers between gods and mortals.[73] The lack of motivation for the Demophoön episode is precisely what gives it its power to resonate with the role of the initiate in the Mysteries; the aura of mystery partially detaches the episode from a concrete place in the narrative and permits it to suggest a far broader set of implications. Moreover, the story, by not allowing Demophoön to die at once, as he does in other versions, and by domesticating Persephone's epic role as the dread goddess of the dead (which receives brief and inexplicit recognition at lines 364–69), prepares more effectively for the beneficence to humankind that the reunited pair of divinities display at the conclusion of the poem. All details of the story are thus apparently shaped to make the Mysteries the outcome of Demeter's and Persephone's contact with mortality. By emphasizing the psychological dimensions of the story for all humankind, the poem develops a theological and cosmological profundity that all other extant versions of the myth seem to lack.

Female Experience in the *Hymn to Demeter*

Scholars have argued, on the basis of the ubiquity and antiquity of Demeter's rite of the Thesmophoria in Greece, that the special emphasis on female experience in the *Hymn* represented the earliest and essential core of the myth and of the rituals developed in association with it. Some scholars even went so far as to suggest that the Mysteries had originally been, as in the case of many other important and early cults of Demeter, exclusive to women.[74] This is unprovable speculation, and we certainly have no historical example of a cult previously exclusive to women becoming open to participants of both sexes. Yet it remains possible that if all-female cults of Demeter such as the Thesmophoria antedated the Mysteries, or coexisted with them from an early date, the nature of these cults and their myths could have influenced mythmaking at Eleusis. In focussing so closely on the experience of mother and daughter and on Demeter's stay among mortal women, the *Hymn*

[73] Bianchi 1964, Rudhardt 1978 (this volume), and Chirassi-Columbo 1975:205. For detailed discussion of the Demophoön episode, see the section below on "Gender Conflict."

[74] Thomson 1972:119–23 makes this suggestion on the basis of the antiquity and possible Egyptian origins of the Thesmophoria (thought to be the oldest cult of Demeter in Greece— see Herodotos 2.171) and even of the Mysteries. See also Allen and Sikes 1904:292 and Kerényi 1967a: 80. Harrison 1903:ch. 4 argues that the Mysteries developed out of the more "primitive" Thesmophoria, Haloa, and other all-female rituals of Demeter. Although the belief of such scholars in a pre-Greek and pre-Olympian Mediterranean religion that emphasized the worship of a mother goddess has been much contested, it is not impossible (though it is unprovable) that the earliest cults of Demeter in Greece were exclusive to women.

shows relatively little interest in aspects of the cult and the myth that related, at least in classical times, more explictly to men: the role of Triptolemos and the origin of agriculture and the male priests of the cult. In other versions of the myth, men also played an important role in Demeter's search for her daughter and in the hospitality accorded the goddess on earth.[75]

We have already seen how Demeter's female quest both resembles and differs from that of male heroes like Achilleus and Odysseus. Both sexes pursue honor and status, but in Demeter's case the recovery of her lost daughter plays an emphatically central role. The female quest is defined by issues relating to marriage and fertility, the male quest by war and kingship. The male quest ends with an acceptance of mortality mitigated by fame, the female quest with a cyclical reunion and separation that also mitigates "death." The next four sections look more closely at the poem's emphasis on female experience and consider how this relates to the mythical founding of the Mysteries in the poem.

Marriage

As noted earlier, the Demeter/Persephone myth became in some instances a paradigm in Greek art and literature for human marriage as a rite of initiation; in marriage the bride could be thought to undergo a symbolic death before a symbolic rebirth and reincorporation into a new household as wife and mother. Just as Zeus in essence "sacrifices" his daughter to the world of death in the *Hymn*, the sacrifice of the daughter by the father is a myth of female initiation in other contexts as well.[76] Attic girls participating in the cult of Artemis at Brauron were probably initiated into adulthood and marriage with the story of Agamemnon's sacrifice of Iphigeneia at Aulis and other closely related myths.[77] In these related myths, a substitution was made and an animal died for the girl, who goes on to maturity and marriage. In other initiatory myths, the girl, like Helen (by Theseus), the Leukippides (by the Dioscuroi), or Oreithyia (by Boreas) is abducted before marriage. Like these myths, the *Hymn* partially undoes the consequences of abduction and "death" for Demeter's daughter Korê in the world above, but it also sacrifices her to the world below as wife of Hades.

By emphasizing in contrast to these other closely related myths the irrevocable and painful consequences of the abduction, the *Hymn* reveals the problematic side of marriage for the bride and develops its narrative on the

[75] In the Orphic tradition, to give an Attic/Eleusinian alternative, Eubouleus and Triptolemos were the lucky informers (Frag. 51K = Pausanias *Graeciae descriptio* 1.14.3).

[76] See Burkert 1983:262 on Persephone's rape by Hades as the father's sacrifice of a maiden.

[77] Iphigeneia had her own cult at Brauron. For the related myths, see Sale 1975, Henrichs 1981, Lloyd-Jones 1983, Sourvinou-Inwood 1988, and Dowden 1989.

divine level as a conflict between genders. Demeter, Hekate, and Persephone are aligned on one side; Zeus, Helios, and Hades on the other.[78] Indeed, one ancient source later than the *Hymn* notes that marriage is repugnant to Demeter because of the loss of her daughter.[79] In this respect the *Hymn* contrasts with the major Homeric epics and resembles, in a manner to be discussed shortly, many later Greek dramas or Hesiod's cosmological poem the *Theogony*.

In the *Hymn* Zeus attempts to impose on Persephone a form of marriage new to Olympus, the divine equivalent of a mortal institution familiar in Homer: in modern terms we would categorize it as patriarchal and virilocal exogamy (a marriage between members of two different social groups arranged by the father of the bride in which the bride resides with her husband). Although in the *Hymn* marriage already exists among mortals on earth, the institution was not always the general rule among the gods.[80] Rape, incest, and promiscuity are perhaps the dominant modes of procreation among divinities in the early phases of the universe during which the majority of gods were born and acquired their powers. Zeus and Demeter, a brother and sister, produced Persephone in precisely this fashion. Although Zeus and Hera (also a brother and sister) and other gods are represented as married, especially once the rule of Zeus over the cosmos has been established, divine marriage, if it functions with any consistency, did not function as earthly marriage does.

Indeed, divine existence is partly defined in epic by the gods' ability to break the rules of human society and avoid the consequences that would have occurred in a mortal context. Mortal marriage in epic entailed an exchange of gifts by the bride's guardian and her spouse-to-be used for the benefit of one or both participating families and a formal ceremony followed by cohabitation in one household and carefully regulated sexual engagement for the purpose of producing legitimate heirs for the husband's lineage.[81] Inheritance and sexual fidelity could not and did not ever play the

[78] It should be noted, however, that Gaia assists Zeus, and Rheia mediates between Zeus and her daughter. The gender conflict here is not as marked or as explicitly emphasized as it is in later tragedy.

[79] Servius on *Aeneid* 4.58. Farnell 1909:3.80–82 and 101–3 notes the rare connection between Demeter and marriage (as opposed to fertility) in mainland Greek cults. By contrast, heroines are linked in cult with all family members except their mothers. Cults of former mortals, then, do not celebrate a relationship that interferes with the woman's primary adult social role, that of married mother.

[80] Rudhardt 1978 (this volume) argues that what makes this divine marriage unique and unacceptable to the two goddesses is Persephone's inaccessibility in the underworld and the separation it occasions. I accept this important point, but I wish to expand on its implictions by formulating it in a different fashion.

[81] Even in the variety of Homeric marriage where the groom would, as in the case of Odysseus with Nausikäa, have lived in the bride's community, Odysseus was to receive wealth and a house where he could take his bride and produce heirs.

same role among immortal beings, whose need to procreate or to regulate procreation did not match that of mortals. In the early phases of Hesiod's cosmology, genealogies can be, in contrast to human ones, represented as matrilineal; children can gain an honored place in the universe as children of the mother and a product of desire.[82] The structure of the universe remained stable precisely because Zeus did not father a male heir who could replace him.

In contrast to mortal marriages, neither divine marriages nor rapes required the same kind of change of residence to which the mortal bride was often subject; nor did they require loss of independence on the part of the female Olympian, who continued to exercise her own perogatives in the sphere allotted to her. In other words, because Olympian gods live as one community, their marriages are in essence endogamous (between insiders) and do not require the separation of the daughter from her natal family. Olympian goddesses may be said in Homer or Hesiod to reside in the homes of their spouses. Aphrodite, for example, is said in *Odyssey* 8 to commit adultery with Ares in the house of Hephaistos, who has paid her father gifts (318, *hedna*) for the bride. But epic frequently treats these residences largely as a place for sleeping (see *Iliad* 1. 605–11),[83] and the regular presence of Olympian goddesses at the assembly of Zeus indicates that a separate residence in no way isolates them from the divine community or inevitably subordinates them to their husbands. Hence Aphrodite, for example, arrives home *from the presence of Zeus* to find Ares awaiting her (8.289–91).

Although sexual fidelity is not at stake in the *Hymn*, Kalypso's complaint at *Odyssey* 5.118–29, makes clear that there was more constraint on the unions of goddesses than on those of gods (although in her examples it was mortals who paid the price for the liaison with a goddess). Here she complains that the gods out of cruelty and jealousy do not tolerate the liaisons of goddesses and mortals. Artemis killed Dawn's lover Orion; and Zeus killed Demeter's lover Iasion with a thunderbolt. Yet the married Aphrodite continues to preside over love legitimate and illegitimate after her adultery; the adultery with Ares outrages Hephaistos, but the incident is quickly resolved by laughter and the promise of a fine from Ares. In the Homeric *Hymn to Aphrodite*, Zeus himself makes the goddess desire the mortal Anchises and

[82] On matrilinear genealogies in Hesiod, see West 1966:35 and 39. The children of Night and Strife are, for example, born parthenogenically, and the children of Styx receive honors from Zeus as her children. The situation of Hekate is discussed below. Such emphasis on the mother does not occur in Homer or later myth, or even in the later phases of Hesiod's *Theogony*—once rule of Zeus is established, patriarchal principle takes over to a greater degree.

[83] Sometimes we see a divine couple pursuing their activities at home. Charis and Hephaistos are both at home when Thetis comes to ask Hephaistos to make a shield for Achilleus in *Iliad* 18. At the same time, epic also pictures goddesses retiring for periods in their temples on earth.

bear his child. Even when major goddesses, like Thetis, are married off to mortals in order to prevent the birth of a divine son who could rival Zeus, the goddess soon returns to her previous element. I should stress, however, that I am not taking into consideration here the marriages of lesser deities, such as Nymphs or Okeanids, whose unions might be imagined (their stories are too unimportant for detailed representation in archaic epic) to entail a more permanent move into another sphere at marriage.

Persephone's marriage with Hades might appear to perpetuate this Olympian endogamy, because it is a marriage to the father's (and mother's) brother. But the inaccessibility of Hades makes it geographically impossible for the marriage to function endogamously.[84] Thus Persephone is subjected to an extreme form of virilocal exogamy in which she is permanently denied access to her parents. As with other aspects of the *Hymn*, this marriage, in which the bride undergoes a symbolic death in the transition from one household to another, brings Persephone closer to human experience. For despite the mitigating conclusion of the *Hymn*, Demeter and Persephone remain forever marked by the encounter with mortal limits: death, marriage, the relentless cycle of the seasons (in cult the goddesses are worshiped for guaranteeing the regularity of the seasons, yet the seasons, insofar as they are linked to Persephone's appearance and disappearance, limit the mother/daughter relation as well).

The opening scene of the *Hymn* hints strongly at Persephone's readiness for sexuality, yet it chooses to envision her marriage as a deceptive and cruel trick foisted by violence on an idyllic mother/daughter relationship.[85] Zeus gives Persephone to Hades without the consent or knowledge of either mother or daughter—as may often have been the case in human society (as opposed to Nausikäa's utopian Phaiakia) at the time.[86] Helios then becomes Zeus's apologist, as the father of the bride keeps his distance from mother and daughter—and hence from the poem's audience—throughout the narrative. Hades needs a wife, and as her uncle and Zeus's brother, as well as a powerful god who can bestow honors on his wife, he is an appropri-

[84] Scarpi 1976:117, 125, 137 notes the endogamy of Olympus but incorrectly considers the marriage to Hades as part of that endogamy.

[85] Ibid.:209ff., following Nilsson, interprets the abduction in the light of Greek traditions concerning marriage by capture. Marriage by abduction survived as a practice in Sparta, but not, for example, in historical Athens. Nevertheless, the theme of abduction and pursuit of girls, possibly leading to marriage, was popular on Attic vases (see Sourvinou-Inwood 1991:58–98. The father of the girl sometimes appears on these vases, but the mother never does). Clay 1989:209.n.33 argues that the scenario does not fit, because Zeus himself plans the abduction. To the degree that the theme is present in the *Hymn*, Hades' marriage by abduction is replaced by an institution that gives a more important role to persuasion and to consent on the part of the bride and her mother.

[86] Zeus's ignoring of Demeter's and Persephone's views on the marriage is also understood by Scarpi 1976:119ff. to be characteristic of Athenian marriage arrangements.

ate husband for Persephone. Yet despite Helios's apology, Hades' abduction does not function as a legitimate marriage. The abduction includes elements in a normal marriage rite—an *engyê* or pledge of marriage between father and groom and the transfer of the bride by chariot to her new residence[87]— only to emphasize the abnormality of a marriage in which the bride, because she initially does not eat in the underworld, has not fully engaged in the final stage necessary to legitimate Athenian marriage at least, cohabitation (*synoikein*).[88]

In Attic marriage the bridal couple was showered with dried fruits and nuts (*katachysmata*) and presented with a basket of bread; the bride ate a quince (and probably a wedding cake made from sesame seeds) on arrival at the groom's house;[89] the bride's acceptance of food (*trophê*) was a form of acknowledging the groom's authority (*kyreia*) over her.[90] Another aspect of the standard marriage rite was the carrying of torches by the bride's mother; in the *Hymn* the bride's mother Demeter carries torches alone and after the event.[91] The abduction comes to resemble marriage more fully only at the point of the final compromise, when Persephone eats and Hades mitigates his original violence with persuasion—a promise of honors to his bride.[92] It is unclear whether Persephone has consummated her marriage—we find her in Hades' bed, an unwilling partner (343–44) still longing for her mother.

Before giving Persephone the pomegranate seed, Hades urges her not to remain depressed but to feel kindly toward him (360–62). Plutarch says that Solon decreed that Attic brides should eat quinces to keep their mouth and their speech sweet (*Moralia* 138D and 279F). The eating of the quince by the Attic bride may also have helped to awaken her desire.[93] As with

[87] See Scarpi 1976:111, 114, 120. In his discussion of the terms for "wife" used in the poem (120), and especially of *parakoitis* (343), which can also mean "concubine," Scarpi 1976:119 nevertheless admits to a certain ambiguity in Persephone's status.

[88] There is of course a danger of anachronism here, because we are not certain whether all these marriage-related elements played a role in archaic Greece as opposed to classical Greece.

[89] In Plutarch's *Life of Solon* 89C, the custom of having the bride eat a quince before the couple entered the bedchamber occurs in a passage where the institution of the heiress or *epiklêros* is under discussion, but at *Moralia* 138D and 279F no distinction is made about the bride's status. For the sesame-seed cake, see the scholiast on Aristophanes *Peace* 869. On the symbolic importance of the bride's eating food in her husband's house, see Erdmann 1934:259 and 320ff. and Sutton 1981:153–54.

[90] Sutton 1981:154.

[91] Clytemnestra at Euripides' *Iphigeneia at Aulis* 734–36 particularly stresses the importance, in her mind, of carrying the torch for her daughter's wedding.

[92] The possible implications of Persephone's new honors will be discussed below. Arthur 1977 (this volume) notes Hades' new use of persuasion in this scene.

[93] Faraone 1990:esp. 237–38. He argues that in the case of the *epiklêros*, the eating of an aphrodisiac may have helped to tame an exceptionally powerful bride (Aristotle *Nicomachean Ethics* 1161a). Apples or quinces were also linked with pomegranates as forbidden foods in cults of Demeter.

Solon's quince, Persephone's eating of the pomegranate seed may signal a shift to seduction, a careful preparation of the bride for sexuality rather than violence. Yet even here the language that Persephone uses to describe her final eating of the pomegranate seed echoes that used to describe the original abduction: "He stealthily put in my mouth a food honey-sweet, a pomegranate seed, and compelled me against my will and by force to eat it" (411– 13). Thus, although from the male perspective Hades' abduction is entirely acceptable, the *Hymn* continues to stress the female resistance throughout.

The *Hymn* thus takes apart the benign cultural institution we see functioning apparently without tension on earth and shows the price paid by mother and daughter in accepting for the first time a marriage that requires a degree of separation and subordination to the male unfamiliar in the divine world. We witness an attempt to achieve a divine version of what Engels called "the world-historical defeat of the female sex." Yet by locating the myth within the context of a human world where marriage with all its variations is a fundamental aspect of the cultural system, the narrative makes the outcome—Persephone's inability to escape maturity and marriage— seem necessary and within limits desirable even for a divinity. Above all, without Hades Persephone would never have acquired her own *timai* or honors separate from those of her mother (although those she acquires from her mother reduce her subordination to her spouse). Nevertheless, the deflection of the challenge to exogamy onto the divine level may reveal as well historical or ideological tensions in the functioning of the institution of marriage in archaic Greek society.[94] (I shall return to this question in the section on "The *Hymn to Demeter* and the Polis.")

Later versions of the myth make Persephone considerably more enthusiastic about her divine husband; in one version she does not even wish to return to her mother.[95] Apuleius's second-century C.E. tale of Amor and Psyche in *The Golden Ass* offers another closely related myth about the struggles of a bride married off to a figure whom she believes to be linked to Death. In this case the mortal Psyche even becomes the active pursuer of the divine Amor (Eros), once she discovers his true identity. Psyche's sisters and Amor's mother Venus block her quest to regain Amor and attempt to destroy Psyche's marital bliss. The *Hymn*, by contrast, does not romanticize marriage. It shows that for mortals, like the daughters of Keleos, the best that could be wished for any young woman is marriage and children, and especially a male heir to propagate the family line. Goddesses, on the other hand, represent a different case altogether. They mature to an age appropriate to their function (they may choose to remain virgins) and do not need marriage to procreate—as Demeter herself did not. Nor do they normally need male protection against violence and rape, as Persephone does in her

---

[94] See Chirassi-Columbo 1975:200.
[95] See Servius on Vergil *Georgics* 1.39 and Lucan *Bellum Civile* 6.698ff. and 739ff.

call to Zeus in the *Hymn*. Rapes among divinities do not have the social consequences that they have on earth, because both male and female children, as the children of mothers, could acquire divine honors without the legitimacy conferred by marriage. Thus, although the marriage of Persephone and Hades cannot be undone, it is hardly surprising that Demeter attempts to reinstate Olympian endogamy.

As might be expected in the case of a goddess who is both eternal virgin (Korê) as well as wife of Hades,[96] the two goddesses finally refuse to be more than partially bound within the confines of the original patriarchal and virilocal exogamous marriage—that is, within a human form of marriage. A compromise takes place which locates all emotional satisfaction in the relation of mother and daughter, even though Persephone may be appeased by the honors she will receive as Hades' wife (or even be readied for sexuality by the eating of the pomegranate seed). Hades, forced by Demeter's famine and Zeus's command to relinquish his bride to her father, will no longer fully possess his wife. Unlike the mortal daughter, Persephone will spend more time with her natal family than with her spouse (in this her marriage more closely resembles the status quo for goddesses on Olympus, although her time is distributed more systematically). Nor does she in any extant version of the abduction myth (including the *Hymn*) explicitly fulfill the normal purpose of Greek marriage by producing a child with Hades (who does not, as eternal Lord of the Dead, need an offspring in any case). Persephone is known to have produced a child in later myth.[97] In the Orphic *Rhapsodies* (frag. 303 Kern), Zeus fathered Persephone's child Iakchos/ Dionysos (see also Orphic hymn 29; Orphic frags. 58, 153, 195, and 303 Kern; and Nonnos *Dionysiaka* 6. 1–168). The Brimos said to be born to Brimo at the close of the rites at Eleusis is sometimes thought to be Persephone's son (the father's identity is also uncertain) but may also be the son of Demeter or even another goddess.[98] The child Ploutos, whom the god-

[96] See Orphic frag. 197 Kern.

[97] Persephone is also called *kallipais*, producer of beautiful children, at Euripides *Orestes* 964, although it is not clear what specific implications this epithet has for herself. Orphic fragments 197 and 360 Kern and *Orphic Hymn* 70 have her produce with Hades the chthonic Eumenides. Elsewhere she mates with Zeus to produce the chthonic nymph Melinoë (*Orphic Hymn* 71), and Tritopatreus, Eubouleus, and Dionysos (Cicero, *De natura deorum* 3.53). In Aeschylus fragment 228 Nauck², Hades is the father of Zagreus (the mother is unnamed). These obscure and probably later traditions are made more difficult to interpret, because Zeus is sometimes understood as having an incarnation in the world below closely identified with the lord of the dead himself. The absence of this theme could of course be due to its role in the most secret parts of the Mysteries. In Claudian's *De raptu Proserpinae*, Pluto wishes to marry because he is childless; but the poem is unfinished and thus leaves the question of offspring open.

[98] See Hippolytos *Refutatio omnium haeresium* 5.8. p. 96 and Clement *Protreptikos* 2.15.1, Likophron *Alexandria* 698 and the scholia, and possibly Apollonios Rhodios *Argonautika* 3.861–62.

desses will send to bestow blessings on earth in the *Hymn*, was generally thought to be the son of Demeter and Iasion, not of Persephone. Within the confines of the *Hymn*, then, it is through her relation to her parents and especially through her mother, not through her husband, that Persephone helps to guarantee fertility on earth. The poem stresses—although this could be for reasons of cult secrecy—the divine adoption of human nurslings, not the birth of an immortal child.

Most important, Demeter's resistance to Persephone's marriage gives it a pivotal place in the universe. A Persephone confined in an inaccessible underworld paradoxically reinforces the separation between the worlds above and below ruled, respectively, by her divine father and her husband, rather than joining them, as would normally be the case in marriage. Zeus's initial plan is barren and treated unsympathetically from the start.[99] The poem never indicates that Zeus planned the final outcome of the story but suggests that it was foisted on him. Events apparently do not go as Zeus expected and a new approach is required to resolve the crisis of the famine.[100] In a fashion unparalleled in epic, Demeter initially ignores the will of Zeus and refuses to abandon the famine. At 334ff. Zeus instructs Hermes to bring Persephone back. Hades then forestalls her permanent departure through trickery. The text gives no indiction that Zeus anticipated Hades' move.[101] If Zeus had planned the marriage to link Olympus to the underworld, there would have been no need for secrecy, nor for Demeter's initial ignorance and cruel separation from her daughter.

It is also Demeter's intervention that makes Persephone finally accessible to her parents as in a normal Olympian marriage, while Hades remains inaccessible in the world below; it is Demeter, not Zeus, who creates the Mysteries and transforms the relation of mortals to herself. A Persephone who is linked permanently through shared honors both to Hades and to her divine mother in the worlds of earth and Olympus can dynamically join the

[99] Rudhardt 1978 (this volume) argues effectively that the resolution of this poem depends on Persephone's return.

[100] This is one of the few important differences I have with the study of Jenny Clay 1989. Clay's interpretation gives all the initiative in the poem to an all-seeing Zeus, whereas the narrative stresses the role of Demeter and her challenge to Zeus. Zeus's plan would make more sense in versions where the underworld is penetrable. As Scarpi 1976:121 points out, Zeus, after being brought to accept a change in his initial plan by Demeter's famine, finally reappropriates his role as head of the family by ratifying his daughter's future. But the offer of new *timai* to Demeter is clearly a new concession, given in recompense to her, just as Tros was compensated with immortal horses for Zeus's rape of Ganymede.

[101] Zeus is not always omniscient in early Greek poetry. In order to distract him from the battlefield, Hera tricks Zeus into sleeping with her in *Iliad* 14. Although in Hesiod's *Theogony* Zeus is not fooled by Prometheus's sacrificial portions, Hyginus *Astronomy* 2.15, where Zeus is tricked, probably indicates an alternate tradition of great antiquity. Ann Suter, in a paper presented at the 1992 American Philological association meeting, documented Demeter's anomalous resistance to Zeus's will.

spheres of the universe and promise the Mysteries and their benefits to humankind. In the end Demeter and Persephone lose some autonomy and gain new powers (as the deities in the other hymns also gain greater powers than before); the "traffic in women" will never become a regular mode of Olympian diplomacy, and Demeter's rupture through her famine of the circulation of honors between gods and humans parallels her blocking of Zeus's free exchange of her daughter among male divinities.[102] Paradoxically then, the *Hymn* makes Persephone's marriage necessary and inevitable, while its conclusion turns on an important modification of the institution originally planned by Zeus.

Gender Conflict and the Cosmological Tradition

By emphasizing the problematic aspects of Persephone's marriage to Hades and by developing its narrative as a conflict between the sexes that ultimately threatens the organization of the cosmos through Demeter's famine, the *Hymn to Demeter* stands in contrast to the major Homeric epics and more closely resembles Hesiod's *Theogony*, later Attic drama, or classical Athenian myths of the Amazons, famed for their resistance to marriage. In Hesiod's *Theogony*, a poem that describes the birth of the universe and the emergence of a divine order, tensions among male and female divinities emerge in each generation of the descendants of the divine ancestors of the Olympian gods, Earth and Sky. At each stage, a male god tries to prevent and thus to control the birth of his children, largely to avoid being replaced by a male successor. The divine children are assisted in their struggle against the father by mothers and grandmothers, just as Gaia (Earth) assists Zeus in his plan in the *Hymn* (8–9). Zeus finally consolidates his power over the universe by swallowing his pregnant consort Metis; he gives birth to the female child Athena from his head but prevents the birth of the male child who would have usurped his power. Finally, Zeus distributes special honors to various (gods and) goddesses, thereby gaining their loyalty and the loyalty of their children. The "civilizing" of the divine realm thus entails a consolidation of male dominance and a male appropriation of the reproductive process. The *Theogony* as a whole demonstrates the superior diplomacy and physical power of male deities; but they require the powers and cooperation of female deities at every phase to succeed. As in the *Hymn*, goddesses retain a far wider range of powers and capacity for independent action than do their mortal counterparts.

[102] Here I again disagree with Scarpi 1976, who argues (esp. 136–37) that the marriage of Korê sanctions the value of women as circulated within the endogamic system of Olympus—despite his awareness that the marriage joins and disjoins Olympus and Hades in a seasonal cycle. Furthermore, endogamy is designed to keep privileges circulating within a narrow group, whereas Demeter deliberately makes mortals beneficiaries in the final arrangement.

The cosmological process produced some acts of rebellion on the part of important female deities, who exploit their maternity to "pursue change and promote succession."[103] In Hesiod's *Theogony*, Earth produces Typhöeus who "would have ruled over gods and mortals" (837), a monster whom Zeus must defeat to maintain his rule. Jealous at the birth of Athena, Hera also tries to give birth by herself to a child who would challenge Zeus's supremacy; but she only bears either the lame god Hephaistos (*Theogony* 927–29) or the monster Typhaon (*Homeric Hymn to Apollo* 305–68). In slaying this beast, Apollo echoes his father's defeat of Typhöeus. In her anger at Zeus, Demeter defies the boundary between gods and mortals in trying to make the mortal Demophoön immortal. Is she also, like Hera, trying to produce an immortal male champion who will challenge Zeus?[104]

The poem gives no explanation for her action, and the mythological tradition offers no precedents that could help the *Hymn*'s original audience to interpret her act with any certainty. The closest precedents are as follows: 1) A goddess like Earth or Hera gives birth, in the latter case by parthenogenesis, to a divine challenger to Zeus and the challenge does not succeed; 2) A divine mother tries and fails to immortalize the child she bore by a mortal (Thetis's attempt to immortalize Achilleus is an example).[105] 3) A goddess immortalizes a mortal lover (Dawn has Tithonos immortalized and Kalypso offers immortality to Odysseus). None of these three scenarios fits. If Demeter as in the first scenario is attempting to provide a male challenger to Zeus, she, unlike her predecessors, surprisingly flees from the gods instead of rebelling directly against Zeus and turns to humanity to acquire a male offspring. Furthermore, it is hard to imagine that a child of entirely mortal heritage could, even when immortalized, challenge the mighty ruler of the universe. Even the immortalized Herakles did not. In a closely related case, Athena fails to immortalize her Attic foster child Erichthonios (another half-divine child whose father was Hephaistos) because his nurses, the daughters of Kekrops, peer into the box in which he is concealed. There is no question here of the child's becoming an equal of the Olympians. Attempts by goddesses to immortalize lovers[106] or children inevitably lead to disaster in Greek myth. In the case of lovers, Dawn forgets to ask for eternal youth for Tithonos, so that he ends up in a state of immortal senility and Odysseus has no interest in accepting Kalypso's offer. All three of these cosmological motifs in any case serve to prepare for failure more than success.

By concealing Demeter's motive for immortalizing Demophoön, the poem permits its audience to supply a range of possible motives for her

---

[103] Clay 1989:13.

[104] This is the view of Clay 1989:226. Another possibility is that Demeter is trying to retaliate by depriving Hades of a victim he is owed.

[105] Medea, who also has divine aspects, similarly tries and fails to immortalize her children.

[106] See Sowa 1984:ch. 2 for examples.

actions yet stresses the inaccessibility of divine motives and plans to mortals. The *Hymn* dwells not only on the disguised Demeter's power and her anger at Zeus, but on her suffering and her pleasure in mortal women and in her maternal role as a nurse. The text partially humanizes the goddess and suggestively juxtaposes her pain at the loss of her only child Persephone with the mortal mother Metaneira's fear that Demeter will destroy her only late-born son. Such parallelism invites the speculation that Demeter is trying to assuage her sense of emotional loss by appropriating Demophoön in order to replace her lost daughter with a male child who cannot, like a daughter, be taken from her by marriage.[107] Nevertheless, narratological considerations are most important here. Demophoön's story serves above all in the *Hymn* to motivate the foundation of the Mysteries (because Demeter has failed to immortalize a mortal) and to stress the tragic inevitability of the mortal lot.[108] Like the Mysteries, the incident plays on the fear and bliss that the goddess can produce in mortals. Finally, Demeter's relation to Demophoön may offer an aetiology for the future relation between Demeter and the initiate. Demeter becomes both to Demophoön and to the initiate a symbolic nurse and mitigator of death (see the commentary on lines 231–55 for further discussion). The first initiates to the cult in this poem are male, and at least at a later period a male "child from the hearth" was initiated for the city. Yet in this version of the myth, it is only as an infant that a male can find a place in the private world of women, where Demeter engages directly with mortals.

By comparing the cosmological strategies used by Demeter and Zeus in this poem, we can see that the maternal politics of Demeter represent a genuine challenge to the patriarchal politics of Zeus in epic, at least insofar as Hesiod, the *Hymn to Demeter*, and to a lesser degree the Homeric poems represent them. In Hesiod's *Theogony* Zeus takes a formal approach to establishing his authority over the universe. Using force, polygamy, ingenuity, and the bait of honor, he prevents the birth of a male successor altogether; divides heaven, the sea, and the underworld among himself and his two powerful brothers; suppresses violent male gods of the earlier generations and distributes powers to all others; mates with goddesses to produce deities whose names suggest the arts of cultured life, and ensures the permanent separation of the worlds of humans and gods.[109] As a result of

---

[107] Clay 1989:225, in dismissing this alternative (suggested by Rudhardt 1978, Arthur 1977, and Rubin and Deal 1980, this volume) tends to underemphasize, in her concern with the cosmological themes of the poem, the poem's stress on the suffering and humanization of the goddess.

[108] Parker 1991:10 suggests that this poem was the first to portray the episode as the origin of the Mysteries.

[109] Zeus does in one sense make the divine world into one endogamous family in the *Theogony*, but his organization of the cosmos does not include Hades or mortals in this family.

the Prometheus episode, humankind is forced to endure an existence radically separate from the gods, and Zeus establishes and makes every effort to maintain the boundaries between mortals and immortals. In the *Hymn to Demeter*, we are not told Zeus's motives for arranging Persephone's marriage directly; Helios, in defending Zeus, mentions only formal considerations—the suitability of so august a bridegroom (84–87). Yet the father, having overlooked both the emotional realities involved and the problematic status of the Olympian bride, is finally forced to modify his position in the goddesses' favor.

Demeter first tries to disrupt Zeus's universal order by making a mortal boy an immortal child and her own; then she goes on strike to win back her daughter. The altered relation between upper and lower worlds emerges as a result of her reunion with her daughter. Unlike Zeus, she is not concerned with the separation of spheres and the transcendence of mother/child bonds, but with a preservation of such bonds and a breaking down of divisions among spheres. Hades becomes linked through Persephone to the world above, and mortals become the symbolic nurslings of the goddesses. The goddesses' relation to initiates is described in the *Hymn* as one of a durable love of one friend or relative (*philos*) for another (487, *prophroneôs philôntai*). Demeter thus softens the boundaries between mortals and immortals that Zeus had consolidated and makes the universe more of a family by uniting its realms, whereas Zeus, by exiling his daughter to the world below, had made it less of one. Demeter's famine reveals that the gods are dependent on humans—for sacrifices—and her own temporary dependence on mortals is a theme of the poem. Furthermore, she throws a new light on the role of the earth in the relations of the cosmos. The divine brothers Zeus, Poseidon, and Hades divided heaven, sea, and underworld among themselves; they left the earth, the mortal sphere, as a territory to be shared among the gods (*Iliad* 15.187–93). Demeter, by demonstrating through her withdrawal her de facto power over that fourth sphere, brings the earth into a new and more beneficent relation to the powers above and below. The *Hymn* thus reinforces the female challenge that Demeter poses to Zeus's rule.

Recent studies have examined the possible differences between men and women as moral and social agents.[110] These studies argue that women more often than men define themselves relationally, and especially by their positions in a family group; when faced with difficult decisions, they are apt to take an approach consonant with their social and familial identities. Men, by contrast, tend to define themselves to a greater degree by bonds outside the

---

[110] Gilligan 1982's views on the morality of care as opposed to the morality of justice have been much elaborated and criticized. For further bibliography, see Gilligan et al. 1988 and Kittay and Meyers 1987. Chodorow 1974 (this volume) served as a partial inspiration for Gilligan.

family and mature in relation to a peer group of other men. They are more likely to approach problems abstractly and formally, and male maturity involves greater detachment from the bonds of intimacy, first from the mother, and finally from the family. In the *Hymn* a similar contrast obtains in the strategies adopted by Zeus and Demeter. Zeus's approach is formal and aims to transcend mother/child bonds, whereas the beleaguered Demeter adopts the relational approach more generally characteristic of women (and the powerless).

The *Hymn*, then, repeats the pattern of sexual tensions among male and female deities found in Hesiod and prefigures the similar tensions that pervade Aeschylus's *Oresteia*.[111] The events of both the *Hymn* and the fifth-century trilogy are triggered by a violent male intrusion into the mother/child bond and the real or metaphorical sacrifice of the daughter Persephone or Iphigeneia;[112] both reach closure and compromise when offended female deities receive new honors in a universe dominated by Zeus. Yet whereas the Erinyes' jurisdiction is changed and circumscribed, Demeter's honors are amplified. Demeter's partial autonomy is represented in her ability to make Zeus capitulate and modify his plans, and in her reception of a *choice* of new honors from Zeus. This is unusual in Hesiod and the hymns. The longer Homeric *Hymn to Aphrodite* (5), for example, establishes new limits on Aphrodite's powers—the goddess, once she herself has been made to desire a mortal, will no longer be able to boast of her power over other divinities; Hermes must to some extent give way to Apollo in the Homeric *Hymn to Hermes*.

The cosmological strategies Demeter uses are not exclusive in Greek literature to the female (the *Odyssey* too, for example, reestablishes order in Ithaka by rebuilding familial bonds, both formally and emotionally, within the household of Odysseus) but are linked to the female in the *Hymn* through the contrast it develops between Zeus and Hades and Demeter as agents. Yet whereas the *Theogony* views female wrath and rebellion as dangerous and disruptive to the divine order and potentially devastating to humanity, the *Hymn to Demeter* emphasizes the creative and positive outcome of Demeter's nevertheless disruptive and dangerous wrath (to say nothing of her love).[113]

---

[111] See Zeitlin 1978 on the *Oresteia* and Arthur 1982 on the *Theogony*.

[112] For a discussion of the "female intruder" pattern in tragedy, in which a female figure steps out of her sphere and disrupts the social order in reaction to a male violation of her domestic interests, see Foley 1982. The *Hymn* is far more tolerant of Demeter's intrusion than tragedy is, however.

[113] Dirk Obbink suggests to me that in attempting to destroy humanity with her famine, Demeter temporarily echoes Zeus's own threats to exterminate humanity in various myths. Nevertheless, Demeter's challenge to patrilocal marriage and her withdrawal from her proper sphere among the gods ends in an acceptance of marriage and the establishment of a civic cult. In the Thesmophoria, women also left their homes, but to put the fertility of married women at

Here Zeus, in being forced by Demeter to modify Persephone's and humanity's future, seems to play a role closer to the one that he plays in Aeschylus's later Prometheus trilogy, where the crude young Zeus, recently come to power, learns through his conflict with the Titan Prometheus that knowledge (the secret about the birth of a son who could replace Zeus that Prometheus learned from his mother) is as important as force and power in ruling the universe and begins to tolerate Prometheus's concern for humankind. (In Ovid *Metamorphoses* 5.341–43 Demeter is, like Prometheus, represented as a giver of cultivation and culture to humanity.) In a parallel fashion, the resolution of the *Hymn* also seems to sanction the right of the divine mother and daughter to be consulted and to consent to marriage.[114] In this case, the *Hymn* would be similar to Aeschylus's later Danaid trilogy, which emphasizes the importance of *peithô* (persuasion) in mitigating *bia* (violence) in marriage.[115]

The section on "The 'Theology' of the Mysteries" (above, this essay) stressed how the cult at Eleusis modified the divine-human relations that we find in the Homeric poems, which emphasized a bleak afterlife and the unwillingness of gods to soften the mortal lot except by promoting human fame and perpetuating the lineage of those they favor. In Hesiod, too, mortals are helpless victims of the struggles among the gods, and their world becomes at best a misleading imitation of the divine and at worst, in Hesiod's *Works and Days*, an Iron Age carrying humanity rapidly to doom. In the *Hymn*, by contrast, the goddesses' involvement in mortality cements through the Mysteries a permanent opportunity for a more intimate and reliable divine/human bond. It is not surprising, then, that the *Hymn to Demeter* also challenges the cosmological strategies of Zeus in the *Theogony* and modifies the perspective of the earlier poem on the role of gender in shaping the universe. The historian Herodotos tells us that "Hesiod and Homer . . . first composed a theogony for the Greeks and gave the gods their names and determined their honors and skills and described their forms" (2.53. 1–2). As Gregory Nagy has recently rephrased this achievement: "The Olympus of Hesiodic and Homeric poetry is a Panhellenic construct that elevates the gods beyond their localized attributes. . . . The evolution of most major gods from most major cities into the integrated

---

the service of the city-state. Epithalamia (marriage songs) could also stress the bride's resistance to marriage and to departure from the mother (see Catullus 62) in the context of celebrating the rite.

[114] This is argued by Ramnoux 1959:122.

[115] In this trilogy, forty-nine sisters kill their cousins, who forced them into marriage against their will. The fiftieth spares her spouse out of love and becomes an agent of reconciliation. The women ultimately move from Egypt to Argos, where they find more acceptable marriages. The Danaids were said by Herodotus (2.171) to have introduced the Thesmophoria from Egypt. Some scholars have argued that Aeschylus's trilogy ended with the institution of this festival. (See Garvie 1969:227)

family at Olympus amounts to a synthesis that is not just artistic but political in nature, comparable with the evolution of the Panhellenic games known as the Olympics."[116]

It seems likely that perspectives on the afterlife that differ from the authoritative cosmological tradition inaugurated by Hesiod and Homer (a tradition that virtually ignored Demeter and did not explicitly link the goddess with Persephone) were of great antiquity in Greece.[117] By incorporating the Eleusinian Mysteries into the Panhellenic epic tradition from a literary perspective, the *Hymn* also makes a bid to acquire a Panhellenic prestige for its alternative religious views and its once local rites.[118] At the same time the Mysteries were potentially antagonistic to the tradition established in epic; we know for example that the Orphics, whose myths and practices in certain respects conflicted with those of epic and the city-state, adopted them. Hence the *Hymn* only uneasily absorbs the cult and its myth into the Olympian cosmos.[119]

The Mother/Daughter Romance

In the *Hymn*, Demeter, once she no longer needs obscurity for her secret strategies with Demophoön, leaves behind the private world of women and demands public recognition from both men and gods. Mortals administer and participate in the Mysteries and can be adopted by the goddess. Nevertheless, the structure of the *Hymn* suggests strongly that the rites originate above all from the divine relation between mother and daughter, and it is presumably the bliss encountered in Demeter's and Persephone's reunion that the mystery initiates shared at climactic moments of the rite. I have argued that structure and characterization in the poem emphasize the important connection between the psychological experience of the goddesses and the founding of the Mysteries. Similarly, the double withdrawal of the two goddesses, unusual in such myths, is reflected in the symbolic doubling of the goddesses in cult, poetry, and the fine arts (see Fig. 7), a doubling that also expresses their indivisible emotional bond. It is to this intense emotional bond between mother and daughter that I now wish to turn.

[116] Nagy 1982:48–49. See also Nagy 1990a:36–82. The same point was eloquently made by Rohde 1898:38–39.

[117] On the relation between the *Hymn*'s representation of reward and punishment in the underworld and that in the Homeric epics, see the Commentary on lines 364–69.

[118] In the *Hymn to Hermes*, Hermes also acquires his powers by challenging Apollo. I agree with Clay's 1989 view (see esp. 15) that the Homeric hymns fill the gap between theogonic poetry and epic, but not with her view of the authoritative role that Zeus plays in this transition. At least to some degree, the hymns aim to challenge and significantly modify earlier epic tradition.

[119] Here I partially disagree with Clay 1989:265.

There have been various psychoanalytic readings of the Demeter/ Persephone myth. Jung and Kerényi, for example, studied the archetypes of the Mother/Maiden and the Divine Child. Contemporary feminists have not surprisingly found the *Hymn*'s depiction of the psychological relation between mother and daughter to be of compelling interest—in particular its unusual focus on the mother and its validation of her grief and anger. After a brief review of several earlier psychoanalytic readings, my own analysis will emphasize how contemporary sociological and psychoanalytic research on the mother/daughter relation can contribute to an interpretation of these aspects of the *Hymn*.

Jung considers Demeter and Persephone to be representative of the archetypes of mother and maiden—figures that operate in the unconscious of both individuals and societies (which have a collective unconscious) and emerge in dreams and myths. In attempting to make clear the rejuvenating effects that Demeter cults may have on the female psyche, Jung argues for a connection between the archetypal relation of mother and daughter and the mitigation of death promised by the Mysteries:

> Demeter and Kore, mother and daughter, extend the feminine consciousness both upwards and downwards. They add an "older and younger," "stronger and weaker" dimension to it and widen out the narrowly limited conscious mind bound in space and time, give it intimations of a greater and more comprehensive personality which has a share in the eternal course of things. . . . The psyche pre-existent to consciousness (e.g., in a child) participates in the maternal psyche on the one hand, while on the other it reaches across to the daughter psyche. We could therefore say that every mother contains her daughter in herself and every daughter her mother, and that every woman extends backwards into her mother and forwards into her daughter. This participation and intermingling give rise to that peculiar uncertainty as regards *time*: a woman lives earlier as a mother, later as a daughter. The conscious experience of these ties produces the feeling that her life is spread out over generations—the first step towards the immediate experience and conviction of being outside time, which brings with it a feeling of *immortality*. The individual's life is elevated into a type, and becomes the archetype of woman's fate in general. This leads to a restoration or *apocatastasis* of the lives of her ancestors, who now, through the bridge of the momentary individual, pass down into generations of the future. An experience of this kind gives the individual a place and a meaning in the life of the generations, so that all unnecessary obstacles are cleared out of the way of the life-stream that is to flow through her. At the same time the individual is rescued from her isolation and restored to wholeness. All ritual preoccupation with archetypes ultimately has this aim and this result."[120]

[120] Jung 1967:162. What he says of mothers and daughters might equally be said of fathers and sons.

Although Kerényi has effectively exposed some of the omissions and contradictions in Jung's discussion of the Korê archetype, Jung's views have served for some as an attractive explanation of the unconscious appeal of the Mysteries.[121] Jung himself, however, had considerably more difficulty in conceptualizing how the Demeter-Korê myth operated in the psyche of the male. The myth does not in his view represent fully the anima (the "feminine" principle in both males and females). For the anima is female in relation to male (the animus, or masculine principle in the human psyche). Although "the man's anima found occasion for projection in the Demeter cult . . . Demeter-Kore exists on the plane of the mother-daughter experience, which is alien to man and shuts him out. In fact, the psychology of the Demeter cult bears all the features of a matriarchal order of society, where man is an indispensable but on the whole disturbing factor."[122] No extended Jungian reading of the *Hymn* exists—Jung focused in this case only on the nature of archetypes. Yet Neumann's Jungian analysis of the narrative of the closely related Amor and Psyche myth in Apuleius's *The Golden Ass* identifies a similar problem:

> The fundamental situation of the feminine . . . is the primordial relation of identity between daughter and mother. For this reason the approach of the male always and in every case means separation. Marriage is always a mystery, but also a mystery of death. For the male—and this is inherent in the essential opposition between masculine and feminine—marriage, as the matriarchate recognized, is primarily an abduction, an acquisition—a rape.[123]

In the Amor and Psyche myth, however, Psyche eliminates Jung's difficulty by rejecting "matriarchy" for the passionate pursuit of Amor.

The sociologist Robert May, in his book *Sex and Fantasy*, also argues that the Demeter/Persephone myth—with its pain and suffering, creative endurance, and ecstatic return to fullness and growth—is the archetypal myth in the fantasy life of women.[124] Similarly, Gilligan and McClelland see the myth as "exemplifying the feminine attitude toward power . . . the strengths of interdependence, building up resources and giving, that . . . characterize the mature feminine style."[125] Neither Jung nor May offers a plausible psychological explanation for the myth's historical appeal to the male initi-

---

[121] Kerényi 1967b:xxvii–xxxiii.

[122] Jung 1967:177. By contrast Kerényi 1967a:146–47 says that "the separation of Mother and Daughter, the yearning of Demeter for her own girl-child, the Kore, must be characteristic of undivided human existence, of men as well as women, but in one way of men and in another of women . . . All human beings and not women alone bear this [the same] origin and . . . duality . . . both the Mother and the Daughter—within themselves."

[123] 1956:63.

[124] May 1980:8–13.

[125] Gilligan 1982:22 and McClelland 1975. Helene Deutsch 1944:292 saw Demeter as "the prototype of the active motherly woman." I owe this reference to Marilyn Katz.

ate. Neumann, however, thinks that the Mysteries offered to the male initiate the opportunity to identify both with his own feminine and pre-patriarchal aspect (here he disagrees with Jung) and with the goddesses' divine sons—both the divine son born to one of the goddesses at the close of the Mysteries and Triptolemos in his role as disseminator of Demeter's grain.[126] We will return shortly to this question.

In Marylin Arthur's (now Marilyn A. Katz) reading of the *Hymn* in this volume, Zeus's intervention provokes a crisis of identity in Demeter that corresponds to the development of the girl at the phallic stage in Freudian theory. Discovering her lack of a penis, the girl withdraws and renounces her own sexuality; she wants to acquire a penis or fantasizes that she possesses it; finally, she identifies with her mother, takes her father as love object, and substitutes for the penis a desire for heterosexual coitus and a baby. Similarly, Demeter, suddenly powerless to resist Zeus and Hades, withdraws and renounces her divinity, tries to compensate for her loss of Persephone, recovers much of her "femininity," and returns and accommodates herself to the male order. The concluding reunion of the goddesses "expresses a female solidarity which is discovered in the context of a patriarchal world."[127]

Arthur herself was fully aware of revisions in Freudian theory about female psycho-sexual development and of the contributions made by the object-relations school of psychology to our understanding of female psychological development, and especially of the mother/daughter relation.[128] Neverthless, the work of Nancy Chodorow (this volume), which combined object-relations theory with perspectives derived from sociology and cross-cultural anthropology, created the opportunity for an interpretation of the *Hymn* that builds on Freudian theory but with a different emphasis. Object-relations psychologists argue that, contrary to Freud's assumptions, gender identity is established in the pre-oedipal phase, probably as early as the first year. The child begins life in a symbiotic state with the mother. Relations with the mother (or another woman), the usual first caretaker in both Western industrialized society and in ancient Greece, permanently shape its psychic reality, and separation from the mother represents the first phase of individuation. The mother treats the boy as other than herself and fosters his

[126] Neumann 1974:323–24.

[127] Spitz 1989 and 1990 and Berry 1975 also offer feminist psychoanalytic readings of the *Hymn*. After the completion of this manuscript, I received from Ann Suter a summary of a paper in which she presented a reading of the *Hymn* from the perspective of object-relations theory (Suter 1991). Suter's interpretation makes Persephone a major actor in her own coming-of-age drama. She picks the narcissus to indicate her readiness to leave childhood behind and refuses to eat as part of an attempt to control her own physical boundaries and thus to separate from her mother.

[128] See especially Arthur's note 6 on modifications of Freudian theory. As will be clear throughout my discussion, I build on those aspects of Arthur's essay that make the most use of such later adaptations of Freudian theory.

independence, whereas she tends to treat the girl as like herself and even an extension of herself. As Chodorow points out, the close affinity between mother and daughter is reinforced, especially in traditional societies, by the different lives of male and female children. Boys leave the household early for relations with peers; the father, the boy's same-sex role model, is often absent. Girls acquire their adult role to a greater degree in daily imitation of their mothers. They leave the world of the family less often and their development is mediated more powerfully by intergenerational relations with other women than by relations with peers (although these still play an important role). The adult female characteristically emerges with more fluid ego boundaries than does the adult male, and an identity more fundamentally structured by intimate relations with others.

Chodorow and other object-relations psychologists accept a modified version of Freud's oedipal crisis as intrinsic to the sexual development of both girls and boys.[129] For such later Freudians, the acquisition of male identity requires separation from the mother at the phallic stage, whereas the acquisition of mature female selfhood requires a continued identity with the mother, along with a transfer of libidinal desire from the mother to the father. In attempting simultaneously to pursue and struggle against maternal identification, girls may have a difficult time establishing a separate identity, and the girl's turn to the father is motivated by an attempt to escape an overwhelming symbiosis with the mother. The phallic phase of a girl's development has come to be viewed by many as transitory and relatively unimportant. Penis envy is not a natural part of female identity, but a conflict to be resolved just as boys resolve the castration complex; the girl tends to envy above all what possession of the penis represents in a patriarchal society.

From the object-relations perspective, then, the fact that women do the mothering is of crucial significance. The complex and ambivalent relation with the mother, established at the pre-oedipal phase, together with later relations among women, plays a far more important role in the development of both sexes than in traditional Freudian theory. The central problem in the girl's transition to adulthood is separation from the mother, yet the continuing attachment between mother and daughter is essential to successful female maturation.[130] Insofar as psychic development affects the imagination, the pre-oedipal phase potentially engenders a longing for symbiotic

[129] Indeed, after Freud himself came to accept (see Freud 1931 and 1933) the importance of the child's pre-oedipal relation to its mother, he adapted Lampl-de Groot's view (1928) that the girl must come to terms with her inability to win her first love object, the mother.

[130] Spitz's two recent discussions (1989 and 1990) of the *Hymn* use the poem to plead for a more mother-oriented psychoanalysis. Earlier analysts, accepting Freud's view that continued attachment to the mother inhibited heterosexual development in the woman, emphasized the necessity of the girl's detachment from her.

closeness with the mother, and a modified vision of subject-object dualism, of autonomy and separation, and of power relations.

I believe that we can extend our understanding of the psychology of the *Hymn* through examining its narrative from an object-relations perspective on the mother/daughter relation, although my own discussion will, like Chodorow's in this volume, be influenced by sociological and anthropological research as well. In following this path we must, of course, beware of inappropriately imposing anachronistic readings on ancient texts and of overlooking certain weaknesses of object-relations psychology—above all its romanticization of the mother-daughter bond, its unproblematic and overly unified vision of subjectivity, and its de-emphasis of the (sometimes debilitating) tensions and ambiguities in the relations between mother and daughter. The French feminist Luce Irigaray, for example, has argued that patriarchy functions to separate women from each other and to cripple or suppress the transmission of a maternal genealogy.[131] The daughter sees her mother as either terrifying and engulfing (the phallic mother) or castrated and thus cannot effectively identify with her or easily accept maternal nurturing in her pursuit of autonomy. Yet Irigaray also sees the establishment of symbolic mother-daughter bonds as essential to women's autonomy and identity. Finally, the relations between the psychoanalytic model and the social/political environment are complex, and we cannot easily dismiss historical variation and differences among women (or men) determined by class, race, ethnicity, and sexual preference.[132] Nevertheless, I hope to show that object-relations theory remains illuminating both for an exploration of the psychology of mother-daughter relations in a traditional society such as archaic Greece and for a poem that deliberately celebrates and idealizes the mother-daughter relation.

As all of the psychoanalytic analyses mentioned above correctly stress, the mother-daughter relation is central to the *Hymn*. The male characters serve as remote and marginal (though critical) catalysts to the action, while the narrative concentrates on the experience of female protagonists in a female world. The psychodynamics of the poem pointedly situate Demeter between her daughter Persephone and her divine mother Rheia and stress the intergenerational chain of relations from mother to daughter. Before turning to close analysis of the mother-daughter bond in the *Hymn*, I shall briefly retrace the major aspects of the relations among Demeter, Persephone, other goddesses, and mortal women as the poem evolves.

At the opening of the *Hymn*, Demeter and Persephone appear as part of a female world (on earth as well, the lives of mortal women are largely separate from those of men). The as-yet-unnamed daughter Persephone is dis-

---

[131] See esp. Irigaray 1981 and 1985.

[132] For thoughtful critiques of feminist object-relations psychology, see esp. Gallop 1987 and Kahane 1988.

covered picking flowers at the remote reaches of the earth with the Okeanidai; later in the poem the virgin goddesses Artemis and Athena are included as part of this group. After the abduction, Demeter's reaction to separation from her daughter is violent. She takes on characteristics of a mourning woman on earth: changed clothing, refusal to eat. We later discover that in the world below Persephone has been grieving equally for her mother, also failing to eat.[133] Demeter is joined by Hekate, who has little to offer but sympathy for the goddess's maternal loss. In later myth and cult, Hekate is strongly associated with both goddesses, becoming at times virtually identical with them; she is thus ideally suited to play the mediating role she adopts in the *Hymn* between mother and daughter, where she both identifies herself with the mother and promises to serve as an attendant to Persephone.

In some versions of the myth, Hekate is said to be Demeter's daughter or to have gone to the underworld to search for Persephone;[134] in others, she was identified with Persephone.[135] In the *Hymn* Hekate ascends to Demeter's side from a cave (25) and promises to attend Persephone in the future. Her links with the moon (which are only certainly attested in the Hellenistic period) and the world below associate her with Persephone, for the moon rises and sets just as Persephone (who later became a moon goddess herself) descends and ascends. In Hesiod she is a Titan, one of the older generation of once-rebellious gods born before the Olympians (of which Demeter is one), but now incorporated with honors into the realm of Zeus.[136] By naming her father, the *Hymn* seems to characterize her as a Titan, and thus from a generational perspective a figure more maternal than daughterly. Yet in Hesiod, as the only daughter of her parents and an eternal virgin, Hekate holds honors, like Persephone or Demeter in some cases, in three realms, in this case earth, heaven, and the sea (*Theogony* 412–15, 427). Like both goddesses, she nurtures the young as a *kourotrophos*.[137]

After discovering Persephone's whereabouts from Helios, Demeter enters an all-female world on earth, where she is gradually (if temporarily) released from her mourning. The marriageable daughters of Keleos come to the Maiden Well for water; the name of the well suggests that virgins draw the water for their nuptial baths from this site. Like meadows, wells were in antiquity often a scene of abduction or molestation of women. Given this suggestive setting, it is not surprising that their age and resemblance to

[133] In Persephone's version of the story, Hades finally forces her to eat.

[134] Callimachus frag. 466 Pfeiffer = Orphic frag. 42 Kern and vase paintings.

[135] The scholiast on Theocritus *Idylls* 2.12, perhaps Euripides *Ion* 1048, and Sophocles *Antigone* 1199.

[136] See Arthur 1977 (this volume) on Hekate's status as a Titan.

[137] She is *kourotrophos* at Hesiod *Theogony* 450–52 and the Scholion to Aristophanes' *Wasps* 804. See the further discussion of these attributes below.

goddesses (and especially Persephone herself) is underlined in the text. This is a world in which women of all ages, including old women, are cared for by other women. The daughters are shocked to find an old woman alone by the well and are eager to find the proper place for her. At Eleusis, it is as if all women are related—potentially mothers and daughters to each other.[138] The daughters express to Demeter pride in the social role of mortal women, who as wives preside over and within the households of humankind (156ff.).[139] Demeter is provoked by their flowerlike beauty and sympathy to wish the daughters happy and fertile marriages, despite her anger over the loss of Persephone to marriage with Hades.

In her lying Cretan tale to the daughters, Demeter represents herself, like her daughter, as a victim of abduction—in this case over the sea.[140] The threat of being sold into slavery supposedly encountered by Demeter perhaps makes an implicit comment on Persephone's "marriage" with Hades and Demeter's own feelings of helplessness. Yet although Persephone was trapped by her captor and will eat the fatal pomegranate seeds, Demeter has refused the temptation of food and eluded the pirates who seized her. In the Cretan tale, mother and daughter become closely assimilated in the mother's imagination. The experience of the one becomes that of the other. The lie also resonates, perhaps accidentally, with an incident in Demeter's own myths. In sources later than the *Hymn*, but potentially known in substance to its author, Demeter herself was twice angered by becoming a victim of rape, once by Zeus,[141] which engendered Persephone, and once, during her search for Persephone, by the god of the sea Poseidon, which engendered an unnamed daughter.[142] In the latter story, Demeter withdraws fertility from the land in anger at her rape and over the loss of her daughter.

At the house of Keleos, Demeter receives gracious hospitality from Metaneira. The maid Iambe cheers Demeter with her provocative joking; if, as seems likely, the jokes addressed female sexuality or female fertility, Demeter is made to laugh responsively at the very aspect of divine/human nature that caused her loss and mourning (see the Commentary on lines 202–4 for

[138] In Jungian terms, the scene stresses the archetypal stages in woman's life: virgin, mother, crone.

[139] Arthur 1977 (this volume) notes that Metaneira makes the choice to hire Demeter. This indicates a certain autonomy for women within the household.

[140] Ibid. (this volume) suggests that by mentioning that a price was not paid for her, Demeter implies that she would accept compensation to mitigate her wrath over her daughter.

[141] Clement *Protreptikos* 2.15.1–2 defines the Mysteries of Deo as Zeus's rape of Demeter and explains her epithet Brimo as a result of her anger at this treatment. Tertullian *Ad Nationes* 2, in asking why the priestess of Demeter is "carried off," suggests that the marriage by violence was Demeter's, not Korê's. See further Burkert 1983:283.

[142] See Pausanias 8.25 and 8.42.2ff.

further discussion) and may offer some mitigation of it.[143] For the moment, we hear no more about Persephone. Demeter ostensibly adopts a female role as a nurse to a highly valued child, although she aims in fact to adopt a divine male offspring.[144]

When out of human folly Metaneira interrupts the immortalization of Demophoön, Demeter angrily turns away from the world of women that has inadvertently betrayed her, takes on her divine identity, and uses her power over the earth's fertility to make the gods capitulate to her will. Only Persephone's eating of a pomegranate seed in the world below ultimately prevents Demeter's total success. The reunion between Demeter and Persephone is mutually ecstatic. Persephone's description of her companions at the time of the rape, in contrast to the original description, names each one of them, thus locating her experience in a context of individualized female presences.[145] Demeter, who has put off her mortal disguise (although she retains her dark cloak) and regained her eternally youthful radiance, has already become the double of her now-mature daughter. Demeter's mother Rheia—who is elsewhere often her mythological double as well—descends to bring the goddesses back to Olympus, and Hekate promises to serve as Persephone's attendant in the future. Persephone will receive honors as the wife of Hades; Demeter accepts additional honors from Zeus. The goddesses will preside together over the Mysteries. The text strongly contrasts the initial helplessness of Demeter, who searches for Persephone in ignorance and then cannot reach her daughter in the world below, with the final powerful strike that wins new honors from Zeus, and the initial helplessness of Persephone, a victim of rape and an unwilling bride, with the powerful rule of the underworld that she will acquire. The Demophoön incident anticipates the nurturant role that the goddesses will adopt toward the initiates in a cult in which mother and daughter were represented as virtually indistinguishable from each other.

The narrative of the *Hymn* is framed by the separation and reunion of mother and daughter, and the *Hymn* extends and develops the implications of their bond through its representation of the worlds of mortal and divine females. In her maternal role, Demeter is linked with Hekate, Metaneira, and Rheia. Although the poem concentrates on the experience of the mother and Persephone is absent for a large part of the poem, the relation of

[143] Arthur 1977 (this volume) argues that in laughing at Iambe's jokes Demeter accepts female sexuality. In an alternative version of the myth, Baubo makes the goddess laugh by exposing her genitals and the baby Iakchos, or she agitates her genitals to make them resemble a child (see the Commentary on 202–4 for further discussion). Hence Iambe's jokes might possibly develop the theme of the birth of a child, especially a male child.

[144] See Arthur 1977 (this volume) on Demeter's "over-valuation" of the male child here. She argues that the competition over Demophoön is the only act of hostility between females in the poem.

[145] Segal 1981:130.

mother to daughter continues to be elaborated in the *Hymn*'s portrait of the daughters of Keleos.

When the poem begins, Persephone is still a child—she reaches for the flower as if for a toy; due to the early age of marriage for a girl, Greek brides often dedicated their toys to gods at marriage. Greek poetry represented a girl's childhood as a protected physical space, an idyllic existence into which time and the outside world intervened very little until the time for marriage.[146] Yet the presence of other females and the physical separation of mother and daughter at the time of the rape suggest something more than a paternal intervention in a blissful infantile unity with the mother. The adolescent girl's attraction to the seductive narcissus and the location of the rape in the flowery meadow (where such divine rapes typically occur) suggest Persephone's readiness for a new phase of life (see the Commentary especially on lines 1–14 and 5–14, for further discussion).[147] Child care in this world, as in ancient Greece generally, is the province of the mother, but other females, both older and contemporary, play an active role in the rearing of girls. Similarly, the fragments of the archaic poets Sappho and Alkman (his Maiden Songs) make clear that the girl's growth to maturity involves active participation, especially in shared religious activities, with other girls and even with older women not their mothers.[148] This is particularly true as the girl nears marriage and maturity—*Odyssey* 6 provides another example in the maiden Nausikaa's group washing expedition, which is provoked by thoughts of her coming marriage.

Mother and daughter each react strongly to their enforced separation. As Chodorow shows, mother and daughter often see themselves as a physical extension of each other. Ego boundaries between Demeter and Persephone are barely developed, for we see each echo the reaction of the other. Neither goddess eats at first, thus expressing a strong sense of physical symbiosis with the other. Persephone leaves the earth lamenting (20) and continues to lament her loss of her mother in the world below (344); and Demeter journeys from heaven to earth, all the while lamenting her daughter's disappearance. Both break their fast by eating "mortal" food. Both are angry and depressed (see 362 for Persephone). Demeter is temporarily alienated from her divine persona,[149] and Persephone is neither maiden nor fully a wife. At the same time, the "aging" of Demeter is the psychological counterpart to the maturation of the daughter. Mourning, a natural part of the gradual

[146] Early Greek lyric represents virgins as naive, innocent, and untamed. Both tragedy, in the portraits of Euripides' Iphigeneia at Aulis or Prokne in Sophocles' *Tereus* (524N), and Hesiod at *Works and Days* 519–26 stress the idyllic and sheltered life of a girl before marriage.

[147] Nevertheless, because sexual feelings in young girls were often initially awakened in an all-female world (see below on Sappho), we should not assume that Persephone is ready for the violent transition to marriage that she is about to encounter.

[148] For a general study of this issue, see Calame 1977.

[149] Arthur 1977 (this volume).

separation of mother and daughter at adolescence, here becomes reality.[150] Yet, we should not, with Berry, see in Demeter's reaction simply the classic signs of depression.[151] Greek funerary lamentation for the dead involved an assimilation of the mourner to the state of the dead; we should recall here the very similar behavior of Achilleus over the dead Patroklos. Demeter's behavior is an appropriate stage in a process that eventually returns the mourner to participation in his or her social world and to the acceptance of the loss of the dead person by following a standard type scene: the mourner sits, eats and/or takes a drink, receives an exhortation to put the death of the loved person into perspective, and eventually does so.[152] In the *Hymn* Demeter sits, temporarily refuses to eat, and receives consolation from Metaneira; she then eats, laughs at Iambe, and takes on the new role of nurse to Demophoön.[153]

In contrast to the mortal society represented in the *Hymn*, the endogamous divine society on Olympus does not normally require radical separation from the natal family upon the daughter's marriage and offers considerable autonomy and authority to its goddesses. In these respects the divine world represented at the opening of the poem is not dissimilar to those discussed in the various anthropological studies cited by Chodorow in the closing pages of her essay in this volume. In East London working-class families, Javanese nuclear families, and Atjenese families in Indonesia, the relation between mother and daughter remains central throughout life. The two live close together. The mother has a clear sense of social identity. She expects to continue an indefinite close relation to her daughter, but she is ready to share the role of rearing the child with other females. The daughter develops an independent identity as head of her own household, but she remains deeply affiliated on a daily basis with her mother and relies on her particularly at important life transitions and events: menarche, marriage, pregnancy, childbirth, child rearing. Other women (often grandmothers) may mediate this relation, helping the daughter to reach a separate identity from her mother. The relation with the mother remains ultimately more important than that with the husband, who is neither as present nor as supportive in her life as the mother. Although in the *Hymn* the paternal presence of Zeus is more dominant than in the latter two of the societies cited by Chodorow, the psychodynamics of the goddesses' relation (as well as their relation with other females) seemingly resonates with that of human

---

[150] Spitz 1990:419. Demeter wanders nine days; the Greeks mourned Hektor for the same time.

[151] Berry 1975:190. See also Hall 1980:78.

[152] See Nagler 1974:174–77 and Burkert 1979:43–45 on the acceptance of seat, food, drink, and consolation as a sign of the return by a mourner to participation in the life cycle.

[153] As Arthur 1977 (this volume) points out, however, she has not yet readopted her full divine identity.

cultures characterized by strong intrafemale bonding, a separation between the lives and worlds of males and females, and endogamous marriage patterns.[154]

The dependence between mother and daughter characteristic of the divine world in the *Hymn* only becomes problematic when it is radically disrupted by the violent intervention of Hades. The separation between mother and daughter that would naturally and necessarily have occurred at adolescence, and would normally have been mediated by participation in ritual with other women, becomes an enforced transition, temporarily harmful to the stability of mother and daughter. Yet despite the devastating effects of their separation, both goddesses in the course of their time apart are prepared for their cyclical separations and their changed relationship; each emerges newly empowered after a period of uncertainty and "loss of identity." Demeter experiences the world of patriarchal marriage from within and receives support in the separate world of mortal women, even though they ultimately fail her. Demeter's encounter with mortal marriage and adolescent girls sets the stage in the narrative for her acceptance of a partial separation from her now-adult daughter.[155] In addition, the mother Metaneira's concern for the male child who is the light of his patriarchal household underlines the impossibility of retreat into a world entirely shaped and controlled by women. Demeter's second attempt to create (or preserve) a mother/child bond that cannot be interrupted by time tellingly fails.[156]

Persephone at first remains isolated as a helpless and unwilling bride in the world below. Yet when Demeter challenges Persephone's marriage directly and publicly with her famine, the mother's intervention (along with Zeus's subsequent command) produces a change in Hades. He (in Persephone's version of the story) forces her to eat the pomegranate seed (see below) but offers the girl a powerful role of her own as queen of the underworld. In short, he gives Persephone a social identity independent from that of her mother;[157] indeed, among the dead Persephone comes to have an awesome power and autonomy that is matched by few other female divinities in the cosmos. (The *Hymn*'s sympathetic portrait of Homer's dread goddess of the underworld is one of its striking features.)

[154] As Chodorow points out, strong mother/daughter bonding can also derive from a shared sense of oppression. Insofar as the society in which this poem was composed does not resemble Olympus, the myth partially compensates, in the context of rituals for the goddesses, for the losses imposed by the separation of mother and daughter at marriage.

[155] On this point see Arthur 1977 and Rubin and Deal 1980:19n.33 (both articles in this volume).

[156] Van Nortwick:56 and 59 argues that Demeter attempts to prolong the mother/child bond in an unnatural fashion.

[157] Persephone rarely has cults on earth separate from those of her mother (Allen, Halliday, and Sikes 1936:116).

Nevertheless, the central emotional relation for both mother and daughter remains their own. Again, we should not import our own cultural assumptions here. Greeks expected women to be loyal to their marriages, but arranged marriages did not necessarily result in a close emotional bond between bride and groom. The bond with the male child was an altogether different matter, and we see this reflected in Demeter's (and Metaneira's) relation to Demophoön in the *Hymn*. The groom can offer status and social identity, as here, but the woman's bonds to her natal family often remained, as we see in many Greek myths, more powerful for her than those to her spouse.[158] The *Hymn* tells us at first that Hades gives the pomegranate seed to Persephone "secretly" (372). If Persephone does misrepresent this story to her mother, by saying that Hades "forced" her to eat it, her gesture may be less the product of affection for her husband (a motif that only occurs in much later versions of the story and may be suggested here by the eating of the pomegranate) than of a desire to please her mother.[159] Indeed, contemporary studies show as typical a daughter's eagerness to protect her mother and preserve their mutual attachment at all costs.[160]

Hirsch has argued that at the conclusion of the *Hymn* Persephone succeeds in enacting the girl's typical bisexual oscillation between mother and father, which successfully concludes in a firm commitment to heterosexuality as well as to a continued and deep-rooted identification with the mother.[161] For Irigaray, Persephone represents divided feminity only partially captured by patriarchy, a paradoxical being who is never alone, "immortally and never more a virgin"[162] but inhabits two mutually exclusive domains as her mother's daughter as well as her husband's wife.[163] Hence Persephone becomes an inscrutable, potentially deceptive figure, never fully known, who inhabits, insofar as she has a self, an ambiguous space between two powerful presences.[164] This emotional oscillation between mother and husband is explicit in later versions of the myth, and structurally the case

[158] See Seaford 1988 and 1990.

[159] Arthur (this volume) and Faraone 1990:237–38 both argue for an element of successful sexual seduction here—especially in the eating of the pomegranate (see the Commentary on lines 371–73 for further detail). Faraone 238 with n.41 suggests that in marriage by abduction (although this may be only a mythical alternative in the historical context in which the *Hymn* was composed) the bride may be required to resist her kidnapper and acquiesce only in the face of irresistible magic.

[160] Low 1982 and 1984:2–3.

[161] Hirsch 1989:101–2.

[162] Irigaray 1991:114.

[163] Ibid.:112–17.

[164] Ibid.:112–17. Making a wordplay on *volé*, *violée*, and *voilée*, Irigaray suggests that "*Kore*-Persephone escapes perspective. Her depth, in all its dimensions, never offers itself up to the gaze, whatever the point of view may be. She passes beyond all boundaries. Withholding herself from appearance, even without Hades. Whence the veils which she is supposed to cover herself with so that she may give herself out to be—what she is not" (115).

here; but the *Hymn* commits Persephone more to accepting than to emotionally embracing heterosexuality. In the world below, Persephone pines with desire—*pothos* (344), a word that often has sexual overtones—for her mother as Demeter does for her (201 and 304); and, as was said earlier, the language she uses to describe the eating of the pomegranate seed echoes the violence of the original abduction and contains no hint of seduction. Indeed, one might argue in Freudian terms that the *Hymn* partially undoes the girl's oedipal crisis, by authorizing and permitting her original passion for the mother.

Too great an attachment between mother and daughter may be in any society psychopathological, but the final emergence of a relation of "mature dependence" between Demeter and her daughter, to use a term borrowed from Chodorow's essay, is in the Greek context both desirable and functional. This is particularly the case in a world of patriarchal marriage, where the development of the nuclear family, which isolated women yet more from nurturing relations with other women, threatened at least in this respect the stability of female identity. At the same time, the text does offer a possible hint of the psychological ambiguity in the figure of Persephone suggested by Irigaray. Persephone's version of the abduction, in a fashion anomalous in epic, differs in a number of respects from that of the impersonal narrator (see further the Commentary on lines 405–40). The poem has already made a striking move from social to psychological reality by making the bride a figure who actively mediates between mother and husband, rather than a figure who mediates (often passively, as a gift from one man to another) between father and husband. As noted above, to the degree that Persephone represents her eating of the pomegranate as force-feeding, the text opens the possibility that she is adapting the story for her mother's benefit; alternatively, the poem suggestively endows her with speech and subjectivity at the moment that she has come into her mature identity as a figure who eternally moves from one sphere of the cosmos and from one powerful adult to another.

At the close of the *Hymn*, the pain of the goddesses' annual separations is again mediated by other females. Chodorow emphasizes the role that other closely related women can play in easing the separation between mother and daughter as the daughter matures. Hekate, who previously assimilated herself closely to Demeter, will stand in for Demeter as a ritual attendant, perhaps even a maternal substitute, to Persephone in the future. Rheia descends from heaven to bring her daughter and granddaughter to new honors on Olympus.[165] Rheia here mediates between Zeus and Demeter. Although she, along with Demeter's grandmother Gaia, has remained allied with the father Zeus until this point, her unusual role of divine messenger,

---

[165] On the importance of Rheia's role, see also Arthur 1977 (this volume).

where Iris or Hermes would have been expected, seems to stress a reconstituting of intergenerational bonds between mother and daughter. Demeter and Rheia feel mutual pleasure in seeing each other, just as did Persephone and Demeter (458, 385).

From at least the fifth century on, Demeter and her mother were closely identified in myth and cult, just as Demeter and Persephone become virtual doubles of each other; Demeter is twice called Rheia's daughter in the poem (60, 75). Rheia, like Demeter elsewhere in the poem (1, 297, 315), is fair-tressed (442; also 60 and 75). Both Hekate and Rheia wear a shining veil in this scene (438, 459; see also 25). The veil presents the image of the female integrated into the patriarchal order and contrasts with the torn veil of Demeter at the start of the poem.[166] The world of women shattered at the outset is thus symbolically regenerated in a new context and with new constraints. Similarly, Demeter's close bonds with the women of Eleusis, severed by Metaneira's spying and the goddess's subsequent wrath, are implicitly reinstated in the founding of the Mysteries, whose initiates are to be loved by the two goddesses.[167] A parallel male case is the relation of Telemachos and Odysseus in the *Odyssey*; Telemachos, who has grown up uncertain of his identity in the absence of his father, gradually matures in searching for his father and discovering their mutual likeness. The poem closes with the rebonding of father, son, and grandfather in a military context.

Clinical experience has shown that when a daughter successfully renews her bond with her mother after adolescence, both mother and daughter discover more fully their own capacities for nurturance.[168] Similarly, the poem's conclusion, which endows the goddesses with greater powers (if less autonomy) than before, is reinforced on a psychological level by the dynamics of the mother/daughter relationship. If the separation between mother and daughter brutally inflicted by Hades and Zeus is unnecessarily radical,[169] the daughter's sexual maturity and a less radical separation from her mother are both necessary and empowering. As Hirsch has argued, Hades (if inadvertently) gives Demeter and Persephone a story and an involvement in a larger world than they would have had in stagnant isolation (or "infantile plenitude."). As Hirsch puts it:

> The cyclicity of the resolution, in which Persephone is to her mother alternately alive and dead, distant and symbiotic, offers an alternative to oedipal narratives

[166] On the veil, see Nagler 1974:52.

[167] Arthur 1977 (this volume) sees the all-night vigil of the women in Keleos's household as a step in reconstituting female bonds on the mortal level.

[168] Spitz 1989:170,n.62 and 1990:418.

[169] The myth includes the possibility of incest between father and daughter. In the Orphic *Rhapsodies* (Orphic frag. 303 Kern) and other versions of the myth, Zeus inseminates Persephone in Crete, thereby producing Dionysos.

structured according to principles of linear repetition. The "Hymn to Demeter" thus both inscribes the story of mother and daughter within patriarchal
reality and allows it to mark a feminine difference. Hades occasions both the
separation and a narrative which will repair the breech.[170]

The cyclical aspects of the narrative bring the psychological and ritual aspects of the cult together. Initiates (in contrast to rites of initiation into
adulthood, for example) could renew themselves by participating in the
rites at Eleusis as often as they wished and, by continually propitiating the
goddesses, ensured the agricultural cycle.

Psychologically speaking, then, the Mysteries logically arise from the
reunion of the separated mother and daughter, who now take on maternal
responsibilities to all humankind. The power of a nurturing maternal figure
to mute the power of death, either literally, as in the case of Demeter's rescue
of Persephone, or through hero cult, as in the case of Demophoön, is
imaginatively extended for the initiate into the world beyond. Just as both
Persephone and Demophoön find all joy in the arms of Demeter, the initiate
renews in death his or her original unity with the mother and dissolves the
anxiety occasioned by all of life's major separations: the first realization of
separateness from the mother, maturity, and death. The closing positive
fantasy of regression into maternal plentitude diffuses the poem's earlier
vision of Demeter as an angry, even vengeful mother, who can be distracted
from her loss of Persephone, abandon Demophoön to mortality, and
threaten to starve with her famine the mortals who treated her with perfect
hospitality while in disguise and who built her a temple once she revealed
her identity. To some extent the conclusion, which as Rich emphasizes
undoes the rape of Persephone and rescues her from death,[171] also obscures
the nature of Demeter's power to affect the world, which is ultimately
limited to a withdrawal of fertility.

Indeed, as Kerényi points out, the resolution effected by Demeter in the
Hymn clashes with cultural realities external to it.[172] Just as Demeter cannot
immortalize Demophoön, there is a sense in which she cannot truly bring
back her inaccessible, "dead" daughter to earth. Insofar as Persephone represents the grain itself, and her disappearances and returns are associated
with the natural cycle, she cannot be truly immortal.[173] Human brides do
not spend two-thirds of their married lives with their mothers, and Persephone's absence from the underworld is never mentioned in accounts of
that place. Nor do mortal women, or even other goddesses, successfully
resist patriarchal authority to the (limited) degree that Demeter initially

[170] Hirsch 1989:5–6.
[171] See the opening quotation in this essay.
[172] Kerényi 1967a:148–50. See also Saintillan 1986:68.
[173] Szepes 1975:30.

does against the plan of Zeus.[174] Yet if the resolution of the myth resists "reality," it does not resist a psychological reality so powerful that it can transcend death and the limits of the universe. The successful maturation of a daughter does involve, and most especially in a traditional society, a symbolic reunity of mother and daughter. In ancient Greek society this seems to have occurred for women in the context of religious cult, particularly in all female cults special to Demeter (see the section on "Women's Rites for Demeter," Part 1 of this volume),[175] and in the repetition of the lives of mother and daughter from one generation to the next. For ancient women, Demeter and Persephone may have represented the extraordinary endurance of the bond between women of different generations in the same family, a bond that carried women through the physical separation from their family that could so radically mark their lives. Even in the case of death, as we see in the funerary lamentations of women in the rural villages of modern Greece, members of a family and especially mothers and daughters can be linked by women's special skill to remember and vividly make present the past.[176]

The *Hymn* idealizes the mother/daughter relation, just as the *Odyssey* idealizes the relation between father and son. The psychology of the Homeric poems, like the rest of Panhellenic epic, serves to celebrate the social context it describes; hence, unlike tragedy, it tends to suppress myths and motifs of intrafamilial conflict.[177] The *Hymn* represents natural strains between mother and a growing daughter as imposed from without, and the *Odyssey* does the same with the relation between father and son. Unlike the tension-fraught mother/daughter relation in the tragic versions of the Klytemnestra/Elektra story, the *Hymn* distances the father psychologically. This is emphasized by Zeus's physical absence throughout the narrative, but it may be partly explained as well by the poem's stress (highly unusual in Western literature) on the mother's rather than the daughter's perspective.[178] Whereas many later versions of the myth include a greater emphasis

[174] If I have seemed to de-emphasize this aspect of the poem, the reason is that it has been so well articulated by Arthur 1977 (this volume).

[175] Bacchic rites also made women forgetful of the separation created by marriage.

[176] See Alexiou 1974, Caraveli 1986, and Caraveli-Chavez 1980. It is very likely, given what we know of women's important role in death ritual in antiquity, that similar traditions obtained then.

[177] The husband/wife relation is an exception to this restraint. The *Hymn* only hints at the potential conflict between father and daughter that might arise in this story, by having Persephone cry out for help to the father who is the cause of her difficulties.

[178] Indeed, the *Hymn* may be said to correct both the romanticizing of the mother/daughter relation in object-relations theory (its idealizing is intrinsic to its genre and not problematic), and the overemphasis on the psychology of the daughter, rather than the mother, in modern psychoanalytic discussion generally. Hirsch's 1989 work has emphasized this latter point. See also Chodorow and Contratto 1982 and Spitz 1989 and 1990.

on Persephone's own experience, or balance her devotion to her mother with a recognition of her emerging heterosexuality and sexual pleasure, this version remains dominated by Demeter; more than all other versions, it validates not only the mother's grief and capacity for nurturance, but her anger, her power, and her insistence on preserving the maternal genealogy against the threat of patriarchy. For, although the text deliberately mutes the effects of Demeter's anger (Demophoön does not die, as in other versions of the myth, and humanity is saved from famine and given the Mysteries) and limits her power, it does not view maternal rage and female desire for autonomy in the same negative terms as does other archaic and classical Greek literature.[179]

Many of the archaic lyrics of Sappho also address the pain caused by the departure of beloved and loving women from her circle. Although, in contrast to the *Hymn*, the fragments ignore the reason for the painful separation, the most likely explanation is marriage. Sappho—unable to achieve the miraculous cyclical reunion of the goddesses—concentrates instead on preserving a memory of an idyllic female-centered past, characterized (as in the *Hymn*) with the imagery of meadows, flowers, and other plants. This memory will serve to unite the separated women and preserve their love. In the following papyrus fragment (frag. 94), Sappho soothes the acute suffering of a departing woman by reminding her of the pleasures she experienced under Sappho's care:[180]

> "Honestly, I wish I were dead."
> Weeping many tears she left me behind
> and said this also.
> "Oh what terrible things we have suffered,
> Sappho. I leave you against my will, I swear."
>
> And I made this reply to her.
> "Go in joy and remember me,
> for you know how we cherished you.
>
> If not, I want
> to remind you . . .
> of the beautiful things we shared.

[179] On maternal rage in Greek literature, see Loraux 1990.

[180] The text of both fragments below (excepting line 17 of frag. 96, where I accept that of Page 1955) is that of Campbell 1982. Ellipsis points represent material lost from the text. I found the translation of Snyder 1989 very helpful in making my own. A fragment of the poet Erinna's *Distaff* also expresses at a later period the same pain over the departure of a beloved friend at marriage. In that poem the poet mourns the death of her childhood friend Baukis, who has recently married and left her friend Erinna alone with the memories of their delightful past.

At my side you decked yourself
with many wreaths of violets
and roses and crocuses.

And many plaited garlands
made of flowers . . .
round your tender neck,

And . . . with much royal
and flowery perfume . . . .
you anointed . . . .

And on soft beds
. . . delicate . . .
you released your desire

And there was no . . .
no shrine . . .
from which we were absent,

. . . no grove . . . nor choral dance . . .

Even women who are separated by great geographical distances (Sardis is in Asia Minor, across the water and some distance inland from the island of Lesbos) can be united, as in Sappho's Frag. 96 below, by the simile of the moon whose light bridges their two worlds. The comparison of the beautiful woman to a goddess in this fragment (Odysseus plays the same compliment to Nausikää in *Odyssey* 6) serves both to praise the mortal woman and to express once again the irrevocable distance between divine and mortal experience. The mortal women have only the fragile weapon of song and the memory of song to assuage their loss.

. . . [Sardis?]
Turning her mind here often . . .

[She revered you]
like a goddess easy to recognize.
Above all she loved your song.

But now she stands out among Lydian women
just as after sunset
the rosy-fingered moon

surpasses all the stars; its light
stretches equally over the salty sea
and over fields with many flowers.

And the dew melts beautifully,
and roses bloom, and tender chervil
and flowery melilot.

But she, often pacing to and fro,
remembers gentle Attis with desire;
Surely your fate weighs on her tender heart.

. . . .

It is not easy for us to rival
the beautiful form of goddesses,
. . . . but you . . .

As a probably older woman addressing unrelated and probably younger women,[181] Sappho can express the necessary "maternal" acceptance of this transition to separation and adulthood in a manner that might be more difficult for the biological mother, as well as a passion preparatory for the experience of adult sexuality. Like Sappho's poetry,[182] the myth told in the *Hymn* probably served in the context of the women's rites of the Thesmophoria to promote women's psychological survival in a context where young daughters are separated at marriage from their family and a circle of other women and to find religious significance in the mother's and daughter's transcendence of their deathlike separation. The *Hymn*, however, addresses a far broader audience, and in this case the emphasis on female experience at the center of an important eschatological cult open to a wide range of participants becomes more difficult to explain.

The Psychology of the Mysteries

The *Hymn to Demeter* assumes a strong division between the private lives of women and the public lives of men in a polis, and even within the household itself. In this it is similar to the picture we receive of Hektor's Troy in the *Iliad*, where Hektor makes a point of stressing to his wife Andromache that women are responsible for the household, and men for war and other issues external to the household (6.490–93). The *Odyssey*, by contrast, establishes somewhat more fluid boundaries between the worlds of the two sexes. There men and women can dine and converse with strangers in the public

---

[181] Intense emotional relations among women in these circles may have occurred between those of nearly the same age as well as between those who are older and younger.

[182] The Spartan poet Alkman's Partheneia, or "Maiden Songs," composed for young women on the verge of marriage (and for the purpose of preparing girls for this transition), also stress the desire of women for women, rather than the desirability of marriage.

sections of the house, and women can directly influence the affairs of men in that context. In the *Hymn* men and women are shown as living separately from each other; the girls go to the well but adult women seem to remain at home, and the daughters of Keleos are concerned to find an old woman alone and outdoors. (In the Orphic version of the myth, by contrast, the mother goes to the well with her daughters [Orphic frag. 49K]). Women are protected by the walls of the city (see 150–51). Even the two goddesses are represented, at least at the opening of the poem, in an exclusively female company. Demeter adopts the disguise of a helpless old woman and lives in an entirely female environment while she is withdrawing from the gods and carrying out her secret designs against Zeus; she moves into a public and male sphere when she returns to her divine shape, commands the building of her temple, and exercises her powers over agriculture (powers intimately connected with fertility) by creating the famine.

Those divine activities that are later imitated in the rites at Eleusis take place in the private sphere of women, whereas men are given a role in making participation in Demeter's secrets accessible to a wider world. (This is a role they actually played, with the help of priestesses, in the Mysteries. The Suda [under the listing Eumolpos] has Demeter communicate the Mysteries to Keleos's daughters [see also Pausanias 1.38.3].) Women's role in presiding over aspects of the rites founded at Eleusis is another omission in the *Hymn* which reinforces the boundaries between male and female worlds.) Metaneira becomes a witness to Demeter's secrets and transmits the goddess's words to Keleos. As in the case of Hesiod's first woman, Pandora, it is feminine curiosity that condemns Demophoön and all humankind once more to mortality.[183] In offering the goddess hospitality, Metaneira and her women engage with Demeter in enacting some of what later became the initial rites at Eleusis (seating Demeter on a stool covered with a fleece and breaking her fast with the *kykeôn* and her silence by *aischrologia*). Demeter mourns among and is consoled by women; child care is an additional solace. In the women's quarters of the house, she first plays the role of nurse to a mortal and reveals her divinity in a frightening epiphany. Iambe is represented as intuitively aware of Demeter's needs; she tells her jokes (secrets) relating to maternity and female sexuality. On the divine level, it is Hekate alone who shares Demeter's search for her daughter, and Rheia who conducts Demeter and Persephone back to Olympus.

Yet the men of Eleusis are the first initiates into the rites; the male child Demophoön may be the first symbolic initiate and during the Mysteries a male "child from the hearth" was initiated for the city. Men build Demeter's temple and later establish her cult. In short, the text seems to stress that the

---

[183] See Ramnoux 1959:139. In Hyginus 147, both parents witness Demeter's secrets, but the father intervenes. See also Servius on Vergil *Georgics* 1.19, Lactantius on Statius *Thebaid* 2.382, *Mythographi Vaticani* 2.97.

Mysteries emerge from the private and even secret world of female experience; on both the divine and human level the male role is to integrate these Mysteries into the larger social structure and to control the access of the initiands to the rites. In sum, mortal women experience Demeter's suffering both in their encounter with her in the poem and, because Demeter's experience is a female one, in the process of their own lives; men are initiated into these Mysteries. A similar cult aetiology occurs in Euripides' *Bacchae*. There Dionysos brings his cult to Thebes with a chorus of Asian women and the maddened women of Thebes are the first initiates into Dionysos's mysteries. King Pentheus is destroyed for prying into the women's secrets. Only after the god establishes the cult in the Theban polis at the conclusion of the play do the men of the city become full participants in rites for Dionysos.

Demeter, as a goddess of grain, and Korê, who is often associated in myth with the grain itself, have, like mortal women in Greek cult, a special symbolic relation to and power over nature. The promise of happiness in the Mysteries was almost certainly linked with the natural cycle itself, with its endless and necessary alternations between procreation and death. The Mysteries and the representations of mortal women in Greek poetry both avail themselves of a common cultural vocabulary. Greek literature tends to link the female more strongly than the male with nature as opposed to culture, darkness as opposed to light, with periphery as opposed to the center, and with the ability to mediate among the spheres of nature, the gods, and humankind. In Greek myth women are more often treated as an undifferentiated race of their own, whereas men are categorized in relation to specific positions in the social hierarchy. In the poems of Hesiod and Semonides, women are created as a separate race from men, who are often described as born from the land that they grow up to defend.[184]

As we saw above, goddesses are not generally limited by the same constraints and associations as are mortal women. Yet to the degree that the poem links the two goddesses with the experiences of mortal women, they take on these same associations.[185] Just as women are often treated in poetry as an undifferentiated group, the goddesses become indistinguishable from each other in cult. The Mysteries involve an undifferentiated group of initiates, who leave behind their roles in the social and political hierarchy, coming face to face with marriage, death, and birth; they occur in a dark and private space; they mediate between earth, Hades, and Olympus. The geographical peripherality of Eleusis itself, its location outside the city, becomes a source of its special distinction.[186] Similarly, at least in the classical city-state, Athens continued to foster the participation and symbolic importance

---

[184] See further, Loraux 1978 on the Greek "race of women."

[185] Women take on comparable associations as participants in the rites of Dionysos.

[186] Geographical peripherality does not, as De Polignac 1984 has shown, mean that a cult is peripheral to a city's religious system. See further below.

of women in the religious sphere even while it excluded them from the rest of public life. It is not surprising, then, that in Greece the Mysteries are imagined to emerge from a "female" experience. Indeed, the degree to which the male initiate engaged in a symbolic identification with female deity may be reflected in the story that the eccentric emperor Gallienus commemorated his initiation by putting Gallienae Augustae in the feminine on his coins.[187]

If the Mysteries in some sense permit universal access to (and imitation of) a secret or private world of the female, and to the mysteries of death, fertility, magic, and even anger connected with her, one can perhaps understand some of its appeal—so puzzling to Jung—for the male initiate. The comic poet Aristophanes' play *Thesmophoriazusae* (*Women at the Thesmophoria*) and other stories about the festival certainly express a combination of fear and fascination about a rite of Demeter from which men are by contrast excluded.[188] In Demeter's festival the Haloa (also held at Eleusis), the women remained within whispering secrets and consuming foods symbolizing fertility, while the men remained outside telling stories about Demeter's gift of agriculture to humankind. This gender distinction at the Haloa perhaps significantly corresponds to two different important Attic/Eleusinian versions of the myth: the Panhellenic *Hymn* stresses female experience and female secrets, whereas those (apparently local) versions of the myth that include the origin of agriculture and the role of mortals in winning the Mysteries through their help to Demeter give (as do the procedures of the Mysteries themselves and most other versions of the myth) a far more prominent role to men.[189]

Demophoön's access to the nursing of Demeter is abruptly cut off in infancy. Similarly, the movement from infancy to youth in Greek myth and cult involved a symbolic or literal break with the mother: the young boy leaves to join peers and tutors, the girl to marry at a young age. Both *Hymn* and cult seem to offer male and female initiates a romantic regression into childhood fusion with the mother and promise an end to the mother's potential anger. Demophoön cries bitterly over the loss of Demeter's embrace: her fragrance, her immortalizing breath, and touch. Persephone, who wastes with desire for her mother in the underworld, is radiant with joy to recover this embrace. Such fusion would in life be dangerous, for permanent immaturity is a psychological death. Myths in which goddesses take mortal lovers, for example, are nearly always permanently disabling to the

---

[187] *Zeitschrift für Numismatik* 38 (1928) 188. See Ferguson 1989:106.

[188] See Detienne 1989.

[189] If we knew more about circumstances in which the *Hymn* was performed, we could better interpret the difference in emphasis on the roles of men and women in different versions of the myth. Was this version or something like it perhaps also or even originally used in all female festivals?

lover (Dawn's lover Tithonos, who won immortality but continues to age, regresses into infantile senility), and girls who reject marriage generally meet with misfortune.

But translated metaphorically to the initiate's fortunate relation to the earth and its fertility, over which the maternal Demeter presides, fusion with the mother—of all sorts—is no longer dangerous. The poem celebrates Persephone's desire to return to the mother's embrace, but the fantasy of male regression into maternal plenitude was by no means an isolated one in the ancient world. In Euripides' *Ion*, the adolescent hero, in a context where the story of the rape of his lost mother Creusa suggests Persephone's abduction, acknowledges the pain that he has felt over losing the nurturance of the mother he never had (308ff.). In Sophocles' *Oedipous the King*, to dream of sleeping with a mother is common and harmless (981–82). For the second-century C.E. writer on dreams Artemidoros, such dreams (apparently common given the number and range of the dreams discussed) can presage good fortune for the male dreamer. In dreams normal (face-to-face) intercourse with a living mother is lucky for laborers, because a trade is a "mother"; for public figures and for those away from home, the dream is lucky because the earth or the native land is "mother" (a point exploited in Aeschylus's tragedy *Seven Against Thebes*); and for the sick the dream is lucky because nature is a "mother."[190]

In the cult at Eleusis, and by the end of this poem, Persephone has become a figure functionally identical with Demeter herself; we do have evidence beyond the poem's own emphasis on Demeter's role as nurse (see especially Sophocles *Oedipous at Kolonos* 1050) that the goddesses served as symbolic nurses to the mystery initiates. We cannot be certain of the language and imagery used in the secret rites at Eleusis, but it may not be illegitimate to borrow an image from an Orphic gold leaf.[191] In the timeless and static world of death, the initiate (of either sex) perhaps imagined becoming a divine "child" eternally nursed in the bosom of Persephone:[192]

> Queen of the dead, pure I come from a pure people.
> And you, Eukles, Eubouleus and the other immortal gods.
> For I claim to be of your blessed race,
> but fate and the other immortal gods subdued me
> . . . . a flash of lightning.

[190] *The Interpretations of Dreams* 1.79. For a translation and commentary, see White 1975.

[191] The gold leaves, generally found in grave mounds, apparently instructed the dead initiate in Bacchic/Orphic rituals (probably related or similar to the rites at Eleusis) about what to do and say as he or she entered the world below.

[192] Nursing could be used in myth to symbolize both adoption and the transition from mortality to immortality. Demeter does not give her breast to Demophoön in the *Hymn*, but after death Herakles nursed at the breast of Hera, who gave up her wrath against him and accepted him as "son" and a fellow divinity.

I have flown out of the sorrowful, wearisome wheel,
I have come with swift feet for the crown of my desire,
I sink into the bosom of Our Lady, the Queen of the Dead
"Blessed and happy one, you shall be a god instead of a mortal."
A kid I fell into the milk.

(Orphic Fragment 32c Kern)

The *Hymn to Demeter* and the Polis

The *Hymn*, unlike Homeric epic and later versions of the myth itself, de-emphasizes the role of specific leaders at Eleusis in favor of representing the cult as given to all. Keleos's role is limited to calling an assembly. He conveys Demeter's instructions to a barely differentiated group of cooperative Eleusinian princes and the whole people to build the temple (271, *teuxontôn pas dêmos upai polin*).[193] The Mysteries are given to specific princes to administer, but their roles in the rites are not, as elsewhere, distinguished. As was mentioned earlier, the women of Eleusis care for each other in a fashion that dissolves the boundaries between households. The *Hymn* saves for its climax the rites and their benefits to every initiate, not the celebration of those who preside over them. By downplaying the importance of the hospitality of individuals to the outcome, and by generalizing rewards and punishments from individuals to humanity, the poem makes repeatedly clear that Demeter's activities are of significance to the whole polis, and that Keleos and his household are in the end largely intermediaries in the creation of the cult. This concern with the city is by no means absent from the Homeric epics.[194] But the *Hymn*'s emphasis on cooperative as opposed to competitive values among the Eleusinian leaders (and their wives), and the importance placed on the founding of cult (both the building of the temple and the later establishing of a hero cult for Demophoön) as a mode of uniting and giving a special identity to a polis lends a new emphasis to elements more latent in Homer.[195]

As a whole, the *Hymn*, as we have seen, aims to be part of the Panhellenic tradition descended from the two great Homeric epics. Yet the pointed contrast between male and female worlds and the stress on the importance

[193] On the status of the leaders at Eleusis, see the Commentary on lines 96–97 and 153ff.

[194] Many have seen a similar interest in the emerging polis in the Homeric portrait of Troy. The society pictured in the epics already has many of the institutions of the later city-state: a public assembly, judicial authority, communal ritual, an urban center with public buildings, and the sense of belonging to a polis (see *Odyssey* 1.170 and *Iliad* 12.243).

[195] At Homeric *Hymn to Apollo* 294–99, a Panhellenic cult is founded at Delphi in a similar fashion. Apollo lays the foundations, the heroes Trophonios and Agamedes lay down a stone footing, and countless men build the temple out of stones. On the association between temple building and public cults, see Kolb 1977 and Shapiro 1989.

of the city are not the only subtle differences in emphasis between the *Hymn* and its famous predecessors. The *Hymn* retains the interest of earlier Pan-hellenic epic in systematizing Greek cosmology; yet the problematizing of divine exogamy and the respect accorded Demeter for her resistance to Zeus's cosmological politics by no means mimics precisely the representation of similar issues in Homer and Hesiod. The *Hymn* closes with the establishment of a modified relation between gods and mortals (the worlds of mortals and immortals are still separate, but Demeter and Persephone promise to mitigate the pain of the mortal lot for initiates) and a new set of possibilities for the afterlife that is again at odds with the Panhellenic epics familiar to us—even though the *Hymn* aims to give the Mysteries status within that earlier tradition.

The *Hymn*'s representation of both Eleusinian society and cosmological politics may thus be partially explained as a response to the evolution of the Greek city-state and may indirectly reflect tensions in the world contemporary to it. Yet even if the differences in emphasis that we see between the *Hymn* and the Homeric epics are primarily the product of thematic considerations rather than historical changes, the *Hymn*'s sensitivity to these issues may well account for the later success of the myth and the Mysteries in the classical city-state. For this reason, it is worth engaging in what is primarily a speculative consideration of the ways in which the *Hymn*'s version of the myth (with its cult) might be a product of one set of historical changes—or an expression of a political and social climate that produced complementary developments in religious, social, and political spheres—and ideally suited to play an important role in the classical polis.

After 750 B.C.E. hereditary privilege began to play a different role in Greek society than it did in the Homeric poems—although it continued to be important. To the degree that the *Hymn*, probably composed from 650–550 B.C.E., downplays hereditary privilege in favor of stressing the relation of the events of the myth to the whole of Eleusis and all its citizens (important and unimportant), it may reflect the beginnings of such a transition, or the political and social climate that enabled this transition, as well as the poem's effort to insert itself into a Panhellenic tradition. In Athens this transition was already in process with the reforms of Solon in the early sixth century (Eleusis was probably not independent from Athens at this time. See the Appendix on "Athens and Eleusis" for further discussion).

Furthermore, it was characteristic of the sixth-century tyrants and, as Aristotle tells us, of democracy, to reduce the number and broaden the base of old aristocratic cults (*Politics* 1319b). The emphasis in the *Hymn* on Demeter's gifts of the Mysteries to a broad and apparently unrestricted group of potential initiates among humankind and its de-emphasis of the role of the priestly families who (at least later) ran the cult may simply reflect the *Hymn*'s ambitions to establish Eleusis as a Panhellenic religious site, yet it could also reflect or anticipate the earlier stages of this broadening of access to religious cults in the archaic polis (it may derive as well from the nature of the goddess and her cults). The whole city builds the temple; noninitiates will not receive the same benefits (*homoiôn aisan*, 481–82) as initiates will. Later texts suggest that initiates themselves received a similar lot in the underworld. Although the *Hymn* is here contrasting the initiate with the noninitiate, a certain equality of opportunity for initiates—which may mean little among the powerless dead—may be implied as well. The word *homoios* was later used of those who had equal access to civic office and earlier of honor (e.g., *homoiês timês*, *Iliad* 1.278).

Whatever the motives for the *Hymn*'s insistence on the cult's accessibility, both the myth and its cult were perfectly adapted to the important role that they acquired in later centuries in Athens. As stressed earlier, the Homeric poems made their promise of immortal fame or Elysion to the aristocratic warrior, whereas the Mysteries gave their benefits to all mortals, regardless of sex and social status. These benefits were won not by good birth and individual achievement, but through initiation and submission to a mass collective experience in which all share equally. Furthermore, hoplites, citizens wealthy enough to purchase arms, played a central role in the army of the city-state. In contrast to the Homeric warrior, they were expected to pursue not individual glory but the glory of their city. They fought side by side, protecting each other with their shields in formations that created a strong dependence between one soldier and the other. The fragments of the archaic poets Archilochos, Tyrtaios, and others already reflect the group ethic of hoplite warfare (and its downplaying of the heroism of aristocratic individuals) by the late seventh century. The Mysteries, by undercutting the need for individual fame to counter the miseries of death, were perfectly adapted to bolster, if only indirectly, this new military ideology.[196] The cult's accessibility served equally well and for the same reasons the ideology of an emerging democracy (or a sixth-century tyranny). In Aristophanes' *Frogs*, for example, the chorus of mystery initiates is virtually equated with the citizen body of Athens.

The *Hymn*'s effort to celebrate Demeter and her important honors within the Olympic order may again represent a double effort to modify Panhellenic epic and to reflect (or anticipate) changing civic realities. Demeter apparently did not begin as a goddess of the city, like those gods associated

---

[196] The massed formations of hoplite warfare are already present in Homer (see Latacz 1977, Pritchett 1985, and Morris 1987:195–201). But the ideology associated with hoplite warfare in the late archaic and classical periods—the de-emphasis of individual glory and the social responsibility of the warrior to the welfare of the whole city—seems to appear first in the late seventh century and reached its height in the Attic funeral orations of the fifth and fourth centuries. The Homeric warrior's commitment to group welfare is sporadic at best. On this ideology see esp. Detienne in Vernant, ed. 1968.

with war or political power (Athena etc.).[197] Like Dionysos, she plays a minimal role in Hesiod or the Homeric epics (although she was important in other archaic poetry, like Pamphos's hymn, or in Orphic versions of the myth). Her cults, though early and widespread, were more often located at first on the borders of cities, not at the civic center—as at Eleusis, where her temple is built on a rise at the edge of the city space.[198] Her powers, extending over agriculture, belong to the world of the country; her special association with female lives and rites link her with a social and religious context separate from the political life that excluded women; initiatory rites such as those at Eleusis often occur in marginal territory as well. Similarly, the cult of Artemis at Brauron at which young girls were initiated was also located at the borders of Attika, and the Thesmophoria, like cults of Dionysos, was thought to have originated outside the city. Demeter inaugurated culture with agriculture and with the "laws" she gave to humankind, but the culture she established is also not civic.[199]

A remote or marginal geographical location for her cults did not mean that Demeter played an unimportant role in the religious life of the polis, however. The agricultural festivals of Demeter and Dionysos became of central importance in the emerging city-state, and there is strong evidence of Attic interest in the Mysteries from the mid-sixth century.[200] From the archaic period on, cults of Demeter and Dionysos played a central role in linking civic and deme cults and in binding rural Attika to the city center.[201] The *Hymn*'s attempt to assert Panhellenic importance for Demeter's cult at Eleusis and to incorporate Demeter's myth into the traditional Olympic cosmology of epic, then, coincided with or anticipated a process of enhancing the role of Demeter and her Mysteries that was consolidated and expanded in the later sixth and fifth centuries.[202]

[197] Other deities, however, such as Hera, who had close links with the family, did have important civic cults at an early date. Demeter herself occasionally became a patron goddess of some cities.

[198] Farnell 1906:vol. 3, esp. 79–80 asserts that the early Demeter was apolitical. The temple at Agrai and the Eleusinion had a similar location (see Richardson 1974:250). Osborne 1985:esp. ch. 8 stresses the important role played by the geographical location of such key cults, which were often dedicated to goddesses, in Attika. On the general issue of the relation between the city and cults located outside the civic center (the *astu* and the *chôra*) in archaic Greek and Attic cults, see De Polignac 1984.

[199] The meaning of Demeter Thesmophoros (see Diodorus Siculus *Bibliotheca* 5.5.2–3) is contested (see, for example, Farnell 1906:76ff. and Brumfield 1981:70–73), but the *thesmoi* or "laws," that Demeter gives are probably traditional customs or perhaps the rites themselves, rather than civic statutes.

[200] Connor 1990 and Kolb 1977 have contested the role of the tyrant Peisistratos in these changes.

[201] See De Polignac 1984 and Osborne 1985 and the discussion under "Eleusis and Athens" in the Appendix to this essay.

[202] On the question of the date of Athenian incorporation of Eleusis and the *Hymn*'s silence on Athens, see again the Appendix on "Eleusis and Athens."

In Attika festivals of Demeter were celebrated at every stage of the agricultural year, and Demeter's temple the Eleusinion was built in a prominent position on the north slope of the Akropolis. Athens began to exploit the propaganda value both of the Mysteries and of its claim to be the site of the origin and dissemination of agriculture. The site of the Mysteries also offered more than ideological advantages to Athens. Its strategic presence on an important border of Attika is discussed in more detail in the first part of the Appendix to this essay. Due to the high quality of its land, Eleusis also became the major source of wheat production in Attika. During the population growth of the archaic age, Athens was forced to import grain from abroad, and Solon enacted laws restricting the exportation of agricultural products except olives and olive oil (Plutarch *Solon* 24). Perhaps in recognition of the importance of the demes to its successful functioning, Athens also continued to give important autonomy to local cults and independence to its demes, of which Eleusis became one.[203]

As we have seen, Demeter resists the exogamous, virilocal marriage that Zeus imposed on Persephone and insists on a partial return to the endogamy standard in Olympian marriages. The poem may, of course, raise general questions about the price paid by mother and daughter in accepting marriage as an institution per se, rather than about specific forms of marriage. Nevertheless, the attempt to establish a closed community played an important role in most emerging city-states in archaic Greece (and perhaps earlier),[204] and the *Hymn*'s problematizing of exogamy and validation of endogamy may reflect this transition. Aristocratic marriage in Homer, exogamous for the most part, often served to create bonds between two powerful and independent leaders from different communities. Through the relation established by marriage, a woman's father and husband could expect advantages beyond the bonds created by common kin and the wealth acquired in an exchange of gifts. Relatives were expected to extend both hospitality and military aid to each other. By contrast, the emerging city-state, and Athens in particular, eventually discouraged marriages that linked Athenians to families outside the city, partly in order to prevent powerful aristocrats from using marriage to play games with foreign policy on their own.[205] Marriages among aristocrats on the Homeric model continued to occur throughout the sixth century and even into the fifth, yet the state's gradual extension of legal control over the household and its increased

---

[203] Osborne 1985:esp. ch. 8 argues that although Athens incorporated Eleusis into its religious system, the process worked both ways. Eleusis's autonomy stemmed from its power as a sacred site, and the participants in the Mysteries temporarily left civic ideology.

[204] Bremmer 1983, citing examples from myth and Bourdieu's argument (1977:58–71) that in uncertain political and economic situations families tend toward endogamous marriage patterns, thinks that Dark Age aristocrats and peasants probably shared this strategy.

[205] Yet, as Herman 1987 has argued, archaic guest friendships remained.

regulation of the lives of women reportedly began with the early sixth-century laws of Solon. In addition, the poem's resolution, which ratifies Persephone's marriage to Hades and the rule of Zeus but also validates the continued emotional unity of mother and daughter, particularly in the context of the cult they will share, anticipates the balance in the classical polis between the wife's general exclusion from civic authority and her important role with other women in religious cult.[206]

Yet the favoring of endogamy over exogamy may not be the only crucial issue here. In one form of Homeric marriage, the father gives his daughter to be the possession of another family and to produce children for that family. This marriage is a form of gift that creates alliances and mutual obligations between the bride's natal and marital families. This gift is potentially reclaimable, but in practice we know of no instance, except in the case of her husband's death, where the bride, once she had entered her husband's household, is reclaimed by her natal family.[207] Instead, exchanges of other kinds continued to circulate between the families linked by marriage, and the bride produced children exclusively for her husband's family. As we have seen, Persephone's abduction by Hades initially failed to create a functional alliance of this kind, and no children are mentioned. But divine affairs in Greek poetry never precisely mimic mortal affairs and these differences should not prevent us from finding significance in the contrast between the original union between Hades and Persephone and the final one.

At the end of the poem, Zeus reclaims his daughter from her husband and retains control (with Demeter) over her capacity to bring fertility to the world above (in the *Hymn* the agricultural cycle is guaranteed by Persephone's yearly return). Hades becomes in essence the permanent guardian of his wife, but she remains her father's possession. Just as the Mysteries, by promising a different and probably better lot in the underworld, offer a compromise between a bleak afterlife and an immortality permanently denied to mortals in epic, Persephone's marriage mediates between giving and keeping the bride. Finally, the original abduction, as might be expected of a marriage between brothers, entailed no offering or exchange of gifts. At the conclusion, Hades has promised honors to Persephone in the world below and predicted the honors that she will receive from Zeus among the living, when she will join her mother in offering benefits to those mortals whom they both love.

This second form of marriage has more in common with, although it by no means exactly resembles, that which emerged in Attika, where a woman

---

[206] Persephone's role is not generally comparable to that of a Greek wife, of course.

[207] The case of Penelope discussed by Lacey 1966 is not really an exception. Penelope can choose to assume that Odysseus is dead and return voluntarily to her father, who will then give her in marriage to one of the suitors. Her situation is anomalous because no one knows whether Odysseus is alive and it is therefore unclear who her guardian (*kyrios*) is.

was pledged (or lent) with a dowry to another family to produce children for it. In the case of the heiress or *epiklêros*, a daughter whose father had died without a male heir was required to produce a male heir for her father's line. Even a married daughter, if childless, could be reclaimed by her family and remarried to a close relative for this purpose.[208] This institution was reportedly already taking shape in Attika in the early sixth-century, because legislation concerning the *epiklêros* was attributed to Solon (Plutarch *Solon* 20.2). I am not claiming here that Persephone is an *epiklêros*,[209] because Zeus has male children by other goddesses and inheritance does not play the same role among divinities as it does on earth (Zeus in particular deliberately avoids producing a male heir who will succeed him). In addition, the offering of honors to Persephone in two spheres does not correspond either to the Homeric exchange of gifts between the bride's father and husband, because Persephone and mortals are the major beneficiaries, or to the giving of a dowry (a premortem inheritance reclaimable on divorce) by the father for the use of the husband. Yet the resulting marriage is still closer to the post-Homeric than the Homeric arrangement.

The parallel between Persephone here and Hekate in Hesiod's *Theogony* may be illuminating. Each goddess is an only female child (*mounogenês*, *Theogony* 426, 448) who is rewarded with special honors in three realms of the universe (*Theogony* 412–15, 427, *Hymn to Demeter* 364–69).[210] Like Persephone, when Hekate is gracious (*prophrôn*, see *Hymn to Demeter* 487, 494) to mortals, she bestows happiness and wealth (*olbos*) on them (419–20) and serves as a nurse to the young (*kourotrophos*, 450–52).[211] Again, Hekate, unlike an *epiklêros*, is not married off to produce a male heir for her father's line; her special honors from Zeus relate to her role as an only daughter of her *mother* (*Theogony* 448), and her birth is unusually recounted in conjunction with the genealogy of her mother.[212] We have seen that

---

[208] On Homeric marriage, see especially Lacey 1966 and Morris 1986 with full bibliography. For a recent anthropologically oriented discussion of the differences between archaic and classical Athenian marriage, see Leduc 1992. An Attic bride was pledged (*engyaô*) in marriage to her spouse. The word *ekdidômi* and its derivatives, often used to describe the giving of an Attic daughter in marriage, was also used for lending. On Attic marriage as a form of transferral that does not imply severance from the person given, see further Wolff 1944:esp. 49. In Leduc's analysis, the dowry accompanying the bride functioned as an interest-free loan, which had to be returned with the bride to her family in the case of divorce. On archaic gift exchange and its relation to marriage, see esp. Kurke 1991:108–62.

[209] As does Clay 1989:213. See further the section on "Marriage," above, this essay.

[210] Demeter produces other children, such as Ploutos, in myth. Yet the *Hymn* makes no mention of other children. She is *mounotokos* (parent of an only child) at Nonnos *Dionysiaka* 6.31.

[211] Clay 1984 argues that Hekate's main function is to determine which mortal prayers are answered.

[212] Schwabl 1970:443. Arthur 1982:68–69 argues that Hekate is like an *epiklêros*, who transmits the patrimony of the old order to Zeus. Hekate is pointedly conceived in a patrilocal,

Persephone's maternal lineage plays an important role in the *Hymn*, although she is still disposed of by her father. Both poems thus seem to attribute a special status in this case to the only child of the mother. In the *Hymn*, because Zeus (with Demeter) partially reclaims an only child from her husband in order to restore fertility to the world above and retains an interest in her to ensure this fertility, Persephone functions to some extent in a fashion symbolically equivalent to the *epiklêros*, but for different reasons better suited to the workings of a divine world. (In later myth, she actually gave birth to a male child for her natal family. Persephone produced Iakchos/Dionysos incestuously by Zeus, and Dionysos, especially through his role in mystic cults, mediated like his mother between the worlds above and below.)

Similarly, although the giving of gifts by the husband to the bride's father does occur in divine marriage (Hephaistos gave gifts to Zeus at his marriage with Aphrodite [*Odyssey* 8.317–20]), the practice has no real significance where Zeus and Hades have already received their own permanent and entirely separate share in the cosmos and have no need of each other's services. Yet because Demeter shares the honors that she receives from Zeus with Persephone, Persephone will not only influence humankind but alter the sphere of her husband and link it in a fashion previously impossible to the world above (we do not know precisely what the Mysteries promised to initiates, but it seems probable that the lot of the initiated and the uninitiated were distinguished, and that the world below thus offered new possibilities to its inhabitants). In this sense, the inheritance that Persephone brings to the world below could be said to function as a divine "dowry." Thus, although the cosmological issues discussed earlier in this essay may be the primary determinant of the final shape of Persephone's unusual divine marriage, it is not impossible that a changing historical climate influenced the way that the *Hymn* imagines it as well.

Insofar as the Athenian polis increasingly attempted through legislation to control marriage and the family in a far more assertive and specific fashion than before, tensions may have arisen. Hesiod's *Theogony*, a poem probably composed close to a century before the *Hymn*, openly emphasizes tensions developing in the changing archaic reality of seventh-century Boeotia: squabbles among petty kings subject to corruption; the unfortunate necessity of marriage (wives are unreliable, an economic liability, and, when adulterous, a threat to male honor), which is most desirable when endogamous; and the importance of retaining and making profitable individual parcels of land. The stable divine world created by Zeus is held up as a model

---

legitimate marriage (the word used for her mother, *akoitis*, is applied to the wives of Zeus's reign). Perhaps the ability of Hekate and Persephone to commute between two worlds is connected to their childlessness.

for humanity to follow. On the question of marriage, the *Hymn* locates itself uneasily between a Homeric acceptance of tradition and Hesiod's marked preference in the *Works and Days* (699–701) for marrying the daughter of a neighbor.[213] Social life in the Eleusis of the *Hymn* is entirely harmonious. Kings act together with an assembly of the whole people to make important public decisions, and women care for each other and look forward to marriage and the running of households. Tensions about the institution of marriage (and especially patrilocal exogamy) in the human social system are displaced onto the divine realm. Yet this displacement may nevertheless indicate an equal concern with the issues. Tensions over marriage and its role in the larger social structure certainly played a role in drama, the major public literature of classical Athens. Aeschylus's Danaid and Oresteian trilogies, Sophocles' *Women of Trachis* or his fragmentary *Tereus*, and Euripides' *Medea* or *Andromache* are among those plays that focus on these issues. These plays certainly use their representation of an earlier mythical era to comment obliquely on contemporary issues. The *Hymn*'s problematizing of marriage and above all of divine exogamy—as well as its (partial) restoration of endogamy—once again uncannily anticipates the concerns of postarchaic society and helps to explain the enduring interest of its myth.

Christianity and the *Hymn to Demeter*

The *Hymn to Demeter* is shaped above all to explain the origin of the Mysteries. The poem suggests that the Mysteries emerge from a breakdown of the boundaries between mortals and immortals, from the attempted imposition of patriarchal marriage on female divinity, and from the particular nature of the mother/daughter bond itself. It is not surprising, then, that the Eleusinian Mysteries are based on the myth of the mother and the daughter, rather than, as in Christianity, on the psychological relation between father and son. The religious experience provided by the Mysteries represented a significant yet apparently complementary alternative to the relation between life and death, divine and human familiar to us from the Homeric epics. Although the complex historical influence of ancient mystery cults on Christianity is beyond the scope of this book, the *Hymn*'s relation to Homer and Hesiod parallels in certain respects that of Christianity to the Book of Job; both Christianity and the *Hymn* stress, for example, the imagery of wheat, communion with divinity, and rites given rather than rites earned

---

[213] The Homeric poems do not, of course, conceal the potential strains in marriage: the adultery of Helen and Klytemnestra are a case in point.

and attempt to mitigate the bleaker, often tragic vision presented in the earlier texts.[214]

Caroline Bynum has stressed in her study of late medieval Christianity that male monastics and mystics defined gender more dichotomously than women did in the same situation.[215] Male monastics used their identification with Christ as Mother to express their difference from the powerful Church hierarchy and their rejection of wealth and power, whereas females used Christ's symbolic motherhood to express their concern with humanity. The men turned to motherhood as a social role that promised emotional fulfillment rather than power, as an opportunity for an oedipal reconciliation with the once-rejected mother. Bodily asceticism was more important to the women, and they associated motherhood with eating, feeding, and suffering. The myth and the Mysteries seem—no doubt coincidentally—to include both these agendas. Zeus ruthlessly separated humans from the gods and condemned them to mortal life in Hesiod's *Theogony*, whereas Demeter (like the maternal Christ) mitigated this separation and mortal suffering through her cult. On the one hand (as in the case of the male mystics), the poem initially emphasizes gender dichotomy and the cult represents an alternative to more hierarchical religious rituals. On the other hand, the physical process of motherhood, eating, and fasting, and the transference of Demeter's love from her child to all humanity play a central role. Although Bynum's study cannot explain the nature and growth of the Mysteries, it might suggest some of the reasons for the *Hymn*'s appeal to initiates of both sexes and for its special and almost exclusive stress, in contrast to other versions of the myth, on maternal experience.

The Influence of the *Hymn to Demeter* and Its Myth

The Homeric hymns never acquired the status of the major Homeric epics in antiquity, and it is in fact difficult to know how well the *Hymn to Demeter* was known and read at most periods. Tracing the role of the *Hymn* in antiquity in relation to the many versions of the Demeter/Persephone myth is a complex task.[216] The poem was apparently known to such authors as Pindar, Bacchylides, Sophocles, and Euripides in the classical period, even

---

[214] A full discussion of this topic would have to include the other mystery cults of antiquity, such as Dionysiac and Orphic rites, above all in the Hellenistic period. For representative bibliography, see Reitzenstein 1927, Nock 1933, Henrichs 1983, and Betz 1991.

[215] 1986.

[216] For a more detailed discussion, see Richardson 1974:68–86.

though they offer alternative versions of the myth.[217] At least one Orphic version of the myth—poems attributed to Orpheus, Mousaios, or Eumolpos—quotes the *Hymn* (Frag. 49 Kern). The eclectic assortment of "Orphic" poems, which seem to record local Attic/Eleusinian traditions about the myth, may have begun to emerge out of a tradition established by a circle of poets who gathered in the court of Peisistratos in the mid-sixth century.[218] Insofar as we can reconstruct the fragments, these poems narrated the wanderings of Demeter on earth, her encounter with rustic inhabitants of Eleusis, her gift of agriculture to humanity (in return for the information given to her by human witnesses), and the dissemination of agriculture throughout the world. Zeus apparently actively intervened with the thunderbolt to ensure the abduction against the opposition of Athena and Artemis. At Eleusis Demeter was met by the queen and her daughters at the well. When the mother, here called Baubo, interrupted Demeter's secret rites with the child, he died. After Demeter revealed herself, she asked who had stolen Persephone. Eubouleus and Triptolemos, the sons of Dysaules, who may have witnessed their swine being swallowed into the earth with Persephone, then offered Demeter information about her daughter and were rewarded with agriculture. The famine apparently did not play a role in these versions. The Orphic version seems to combine the *Hymn's* version of the abduction of Persephone and the nursing of a male child at Eleusis with the tradition that motivated Demeter's gift of agriculture to humanity.

The learned Hellenistic poets showed great interest in the *Hymn*. Antimachos, Kallimachos, Nikander, Philikos's *Hymn to Demeter*, and the lyric hymn to the Mother of the Gods apparently know of the *Hymn*; and Apollonios's description of Thetis's attempts to immortalize the baby Achilleus (*Argonautika* 4.869ff) shows a direct influence. In the Roman period, Ovid (*Metamorphoses* and especially the *Fasti*) responded to the *Hymn*,[219] and Claudian (*On the Rape of Proserpina*) may have known it. Philodemos in his *De Pietate*[220] quotes line 440 of the *Hymn*. He objects that Homer's description of Hekate as an *opaôn* (attendant or servant) of Persephone is demeaning for a goddess. Both Greek and Latin poets present their own version of the story, and their attitudes to or knowledge of the *Hymn* are hard to evaluate. The poem's version of the myth—as is the case with other myths in

---

[217] Bacchylides fr. 47 Snell, Pindar fr. 137a Snell, Sophocles frag. 837 Radt, Euripides *Helen* 1301ff. See Richardson 1974:69.

[218] This speculation derives in large part from Herodotos 7.6, which suggests that in the mid-sixth century there already existed in Athens a body of work attributed to Mousaios. For discussion, see Malten 1909, Richardson 1974, and Graf 1974. As Jenny Clay argued in a paper presented at the 1992 American Philological Association meeting at New Orleans, the Orphic appropriation of material from the *Hymn* in frag. 49 Kern attests to the prestige of the poem in the tradition.

[219] Hinds 1987 argues for direct influence.

[220] Herculaneum Papyrus 1088:fr. 6.12–16. See Schober 1988:87 and Luppe 1985.

antiquity—was never canonical, even if the mythographer Apollodoros (*Bibliotheca* 1.5.1–3) apparently paraphrased the *Hymn* and echoes its language at several points.

The myth of Demeter and Persephone remained of interest throughout later Western art and literature, but direct influence of the *Hymn* reemerges only after the discovery of the single surviving medieval manuscript (dated to the early-fifteenth century) in 1777. In what follows I shall attempt a selected survey of late-nineteenth- and twentieth-century works in English that are influenced by the *Hymn*, or by the *Hymn* and other related versions of the myth (especially those of Ovid).

Victorian poets showed a special interest in the *Hymn*.[221] Tennyson dedicated his "Demeter and Persephone" of 1889 to the Greek Professor R. C. Jebb who had provided him with classical sources for the poem.[222] Writing at the age of 80, Tennyson confronts humanity's hard condition. His Demeter narrates her sufferings and hopes for an era of "younger kindlier gods" and the love of the mother and daughter goddesses for a humanity to whom they would offer perpetual abundance and a dissolution of fear and death. The poem thus suggestively begins with the reunion of mother and daughter:

> Queen of the dead no more—my child! Thine eyes
> Again were human-godlike, and the Sun
> Burst from a swimming fleece of winter gray,
> And robed thee in his day from head to feet—
> 'Mother!' and I was folded in thine arms.[223]

Meredith's "The Appeasement of Demeter" (1887) dwells on the sterility caused by Demeter's famine. Iambe, pitying the dying earth, makes Deme-

---

[221] In the nineteenth century I am largely confining myself to poems directly influenced by the *Hymn*. Shelley's earlier "Song of Proserpine" and Mary Shelley's verse drama "Proserpine" are based on Ovid, although a love of things Greek was perhaps a more fundamental motive for their reworking of the myth. Mary Shelley's drama, which was written after the death of her daughter, stresses the mother's point of view. The poem laments male intervention in a female pastoral paradise and celebrates Ceres' creativity, capacity to produce fertility, and devotion to her child. Elizabeth Barrett Browning's *Aurora Leigh* adapts the Persephone myth in its treatment of the raped Marian Erle (see further Gubar 1979:304–5). Keats's "Ode on Melancholy," Milton's *Paradise Lost* 4.268–71 and letter to Diodati (1637; the latter equates the search for the beautiful to Ceres' search for Proserpina), Spenser's "The Garden of Proserpina" in The *Faerie Queene*, and Shakespeare's *Winter's Tale* are among the well-known English poetry that makes passing references to the myth of Ceres and Proserpina (see also Thomas Campion's "Proserpina."). Richard Watson Dixon's pre-Raphaelite "Proserpine," which does respond to the *Hymn*, and Maybury Fleming's "To Demeter" (in Stedman 1900:566) are not discussed here. For further discussion of nineteenth- and early-twentieth-century poetry influenced by the *Hymn*, see Bush 1969 and Mayerson 1971.

[222] Ovid, the *Hymn*, and Claudian.

[223] Reprinted in Ricks 1969.

ter laugh over the pathetic efforts of two starving and enfeebled horses to mate.

> She laughed: since our first harvesting heard none
> Like thunder of the song of heart: her face,
> The dreadful darkness, shook to mounted sun,
> And peal on peal across the hills held chase.
> She laughed herself to water; laughed to fire;
> Laughed the torrential laugh of dam and sire
> > Full of the marrowy race.
> Her laughter, Gods! was flesh on skeleton.[224]

The poem above all celebrates the role of laughter, which has the power to break the curse and revive the earth. In "The Day of the Daughter of Hades" (1883), which Meredith considered his best poem, he invents a daughter of Persephone and Hades, Skiageneia, who shares one day on earth delighting in the beauties of nature with the youth Callistes. Swinburne's "Hymn to Proserpine" celebrates paganism over Christianity; in "The Garden of Proserpine" the poet, weary "of tears and laughter," longs for Persephone's world of death; but "At Eleusis" responds directly to the *Hymn to Demeter*. This intensely lyrical poem is narrated by Demeter, who stresses her power as an artist of nature, carving "the shapes of grass and tender corn" and coloring "the ripe edges and long spikes/With red increase and the grace of gold." Her attempt to immortalize the child, here named Triptolemus, powerfully mingles maternal love and danger:

> Unswaddled the weak hands, and in mid ash
> Laid the sweet flesh of either feeble side,
> More tender for impressure of some touch
> Than wax to any pen; and lit around
> Fire, and made crawl the white worm-shapen flame,
> And leap in little angers spark by spark
> At head at once and feet; and the faint hair
> Hissed with rare sprinkles in the closer curl,
> And like scaled oarage of a keen thin fish
> In sea water, so in pure fire his feet
> Struck out, and the flame bit not in his flesh,
> But like a kiss it curled his lip, and heat
> Fluttered his eyelids; so each night I blew
> The hot ash red to purge him to full god.[225]

In Robert Bridges's mask "Demeter," composed for the ladies at Somerville College in 1904, Demeter learns sympathy for humanity in nursing

---

[224] Reprinted in Bartlett 1978.
[225] See 1924–27, Vol I.

Demophoön.[226] Yet she comes to think that saving one mortal would be meaningless, and she institutes her Mysteries to help humankind to accept and even embrace suffering. Persephone, who begins the poem with an innocent obsession with the beauty of flowers, learns the nature of good and evil in the world below. Accepting the power of fate and goodness to prevail over all, the mother and her now-mature and wise daughter become equal partners in assuaging the lot of mortals.

Walter Pater's half-poetical, half anthropological essay "The Myth of Demeter and Persephone"[227] sees the myth itself as a reflection of the earlier religion of Greece that had "but a subordinate place in the religion of Homer."[228] The *Hymn* represents the second "conscious, poetical or literary, phase" of Greek myth in which poets transformed products of the half-conscious, popular imagination by interweaving incidents and developing emotions to create a powerful narrative.[229] Yet the *Hymn* still preserves traces of the earliest phase—Demeter is both "Lady of Sorrows" and earth itself.

> The myth of Demeter and Persephone, then, illustrates the power of Greek religion as a religion of pure ideas—of conceptions, which . . . because they arose naturally out of the spirit of man, and embodied, in adequate symbols, his deepest thoughts concerning the conditions of his physical and spiritual life, maintained their hold through many changes, and are still not without a solemnising power even for the modern mind.[230]

Helen Hunt Jackson's "Demeter" (1892), on the other hand, sees the myth as a "legend of foul shame to motherhood!" because Demeter was willing to sacrifice other children for her own.

Pater's Victorian romanticizing of Greek myth and poetry set the stage for the reappropriation of ancient myths in a different vein by the Imagists, above all Ezra Pound and H.D. (Hilda Doolittle). H.D.'s "Demeter," "At Eleusis," and "The Mysteries" interweave the myths of Demeter and Dionysus/Iacchus, her foster child at Eleusis.[231] In H.D.'s "Demeter," the goddess, seated in her temple, rejects the sacrifices offered to her as "useless." Greater than other gods and in essence unknowable, she has learned the secrets of death, birth, and nature through her love for the motherless Dionysus, "the child of my heart and spirit," and her daughter Persephone.

[226] See Bridges 1912.

[227] Pater 1911.

[228] Ibid.:81.

[229] Ibid.:91. The statues of Demeter by Pheidias, Praxiteles, and others embody the third or "ethical phase" in which "the persons and the incidents of the poetical narrative are realised as abstract symbols . . . of moral and spiritual conditions."

[230] Ibid:151.

[231] 1925 and 1983. A section of H.D.'s "The Mysteries" is quoted at the end of Arthur's article (1977) in this volume.

The poem closes by recording the empowerment that this love for her daughter has produced:[232]

> *What of her—*
> *mistress of Death?*
>
> Form of a golden wreath
> were my hands that girt her head,
> fingers that strove to meet,
> and met where the whisps escaped
> from the fillet, of tenderest gold,
> small circlet and slim
> were my fingers then.
>
> Now they are wrought of iron
> to wrest from the earth
> secrets; strong to protect,
> strong to keep back the winter
> when winter tracks too soon
> blanch the forest:
> strong to break dead things,
> the young tree, drained of sap,
> the old tree, ready to drop,
> to lift from the rotting bed
> of leaves, the old
> crumbling pine tree stock,
> to heap bole and knot of fir
> and pine and resinous oak,
> till fire shatter the dark
> and hope of spring
> rise in the hearts of men.
>
> *What of her—*
> *mistress of Death?—*
> *what of his kiss?*
>
> Ah, strong were his arms to wrest
> slight limbs from the beautiful earth,
> young hands that plucked the first

---

[232] H.D.'s "Psyche" also links Persephone with Psyche's quest for Amor. For further discussion of a prepatriarchal empowering mother/muse/goddess figure in H.D., which helped H.D. to come to terms with her own self-effacing and unsupportive artist mother, see Friedman 1990. For further references to Demeter and Persephone in H.D.'s longer poems, such as *Helen in Egypt* and *Trilogy*, see Gubar 1979:306–7 and Friedman 1981. For H.D., the Eleusinian Mysteries encouraged a unity of mind, body, and spirit fragmented in later Western culture.

buds of the chill narcissus,
soft fingers that broke
and fastened the thorny stalk
with the flower of wild acanthus.

Ah, strong were the arms that took
(ah, evil the heart and graceless),
but the kiss was less passionate!

In "Art and Women," Rachel Annand Taylor contrasts the dearth of women artists with the centrality to art of the mysteries with which women and Demeter are connected—"Our broken bodies still imagining/The mournful Mystery of the Bread and Wine."[233] In Dorothy Wellesley's "Demeter in Sicily," a visit to Sicily, with its Greek ruins and traditional agricultural cycle, awakens in the poet both a sense of Demeter's continued divinity and an uncertainty that she and her relation to her daughter can be truly understood in a modern world:

Cease weeping: now for thee the almond springs.
Stay sighing then,
Demeter, goddess still.
For in this strange, this iris-region wild
I dream that dreadful things
Forever hold thy child.

How shall I know
If these thy worshippers remembember thee?
As I, these lighted days,
Who may not push the plough about the tree
Nor break the favoured bough
To deck an altar by a sighing sea,
Where comes bright foam to little coloured bays.[234]

Particularly in "The Pisan Cantos" and "Rock Drill," Eleusis, Demeter, and Persephone play a central role in Ezra Pound's mythical descents into the underworld. As Lillian Feder remarks: "Pound equates mystery, truth, ritual, and poetry, all of which could be combined through participation in ancient rites such as were practiced at Eleusis. In Pound's view the modern world has violated the tradition of Eleusis."[235] "Absent from modern society, myth and ritual remain in the mind of man; Pound asks rhetorically

[233] Reprinted in Bernikow 1974:146. The poem was composed in the early 1900s.
[234] Reprinted in Ibid.:162–64. The poem was composed in the 1930s.
[235] Feder 1971:202. Feder has an excellent discussion of Pound's use of the Demeter/Persephone myth with further bibliography. See also Davenport 1981:141–64, "Persephone's Ezra." Frederic Manning's evocative "Kore" (1910) partially inspired Pound's interest in Persephone.

whether 'a modern Eleusis [is] possible in the wilds of man's mind only?' "[236] In *Guide to Kulchur*, Pound says: "Eleusis did not distort truth by exaggerating the individual, neither could it have violated the individual spirit. Only in the high air and the great clarity can there be a just estimation of values."[237] "Great intelligence attains again and again to great verity. The Duce and Kung fu Tseu equally perceive that their people need poetry; that prose is NOT education but the outer courts of the same. Beyond its doors are the mysteries. Eleusis. Things not to be spoken save in secret."[238] Using Eleusis, Pound constructs an idealized past, "an image of a perfect civilization, which can be described only in myth and summoned only in ritual."[239] Demeter's mourning and the accompanying barrenness of the earth is played off against the rebirth of Persephone through her empowering experience of death; "for Persephone, love and death are one, also the prelude to her reign as a goddess of fertility."[240] "The strength of men is in grain." (Canto CVI)

Edgar Lee Masters is one of the last poets to offer a reworking of the *Hymn* closely based on the original text. In his "Persephone" (1935), by interweaving motifs from the Homeric *Hymn to Hermes* concerning Hermes' invention of the lyre, Masters links Persephone's return with an image of poetic and almost Christian rebirth:[241]

> Then the dawn came up as fresh as jonquils;
> There were blossoms in coverts, fields and hills;
> There were songs in the sky;
> There were musical tongues in the teeming sea
> That chanted hymns to the April morn.
> For Demeter walked with Persephone
> Over the land of the springing corn.
> And men rejoiced, they sang believing
> In Earth from Heaven life receiving,
> In life that does not die.

Among interesting adaptations of the myth is A. D. Hope's "The Return of Persephone."[242] Persephone's departure to earth is envisioned as a com-

---

[236] Feder 1971:92, quoting Pound 1938 (1968):294.

[237] Pound 1938:299.

[238] Ibid.:144–45

[239] Feder 1971:204.

[240] Ibid.:205, also 203. See especially the last six cantos of "Rock Drill."

[241] Masters 1935:24. Nathaniel Tarn's stunning ten-poem sequence in *The Persephones* (1974) makes many explicit borrowings from the *Hymn* but was too long and complex for quotation here; see below for Jenny Joseph's novel, which includes verse sections closely based on the *Hymn*. Mrs. Charles Manning's "Persephone" (1881) offered an explicitly Christian version of the myth in which Persephone, returning to her mother only in dreams, reconciles her to the loss of her daughter through a vision of a Christian afterlife.

[242] Hope 1986. In John Drinkwater's "Persephone" (1926), Persephone is won over by

ing to life, a regaining of virginity and girlhood that provokes envy in the god of the dead. Persephone's love for Hades begins at this moment:

> And still she did not speak, but turned again
> Looking for answer, for anger, for command:
> The eyes of Dis were shut upon their pain;
> Calm as his marble brow, the marble hand
> Slept on his knee. Insuperable disdain
>
> Foreknowing all bounds of passion, of power, of art,
> Mastered but could not mask his deep despair.
> Even as she turned with Hermes to depart,
> Looking her last on her grim ravisher
> For the first time she loved him from her heart.

In Amy Clarke's play *Persephone* (1925), Demeter, having made the error of aspiring to a marriage with Zeus for Persephone, is tricked into assenting to a marriage with Hades. When she discovers the deception, she descends to the underworld to rescue her daughter, who is then reluctantly revived by the music of Echo and Pan. Persephone, once a companion of Pan and a lover of wild nature and flowers, is irreversably marked by her stay in the underworld. Out of pity for the dead, for whom she is the only glimmer of light in darkness, she has promised Hades to remain with him and voluntarily returns below. Pan and his cohorts still expect her return in spring, but Demeter is without hope. She becomes once more a beneficent Promethean figure who labors to work the earth for humankind.

In Robert Lowell's "The Mills of the Kavanaughs," the protagonist Anne Kavanaugh, the widowed inheritor of the estate of the Kavanaughs, thinks of herself as Persephone, "the goddess," as Lowell's introductory note describes her, "who became a queen by becoming queen of the dead" and who is present in the garden as "a maternal nineteenth century/ Italian statue"

Hades' gentle reign over those below. She moves from friendship to love for her abductor, yet, "his equal in immortal nature now," she remains "tenderly resolute" in her submission to the "supreme decree" that returns her to earth each spring. For some other adaptations not discussed here, see William Carlos Williams's *Kora in Hell. Improvisations* (1921), William Rose Benét's "Sung to Persephone" (1933), Ronald Bottrall's "Proserpine at Enna" (1961:154), Nathaniel Tarn's "Persephone's Down" (1964:28), Stanley Kunitz's "For Persephone" (1979:216), John Peale Bishop's "The Coming of Persephone," (1948:72), Philip Martin's "Myths," (1970:6), Nancy Willard's "The Animals Welcome Persephone" (1974:23), Carol Rumens's "Persephone in Armenia" (1988:80), Helen Lawson's "Persephone" (in Stratford, ed. 1988:70), Edward Sanders' "Demeter walking th' corn furrow" (in Allen and Butterick, eds. 1982: 367–72), Mildred J. Nash's "Demeter's Daughters" (in O'Brien, Rasmussen, and Costello, eds. 1981:20), Helen Lawson's "Persephone" (in Stratford, ed. 1988:2.182), Natasha Yim's "The Abduction of Persephone" (in Stratford, ed. 1988:1.181), and Rita Dove's "Persephone Abducted" (1992:22). Robert Graves' "Escape" (1927:58–59) and Robert Duncan's "Persephone" (1966:3–4) refer to Persephone in poems about war.

beckoning to "a mob of Bacchanals/To plunge like dogs or athletes through the falls, /And fetch her the stone garland she will hurl."[243] Engaged in a ritualized card game with the Douay bible and a dialogue with her dead husband, Anne recalls the violence and madness that pervaded her past life. One of thirteen children of an impoverished family, she met Harry Kavanaugh picking flowers. The statue of Persephone with her bacchanals comes to life as the air is "orgied" and Harry's setters yap and nip at the goddess's heels. Like Persephone, Anne is both empowered and victimized by her marriage to Harry/Hades, who once tried to kill her and died mad. The poem concludes with Anne rowing down an autumnal (and avernal) river:

> "Soon enough we saw
> Death like the Bourbon after Waterloo,
> Who learning and forgetting nothing, knew
> Nothing but ruin. Why must we mistrust
> Ourselves with Death who takes the world on trust?
> Although God's brother, and himself a god,
> Death whipped his horses through the startled sod;
> For neither conscience nor omniscience warned
> Him from his folly, when the virgin scorned
> His courtship, and the quaking earth revealed
> Death's desperation to the Thracian field.
> And yet we think the virgin took no harm:
> She gave herself because her blood was warm—
> And for no other reason, Love, I gave
> Whatever brought me gladness to the grave."[244]

In Robert Kelly's *The Book of Persephone*, Persephone, her body, and the earth, the darkness, and the world of the dead with which she is identified, become a source of inspiration and a refuge from the world of light and inexorable time: "& then I knew she is the glade, or glad/ comfort in the steady sun, time beating down."[245] As a muse figure with a dark, ambiguous mind, she is

> flicker of a something
> I am allowed to interpret,
>
> she passes
> leaving dew on the grass behind her,

---

[243] Lowell 1951:2–3. For a detailed discussion of the poem, see Feder 1971:20–22.
[244] 1951:21.
[245] Kelly 1978. See also "Kore Kosmou" in Kelly 1978. In a similar vein, Robert Creeley's "Kore" (1982) makes Kore into a muse figure who has just risen from the earth.

disturbance of her journey through me,

this perturbation, this literature.

For Plutone (Hades) himself, Persephone is also an enigmatic source of intellectual and physical attraction:[246]

> "I understood the day
> as well as I was able,
> sense of my body helping to hold.
> I saw the girl then, bent down to recover
> one of those dark blue flowers herself—
> half aloud she was asking Do they
> after all have white centers, white
> or pale yellow deep in the heart?
> The grace of her bending low
> to serve her intellectual desire
> gave me such pleasure that I took hold.
> Constrained by my travel she came along
> willing unwilling, who can say,
> still speaking softly to the flower
> till she came to my House.
> . . . .
> At times I persuade myself
> I am or become the stalwart dark blue flower
> in whose service she once bent low."

Adopting the male perspective on the goddess throughout, the book's poems alternate between viewing the goddess/the earth as a source of knowledge and as a figure of masculine exploitation:

> she endures in an angry turbulent sullen adolescence she
> breathes
> she consents that we fuck her it is the saddest imagination
> that the wheat springs up to be eaten in that obedience
> . . . .
> my formless greed reaches down to pull her naked into this
> cheap light of my fancy I will caress her no more here
> I will leave her to speak to me what she desires or silences
>
> or silence me in the overarching fact of her impeccable form.

[246] I am grateful for a letter in which Robert Kelly informs me that this passage alludes to an aria from Monteverdi's *Il Ballo dell'Ingrate*; Kelly's king, however, "is beginning to be concerned with justifying himself."

Overall, the poet uses Persephone to express man's simultaneous exploitation of and desire for women.[247]

Margaret Atwood's sequence of poems *Double Persephone* stresses above all the cycle of life and death. "Persephone Departing" is the first of four poems in the book to meditate directly on the goddess's implication in these themes: [248]

> From her all springs arise
> To her all falls return
> The articulate flesh, the singing bone
> Root flower and fern;
>
> The dancing girl's a withered crone;
> Though her deceptive smile
> Lures life from the earth, rain from the sky,
> It hides a wicked sickle; while
> Those watching sense the red blood curled
> Waiting, in the center of her eye;
>
> But the stranger from the hill
> Sees only the bright gleam
> Of a slim woman gathering asphodel,
> And lashes his black team.

Women poets in particular have used the Demeter/Persephone myth to mark phases and transitions in the female life cycle.[249] In Kathleen Raine's "Transit of the Gods," the aging poet has outlasted the influence of "The Virgin, Aphrodite, and the Mourning Mother." "For in her theater the play is done." Yet even now "I . . . Wait for the last mummer, dread Persephone/To dance my dust at last into the tomb."[250] In Sylvia Plath's "Two Sisters of Persephone," the two Persephones in the worlds above and below become alternative and limiting fates for woman: the spinster office worker computes in the dark "problems on / A mathematical machine," while her sister "sun's bride. . . Grows quick with seed" and "bears a king."[251] In Carolyn Kizer's "Persephone Pauses," Persephone is the moon goddess,

---

[247] In a letter, Kelly says that "the whole book seems to me about the terrible repentance of being a man, in a world that does to women what it does, and desires them in the very article of their victimage. . . . I was questioning the relationships between male desires, projections, possessions, entrapments, entitlements false and true."

[248] Atwood 1961. I cannot do justice to this sequence of poems here.

[249] In Keith Abbott's "Persephone" (in Codrescu 1989:369), a father envisions his daughter, leaving for Paris to become a writer, as Persephone.

[250] Raine 1956:83.

[251] Plath 1960:31–32.

locked into a cycle with a lover whose sensuality alternately attracts and repels her:

> . . . But then, the grim
> Tragedian from the other shore
> Draws near my shade. Beneath the brim,
> In motions formal and austere,
> We circle, measure, heel to hem.
> He profers me an iron plate
> Of seedy fruit, to match my mouth.
> My form encased in some dark stuff
> He has bedizened, keeps me hid
> Save for that quivering oval, turned
> Half-moon, away, away from him
> And that excitement of his taste
> He suffers, from my flesh withdrawn.
> But this unwilling touch of lust
> Has moved some gentle part of me
> That sleeps in solstice, wakes to dream
> Where streams of light and winter join.
> He knows me then; I only know
> A darkened cheek, a sidelong lower,
> My nerves dissolving in the gleam
> Of night's theatrical desire,
> As always, when antagonists
> Are cast into the sensual
> Abysses, from a failing will.
> This is my dolor, and my dower.[252]

Joan Aleshire's "Persephone" links her own experience of following a man into the dark after a party with Persephone's attraction to Hades; she wonders whether the goddess had not "grown tired of living with her mother," in "endless mildness, all that perfect light."[253] Edna St. Vincent Millay's "Prayer to Persephone" asks Persephone to care for a dead child in the world below, and in Olga Broumas's "Demeter" the myth evokes the frightening dependence of child on mother, the "tears of a mother grieving a mortal child," and the treatment of the mother/daughter theme in the works of fellow women poets.[254] In Kate Ellis's "Matrilineal Descent," Demeter and Persephone serve as a paradigm of the unified female psyche, in which

[252] Kizer 1961.
[253] Aleshire 1987:33.
[254] Millay 1956 and Broumas 1977.

mother and daughter can separate and unite, descend and return with predictable ease.[255] Ellis's self is by contrast divided. Feeling unloved by her mother and hating a favored sister who almost died as a child, Ellis makes a symbolic descent in dreams to recover her lost self. She becomes dream mother to her sister and child to a close friend.

Michèle Roberts's cycle of poems, "Persephone descends to the underworld," "Demeter grieving," "Persephone voyages," "Demeter keeps going," "Persephone pays a visit to Demeter," and "Persephone gives birth" tracks the relation of daughter to mother from the first engagement with the lover to reunification with the mother at the birth of a child.[256] In the first poem of the sequence, the daughter is reluctant to leave beloved women for the lover who is death. Her mother authorizes the departure.

> this spring my lover
> came for me again; this
> time my mother did not
> hold me back; she blessed me; she
> suggested it
> was about time; then she released my wrist
>
> my lover is a dark man
> we embrace in the garden, in the grave; his
> twisting root is clotted with my black earth
> as I break open, and take him in
>
> this time no return is possible; this
> time he has me; this time when we go
> underground we go together
> though I shall be crying loudly
> for the mother and women lovers I leave behind.

Demeter generates fertility on earth while waiting for her daughter, and the daughter returns for a visit to her mother. The sequence concludes with birth as "in the churchyard/Persephone in her bone nightgown/squats down." In Enid Dame's "Persephone," by contrast, the transition from mother to "husband" is never fully effected for the daughter.[257] The girl remembers life with the mother, even when she is scolded, as a domestic paradise:

> I wanted to spend
> my life in her kitchen,

---

[255] Tulloss, Keller, and Ostriker 1980:31–34.

[256] Roberts 1986.

[257] Dame 1992:10–11. By contrast, Mary Winfrey's "Demeter's Song" (in Newman, ed. 1978:16) celebrates the daughter's escape from rape and return to her mother.

quietly watching
her capable fingers
build fires,
strip corn ears,
crack warm eggs
against a blue bowl.

I wanted to be
a part of that room:
cat on the windowsill
sprawled among flowerpots,
cast iron kettle,
milk sliding down
her sweet throat.

Sometimes she'd pace the room
caged tiger   tail flashing.
Sometimes she'd cry.

After all, it was no picnic
dragging the earth into fruit
too many seasons   too many months
too big a job
for one woman.

The girl is abducted by an older man and lives in a world too dark to see her lover's face:

He says,
"You're my little girl now."
He smells like old clothes.
His body sprouts fingers
thicker than carrots.

They grip me knobbily.
He rocks back and forth
like a leaky old boat
shakes on the ocean.

He shipwrecks inside me
every night.

When he kisses me
later
I call him "Mama."

Josephine Donovan has studied the Demeter/Persephone myth in the work of the novelists Edith Wharton, Willa Cather, and Ellen Glasgow (with an appendix on Virginia Woolf and Colette), where the myth is used to allegorize the transition from a matricentric preindustrial culture to patriarchal captivity under capitalism and industry.[258] Guy Davenport has argued that in the fiction of Eudora Welty, especially *Delta Wedding* and "Going to Naples," "there is the same understanding as in Claudian's poem [*De raptu Proserpinae*] that Persephone's innocence and vulnerability are to be seen as a civilized order menaced by invasion."[259] Of Meridel le Sueur's many adaptations of the myth, the most ambitious is her novel, *The Girl*.[260] The working-class Girl, violently initiated into sex by her boyfriend Butch,[261] closes the novel by giving birth in prison to a daughter who has the name and the face of her dead friend Clara: "Clear Light, the baby. Clara! . . . Claro clara cleara light yes."[262] "*The Girl* suggests that Persephone's reemergence from the land of the dead (like Clara's return) is consonant with, if not the same as, the resurrection of Christ, the rising of a submerged lower class, and biological birth. Through this attemped conflation, le Sueur seeks to realize the novel's religious and political themes, its desire for . . . transcendent truth and for social justice."[263] In the course of the novel the naive, nameless Girl gains (like Korê) her own voice and sense of authority: "Nobody can shut me up."[264] Both the Girl's conversion to radical union politics and the final revelatory birth, described with language suggestive of the maternal secrets of Eleusis, take place in a circle of women, the "great Mothers" (all the main male characters are dead, although a few unnamed men view the scene from a distance), and the novel implies that maternity—reproduction, suffering, and the giving of nourishment—and cyclicity offer a necessary alternative (political and artistic) to exploitation and seizure.[265]

[258] Donovan 1989. Gladys B. Stern's *Debonair: The Story of Persephone* (1928) is not discussed here. On H.D.'s *Her* and *Kora and Ka*, see Friedman 1990. Gubar 1979 argues that the Persephone myth stands behind the plots of novels such as Margaret Atwood's *Surfacing* and Toni Morrison's *The Bluest Eye*, as well as Thomas Hardy's *Tess of the D'Urbervilles*. Doris Lessing's *Summer Before the Dark* and *Briefing for a Descent into Hell* are also novels of descent and rebirth.

[259] Davenport 1981:251–52, from a discussion in "That Faire Field of Enna."

[260] Her first story (1927, rep. 1982), "Persephone," based on a reading of the *Hymn*, tells of a daughter who is dying after being abducted from her mother, and the grief of her mother, who began as a symbol of the successful farmer in a midwestern town and then ages and haunts the town wells. She also wrote a parody of the myth in tough street-guy language, with Pluto playing the role of a gangster (see Yount 1978:91–92). See further le Sueur 1982:251ff.

[261] She is also given by Butch to be raped by another man.

[262] le Sueur 1978:143.

[263] Gelfant 1991:198.

[264] le Sueur 1978:113.

[265] See further Gelfant 1991:esp. 195 and 207n.27. The novelist and her heroine claim to be transmitting stories told to them by other women.

Finally, Jenny Joseph's *Persephone*, which opens with an epigraph from the *Hymn*, interweaves verse recounting the myth of Demeter and Persephone with short prose pieces that reinforce the narrative from the perspective of modern Demeters and Persephones.[266] This experimentally cyclical narrative uses its collective voices to move from loss, rape, despair to rebirth and renewal and ends where it began, suggesting that without suffering there can be no fruition, no control of death. Although the two goddesses are doubles of each other, the figure of the mother is static, embroiled in child care, harvest, and the world above; it is as daughter that Persephone travels, empowered by mysteries that the mother "does not want to look at" or has forgotten in the world below.[267] Like Joseph's novel, twentieth-century versions of the myth, even when they give considerable voice to the mother, tend, unlike the *Hymn*, to emphasize the quest of the daughter and/or to make Persephone the central figure in the narrative.

The *Hymn* has attracted renewed interest in the twentieth century from psychoanalytic critics, sociologists, literary critics, and writers. Jungian and feminist psychoanalysts, Chodorow, Gilligan, Irigaray, and Hirsch have been discussed above. Adrienne Rich's *Of Woman Born* inaugurated the feminist reappropriation of the myth.[268] Whereas Rich focuses on the mother/daughter relation, Luce Irigaray, in objecting to the elements of Western culture and religion that are predicated on violence, sacrifice, and an indifference to the environment, turns to the myth for its respect for the natural cycle and the mother's insistence on being "fertile *with her daughter*."[269] She asks:

> Perhaps this means recognizing that we are still and continue to be *open* to the world and to the other simply because we are alive and sensitive, subject to time and to the rhythms of the universe, a universe with which we share certain properties—properties which are different depending on whether we are men or women. We are not living, for all that, in primitive societies, nor in a culture at pains to take its rhythms from the moment, the hour, and the season, so as to respect natural products and to respect ourselves as one of these. If we were, then sacrifice might seem pointless? Winter isn't summer, night isn't day, not all parts of the universe equal each other. These rhythms ought to be sufficient to permit us to constitute societies. Why hasn't man been satisfied with them? Where does he get this excess of violence that he then needs to get rid of? Has his growth been stunted or stopped? . . . . [270]

Nevertheless, there is no question of us simply returning to the earth god-

---

[266] Joseph:1985.
[267] Ibid.:210.
[268] See the opening quotation in this essay.
[269] Her italics 1986:9.
[270] Ibid.:17.

desses, even if that were possible. A return to them would require that they be upheld, and that we establish (or re-establish?) a form of sociality based on those values and that fertility. It's not enough to restore myths if we can't celebrate them and use them as the basis of a social order. Is that possible?

Let us grant that it is possible: will Gaea and Demeter be enough? What will we do with Core? And Persephone? . . . Aren't we always at least two? How can we unite the two within us? Between us? How can we affirm together these elementary values, these natural fertilities, how can we celebrate them and turn them into currency while becoming or remaining women?[271]

Spiritual feminists who are interested in drawing on pagan traditions to (re)create a more female-centered religion have been particularly attracted to the *Hymn*. For many such readers, the poem preserves traces of a pre-Olympian and prepatriarchal religion of the early Mediterranean, in which the central deity was female and which celebrated female fertility and bonds among women. New hymns and rites in honor of the goddesses have been created, and new psychotherapies based on goddess archetypes (Demeter is one of them) have developed.[272] In wishing to celebrate female fertility they (and some of the women writers quoted above) pointedly differ from other feminists, who have objected to the myth precisely because it seems to reinforce essentialism by linking female authority with the female body; from this critical perspective, the myth condemns women to "an endless breaking . . . on the wheel of biological reproduction."[273]

For many feminists, the *Hymn*'s version of the myth is marred by its inscription into patriarchy. The spiritual feminist Charlene Spretnak, for example, imagines that an earlier version of the myth lacked the patriarchal rape. In her reconstruction, Persephone descends voluntarily to the underworld to care for the neglected dead.[274] Similarly, the feminist theologian Mary Daly argues that the myth "expresses the essential tragedy of women after the patriarchal conquest." Demeter should not have allowed Persephone to return to Hades or have shared her secrets with men: "It was fatal for her to undervalue the power of her own position and set aside her anger, just as it was fatal that she taught the kings of the earth her divine science and initiated them into her divine mysteries."[275]

Classicists have taken up this issue in the context of Greek culture. Marylin Arthur's essay in this volume develops the suggestion that the poem could be subtitled "How to Be a Mother Goddess in a Patriarchal Society."

[271] Ibid.:11.

[272] For a hymn, see Starhawk 1989; for new rites, see Christ 1987; for the therapy, see Woolger and Woolger 1987 and Bolen 1984. For many, the Demeter myth has become a far more central psychological paradigm in female psychology than the Freudian Electra complex.

[273] Chesler 1972:240. See also 266.

[274] Spretnak 1978:103–18. This movement is too complex to address in detail here.

[275] Daly 1978:84.

Along the same lines, Saintillan has argued that the castration of the god Ouranos or Heaven by his son Kronos introduced the disorder of death and revenge into the Greek cosmos; thus a second separation, that of Demeter and Persephone, was required to order the relation between Heaven, Earth, and Sky and between life/fertility and death. The agricultural cycle, Demeter's role as mediator on earth between heaven and Hades, and the marriage and eternal return of Persephone were all "necessary" to link the natural cycle with human culture, which is characterized by its political hierarchy, its exchange of gifts to control revenge, and its regulation of sexuality by marriage. The myth creates the fiction that nature is preserved and reproduces itself by the same process that rules gift exchange in society. Just as Zeus's intervention is necessary to assure the marriage and "return" of Persephone, royal (and male) authority is needed to regulate a nature that can only be controlled and ordered if it resembles culture. This resolution is a fiction (like Kerényi, he argues that Persephone's return is imaginary and that humans get a mere symbolic substitute for immortality in Demeter's grain) that later Greek rationalism exploded when it insisted on viewing human culture as conventional rather than as fundamentally linked to nature.[276]

Insofar as the myth justifies imposing marriage on women and relegates authority to the female exclusively in the area of religious cults associated with fertility, the *Hymn* clearly does serve a patriarchal agenda. Nevertheless, within the limits of patriarchy, Demeter ultimately stages a far more decisive resistance on behalf of herself and her daughter than occurs in any other context in Greek literature. To return to the quotation from Adrienne Rich that opened this essay: "Each daughter, even in the millennia before Christ, must have longed for a mother whose love for her and whose power were so great as to undo rape and bring her back from death. And every mother must have longed for the power of Demeter, the efficacy of her anger, the reconciliation with her lost self."

APPENDIX

Eleusis and Athens

Some scholars argue that the *Hymn* was composed at Eleusis in the late seventh or early sixth century, before Athens integrated Eleusis and the Mysteries into its political and religious life and probably transformed both

[276] Saintillan 1986.

the cult and its myths in the process. From this perspective, the story of Triptolemos and the gift of agriculture may have been invented or more likely emphasized—it is after all a story about Eleusinians—to serve Athenian imperial ambition, whereas the *Hymn* reflects an earlier reality and the cultural agenda of an Eleusis as yet independent from Athens. Attic legends about the early relations of Eleusis and Athens sometimes make Eleusis (led by Eumolpos or his son) the aggressor in wars that ultimately led to the political integration of the two cities. Myths placed these wars between Athens and Eleusis during the kingship of Erechtheus (late Bronze Age), and the union (*synoikismos*) of the twelve independent communities of Attika at the time of Theseus.[277] (Pausanias 1.38.3 tells us that after the defeat Eleusis was to be subject to the Athenians in everything but carry out the Mysteries independently.) Finally, Herodotos (1.30) tells us that Tellos the Athenian died fighting at Eleusis against Athens' neighbors (although these unnamed neighbors are not necessarily the Eleusinians).[278] These legendary events are, aside from the *Hymn* itself, the only explicit evidence for Eleusinian independence from Athens, which may have ended as early as the thirteenth century.[279]

Recent reassessment of the archaeological evidence does not support the view that Eleusis was independent of Athens during the period at which the *Hymn* was composed. Robin Osborne has argued that culturally Eleusis was a part of Attika from as far back into the Dark Ages as it is possible to go.[280] More specifically, there was a gradual expansion of settlement and cult activity in eighth-century Attika, followed by some contraction in settlements (habitation sites and burials), but continued expansion of cult activity far from the city center of Athens (with substantial material goods devoted to it) in the seventh century. Pottery and burial practice do not significantly distinguish Eleusis from the rest of Attika either at this period or earlier.[281]

[277] On the mythical wars between Athens and Eleusis, see Pausanias 1.36.3 and 1.38.3, Apollodoros *Bibliotheca* 3.15.4–5, and the fragments of Euripides' *Erechtheus*. For Theseus's unification of Attika, see Thucydides 2.15 and Plutarch *Life of Theseus* 10, where Theseus takes Eleusis from Megara.

[278] Padgug 1972:139 assumes that Megara is meant.

[279] Padgug 1972 builds a coherent if speculative case, with full bibliography, for the annexation of Eleusis at this early date. He is by no means the only historian who has concluded that Eleusis was already part of Attika in the seventh century.

[280] Osborne 1989 has full citation of evidence and further bibliography on the seventh century. This discussion draws above all on a paper presented by Osborne at the 1991 Archaeological Institute of America Meeting in Chicago. Although he discusses evidence from the Dark Ages onward, I have only noted the evidence he cites for the period at which the *Hymn* was probably composed. Prior to the eighth century, in the Sub-Mycenaean and Protogeometric periods, there seems to have been a great contraction of settlements in Attika.

[281] Osborne 1991 notes that the Protoattic pottery found at both Eleusis and Athens in the seventh century was limited to Attika in its distribution. This would place Eleusis within a nexus of cultural exclusiveness.

Athens' active interest in the Mysteries at Eleusis is well documented from at least the mid-sixth century.[282] Yet, as Osborne argues, the evidence for the growth of rural cults throughout Attika and the territories that it later controlled predates the sixth century. Thus this mid-sixth century evidence may simply reflect the Athenians' desire to absorb the Mysteries into their own changing religious system or, more probably, to restructure their place in it, rather than the political incorporation of Eleusis.

The argument that the relations between Athens and its extra-urban cults such as that at Eleusis were atypical by the standards of other contemporary Greek city-states does not on closer examination stand in the way of accepting this last hypothesis. Osborne also questions De Polignac's argument that Athens represents an exception in the development of extra-urban cults in early Greek city-states.[283] De Polignac argued that most extra-urban cults founded in the eighth or seventh century in Greece were situated on what had once been Mycenaean sites (even though cult activity had ceased at these sites in the intervening period). Major cults and temples were established on the borders of territories by emerging archaic city-states in order to mark boundaries and consolidate a specific territory under their control; roads and processions to these extra-urban sanctuaries reaffirmed control over this territory and helped to include nonmilitary members of the society in a civic identity. Deities who occupied these extra-urban sanctuaries were (like Demeter) most often female—Athena, Artemis, Hera, and Apollo—and their cults frequently involved promoting agricultural fertility and the nurture of the young. Herodotos's assertion (Histories 9.97; see also Str. 633) that the migrating Ionians took with them the cult and hereditary priesthoods of Eleusinian Demeter, supports the view that the cult at Eleusis was already widespread in Greece in the late Bronze Age.[284] Yet the evidence for an Eleusinian cult of Demeter in the Mycenaean period has recently been questioned by archaeologists and there seems to be no important activity at the site from the Mycenaean period until the eighth century.[285] Eleusis was on an important border of Attika: opposite Salamis on the West coast of Attika, on the trade route where roads from Attika,

[282] E.g., the building of a new Telesterion at Eleusis and an Eleusinion at Athens, new fortifications, the Orphic myths, and vase paintings with Eleusinian motifs. See Richardson 1974:9–10 and Boardman 1975:4–5. The date of the building of the first Eleusinion (many other small Eleusinia appeared throughout the Attic demes in the classical period) is uncertain. The building remains date from the early fifth century, but inscriptions suggest earlier occupation. The archaic "Solonian" Telesterion may indicate involvement earlier in the century. See Richardson 1974:10.

[283] De Polignac 1984 and Osborne 1991. Calame 1990:361–62 raises additional problems about De Polignac's interpretation of Athens.

[284] See Richardson 1974:18 and Graf 1974:274–77. The exact date of the Ionian migrations remains controversial.

[285] See Darcque 1981 and Parker 1988:102n.31.

Boeotia, and the Peloponnesos met. Both Solon and Peisistratos would have found Eleusis of strategic importance in their wars against Megara. The procession at the Mysteries, at least at a later date, went from Athens to Eleusis.

Yet despite Eleusis's potential for conformity to his pattern in certain respects, De Polignac saw Athens as an exception, with a concentric rather than bipolar development of cults. In his model of Athens, the city center was always of paramount importance from the Mycenaean period on; extra-urban cults were founded or appropriated from the center; processions, like the Panathenaiac procession, were sometimes made to the center rather than from it, as in other cities; in Attika the interest in important extra-urban sites like Eleusis or Brauron came only in the sixth century rather than in the seventh or eighth centuries (although evidence of cult activity at these sites predates the sixth century). On this issue of date, De Polignac raises a significant question. Yet, Osborne argues, important shrines outside Athens could in fact have functioned as they did in other cities even if, as in the case of Eleusis, the cult was, in contrast to isolated temples like the Argive Heraion, located in a settlement. Athenian cult practices and politics seem on his evidence to be linked from at least the eighth century, although the remains are more monumental in the sixth century (as elsewhere).[286] Even if the cult at Eleusis was open to outsiders, as opposed to marking the limits of a community as in De Polignac's other cases, it could signal the unusual power and capacities of Athens without compromising the ability of other exclusively Athenian cults to maintain the integrity of the community.

Yet if the *Hymn* was likely to have been composed at a time when Eleusis was already part of Attika, it is still necessary to consider the poem's silence on matters Athenian. Kevin Clinton has alleged that such omissions indicate that the *Hymn* was not composed for a local audience and that the author of the *Hymn* was unfamiliar with Eleusis and many details of the cult, and thus not from Attika.[287] This is no trivial issue, in that both the relation of the

---

[286] There is also in Osborne's view no hard evidence that the tyrant Peisistratos, as is generally supposed, founded or promoted major cults (such as that at Eleusis) in Athens in the mid-sixth century. See also Connor 1990 and Kolb 1977.

[287] Clinton 1986. Cassolà 1975:34 also suggests that the poet of the *Hymn* may have been a stranger to Eleusis. In a paper presented at the 1992 American Philological Association meeting at New Orleans, Clinton revised his original view. He now links the poem to Eleusis (if not to the Mysteries) but thinks that the body of its myth originally served as an aetiology for the Thesmophoria. The dearth of visual evidence, even in the classical period, where the cult at Eleusis was known to be important in Athens, makes it difficult to assess its implications. (See Shapiro 1989:67–83 and Peschlow-Bindokat 1972.) Demeter is represented rarely in Attika before the mid-sixth century B.C.E., and there is no hint of the goddess's association with Eleusis. Representations of Persephone begin about 540 B.C.E., but they do not initially link the goddess with her mother or the cult. Fragments of vases that apparently relate to cult activity at Eleusis appear from the first quarter of the sixth century to the last. Yet in the case of mythological scenes, only representations of the two goddesses with Triptolemos became

Hymn to the cult at Eleusis and the possibility of locating the poem in a social and religious context are at stake. Clinton argues as follows: Eumolpos, by later tradition the first priest of the Mysteries, is given no special role in the *Hymn*. The poem is silent on his priestly role and that of the daughters of Keleos, the prototypes for the first priestess of Demeter. There is no mention in the *Hymn* of the priestly family important in the later Mysteries, the Kerykes. In the *Hymn* the obscure Demophoön is given a central role later usurped in myth and cult by Demeter's nurslings Triptolemos and others. The role of Hekate is in Clinton's view also marginal at Eleusis, and the names Hades or Aidoneus and Persephone (rather than Ploutô and Korê) are taboo in later Eleusinian inscriptions. Demeter's founding of agriculture in Attika is omitted in the *Hymn*, and the poet seems to have little or inaccurate knowledge of the local topography at Eleusis.

As Parker has recently noted, however, all Clinton's sources for this condemnation are decidedly late.[288] The names Persephone and Hades were used not only in epic (the *Hymn* is stylistically in this tradition) but in Eleusinian contexts in Attic drama (Euripides *Suppliants* 271, Aristophanes *Frogs* 671).[289] Hekate does have a role in Eleusinian iconography and many scholars have argued for an important symbolic link betwen Demophoön and the founding of the Mysteries.[290] Even Clinton seems hesitant on the question of topographical detail,[291] and he tends to play down those parts of the poem that do correspond to what we know of the public— preliminary and not secret—parts of the rite at a later date: the journey to Eleusis, the story of the rape, the torchlit search for Persephone, the acts of sitting on a stool, and fasting, the drinking of the *kykeôn*, the hint at *aischrologia*.[292] The poem also develops the themes of sight and hearing,

---

popular, and even this occurred largely in the classical period. The rape of Persephone was represented for the first time well into the fifth century and rarely thereafter. Hence the evidence from visual sources is largely negative, although the gradual increase in representations of the goddesses from the second half of the sixth century on might reflect a growing Athenian interest in the cult.

[288] Parker 1991:16n.22.

[289] See Parker 1991:16n.22. The name Persephone appeared in Pamphos's *Hymn to Demeter* (Pausanias 8.37.9), which was composed for an Athenian audience, and on local pots as well (see Schwartz 1987:39nn.58 and 61). In a fragment of an Attic calendar of 403–02 B.C.E. (Sokolowski 1962:10.63), sacrifices are offered to Pherephatta (=Persephone) in an Eleusinian context.

[290] See Parker 1991:16n.22, Schwartz 1987:253 on Hekate, and my Commentary (this volume) on lines 231–55 on Demophoön's relation to the Mysteries.

[291] Clinton 1986:44 agrees with Richardson 1974 that the Telesterion could be described as being on a "jutting hill." Richardson 1974 (Appendix 1) argues that the wells Parthenion and Kallichoron, and hence the well found near the Telesterion, are one.

[292] Clinton 1986:43n.5 argues that the tradition that initiates covered their heads or sat on a fleece derives from visual representations of Herakles, which may have a dubious connection with Attic Eleusis. This argument cannot disprove the possibility that inititiates did perform these actions, however.

light and darkness, and the transition from fear to joy thought to be central to the secret rites as well. I would even argue (see the Commentary on lines 490–95) that the poet hints, by claiming a livelihood from Demeter at the close of the poem, that he is an initiate (a possibility not denied by Clinton in any case).

Clinton's argument also assumes that the poem aims to reflect to some degree contemporary experience and practice. The Homeric features of the poem's social world, however, suggest that it aims to recapture an earlier, mythical period when the Mysteries were founded—a period when Eleusis might easily be imagined to be independent from Athens.[293] The myths concerning the wars between Eleusis and Athens and the unification of Attika under Theseus mentioned above were Athenian. Hence even an Attic poet telling the story of the founding of the cult at Eleusis could set his tale at a time prior to Athenian presence in Eleusis without being inconsistent with local tradition.[294] In fact, an archaizing poem would not only have no reason to mention Athens but would enhance the cult's claim to immemorial antiquity by ignoring the city. Furthermore, as we shall see, the omissions that trouble Clinton can be deliberate rather than a reflection of ignorance.

Finally, I want to stress that Clinton's theory fails to explain how or why the *Hymn* would have been composed. The rape of Korê was a popular subject at this period, he says, and thus a non-Athenian would want to sing about it. As proof he reminds us that we also know of Pamphos's *Hymn to Demeter* and a poem attributed to Homer with different names for the daughters of Keleos than in our hymn. In fact, we do not have evidence for a non-Attic interest in the myth or the cult of the kind Clinton posits. Pausanias tells us (7.21.3) that Pamphos wrote the most ancient *Athenian* hymns before Homer, and his poem seems by Clinton's standards to fit Attic tradition and a local audience better.[295] The Orphic versions of the myth do make more reference to local Attic myths and features of the rites; but it is generally assumed that they reflect early Attic traditions. On the other hand, the major Homeric epics and Hesiod show little interest in Demeter and Persephone (their names are not even linked in Homer). Similarly, although the story of the founding of well-known shrines was a typical hymnic theme, it is unclear to what degree Eleusis, unlike Delphi, whose oracle clearly has

---

[293] Padgug 1972:137–38 with further references.

[294] My point is that it would help to consider the *Hymn*'s failure to mention Athens in light of the way that Athenian poetry generally treats the origins of Attic cult. Euripides' play *Hippolytos*, for example, barely mentions the Attic cult of Hippolytos in the precinct of Aphrodite in Athens. If the Athenians simply invented myths about an earlier conflict between Eleusis and Athens, it would also be important, in evaluating these issues, to explore when and why this invention occurred.

[295] See Richardson 1974:74 on Pamphos and the Attic tradition.

Panhellenic status in Homer, was an important Panhellenic site at this period.[296] We do not even know whether there were restrictions on initiation
at Eleusis in the late-seventh or early-sixth centuries, although I think,
because the *Hymn* mentions none, it makes sense to assume that the poem is
directed at a larger than local group of potential initiates.[297]

I would conclude, then, that neither the poem's probable date of composition nor its purported non-Attic authorship can explain the absence of
features of the cult associated with Athens; nor does the poem represent an
Eleusinian version that deliberately repressed Attic presence in the myth, as
Walton argued.[298] Nevertheless, we still have not offered a full explanation
of the shape of our *Hymn*. Parts of the *Hymn*'s own narrative, as mentioned
earlier, have no logical motivation, whereas the later versions do, and there
are traces in the poem of the versions omitted by our poet.[299] It seems far
more likely, then, that such "gaps in motivation" or distinctive features of
the *Hymn*'s version of the myth are rather the result of the poem's deliberate
modification and adaptation of inherited versions. In general, more than
one version of an aetiological myth explaining a particular Greek cult could
exist (even contradictory versions) without causing its participants discom-
fort. Because, as we stressed earlier, Greek religion had in every respect no
official theology and poets were free to draw on tradition to create their own
version of a myth, we have no reason to think that the *Hymn* was ever, as
some earlier critics thought, the "official" Eleusinian version of the myth at
any time, but *a* version designed at Eleusis for audiences (including audiences at Eleusis) who had more than a strictly local interest in the
narrative.[300]

The *Hymn to Demeter* as a Panhellenic Poem

Let us come back to the questions asked in the section "Variants of the
Myth" (above, this essay) about why the *Hymn* might have avoided empha-

[296] E.g., the *Hymn to Apollo* includes the founding of Apollo's cults at Delos and Delphi. See
Parker 1991:3.

[297] Parker 1991:6 stresses that the poem's audience must be potential initiates. The only
evidence that the cult was restricted at an earlier date is mythical: Herakles and the Dioskuroi
were made citizens before initiation. These myths may have more to do with Athens' attempt to
appropriate these heroes for itself by making them citizens than the state of requirements for
ordinary initiates, however.

[298] Walton 1952.

[299] See my Commentary (this volume) and Clay 1989 passim for examples.

[300] Richardson 1974:12 suggests the Eleusinian games or the Balletys for Demophoön as a
possible occasion for recitation of this poem in Attika. I agree with Clinton 1986:48 that a
poem composed exclusively for a local audience would probably be considerably different from
this hymn, although there were likely to have been variations in versions aimed at such a local
audience as well. Parker 1991:5 and 16n.22 cites Athenian variations on the story of
Triptolemos.

sizing those aspects of the myth that stress the origin of agriculture, ignored or de-emphasized some local features of the cult and its officials, and left parts of the story "unmotivated," where other versions do not. Of course, no poet would have risked divulging any part of the Mysteries but the preliminaries. Ancient sources emphasize the secrecy of the final initiation and the dangers of revealing any part of it. But the Panhellenic context in which the Homeric hymns were probably presented would further encourage an archaic Greek poet to avoid or downplay regional versions of the myth and local details.[301]

As said earlier, these hymns were at least theoretically composed and sung by poets as a prelude to the recitation of other epic poems, such as we have preserved in the *Iliad* or the *Odyssey*.[302] Poetic contests and other occasions for such recitation would have occurred not just in one locality, but in many parts of Greece. Although we know almost nothing about the occasions at which the Homeric hymns would have been performed—public festivals and poetic contests and/or feasts at the courts of nobles—a Panhellenic movement in poetry was clearly in full flower by the end of the eighth century B.C.E. when the major Homeric epics were probably composed; and Jenny Clay has made a strong case for the Panhellenic orientation of all the major Homeric hymns.[303] This movement paralleled the development of Panhellenic religious sites, like Delphi, and the emergence of Panhellenic athletic games at Olympia and elsewhere.

As noted above, Clinton's argument supports the assumption that the poem aims at an audience unlikely to be strictly local,[304] and the *Hymn* seemingly makes a bid for Panhellenic status by emphasizing the collective nature of Demeter's gifts to humankind. Demeter removes and restores the fertility of the whole earth; the poem treats her as a goddess with cults outside Eleusis. To the degree that the *Hymn* aims to adapt local material to suit a Panhellenic perspective, then, it must be addressing a wider audience of potential initiates. There is no reason to believe that a Panhellenic version

[301] Clay 1989:6–7 argues that the Homeric hymns give no internal evidence confirming that they were recited in a strictly local context.

[302] For the controversy on the nature of the hymns, and whether they served as *prooimia* (preludes) to epic, see Richardson 1974:4, Clay 1989:3–4, and Nagy 1990b:353–60 with further references. Although the hymns were originally *prooimia*, the longer hymns may have become independent performances that still preserved the form of *prooimia*. See the beginning of the Commentary (above) for further discussion.

[303] See Clay 1989:9ff. and passim, who, following the lead of Nagy (esp. 1982 and 1990a:36–82), also attempts to explain the cosmology of the hymns and their avoidance of local concerns through their Panhellenism. The best evidence that a Panhellenic movement in poetry existed is the nature and later status of the poems themselves, with their avoidance of local detail and local hero cult; in addition the Greeks believed that Homer and Hesiod systematized their views about the gods and their cosmological struggles. See further below. Clay, on the other hand, accepts Clinton's arguments.

[304] Clinton 1986.

of the founding myth could not have been generated in and performed at Eleusis (and/or Athens); indeed, it would make strategic sense for Eleusis (and Athens) to encourage this development. Athens itself was soon to establish the recitation of the Homeric epics at its own Panathenaic festival and to promote a Panhellenic status for the Mysteries. Indeed, Athens invited Panhellenic participation in all three of the major festivals it promoted in the course of the sixth century: the Panathenaia, the City Dionysia, and the Mysteries.

The version of the myth represented in the *Hymn* is thus not fundamentally antagonistic to local myths or misinformed about the rites performed at Eleusis; it complements other versions but aims to represent the rites from a Panhellenic perspective. Reasons of genre can thus go some way toward making sense of the particular version of the myth found in the *Hymn* and its silence on Athens' role in the cult.[305] There were many competing Greek versions of Demeter's search for her daughter, and the Sicilians also claimed to have been the first to receive the gift of agriculture from the goddess. The *Hymn to Demeter* deftly avoids choosing among different local claims about which mortals were the first to inform and help the goddess, through bypassing that version altogether in favor of divine witnesses and locating the abduction at the ends of the earth. The poem thus inserts itself into a Panhellenic tradition by making the question of hospitality a non-issue. Diodorus Siculus (*Bibliotheca* 5.69.3) says that everyone agrees that the abduction of Persephone took place in Sicily; this is not true, but he may be correct that Sicily was the most widely acknowleged site for the abduction. Athens' claim to be the site of the abduction would thus represent a minority local view to be avoided before a Panhellenic audience. As a Panhellenic poem, the *Hymn* also ignores Athens' exclusive claim to the origin of agriculture and does not drown its audience in details about the local priestly hierarchy or esoteric local taboos. By contrast, there were, as far as we know, no competing claims for important Mysteries of Demeter at this early date, and ancient sources generally agree on the antiquity and the priority of the Mysteries at Eleusis. Cicero (*Against Verres* 2.4. 106–8) shows that the Sicilians contested the Athenians' claim on agriculture but viewed the Mysteries as imported from Attika. Diodorus Siculus *Bibliotheca* 5.4.4 similarly concedes their antiquity in a context where he is claiming the founding of agriculture for Sicily. Hence the *Hymn*'s focus on the founding of Panhellenic Mysteries is ideal for a Panhellenic audience.[306]

[305] In making this argument, I am aware that it is dangerous to generalize from the Panhellenic poetry now available to us, which was selected out for preservation at a later date, as to the nature of Panhellenic poetry at the time the *Hymn* was composed.

[306] The Mysteries were sometimes said to have originated in Crete (Diodorus Siculus *Bibliotheca* 5.77.3). As Clay 1989:8–10 emphasizes, the hymns follow the major Homeric epics and Hesiod in aiming to represent a synthetic and Panhellenic divine cosmology.

Versions of myths in the *Iliad* and *Odyssey* were also apparently chosen to be appropriate and tasteful for a broad, Panhellenic audience.[307] In aiming to praise, poems in the Panhellenic epic tradition (above all the two great Homeric epics that have clearly influenced the *Hymn*)[308] often favored discreet or euphemistic versions of a myth over ones that emphasized an unfavorable portrait of gods or humans, or intrafamilial violence and explicit sexuality—myths such as we find in later tragedy or even the poems of the Epic Cycle. The *Hymn* is euphemistically silent on the content of Iambe's jokes with Demeter (probably explicitly sexual) and does not have the baby Demophoön die when abandoned by Demeter as he does in some other versions.[309] The *Hymn* creates an Eleusis and a royal household that would fit comfortably into Homer and in no way resembles the rustic households of Keleos, Dysaules, Baubo, and others in alternative Attic versions of the myth. Whereas the witnesses to Persephone's abduction in these other Attic versions are often pastoralists, the Eleusinians of the *Hymn* are settled agriculturalists in a well-organized polis. Thus, in its style, tone, and choice of themes for emphasis, the *Hymn*'s version of the myth is well adapted for the Panhellenic (rather than strictly local) context for which it was composed.

[307] On the euphemism of Homeric epic, see Wehrli 1934:80, Deichgräber 1950:529, and Richardson 1974:59.

[308] For a detailed comparison, see Richardson 1974:31–33.

[309] Orphic frag. 49. 100ff. and Apollodoros *Bibliotheca* 1.5.1. See the Commentary on lines 202–4 for detailed discussion of Iambe.

PART THREE

FURTHER INTERPRETATION:

CONTRIBUTED ARTICLES

WITHDRAWAL AND RETURN: AN EPIC STORY PATTERN IN THE HOMERIC *HYMN TO DEMETER* AND IN THE HOMERIC POEMS

Mary Louise Lord

T HE PURPOSE of this paper is to show that the story of Demeter's withdrawal and return in the Homeric *Hymn to Demeter* shares an epic pattern that is discernible also in the Homeric poems.[1] The narrative of the *Hymn*, built upon recurrent epic and mythic themes, may be seen to reveal a structure found in other stories in verse that have long existed in tradition.

It has been observed that certain story elements tend to belong together and to recur in essentially the same pattern or grouping of themes. A. B. Lord has shown in *The Singer of Tales*[2] that in traditional stories there are complexes of themes held together by a strong force or hidden tension that works both "by the logic of the narrative and by the consequent force of habitual association." Long absence of the hero, for example, has been demonstrated in a number of songs to attract the themes of deceptive story and recognition.[3] Although the pattern normally demands a certain order of its component elements, there may be a shifting of parts within the group according to the needs of a particular narrative. The basic pattern is nonetheless recognizable. For the sake of emphasis, and because the forces of association are so strong, repetitions or reduplications of some elements in the pattern frequently occur.

The narrative pattern that I shall trace centers on the following principal elements with accompanying themes: (1) the withdrawal of the hero (or heroine), which sometimes takes the form of a long absence—this element is often closely linked with a quarrel and the loss of someone beloved; (2) disguise during the absence or upon the return of the hero, frequently

---

[1] This article was originally published in *Classical Journal* 62 (1967):241–48. It has been very slightly abridged (eight sentences cut) and some of the notes have been cut. Additional minor alterations have been made to conform with the editorial style of this volume.

[2] Lord 1960:96–98.

[3] Ibid.:97.

accompanied by a deceitful story; (3) the theme of hospitality to the wandering hero; (4) the recognition of the hero, or at least a fuller revelation of his identity; (5) disaster during or occasioned by the absence; (6) the reconciliation of the hero and return. These themes are listed in the sequence in which they occur in the Homeric *Hymn to Demeter*. As each element is discussed, related themes from the *Iliad* and the *Odyssey* will be cited.

That the pattern of withdrawal and return or of absence and return is basic to the plot of the *Iliad* and of the *Odyssey* and that it is prefigured in the myth of Persephone have been pointed out in *The Singer of Tales*:[4]

> The essential pattern of the *Iliad* is the same as that of the *Odyssey*; they are both the story of an absence that causes havoc to the beloved of the absentee and of his return to set matters aright. Both tales involve the loss of someone near and dear to the hero (Patroclus and Odysseus's companions); both contain the element of disguise (the armor in the *Iliad*); in both is the return associated with contests or games and followed by remarriage (Achilles with Briseis, Odysseus with Penelope) and, finally in both a long period of time is supposed to elapse or to have elapsed.
>
> The story of the Trojan War is a simple one of bride-stealing and rescue. It belongs primarily to Menelaus, Paris, and Helen, and might have remained uncomplicated even if the struggle did call forth the armada of Achaeans and a host of Trojan allies. But bride-stealing in epic was mythic before it became heroic and historical. The rape of Persephone in all its forms as a fertility myth underlies all epic tales of this sort, and until the historical is completely triumphant over the mythic, all such tales are likely to be drawn into the pattern of the myth.

The remarks that follow will be concerned not so much with the seasonal withdrawal and return of Persephone, as with the withdrawal of Demeter from Olympus to humans and her eventual return to the gods.

By citing Homeric parallels for narrative elements in the *Hymn to Demeter*, I am not suggesting literary indebtedness, but instead similarity in the use of old and widespread epic themes. In Homer there is no reference to the rape and return of Persephone, and the names of Demeter and Persephone are not linked. Demeter's role in the Homeric poems is negligible. Her precinct, "flowery Pyrgasos," is mentioned in the "Catalogue of Ships" (*Iliad* 2.695–96). The phrase "the corn or meal of Demeter" (*Dêmêteros aktê*) occurs twice in the *Iliad* (13.322; 21.76), and in *Iliad* 14.326 Demeter is listed in the catalogue of mortal women and goddesses loved by Zeus. In the *Odyssey* (5.125) Kalypso relates that when Demeter lay with Iasion in the thrice-plowed field, Zeus killed him with his thunderbolt. It is in association with Hades that Homer mentions Persephoneia (*Iliad* 9.569; *Odyssey*

---

[4] Ibid.:186.

10.491), the daughter of Zeus (*Odyssey* 11.217). In the *Iliad* she is called *epainê*, "the dread goddess" (*Iliad* 9.457, 569), and in the *Odyssey* her epithets are *agauê*, "noble" (11.213, 226, 635), and *hagnê*, "pure" or "holy" (11.386). The poet of the *Theogony* (912–14) includes Demeter among the divine marriages of Zeus and in three lines briefly alludes to the rape of Persephone by Hades, carried out with the consent of Zeus.

In the pattern of withdrawal and return in the Homeric *Hymn to Demeter*, the absence of Demeter (Theme 1) is a withdrawal from the assembly of the gods to the world of humans. After the abduction of Persephone at the beginning of the *Hymn*, Demeter hears her daughter's voice and hastens over land and sea in search of her. For nine days she wanders over the earth with kindled torches and refuses to taste nectar and ambrosia and to bathe (47–50). On the tenth day she goes, accompanied by Hekate, to Helios, who explains that Zeus has given Persephone to Hades in marriage and that the latter has snatched her down to his murky realm. At this point the quarrel theme (77–87) becomes apparent and motivates what would seem to be Demeter's second and much longer withdrawal from the gods. Earlier in the poem (3, 30) we are told that it is with the permission and counsel of Zeus that Hades took Persephone. Although a quarrel is not enacted, Demeter's anger against Zeus is clearly stated. Helios in revealing to Demeter the fate of Persephone tries to convince her that Hades, her own brother and lord of a third portion of the world, is no mean son-in-law and that it is not fitting for her to cherish in vain her "unapproachable wrath" (82–83). But more terrible and more savage ("doglike," *kunteron*) grief comes to her, and in anger against Zeus she thereupon avoids the assembly of the gods and high Olympus and comes to the cities and rich fields of humans (90–93). This withdrawal of Demeter occupies the major portion of the narrative. It is caused essentially by the loss of her daughter but is immediately precipitated by her anger against Zeus.

In the *Iliad* a quarrel, provoked by the loss of Briseis, is the active force in the withdrawal of Achilleus from battle. This vital action, once announced, is preceded by a version of the theme in briefer compass, that is, Agamemnon's angry refusal to ransom Chryseis and Chryses' withdrawal to pray for Apollo's vengeance. Chryseis is restored to her father, but Agamemnon's further anger leads to the quarrel with Achilleus over Briseis.[5]

Another parallel to the withdrawal in anger is found in the story of Meleager used by Phoenix (*Iliad* 9.524–605) as an exemplum to urge Achilleus to accept Agamemnon's gifts and to return to the fighting. Meleager withdraws from the defense of Kalydon in anger at his mother's curses. She has invoked these upon him because of her grief over the killing of her brothers at the time of the tumultuous division of the boar's head and

---

[5] For these interlocking patterns, see ibid.:188–90.

hide. It is true that the loss of loved ones is felt by Althaia rather than by Meleager, but the lesson for Achilleus is plain. It is striking that both the *Iliad* itself and the Meleager story within it begin with an affronted deity who sets the devastation in motion.[6]

Unlike Meleager, Achilleus is not persuaded by the embassy to rejoin the battle. His angry refusal of Agamemnon's gifts leads to a renewal of the quarrel and the subsequent loss of Patroklos, whose death (with that of Hektor for the Trojans) provides the most important bereavement in the *Iliad*. With the loss of Patroklos we have, interwoven in the pattern of withdrawal in anger, the theme of the "death of the substitute," realized by the slaying of Patroklos in the armor of Achilleus.[7]

The introduction of the death of the substitute raises the question that can only be posed here, whether Persephone, as "the younger double of her mother,"[8] may be said to die (and be revived) as a "substitute" for her mother. A closer parallel to the death of Patroklos for Achilleus is seen in the death of Enkidu for Gilgamesh. In Tablet 7 of *The Epic of Gilgamesh*, Enkidu dreams that the gods debate which of the two heroes should die for having slain the Bull of Heaven and Huwawa. When Enkidu lies ill, Gilgamesh mourns that he has been "cleared at the expense of his 'brother.' "[9]

In the *Odyssey* the use of the theme of withdrawal or long absence, associated with anger and the loss of a loved one, is not so clear-cut as in the *Iliad*. Odysseus's long wandering after the fall of Troy, however, could be said to be caused in large measure by the anger of Poseidon and by Polyphemos's prayer to his father that Odysseus may return to his home "late and in evil plight, having lost all his companions, in the ship of strangers, and find woes in his house" (*Odyssey* 9.534–35). Although the loss of his companions is not the reason for Odysseus's absence, it is an important element in the return story and is given prominence at the beginning of the poem (1.5–9).

In the *nostoi* of Agamemnon and of Menelaos, which in the *Odyssey* provide foils to the return of Odysseus and which follow some parts of our story pattern, the quarrel theme is conspicuously present as a prelude to the journeys and misadventures of the heroes. Nestor, relating to Telemachos (*Odyssey* 3.132ff.) the baneful return devised by Zeus for the Achaeans, tells how Athena, as a result of her destructive wrath, caused strife between the Atreidai over whether they should appease the goddess with sacrifice before departing. Their noisy disagreement helps to account for the separate returns of the brothers and for the fact that Agamemnon did not have the help of Menelaos either in preventing or in avenging his death.

---

[6] For the anger of Apollo, see *Iliad* 1.8ff.; in the Meleager story, note the anger of Artemis, *Iliad* 9.533ff. One thinks also of the wrath of Artemis, the prevention of the sailing of the Greek host, and the sacrifice of Iphigeneia at the beginning of the Trojan War.

[7] Lord 1960:190.

[8] Rose 1959:91.

[9] Pritchard 1950:85–86.

The absence of Demeter is in one respect unlike that of Achilleus or that of Odysseus (in the *Odyssey*), because her withdrawal is combined with a search or quest for her daughter. While recognizing this important difference, we must remember that the larger context of the Trojan War is concerned with bride-stealing and the attempt to regain Helen. The *Iliad* itself begins and ends with a parent (Chryses, Priam) seeking the return of his child.[10] Furthermore, one of the intrusive patterns in the *Odyssey* is Telemachos's quest for news of his absent father, an initiatory exploit for Telemachos.

The element of disguise (Theme 2) occurs in the Demeter story when the goddess for a long time disfigures or emaciates her form (94) so that no mortal knows her. She is like an old woman born long ago (101). Gods appearing on earth among humans regularly disguise their appearance and divinity. Demeter's disfigurement is also a sign of mourning. In her first search for her daughter she tore the headdress on her divine hair in keen sorrow and threw off her dark cloak (40–42). For nine days she wandered over the earth and refused to taste nectar and ambrosia and to bathe (49–50). We are reminded that when Achilleus hears the news of Patroklos's death, he takes the sooty dust in both hands and pours it over his head and disfigures his fine countenance, and black ashes settle on his chiton (*Iliad* 18.23–25). He also refuses food and drink (*Iliad* 19.210, 320). Athena's method of disguising Odysseus is to wither his limbs, make him lose his hair, give him the skin of an old man and dim his eyes, as well as to provide him with the garb, staff, and wallet of a beggar. A foreshadowing of his disguise is the self-disfigurement and beating Odysseus endures, as well as the rags he wears, in his feat of entering Troy by night (*Odyssey* 4.242ff.). The element of disguise also enters the Agamemnon story, when Agamemnon's shade advises Odysseus to return home "secretly," *krybdên* (*Odyssey* 11.455), a precaution that Agamemnon himself should have taken.

When Demeter meets the daughters of Keleos, she tells them a deceitful story that her name is Dos (or Doso) (122) and that pirates brought her against her will from Crete to Thorikos where they landed to have food and that she escaped while the meal was being prepared (122–32). This story closely resembles a part of one of five versions of Odysseus's deceptive story, that he came from Crete. As the last incident of his long and circumstantial account to Eumaios, he describes how the crew of the Thresprotian ship tied him under the ship's benches and disembarked. While they took supper on the beach, he made his escape with the help of the gods (*Odyssey* 14.345ff.).[11] The multiforms of Odysseus's deceptive story by their very number indicate the emphasis that was placed on this element in the plot of the *Odyssey*.

[10] See Levy 1953:181n.4 and Sheppard 1922:207ff.
[11] Cf. also the reference to the need for supper in the deceitful story in *Odyssey* 13.280.

Theme 3: The encounter at the Maiden Well of the disguised Demeter with the daughters of Keleos, who lead her to their mother Metaneira, might seem to be a theme that stems solely from the topography of Eleusis, which Mylonas has been able to equate closely with references in the *Hymn*.[12] Hospitality to a wandering stranger by maidens at a well or at washing troughs is a theme familiar, however, from the gracious reception given to Odysseus by Nausikäa, who sees that he reaches her mother Arete. A second version or multiform of the theme immediately follows in the *Odyssey* when Nausikäa tells Odysseus to wait by a spring in the grove of Athena (*Odyssey* 6.291–92). Soon (*Odyssey* 7.19–20) Athena appears, disguised as a young girl carrying a pitcher, and conducts him to the palace. In a third instance of the theme, in Book 10, Odysseus's men meet a maiden drawing water, the sturdy daughter of Laestrygonian Antiphates. She had come to the clear-flowing spring Artakia. She too leads strangers to home and mother, but here "mother" is a monstrous hulk of a woman, and her menfolk are even more dangerous; the results are disastrous (*Odyssey* 10.105ff.).

The theme of the maiden at a well is usually associated with finding a husband. Marriage is clearly in Nausikäa's mind when she goes to wash the clothes, so that it is not surprising that Odysseus prays to the gods to grant her a husband and a happy home (*Odyssey* 6.181–84), just as Demeter wishes for the daughters of Keleos husbands and children (136). An unmistakable and definitive use of the theme is found in the story of Rebekah at the well in *Genesis* 24, which recounts how the servant of Abraham found a wife for Isaac from Abraham's own people.

In the *Hymn to Demeter* the use of the theme of hospitality at a well is a natural and traditional way of having the disguised Demeter conducted to the palace of Keleos and to an audience with Metaneira. Pamphos, in a lost hymn to Demeter referred to by Pausanias (1.39.1), also had Demeter met by the maidens of Eleusis at a well, although a different well (the Anthion), from the Parthenion Well of the Homeric *Hymn*.[13]

In receiving Demeter, Metaneira bids her to be seated, but the goddess will not sit on the shining couch. She remains silent with eyes cast down until Iambe places a stool for her and covers it with a silvery sheepskin. When Odysseus returns as a beggar to the palace in Ithaka, he is given a humble seat on the wooden threshold (*Odyssey* 17.339). His abasement or vilification is much more violent than that of Demeter. During the course of his many adventures, he is taunted by the Phaeacian Euryalos at the games (*Odyssey* 8.158–64), kicked by the goatherd Melanthios (*Odyssey* 17.233), and hit with a footstool by Antinoös (*Odyssey* 17.462). Is it possible, how-

---

[12] Mylonas 1942:23–24, 64–81.
[13] Ibid.:65ff.

ever, to find a closer thematic correspondence with the Homeric *Hymn to Demeter*? It may be that the raillery and the mocking of Odysseus by the suitor Eurymachos, who makes fun of his baldness, correspond to the jesting of Iambe to make Demeter smile (202–4). Iambe's joking is mentioned also by Apollodoros (1.5.1), who associates it with the jesting of the women at the festival of the Thesmophoria.

Metaneira next offers sweet wine to the goddess, but Demeter declares that it is not lawful for her to drink it.[14] She orders instead a mixture (*kykeôn*) of barley meal, water, and tender pennyroyal, which she receives "for the sake of the rite" (*hosiês heneken*). In Homer the drinking of the *kykeôn* could be a somewhat special event associated with hospitality, but it was not a ritual. In the *Iliad* (11.624–42) a *kykeôn* is served to Nestor and Eurymedon, made of Pramnian wine, grated cheese, and white barley, which quenched their parching thirst after battle. Ovid's story (*Metamorphoses* 5.449–61) of the boy who was turned into a spotted lizard after he had mocked Demeter and called her greedy in drinking the barley mixture so avidly, also suggests that the *kykeôn* could quench thirst. The example of *kykeôn* in the *Odyssey* (10.234ff.), Kirke's mixture of cheese, barley, honey, and Pramnian wine, does not of itself transform Odysseus's men into swine but has to be spiked by the addition of baneful drugs (*pharmaka lygra*).

Demeter is duly accepted into the household of Keleos and appointed to be the nurse of the child Demophoön. In order to make him immortal, Demeter anoints him with ambrosia and puts him secretly into the fire at night to burn away his mortality. She is frustrated in this attempt by Metaneira, who, spying on the goddess, cries aloud at the sight of her child in the fire. Demeter snatches him out of the hearth and throws him to the ground, declaring that in no way can he escape death yet will have honor because she has been his nurse. A similar story is told in Apollonios's *Argonautika* (4.869ff.), that Thetis attempted to make Achilleus immortal by this same method, that is, by anointing him with ambrosia and putting him into the fire, but was thwarted by Peleus. In the *Iliad* we hear only of Thetis's dissatisfaction with Peleus as a husband and that he lies in his halls spent with age (*Iliad* 18.432–35), but we are repeatedly reminded of Achilleus's mortality and that not even his mother can save him from death.

When Demeter first enters the palace of Keleos, there is an epiphany (Theme 4) of the goddess, partial and somewhat premature. She fills the door with a heavenly light and her head reaches the roof (188–89). The epiphany is partial because she is still unrecognized, and premature because it anticipates the climactic scene later in the poem when it is time for her divinity to be fully revealed. The earlier hint of the goddess's majesty may be

---

[14] Demeter's cult was generally wineless, but there were exceptions as at the Haloa. See Allen, Halliday, and Sikes 1936:152–53.

compared to the beautification of Odysseus by Athena when he has washed away the scurf of the sea and appears godlike to Nausikäa, although still a stranger and not recognized as Odysseus (*Odyssey* 6.224–37). Demeter's anger at Metaneira's interference with her treatment of Demophoön is the culminating event that causes the goddess to reveal herself and to demand appeasement: "I am Demeter, held in honor, the greatest help and joy to the immortal gods and to mortals" (268–69). Her demand to be conciliated leads to the aetiological part of the *Hymn*, in which she bids all the people to build her a great temple and an altar beneath it, under the city and its steep wall on a projecting rock. She says, "I myself will prescribe my rites so that performing them undefiled you may appease my heart" (273–74).

Thereupon comes the epiphany or revelation of the goddess in glory. Her old age is thrust away, fragrance is shed from her garments, radiance shines from her immortal body, and the house is filled with the brilliance of lightning (275–80).

Quite like this epiphany is the appearance of Achilleus in glory at the trench (*Iliad* 18.203–31). Before he receives his divine armor, he is ordered by Iris at Hera's command to go forth to the trench to show himself as he is and to reveal himself to the Trojans. Patroklos had earlier appeared in the borrowed armor of Achilleus as a disguise, first suggested by Nestor (*Iliad* 11.795ff.), in order to confuse the enemy into believing that he was Achilleus. Achilleus must now reveal his true self, wearing the aegis of Athena. His dazzling epiphany is marked by a golden cloud and by a flame blazing from his head. His voice strikes dismay into the Trojans and thereupon twelve of them perish (*Iliad* 18.197–231).

The multiplicity of the recognitions of Odysseus upon his return may be regarded as a means of testing his relationship with each of the members of his household. We are reminded that in some versions of the return story, as with Agamemnon, the hero returns to an unfaithful home.

Theme 5: Even after the building of Demeter's temple and altar, her sorrow over the loss of Persephone is not diminished. Terrible havoc follows as she stays apart from the gods. The ground will not send forth the seed, for Demeter has kept it hidden. Oxen draw the plough in vain, and much white barley falls useless upon the ground. Cruel famine threatens mortals, and the gods also are deprived of their gifts and sacrifices.

At the beginning of *Iliad* 9 (2–3), fearful panic, companion of chilling fear, takes hold of the Achaeans, and all their best men are smitten with unbearable grief. This despair leads first to an assembly in which Agamemnon advises returning to Argos, and then to a council where he accepts the proposal to appease Achilleus and restore Briseis to him. In Book 16 (21ff.) Patroklos draws such a vivid picture of the crisis among the Achaeans and of the wounding of their best fighters that Achilleus consents, not to return to battle himself, but to let Patroklos fight in his armor. These two scenes of panic are linked by the same simile, for the distraught heroes, Agamemnon and Patroklos, are both said to weep like a spring of dark water that pours its murky stream down a steep cliff (*Iliad* 9.14–15; and 16.4–5).[15]

Havoc caused by the absence of the hero is reiterated throughout the *Odyssey* in the descriptions of the insolence of the suitors and their damage to the property of Odysseus. Destruction occurs also during the absence of Menelaos. When he tells Telemachos of his sorrows during his many years away from home and his wandering, he mentions not only the murder of Agamemnon but also the ruin of his own house and expresses the wish that he may now have even a third of his former wealth (*Odyssey* 4.90ff.).

Theme 6: In the Homeric *Hymn to Demeter* Zeus sends emissaries to plead with Demeter: first Iris, then all the gods each offering beautiful gifts and privileges: but she stubbornly refuses them all. We are reminded not only of the embassy to Achilleus with its splendid offer of gifts, but also of the story of Meleager (*Iliad* 9.574–99), who is entreated to return to the defense of his city by the offer of the richest land in Kalydon.

Just as there are in the *Iliad* two important reconciliations—one when Achilleus finally accepts the gifts and Briseis and the other at the end when he ransoms Hektor's body—so in the *Hymn* Demeter is first reconciled by the building of her temple. Her final reconciliation with Zeus, however, and her return to Olympus are achieved only when Zeus and Hades agree to release Persephone to her mother, a restoration made conditional by Persephone's having eaten food, the pomegranate seed, in the other world. When Rheia carries to Demeter Zeus's offer of honors among the gods and the return of her daughter for two-thirds of the year, the goddess does not refuse but makes the rich lands burgeon again with fruits and flowers.

We might add that the *Odyssey* ends most appropriately, not at 23.296, after the recognition of the hero by Penelope, but after reconciliation, when the blood feud caused by the death of the suitors is stopped and Athena places a covenant of oaths between the contending forces.

The pattern of Demeter's withdrawal, reconciliation, and return is at times closer to the pattern in the *Iliad* and at other points nearer to the *Odyssey*. For a story that is found in neither of the Homeric poems, these thematic correspondences are remarkable in number and in kind. They help reveal the vitality and multiformity of the elements from which epic tradition is formed. Our notions of the sorrows of Demeter and their connection with the Eleusinian Mysteries have been so heavily overlaid with additions from the Orphic and Dionysiac cults and with syncretisms of many kinds that it is useful to examine the structure of the Homeric *Hymn to Demeter* in the light of other narratives current at approximately the same time.

---

[15] The pairing of these similes is noted with somewhat different emphasis in Whitman's chart of the geometric structure of scenes in the *Iliad* (1958).

SOME FUNCTIONS OF THE

DEMOPHOÖN EPISODE IN THE HOMERIC

HYMN TO DEMETER

Nancy Felson-Rubin and Harriet M. Deal

T HIS STUDY focuses on the functioning of the Demophoön narrative, enclosed in the Homeric *Hymn to Demeter*, within the larger narrative of Persephone's abduction and partial restoration.[1] On a dramatic level, the Demophoön episode furthers the character development of Demeter, retards the resolution of the plot, and allows focus to fall first on Demeter, then on the reunion of Demeter with Persephone. The episode helps to develop and express certain values and beliefs pertaining to divinity and mortality, male and female experience, sexuality and virginity, fertility and infertility. Though much has been written about these values and beliefs as they are expressed in the *Hymn*, and to some extent about the effect of the Demophoön episode on their expression, our focus on this narrative sheds new light on these issues.

Our method has been to compare the narrative sequence of events which constitutes the Demophoön episode with the sequence surrounding Persephone. In each, the actions seen from the three main characters' points of view (the outsider/instigator, the mother/protector/obstructor, and the child/victim) are woven into a composite narrative syntagm. Through narrative analysis, we determine that the two composite syntagms form a paradigmatic set. The intervening Demophoön narrative both parallels the primary Persephone narrative (a paradigmatic relation) and forms part of it (a syntagmatic relation). As we examine the narrative structure, we also note semantic elements shared by the two composite syntagms, particularly as they reinforce parallelisms that we had already detected in the narrative structure itself, or as they underscore significant differences.[2]

---

[1] This article was originally published in *Quaderni Urbinati di Cultura Classica* 34 (1980) 7–21. The notes have been substantially cut and there is one small cut in the text (two paragraphs). Additional minor alterations have been made to conform with the editorial style of this book.

[2] The terms describe two types of relations between units in any system, those along a paradigmatic or selective axis (the classification of units according to similarities and contrasts) or along a syntagmatic or combinatorial axis (the combination of units drawn from different paradigmatic classes).

In each composite syntagm, an outsider instigates action that separates a child from its mother. In each, the chain of events from this outsider's point of view proceeds as follows. A need (Hades' for a wife, Demeter's for a substitute child) leads to a request (Hades' to Zeus, Demeter's to the daughters of Keleos and to Metaneira), which is then granted. By a second procedure (Hades' violent abduction of Persephone, Demeter's subjection of Demophoön to the fire), the outsider acquires some degree of control over the child. Interrupted (by a messenger from Zeus, by the child's mother), the outsider releases the child. This release coincides with an event (the "force-feeding" of the pomegranate seed, the establishing of a role for Demophoön in Demeter's rites) that assures the outsider partial retention of the child.

From the point of view of the bereft mother, the narrative chain follows the same sequence, with specific events varying slightly. In the outsider's request for her child, the mother is not fully informed—either not consulted at all in Demeter's case or duped by disguise and deceit in Metaneira's. Each mother remains ignorant of the violent or apparently violent act committed by the outsider upon her child. Each, discovering this act, believes the child has been or will be annihilated at the hands of the stranger. Grief and anger lead each to obstruct a divine plan (Demeter, the will of Zeus; Metaneira, the plan of Demeter). This interference eventually causes the outsider to return, or promise to return, the child (Demeter voluntarily, Hades under constraint). Each mother then partially yields to the outsider (Demeter by a resigned acceptance of Persephone's intermittent residence with Hades, Metaneira by a silent and awed acceptance of Demophoön's ritual bond with Demeter).

From the child's viewpoint, the narrative chain begins with the transfer to the control of an outsider. Subsequent exposure to a violent or apparently violent act alters the child's ontological state: Persephone's abduction to the underworld symbolizes death, and Demophoön's subjection to fire is part of an immortalizing process. Honors and powers follow (for Persephone as Hades' wife and queen of the dead, for Demophoön as part of Demeter's immortal rather than his mother's mortal realm). This absorption into the realm of the "other" is abruptly arrested by an intrusion causing each outsider to relinquish the child. The release is not total, however, because each child retains a partial bond with the outsider. Thus the final outcome is a compromise: Persephone is restored to Demeter two-thirds of the year but remains the honored wife of Hades and queen of the dead for one-third; Demophoön, though no longer the nursling of Demeter and no longer potentially immortal, is joined to the goddess through rites and the games instituted in his honor.

The two composite syntagms are sufficiently parallel at a concrete level to warrant their placement in a paradigmatic set. The abstract sequence for both is: *desire, request, granting of request, violent procedure, possession of child, obstruction, outcome of obstruction, concession, final outcome.* Certain semantic features confirm this paradigmatic relation. Such features include verbal echoes, symbols, actions, metaphors, and descriptive terms, especially when they occur at the same point or step in the parallel syntagm.

At *desire* both Hades and Demeter have a legitimate kinship relationship that is unfilled. At *request* and *granting* of request, both outsiders are immortals whose power greatly exceeds that of mother and child combined. In Demeter's case this is emphasized (in spite of her disguise and seeming dependence on Metaneira) by her first epiphany. Both outsiders intend a protective relationship with the child. Both mothers remain ignorant, either of the request itself (Demeter) or of its true nature and implications (Metaneira). In neither case is the child consulted. In both the child has an almost symbiotic relation to its mother. Both children are designated *thalos*, "flower" (in 66 Persephone is the *glukeron thalos* of Demeter; in 187 Demophoön is the *neon thalos*, of Metaneira).

At *violent procedure* secrecy and deceit surround both acts. That no one except Helios has witnessed the abduction, and no one except Helios and Hekate has heard Persephone's cries, parallels the secrecy with which Demeter "keeps hiding" baby Demophoön in the fire-at night, in secret from his parents (239–40: *nyktas de krupteske . . . lathra philôn goneôn*). This use of *krupteske* for Demophoön also corresponds semantically to Persephone's descent under the earth (431, *hypo gaian*) and into darkness (80). Both mothers view the outsider's *secret procedure* and *possession of child* as a form of death. Both initially react to the perceived loss in a helpless, ineffectual manner (Demeter by wandering everywhere in search of information about Persephone and by withdrawing from the company of gods; Metaneira by lamenting). Both mourn, Demeter for her lost Persephone, Metaneira in fear for Demophoön's life (246, *deisas'*). Demeter's mourning ritual, elaborated several times (40ff, 90ff, 200ff, and 304), includes such gestures of grief as tearing her headdress, refusing food and other comforts, wearing dark mourning clothes, wailing, etc. For Metaneira, mourning is suggested by the use of words commonly associated with grief or anguish over the dead,[3] and also by her gesture of beating her thighs, which, although not a formal mourning gesture, is suggestive of similar self-abusive mourning

---

[3] Important too is the verbal echo in the *Hymn* itself, 82, when Demeter is asked by Helios to cease her *megan goon*. The mourning of both Demeter for Persephone and Metaneira for Demophoön results in the ultimate release of each child from apparent death. It may well be that in these two contexts of the *Hymn* mourning has some magical efficacy. Compare the magical effect of Metaneira's intrusion itself on Demeter's ritual. Such magical efficacy might explain why Demeter goes into mourning several times in the course of her search for Persephone: by doing so, according to mythic logic, she might actually bring about Persephone's return from the dead. Such logic underlying her actions may be valid even though the word *goos* only appears once for Demeter (82), and even though she may be quite unaware of the efficacy of her lamentation.

acts. Moreover, Helios rebukes Demeter for excessive and vain grief (82, *katapaue megan goon*, "cease your great lament"), and later Demeter rebukes Metaneira and all mortals for vain grief and ignorance (256ff). Though the two mothers obstruct an outsider in different ways, in both cases the outcome of obstruction for child/victim is a second ontological change whereby Persephone returns to the upper world (light, immortality), and Demophoön, deprived of light and immortality, returns to a mortal state. In the interval between this change and the revelation of the partial bond remaining between outsider and child, there is scant time for either mother to react to what appears to be the unconditional return of her child.

At *concession* the outsider retains a partial bond with the child. Persephone's swallowing of the pomegranate seed renders permanent her ties with Hades and hence simultaneously with cyclic death and seasonal fertility. Demophoön, because of prior contact with Demeter, will continue a bond with her (as she explains to Metaneira in 263–64) and hence with some form of immortality (undying honor). In each case, the permanent bond with an outsider resulted from eating or receiving nurture. Moreover, the violence or force of Persephone's swallowing (413, *akousan de biêi me prosênangkasse pasasthai*, "against my will by force he made me eat") may parallel Demeter's angry abandonment of Demophoön to the ground, while Persephone's general claim to be helpless corresponds to Demophoön's literal helplessness as an infant. At *final outcome*, when each outsider proclaims honors for the child (*timas megistas*, for Persephone in 366, *timê* for Demophoön in 263), both the young goddess and the young hero are honored with annual, perpetual rites. Further, Persephone has reached maturity through her marriage to Hades, and, although Demophoön does not explicitly reach manhood in the course of the *Hymn*, Demeter's tacit acceptance of the responsibility to raise him to "a measure of manhood" in 166 and 221 (*hêbês metron*) implies his eventual maturity.

These semantic correspondences reinforce the paradigmatic relation between the two composite syntagms at corresponding steps in each narrative. But distinctions and discrepancies are present as well, breaking the analogies even as they are being established and disturbing the neatness of the parallelisms. Some of the discrepancies are not exact opposites, but qualitative differences. At several places, semantic features are inverted: what is positive for a character in one tale may be negative for the corresponding character in the other at a comparable step. Further, the same state may occur at different but chiastically related points in the two narrative syntagms.

Consider first Persephone and Demophoön. At *violent procedure*, where Hades forces Persephone to reside in the dark underworld, Demeter offers Demophoön light and immortality. As they move in opposite directions— Persephone into darkness and mortality, but on a *golden* chariot, Demophoön into light and immortality, but *hidden by* Demeter in the fire—the young girl screams and exhibits a need and longing for her mother, while the infant offers no resistance and shows no such need. She grieves and mourns; he does not. Persephone remains unchanged in the underworld, while Demophoön, anointed with ambrosia (237) and stimulated by the presence of Demeter, grows miraculously. At *possession of child*, Persephone dies symbolically, but Demophoön is undergoing a symbolic purification and immortalization. At *obstruction* by the mother, Persephone is joyful, Demophoön insatiably angry: just as Persephone screamed at separation from her mother and now rejoices at the prospective reunion, so Demophoön, who had not protested earlier when separated from his mortal mother, now cries incessantly. At *outcome of obstruction*, Hades' "wry" or amused smile (357) contrasts with Demeter's anger (251) and verbal abuse. Persephone's reemergence from the underworld symbolizes immortality but also epiphany; Demophoön's abandonment to the ground and his separation from the fire's immortalizing power both mark his mortality.

The two offspring participate in mortality and immortality, in darkness and light, in contact with and separation from the earth, in grief and joy at different but chiastically related points in their respective composite syntagms. Persephone's reemergence at *final outcome* also parallels Demophoön's incipient immortalization at *violent procedure*. We recall that at *violent procedure* Demophoön's growth inspired wonder (*thauma*), while Persephone is a "wonder to behold" (*thauma idesthai*) at *final outcome*. His final mortality is like her earlier symbolic mortality. His ultimate separation from fire and light and his contact with the earth are like her earlier descent into the dark earth. Persephone has moved from separation from Demeter to partial reunion, Demophoön from union to partial separation. The chiastic inversions serve to allow Demophoön to recede into the background, once he has been granted his final compromise position vis-à-vis Demeter. They also bring the focus on Demeter as the source of joy. For both offspring the happier state is in the presence of Demeter.

At parallel points in the two composite syntagms, Demeter and Metaneira as mothers/obstructors differ in important and striking ways. One early difference is that, until she herself eye-witnesses his exposure to the fire, Metaneira has no idea that she may be "losing" Demophoön, whereas Demeter knows immediately upon hearing Persephone's scream that her daughter has suffered some disaster, although she does not know exactly what has happened until Helios who witnesses everything informs her. Later on, when Demeter interferes with Hades' possession of Persephone, she does so through an active plan, by suppressing the grain in the earth. At this point, her power with respect even to other immortals is impressive. Metaneira, on the other hand, has no exceptional power; she interferes in Demeter's immortalizing of Demophoön by accidentally and unintentionally breaking the taboo against witnessing a magic spell. Furthermore, Demeter does not confront the outsider directly, as Metaneira does. Metaneira screams in helplessness at what she regards as the stranger's destruction of her son, while Demeter exerts power in a purposive manner. Once Demeter has withheld the grain, Zeus offers her "whatever honors she would choose" (328), but Metaneira is not treated with like deference by Demeter. Metaneira's and Demeter's obstructions differ enormously in implication, because Demeter's withdrawal has cosmic effects, while Metaneira's intrusion in Demeter's plan remains on a personal level: it directly affects only the fate of her own child, though it may well have symbolic implications for the whole of humankind.

Further, Metaneira's obstruction causes Demeter to reveal herself with Metaneira as a witness. Metaneira has no comparable manifestation of power. And, although Metaneira's interference precipitated *Demeter's* self-revelation, Demeter's interference ultimately causes *Persephone* to emerge from darkness into light. Thus, in the embedded tale, the actual figure who moves from hidden to manifest is the outsider/ intruder (Demeter), while in the main narrative it is the child/victim (Persephone).

The effect of these discrepancies is to disrupt the relationship between the two composite narrative syntagms. Because it is Demeter who reveals her divinity and power and undergoes a full epiphany, while Demophoön is separated from immortality and light and his mother is dismissed as foolish and shortsighted, Demeter is brought into prominence.

This emphasis on Demeter, together with the evanescence of Demophoön and Metaneira, allows a more general focus on humans and their relationship to the gods. With the inauguration of the Mysteries, the focus of the poem shifts from Demeter's relationship with Demophoön to her relationship with humankind as a whole, especially from her preoccupation with his mortality to a concern for the mortality of all people. Although Demeter after her encounter with Demophoön and Metaneira does not attempt to immortalize the human race, or individual members of it, she does introduce rites that promise the initiate blessedness and a happier portion (*aisa*) after death (480–82).

Demeter's withdrawal to the temple just built at her instruction marks her seclusion from both gods and humans. She no longer chooses to sojourn among mortals, disguised as one of them, nor does she yet rejoin the Olympian realm. At this point her longing for Persephone, submerged or unexpressed during the Demophoön encounter, reappears (304, *pothôi*) and the main narrative line resumes. It is interesting that a similar longing is attributed to Persephone (344, *pothôi*) at approximately the same narrative moment, as she sits beside her husband in the underworld. The resumed narrative centers upon Demeter's relationship with the other gods and her attempt to reclaim Persephone. As the power shifts in favor of Demeter over

Hades, Hades (like Demophoön and Metaneira earlier) recedes into the background. Literally and verbally, light falls upon the joyful reunion between divine mother and daughter.

The resolution of the Demophoön episode not only refocuses attention on Demeter's relationship to the gods and her recovery of Persephone, but also, on a dramatic level, motivates significant changes in Demeter's character. For as her verbal abuse of Metaneira indicates, Demeter has come to see that shortsighted and ineffectual interference in divine plans belongs to the realm of humankind and characterizes human folly. Her own initial and ineffectual withdrawal from the gods was in fact like Metaneira's failure to recognize and accept divine gifts. But now Demeter has changed as a result of confrontations within the Demophoön episode.[4] This change is marked by her resumption of divine form just as it is by her condemnation of mortal folly. Thus, again on the dramatic level, she is motivated to a fuller knowledge of her own power and of her own prerogatives vis-à-vis the other gods. She no longer pretends to be mortal or seeks consolation through the "adoption" of a mortal child but instead exercises the power (inherently hers as a fertility goddess) to oppose the actions of Zeus and Hades in an *effectual* manner. Further, she is able not only to exercise this power but also eventually to know and accept its fated limits: that, although her power to suppress fertility wins release for Persephone, it cannot undo the effect of the pomegranate seed. Her ability to predict how Persephone, in consequence of swallowing the seed, will spend each year contrasts markedly with an earlier utter ignorance of the details of the abduction of her daughter. Her awareness and acceptance of the partial but irreversible bond that Persephone now has with Hades also contrasts with an earlier unwillingness either to acknowledge or to accept any bond between them.

Demeter's new awareness of her own power and her new acceptance of its limits have at least two broad implications for humankind. First, her own return to immortal form and her acceptance of failure to immortalize Demophoön clarify the division between the human and the divine. Demeter now realizes the nature of her divinity and the degree of her separation from that which prevents Demophoön and all mortals from attaining either immortality or divine knowledge. Thus she abandons the effort to immortalize

---

[4] Demeter's other encounters during the Demophoön episode also affect her development. For example, from observing Demophoön's sisters, the daughters of Keleos and Metaneira, she sees that young girls *can* enter womanhood with confidence. Her encounter with Keleos's daughters provides her with a model for her own relationship with her daughter. Unable to see any benefits or blessings in Persephone's marriage to Hades (despite Helios's assertion that Hades is no unworthy son-in-law), she can, however, comfortably and graciously wish the daughters of Keleos good husbands and children. They are similar to the unwed Persephone in age and manner and marriageability but are mortals and not "blood" relations of Demeter. Hence Demeter is able to see them "objectively" in their readiness for an end to innocence, for entry into marriage and sexuality.

Demophoön, aware of the impossibility of its success, yet uses her power as a goddess to establish rites that bring him undying honor, and other mortals a happier portion after death. This exercise of her power is contingent upon her awareness of its limits. Her acceptance of the difference between the divine and the mortal recalls Zeus' resigned acceptance of his son Sarpedon's mortality in *Iliad* 16.419ff. What keeps Zeus from rescuing his son Sarpedon—and hence behaving like a shortsighted human father—is an awareness of the total picture and of what will happen if he, of all the gods, starts acting like a human. Hera reminds Zeus of the cosmic chaos that such behavior will effect. In both the Sarpedon and the Demophoön episodes, a god comes to accept the limits of his or her power. In Demeter's case this acceptance receives even more emphatic expression later on in her acquiescence to Persephone's destiny.

A second implication of Demeter's new awareness and new acceptance is that it assures within the mythic narrative a dependable, permanent, cyclic fertility of crops. That this myth and others of its type address the issue of cyclic fertility is obvious and has been thoroughly discussed by others. The return of Persephone in itself symbolizes the return of crops, though Demeter's actual restoration of the grain takes place a little later in the narrative. What is clear from our analysis is the contingency of this permanent cyclicity on Demeter's willingness to accept the binding power of the pomegranate seed. It is Demeter's acceptance of her daughter's intermittent residence in the underworld, as much as Hades' and Zeus's recognition of Demeter's prerogatives, that assures cosmic stability and predictability. Because of it her power over grain is no longer ill-defined and easily threatened (e.g., by Hades and Gaia in collusion with Zeus) nor exercised in an erratic manner (by Demeter herself). And because Demeter gains the pivotal awareness crucial to the resolution of this conflict through her confrontations in the Demophoön episode, the centrality of that episode becomes quite clear.

CONCERNING THE HOMERIC

HYMN TO DEMETER

Jean Rudhardt

TRANSLATED BY LAVINIA LORCH AND HELENE P. FOLEY

T HE ACT of distributing *timai* (honors) constitutes an essential expression of Greek mythical thought.[1]

A

In invoking the Muses, the author of the Hesiodic *Theogony* defines his project in the following manner:

> Hail, children of Zeus! Give me an alluring song and celebrate the holy race of immortals who live forever, those who were born from Earth and starry Sky or from dark Night and those whom salty Pontos nourished. Tell how, at the beginning there came to being in the world of the gods the earth, the rivers, the limitless sea with its restless billow, the shining stars and the vast heaven above, and the gods who were born from them, givers of good things. Tell how for the first time they divided the goods, distributed both wealth and honors among themselves (*hos timas dielonto*) and how they lived on Olympus of the many vales.

> (104ff.)

In thus announcing the plan of his work, the poet presents the distribution of *timai* as the outcome of events that produced the different divinities in succession. In his prologue he says, speaking of Zeus: "He who reigns in the heavens and holds thunder and scorching lightning ever since he overcame his father Kronos; he distributed everything equally among the immortals and defined their honors and their duties" (*epephrade timas*, Hesiod *Theogony* 71–74). Thus it appears that the distribution of *timai* must have taken place after the victory of the sons of Kronos in an Olympic society subject to the authority of Zeus.

[1] This article was originally published in *Museum Helveticum* 35, Fasc. 1 (1978):1–17. The beginning of the article has been cut and some of the notes are slightly abridged; the final note has been eliminated. Additional minor alterations have been made to conform with the editorial style of this book.

In reality, things are more complex. The distribution takes place progressively and involves several episodes, all dependent on events that accompany the birth, struggles, and conflicts of divine beings.

Aphrodite, for example, receives her attributes from the moment she is born (*tautên ex archês timên echei êde lelongche/moiran*, Hesiod *Theogony* 203–4). Certain divine attributes are therefore already defined before the accession of the Olympians; it will be up to Zeus to confirm them. At the beginning of the conflict between the sons of Kronos and the Titans, he calls the gods together. He promises those who take his side that they will continue to enjoy their *timai*, if they already have them (399, 903–6). If they do not have them as yet, he promises to bestow *timai* on them justly. We shall see him in fact confirm the *timê* that Hekate had received among the Titans (412ff.) and give *timê* to Styx and the Fates (390–96). Without always using the word *timê*, the *Theogony* implies a lot of similar conferring of honors (346–48, 926, 929, 939). If, therefore, the distribution of *timai* begins very early in the cosmogony, if the Titanomachy (Battle of the Titans) itself contributes to it, the process comes to fulfillment and becomes definitive under the reign of Zeus. The prologue of the poem had announced it. The concluding verses of the Titanomachy confirm it: "When the blessed gods had come to the end of their painful struggle and they had resolved by force the conflict over *timai* (*timaôn*) with the Titans, then, inspired by Gaia's wisdom, they urged Zeus to take power and reign over the immortals. And Zeus distributed among them their honors and duties" (881ff.).

The image of the distribution of *timai* is not a Hesiodic invention. Familiar to Greek thought, it serves from Homer on to signify the establishment of order in the world and among the gods. One recalls Poseidon's words in the *Iliad*:

> We are three brothers, sons of Kronos and born of Rheia: Zeus, myself, and as a third, Hades, King of the Dead. The universe was divided into three parts and each received his fiefdom (*timê*). As for me, the lot determined that I live in the foamy white sea; Hades received the misty darkness, and Zeus the vast heavens in the ether and the clouds. Yet the earth remains common territory, as does high Olympus.
>
> (*Iliad* 15.187–93)

By thus affirming his background as a son of Kronos and the legitimacy of the power that he exercises in his particular domain, Poseidon is justifying his resistence to the will of Zeus. In context, however, his discourse appears incomplete and remains imprecise. The earth is of course generally accessible to the gods, but they fulfill different functions, and, although they participate in the Olympian assembly, Zeus presides over it. He reigns over them and gives them orders, and Poseidon himself ends up obeying him.

Thus the *Iliad* does not ignore the preeminence of the *timê* vested in Zeus. This preeminence, which is clear in Hesiod, is confirmed in one of the most ancient of the Homeric hymns, the *Hymn to Aphrodite*. In this Hymn Zeus is designated as the one who received by lot the greatest *timê* (*Hymn to Aphrodite* 37).

It is understandable that the defeat of the Titans excludes them from the final distribution of *timai* and that Zeus presides over the distribution of these *timai* among the younger gods. Their distribution among the sons of Kronos is potentially problematic. According to the *Iliad*, it takes place by a drawing of lots. In the Hesiodic *Theogony*, we have seen that Zeus proceeds with the distribution once he is given the power by the other gods. According to the Homeric *Hymn to Poseidon*, the gods confer a double *timê* on Poseidon: the prerogative of taming horses and of saving ships (*Hymn to Poseidon* 22, 4–5). Such variations are proof of the great freedom of Greek mythical thought. They also indicate, however, the manner in which the use of such variations converge. The poets employ a similar image, although in different ways, to explain the divine ordering of the world. They unanimously recognize Zeus's final preeminence. They admit, furthermore, that the distribution of *timai* is not the product of his initiative alone and does not take place suddenly. In the Hesiodic *Theogony* itself, where Zeus takes over after the Titans' defeat, the Kyklopes had already, from the beginning of the Titanomachy, given him the lightning bolt, the instrument and symbol of his sovereignty (*Theogony* 141).

The Titanomachy constituted a crisis whose outcome was to determine the distribution of the spheres of influence, of *timai*, among the gods (*Theogony* 882). For every new circumstance, conflict or crisis is the principal mode of distribution. Even under the reign of Zeus, this distribution will continue to take place through crises.

According to Apollodoros, the object of Athena's and Poseidon's contest for the possession of the Akropolis is a distribution of *timai* (*Bibliotheca* 3.14.1). According to the Homeric *Hymn to Hermes*, the outcome of Apollo's and the son of Maia's dispute is the expansion of the province of the son of Leto and Zeus's definition of Hermes' *timê* (*Hymn to Hermes* 471, 516, 573).

The distribution of *timai*, however, does not simply define the gods' prerogatives. According to the Hesiodic *Theogony*, the conflict between Zeus and Prometheus took place "when gods and mortals made a decision [or division] for themselves at Mekone" (535–36). The verb that is used, *hot' ekrinonto*, is the same one that designates the decision concerning the possession of *timai* after the Titanomachy: *epei . . . timaôn krinanto* (881–82). The conflict between Zeus and Prometheus is thus a crisis similar to the Titanomachy. The scholiasts confirm this, pointing out that its purpose was the distribution of *timai*; one scholiast specifically states that it concerned humanity. There the gods decided, he says, what is divine and what is human: *ekrinonto ti theos kai ti anthrôpos*.

We know that humans existed before Prometheus's intervention. Their mortality distinguished them from the gods, but they were not clearly separated from the gods and they did not have their proper status or way of life. By striking trees with his lightning bolt, Zeus gave them fire and thus a means of subsistence that they received passively. Prometheus's trickery irritates Zeus, who now no longer sets trees on fire for humans' sake (*Theogony* 561ff., *Works and Days* 47–50). Its first effect is therefore to separate humans from gods. Prometheus then steals fire to bring to humans. But this is a one-time action. Humans must learn to preserve fire in the fennel stalk (*Theogony* 565ff., *Works and Days* 50–52): survival for them now depends on their knowledge and their activity. Hesiodic pessimism insists on the negative aspect of this transformation. Yet, as with all the cosmogonic crises, the decision at Mekone had a positive aspect, which the scholiast highlighted. It defines what humans will be from now on. Later versions of the myth of Prometheus confirm this. Iapetos's son puts humans under an obligation but supplies them with the means to work and at the same time offers them the possibility of creating a civilization for themselves (Aeschylus *Prometheus Bound* 106–13, 436–506). Thus, separated from the gods and capable now of living with this distance, humans receive what will constitute their specific function and mode of existence: the crisis Prometheus instigated has defined their *timê*. Later versions of the myth will say that he created humanity.

The fire Prometheus gave mortals will also be an instrument of sacrifice. Established at a later time by his son Deukalion, sacrifice reproduces in the victim the unequal portions already established by Prometheus to fool Zeus. By thus recalling the gesture that inaugurated the process of separation between gods and humans, sacrifice reestablishes a communication between them that is necessary to both and that transcends the distance that it does not presume to abolish.[2]

In the circumstances thus defined as common to all mortals, other episodes that distribute *timai* characterize the particular situation of certain communities. The contest of Athena and Poseidon for the possession of the Akropolis does not simply change these two divinities' prerogatives. Kekrops' role as witness and judge in favor of Athena is decisive and defines at the same time the religious identity of the city: it is called Athens from this moment on (Apollodoros 3.14.1). In other cases Zeus confers a particular privilege on certain races in a more direct fashion. Thus, according to Pin-

---

[2] Rudhardt 1970.

dar, he confers the kingdom of Iolkos as a *timê* on Aeolos and his descendants (*Pythian* 4.106ff.[189ff]).

B

1. The events recounted in the Homeric *Hymn to Demeter* must be situated in this undoubtedly vast and ill-defined but coherent context.

When Demeter, withdrawn inside the temple of Eleusis, ceases to guarantee the growth of plants, Zeus, to convince her to take up her activities again, promises her that she will have among the immortals the privileges and duties, the *timai*, of her choice (*Hymn to Demeter* 326–28). Once she has obtained satisfaction by Persephone's release, Zeus affirms this promise so that Demeter will come back to Olympus and once again make plants grow. Speaking for him, Rheia tells the rebellious goddess who is, nevertheless, already about to obey: "he has promised to give you the *timai* of your choice among the immortal gods" (443–44). The poem's last lines, which sing of the glory of Demeter and Persephone, now returned to Olympus after the establishing of the Mysteries, imply the fulfillment of that promise.

Similarly, Zeus grants a wife to his brother Aidoneus, whose portion was not yet complete (*Hymn to Demeter* 3, 78–80). Just as he is about to let Persephone leave the world of the dead, Hades, certain that he will see her return one day to him, tells her, "You will reign over the infernal kingdom, you will have very great *timai* among the immortals" (365ff.).

Finally, humans also receive their share. Although she fails to immortalize Demophoön, Demeter announces that a rite will be celebrated in his honor and that he will enjoy an "undying *timê*" in the future (263). Because she then promises the princes of Eleusis that she will establish the Mysteries (273–74), there is reason to believe that they too profit from the same kind of distribution.

Thus, in order to understand the meaning of the *Hymn to Demeter*, one must try to define the nature of the new *timai* that the crisis recounted in the *Hymn* finally confers on these three gods and perhaps on mortals.

2. Here is the initial situation. The drama explodes at a very specific moment of mythical time. Zeus is king of the Olympians: the three sons of Kronos have received their share (Zeus, 3, 78, 313ff., 321ff., 348ff.; Hades, 17ff., 79ff.; Poseidon is not mentioned but the *Hymn* refers explicitly to the division of the universe into three portions, 85–87). The distribution of *timai* is nearly complete. Let us take, however, a closer look.

The great regions of the world, the sky, the earth, and the sea, have received their clearly defined place. On high the gods reign on Mount Olympus (91–92, 484–85) but are by no means confined to it. They can come down from Olympus and move all over the earth (27–29, 324–26)—

which for them remains a common domain, as we learned from Poseidon's words in the *Iliad*. Below lies Erebos, dark and misty, inhabited by the dead (80, 335ff., 349). A boundary separates it from the world above. All of Greek tradition teaches us that humans cross that boundary only once, when they die, and that they never will be able to cross it again. This rule seems to have been established prior to Persephone's abduction. By stressing both the power of Hades, lord over countless people (9, 17, 31, 84ff.), and the power of his future wife to whose authority all the living are subjected (365), the *Hymn* makes clear that the dead will never escape from their empire. If the *Hymn* coincides with tradition on this point, it reveals something else that, although less immediately evident, is crucial: with one exception, gods cannot cross the infernal barrier.

Unless we accept this impermeability, the myth of Demeter, Hades, and Persephone is incomprehensible. No marriage in all of Greek mythology provokes a drama like the one of Hades and Persephone. Marriage does not tear away a young wife from her mother in this manner. Normal divine marriages do not separate them definitively. In the world above, wherever they may reside, gods are accessible to one another as much as they want to be. If Demeter, if Persephone could cross the infernal barrier, marriage with Hades, like other divine marriages, would not cause the crisis narrated in the Eleusinian hymn.

When Hades snatches her into his chariot, the shy Persephone is deeply shocked. She remains confident, however, as long as the chariot runs over land and sea. Raped by a god who terrifies her, she still hopes to see her mother and the other gods again (35–36). She loses this hope, however, at the exact moment that she moves into the world below, and she gives the piercing cry that alarms Demeter (38–39).

Similarly, Demeter, frightened by this cry, understands that disaster has struck her daughter. She is tormented by worry and pain, but, because she seeks Persephone, she still hopes to find her. On the other hand, when she finally learns that Hades has snatched Persephone and brought her underground to make her his wife and the queen of the infernal kingdom, this flattering news completely destroys her (90). Even more significantly, she ceases to search for her daughter, knowing she cannot reach her.

The *Hymn* furnishes us with yet another indication of the gods' inability to cross the infernal barrier as a general rule. At the peak of the crisis, Zeus sends messengers to Demeter and to Hades in order to bend their conflicting wills. He first sends Iris to Demeter on this mission and then in succession all the gods. Although Demeter is shut in a temple, she still belongs to a world accessible to them (314ff., 325ff.). In order to reach Hades, on the other hand, Zeus must have recourse to the only god who has the power of crossing the infernal barrier: Hermes (334ff.). The special function, in fact, of this god, the god of crossings, is to accompany the dead in their descent to the subterranean world. Several gods in addition to the three sons of Kronos have, we note, received their *timai*. Iris and Hermes are already fulfilling the function of messengers that they will later retain.

Demeter, on her part, has *timai* from the onset of the drama. *Potnia* and *anassa* ("Divine Mistress," 47, 54, 118; 75), we hear her declare, "I am Demeter, holder of *timai*" (268). Her epithets show that she is the bestower of the harvest. She ensures the growth of vegetation (4, 54, 192; see also 269). This is her function prior to Persephone's marriage, because it is precisely what she will cease to fulfill in trying to undo the marriage (305ff.). The *Hymn* teaches us many important things about how she fulfills this function. I shall indicate only one of them. Demeter's action concerning vegetation is the result of her participation in the society of gods and of the only form of communication that she retains with the other gods. She need only retire from society, break off this communication by locking herself into a temple, for the plants to cease growing (302ff.). In order to put an end to the sterility of the fields, the gods will simply ask her to return among them (321–22, 460, 469; see also 354–55).

Persephone plays with other young maidens. At the same time, she needs to know her mother is near, because she is so attached to her. She is a nubile virgin, but still enough of a child to remain passive during the entire drama in which her fate is decided. When it begins, she has no particular *timê*.

We already know Hades' *timê*. He reigns over the countless dead. Yet, a bachelor living beyond the barrier that gods may not cross, he is cut off from them. At the most, he might see Hermes who brings him a message from Zeus. He does not leave his kingdom. A veritable miracle will be required to permit him to ascend to the world above (see the discussion of the miraculous flower and its function below).

As for humans, they use fire; they work and live in regulated towns: they have a civilization (93ff., 96ff., 151ff.). The Promethean crisis, therefore, has already taken place. Let us note in passing that they are acquainted with agriculture and cultivate cereals, barley at least (305–9). Let us note, finally, that sacrifice has already been established. In fact, it is the threat of seeing the gods deprived of the *timê* of sacrifice that will determine Zeus's behavior (310ff.; see 353–54).

3. We know that the crisis unfolds in several stages.

a) It is set off by a decision on the part of Zeus: to give Persephone to Pluto as wife and make her the queen of the dead (3, 77ff.). His behavior is remarkable in two ways. He leaves Demeter and Persephone entirely in the dark as to his designs and veils them in deep secrecy (the secret extends to the whole universe; see 44–46). This precaution suggests that he anticipates Demeter's and Persephone's resistence to his plans. Were they to be forewarned, they would refuse to be separated by the infernal boundary. If, however, Persephone were to find herself drawn across it but once, the situation would be irreversible and the two goddesses would not be able to create any obstacle to his plan. On the other hand, with the aid of Gaia, he creates the miracle I have already mentioned: he has an extraordinary flower grow on the plain of Nysa (8ff., 428ff.). This is a trap meant to create two complementary effects. First, he must seduce Persephone and incite her to make the gesture that will deliver her into the power of Hades. She must in fact participate in the act that will determine her fate, just as later she will have to eat the pomegranate seed in order to be bound to the infernal world. And second, he must open a gap through which Hades might pass in the boundary that separates the two worlds.

The trap is successful. When Persephone with both hands rips out the stem of the miraculous flower, the earth gapes. Through the fissure thus created, Hades rises from the depths and snatches the maiden (15ff., 429–30). Alerted by the cry she lets out, Demeter seeks her over the entire earth until Helios at last informs her of her daughter's fate (75ff.). The goddess at that point interrupts her quest.

At the end of this first episode, it appears that Zeus's design has worked. Hades receives a wife. At his side, Persephone will reign over the dead. Yet, if the god of the Underworld finds a companion, Demeter loses her daughter. Her despair sets off the second episode of the drama.

b) Full of anger and sadness, she leaves Olympus. Even though Persephone is immortal, her marriage to Hades steals her away from Demeter just as death snatches a daughter away from her mother here on earth. The suffering that strikes the goddess draws her closer to humanity. She goes among humans in the guise of an old woman. She arrives at Eleusis where she is welcomed warmly. Without recognizing her, the Eleusinians give the mother who has recently lost her child a child to bring up. She bestows all her care upon that child and, seemingly finding in him a substitute for Persephone, she attempts to immortalize him (88–242).

In order to compensate for the calamity that for her stems from the order established in the universe (where the boundary with the Underworld is uncrossable), Demeter appears at this point to disregard or question the basic distinctions of that order: that which separates the mortal from the immortal. A humanized goddess, she attempts to divinize Demophoön.

c) The attempt proves impossible. The inevitable blundering of mortals makes her fail. This sets off the third episode of the crisis (243ff.). Assuming once more her divine form, Demeter behaves again like a goddess. She orders humans to build a temple for her and announces to them that the Mysteries will be established (250ff., 270–72, 273–74). At the same time, because she lost Demophoön among humans, she begins her struggle with the gods to get Persephone back.

Shut inside the temple that was built by the Eleusinians, she cuts herself off from the gods and makes vegetation cease growing (302–9). This strike deprives human beings of food and threatens to exterminate them. By destroying both the actual material of the sacrificial offering and those who offer it, she makes sacrifice impossible (310ff.). Frightened, Zeus begs her to reintegrate herself into the company of the gods so that she may fulfill her proper function. She refuses to obey until Persephone is returned to her (329–33).

Thus, after her attempt to abolish the distance between humans and gods, she now threatens to break the indispensable relation that sacrifice, over and above that distance, establishes between them.

d) This pressure leads to the final episode of the crisis. Zeus commands his brother to return Persephone. He obeys. Yet, before Persephone takes her leave of him, he offers her the pomegranate seed that, by binding her to the world of the dead, will force her to come back to him. If he did not take this precaution, Persephone, once she had returned to the world above, would remain on the other side of that forever insurmountable infernal boundary. Persephone eats what is offered to her, as unaware as she was when she picked the miraculous flower. Hermes, the god of crossings, then leads her to her mother's side, fulfilling Zeus's order (334–83).

From that moment on, her destiny is sealed. She is once again with Demeter, who is already aware of Hades' trap and has foreseen the compromise that would satisfy both herself and the king of the dead (393–404). She agrees to it in advance and Persephone accepts it immediately. The prospect of her periodic return to the Underworld does not mar the common joy of mother and daughter (434–37). It is therefore not the marriage with Hades that tormented them. They were only suffering at the idea of a definitive separation.

Soon Zeus has Rheia tell them what they already know. Demeter should resume her activities. She will receive new *timai*. From now on Persephone will spend one-third of the year in the Underworld with Hades and two-thirds among the other gods (445–47, 463–65). Demeter, satisfied, obeys. She establishes for humankind the Mysteries that she had promised them and, once again fulfilling her function, she returns to Olympus (470–84).

4. At the end of the crisis, what transformations have the protagonists undergone in their own world? What are the new *timai* that they have obtained?

a) The answer is clear in the case of Persephone and Pluto. In conformity with Zeus's first plan, Hades is no longer alone. The divine maiden has become his wife and along with him reigns over the dead. She is not, however, locked into his kingdom. Each year she ascends to Olympus among the other gods where she is with her mother. She therefore periodically crosses the boundary with the Underworld, alternately moving from Erebos to Olympus. Queen of the kingdom of the dead, she has her seat among the Olympians (484). In this way she establishes a regular relationship between the members of the Olympian assembly and Pluto and abolishes the rift that previously existed among the gods. This is her basic *timê*.

b) Several modern scholars view Persephone as the symbol or personification of cereal grains. In the opinion of some of them, her sojourn underground corresponds to the sowing of the grain in the earth in which it is buried and her return to Olympus to the growth of the grain in the fields. In Nilsson's view, she symbolizes instead the grain that is preserved in *pithoi* (jars) underground and when she returns, she represents that same grain that has been taken out for the sowing. Some texts might support such interpretations, but the Homeric *Hymn* does not. By clearly associating Persephone's return with the flowers of spring, the *Hymn* excludes Nilsson's interpretation but also renders obsolete those of his predecessors. In fact, the poem does not establish any true coincidence between Persephone's presence or absence on earth and the life or death of vegetation. Once Persephone, raped by Hades, has disappeared into the Underworld, vegetation continues to prosper. Only much later will it cease to grow. The fields will become sterile when Demeter—after having sought out her daughter, learned of her marriage, wandered among humans, reached Eleusis, nourished Demophoön, and attempted to immortalize him—will shut herself in her temple and cease to fulfill her divine function (39ff., 302ff.). Analogously, once Persephone emerges from the Underworld and returns to the earth's surface, vegetation does not start growing again. Demeter recovers her daughter, asks her questions, and the two goddesses give themselves at length to the pleasures of reunion. The fields do not turn green. In order for Demeter to agree to resume her activities, Zeus must intervene and offer the command and the promises that he has Rheia give the goddess. Only then does the grain sprout and the earth cover itself with flowers and leaves (384, 470ff.). Thus the life of all vegetation, the growth of all grains, depend exclusively on Demeter.

At the end of the crisis, if one establishes a chronological relation between Persephone's return and the spring growth of plants, Demeter's activity is from now on subject to a rhythm and this rhythm is tied to Persephone's fate. In order to understand this relation, one must heed the teaching of the myth.

Demeter's revolt caused all vegetation to stop growing. Apparently this is the first such arrest and the goddess had never interrupted her activity before. Plants, therefore, had constantly grown and borne fruits in a year where seasons had not been differentiated. In its description of the drought year brought on by the divine strike, the *Hymn* mentions neither spring nor summer nor winter. "Earth," it says, "did not bring forth the grain" (305–7). It does not mention the time of year at which it would have been normal for the grain to grow. During all this time, humans labor and sow as though they had no worry about the calendar (308–9). Once the goddess is satisfied and resumes her activity, the fields cover themselves with a "mane of slender ears of corn in a burgeoning spring" (453–55, 471). This was probably the first spring.

However this may be, the yearly return of Persephone is the result of a bargain. Zeus agrees to it insofar as Demeter resumes her activity, and Demeter accepts the terms. Things are no longer what they used to be, however. Each year Persephone leaves her mother and is reunited with her husband. She can never come back. When Demeter slows down her activity for a few months, this pause now recalls her original strike. In this fashion the goddess reminds the gods of their deal, but she soon resumes all her functions and thus assures them that she scrupulously respects that deal. Plants grow and it is springtime. Persephone now returns, in conformity with the agreement that has clearly been respected by Demeter. On this issue the text of the *Hymn* is perfectly clear. Persephone's return does not precede springtime. It does not make plants grow. The goddess returns once flowers are in bloom (401–3). Although the crisis did not create the first winter and the first spring, it did at least bestow a new meaning and seriousness on the annual cycle of plant growth. Thus Demeter fully deserves the epithet *ôrêphoros* (54, 192, 492, "bringer of seasons") that the *Hymn* insistently uses for her. She truly is the creator of the seasons.

c) But the *Hymn* is above all the story of the establishment of the Mysteries. The Eleusinian cult is one of the *timai* that the two goddesses won for themselves. It completes the portion set aside for humankind. The *Hymn* teaches us that the Mysteries procure for their initiates advantages both in this world and in the Other World (480–82).

Here on earth the two goddesses offer their protégés prosperity (486–89). This prosperity is the result of the successful harvests that a vegetation goddess can naturally ensure. Yet a crisis has taken place. Demeter had at one time resolved never to allow vegetation to grow. She could refuse once again. Now humans had been partially responsible for her dreadful strike: they had irritated her when they prevented her from immortalizing Demophoön. By altering her mood, they could once again influence the way in which she fulfills her function. The Mysteries give them the means by which to appease her, please her (274), and prevent another estrangement on her part. Yet beyond the immediate benefit derived from a good harvest, the performance of the Mysteries has another effect. Persephone must return to the Upper World when spring is in full bloom, a bloom that reflects Demeter's respect for her contract with the gods. If Demeter reneged on it, Persephone would not return. By pleasing the goddess through the celebration of the Eleusinian rites and by thus reinforcing the regularity of her intervention in the rhythm of the seasons, humans contribute to Persephone's return. Through the cult they become associated with the divine economy, just as they had through myth been associated with the establishment of divine laws.

Respectful of the secret of the Mysteries, the *Hymn* allows us to be ignorant of the benefit that the initiates can receive once they die. Yet it teaches us two things on this matter.

Demeter promises mortals to establish the Mysteries at the high point of the crisis, just as she is about to start her strike (273–74). In fact, however, she creates the Mysteries much later, once Persephone has been endowed with the power of crossing the infernal barrier (473–79). If she waits so long to keep her promise, it must be that the power that Persephone acquires at that time is necessary for the rite to function properly.

In spite of the distance that the mythical events involving Prometheus created, sacrifice allows humans to address themselves to the gods. They can thus exert an influence on their present condition on earth. There is, however, only one god, Hades, with whom they cannot communicate in this way, because he does not reside on Olympus. He lives beyond a boundary that cuts him off from other gods. He remains inaccessible to ordinary sacrifices. Humans cannot, therefore, by addressing themselves to him, exert an influence on their future existence in his kingdom. Hades, in fact, has almost no cult in Greece that is not linked to Persephone. The privilege that Demeter's rebellion gives her daughter will change the situation. Associated with the Uranian gods during one period of the year, Persephone is accessible to cult just like all the gods. Sharing her power with her spouse during another period, she can satisfy down in the Underworld the wishes she received from humans. Through her as an intermediary, humans retain the hope of bettering their fate once they die. On this issue, it is Persephone who bestows on the Eleusinian rites their efficaciousness.

The *Hymn* teaches us something else in addition. At the very moment when Demeter announces the creation of the Mysteries, affectionate relations of a new kind have been formed between her and humanity. Due to her motherly love, Persephone's rape had wounded her. It is as a suffering mother, humanized by suffering, that she came among humans. Received by them with trust and sympathy, she fed one of their children and adopted him to the point of wishing to immortalize him. Certainly their behavior destroyed her plans. Yet, although it did distance her, it did not erase her understanding of humanity's worries. On the contrary, it deepened this understanding. She knows that the boundary with the Underworld torments them just as it makes her suffer personally. Within the limits of the new situation that she will soon impose on Zeus, she wants to render that boundary permeable for humans by giving them the only means by which they can act in relation to the limits that define the sacred order of things: the instrument of ritual.

Because of her power to cross periodically the boundary with the Underworld, Persephone is indispensable to the functioning of this ritual. Once she acquires it, the Mysteries are established. She must also, however, share her mother's feelings. Clearly she suffered from the separation as her mother did. The two goddesses have similar dispositions. In fact, the Mysteries address the two of them. Their mutual affection is beneficial to humankind: "Among mortals on earth, blessed is he to whom their love is shown" (486–87).

Love, however, is elective. Among humans, it is the Eleusinians who received Demeter. The love of the goddesses is addressed to the initiates.

Thus the divine mother's love was the moving force behind the entire drama from which the Mysteries arose. It inspired the creation of the Mysteries. It cannot remain indifferent to their fulfillment nor detached from the effects that result from them. If we bear in mind the importance of these feelings in the entire mythical crisis and the moving aspect of the rituals it evokes, we would tend to believe that the assurance of that love is the most precious benefit that the initiates derive from the Mysteries. They assure humans a good harvest; but such material advantage is in fact the result of the love the two goddesses feel toward them. The *Hymn* is quite explicit on this point (486–89). We do not know what concrete advantages they hope to acquire in the Other World, but the relationship of affection that the initiates are convinced they have created with Demeter and Persephone is undoubtedly strong enough to assure them of its permanence. The goddesses will not cease to love them once they have died. In one way or another, thanks to Persephone who crosses the boundary of the Underworld, they will feel the effects of this constant love in the world beyond.

5. In short, the Eleusinian crisis defines the new *timê* of Pluto, who now has a wife and through her is in contact with the gods above. It defines that of Persephone, who becomes queen of the dead but periodically lives on Olympus and thus assures a form of regular communication between the world of the living and that of the dead, between Zeus and Pluto. It defines the *timê* of Demeter, whose rhythmic activity produces in the seasons visible proof of the divine management of earthly existence. Without abolishing the boundary with the Underworld, the Eleusinian crisis keeps this boundary from creating a break within divine society. It modifies the relationship between humans and gods and, without saving them from their mortal condition, it gives them the hope of bettering their lot in the Other World.

The Promethean crisis had created between humans and gods a distance that is fitting given their different natures. Over and above that distance, the establishment of sacrifice had recreated between them the communication needed for the world to remain coherent. In accomplishing their function within this order, all the gods and Zeus, in guaranteeing it, will protect mortals insofar as the latter play out their proper role. Yet, as efficient as it may have been, this protection remained remote. The Eleusinian crisis clothes it in a new warmth. It reveals within the divine—which it presents as otherwise terrifying—a capacity for suffering and for affection. For the privileged mortals of Eleusis, these feelings will from now on color their relation with the cult.

All these transformations are interdependent. They were initiated by Zeus; but, because the ancient order opposed him, they were fulfilled, along with all the redistribution of *timai*, during a long crisis in which all concerned played a role. Nevertheless, the outcome of this crisis is agreed upon by Zeus, who will guarantee the order finally created. In their conviction that they are loved by the two goddesses, in their hope for what concerns the Other World, the initiates know that they do not transgress the limits of their condition and do not offend the will of Zeus.

POLITICS AND POMEGRANATES
REVISITED

Marilyn Arthur Katz (Marylin Arthur)

I T HAS NOW BEEN nearly twenty years since I wrote "Politics and Pomegranates," and it is not the essay I would write today. It was composed originally for a 1975 conference on "New Approaches to the Study of Classical Antiquity," and it was designed as an experiment in juxtaposing psychoanalytic theory with literary criticism. At the time, I wanted to see whether I could avoid the subordination of text to theory which had always been the hallmark of so-called "applied analysis." As one critic later put it, "The relationship between 'literature and psychoanalysis' . . . is usually interpreted . . . as implying not so much a relationship of coordination as one of subordination, a relationship in which literature is submitted to the authority, to the prestige of psychoanalysis."[a]

"Politics and Pomegranates" was an attempt to achieve this kind of "coordination." I wanted to "elucidate a common structure underlying both [the ancient text and the modern theory]."[b] More specifically, I aimed at offering a structuralist analysis of the narrative dynamics of the poem, at a time when there existed in the literature only one literary study of the hymn.[c] And I also wanted to juxtapose against this interpretation the analytic logic of the Freudian paradigm of female psychosexual development.

Indeed, the Freudian theory of female psychosexual development appeared to me to embody and illustrate a cultural logic analogous to that found in the Homeric *Hymn to Demeter*. In both, the strategies of resistance to patriarchal domination have an internal logic and coherence, and both culminate in a validation of the patriarchal order. The juxtaposition of Freud and Demeter, I thought, could serve both to demonstrate the structural unity of the poem and to clarify the ideology underlying the psychoanalytic theory.

The analogy also seemed particularly useful in explaining the meaning of the central section of the hymn encompassing Demeter's sojourn among human beings. This section previously had been understood simply as ae-

---

[a] Felman 1978:5; emphasis in the original.
[b] Peradotto 1977:5.
[c] Lord 1967 (reprinted in this volume).

tiological, and I wanted to argue instead that it constituted the narrative core of the poem and that it was critical to transforming the withdrawal theme into the central motif of the poem.

In the years intervening, "Politics and Pomegranates" has gained recognition almost exclusively as a feminist/psychoanalytic interpretation of the poem. Its contribution to the history of literary analysis of the poem, in other words, has fallen victim to the power of the psychoanalytic paradigm. For its readers, however kindly intentioned, have imposed upon the essay the very subordination of text to theory which I had attempted to avoid.

Consequently, it is not without misgivings that I have agreed to send forth "Politics and Pomegranates" in its original form once again, knowing full well that, like the written word of Plato's *Phaedrus*, "it has no capacity to protect or defend itself" (275e6). Wherefore these brief remarks, which are meant to serve as the "help" that in Plato's view the written word always requires of its parent (ibid.), and my hopes that the reader's interest in the psychoanalytic aspects of my discussion will not be allowed to occlude the literary aspects of my analysis of the Homeric *Hymn to Demeter*.

Summer 1992

POLITICS AND POMEGRANATES:

AN INTERPRETATION OF THE HOMERIC

HYMN TO DEMETER

Marylin Arthur

Introduction

THERE IS PROBABLY no other Western culture in which the antagonism between the sexes occupies so central a place in literature and art as classical Greece.[1] The archaic poet Hesiod who, along with Homer, "gave the Greeks their gods" (in the sense of canonizing the tradition), organized his epic poem the *Theogony* around the basic polarity between the male and female gods. The triumph of civilization, achieved in the third generation, was contingent upon Zeus's abilities to subdue and appropriate the female force. Zeus's battle with the giants and monsters produced in the earliest era of existence when female power reigned supreme, and the birth of the goddess Athena from his head (signifying his appropriation of the female capacity for generation), were both popular subjects of artistic representation during the classical period.

The Homeric hymn to Delphian Apollo, likewise, makes Apollo's successful institution of his oracle depend upon his conquest of the rival and earlier female spring-deity, Telphousa. In that hymn, a subordinate quarrel between Hera and Zeus reinforces the message of the main story. Another example: Theseus's most important victory, the defeat of the Amazons, led to the foundation of the city of Athens. Many vase paintings and public monuments kept this myth alive during the historical period: Mikon's paintings on the walls of the Stoa Poikile in the Agora, the western metopes of the Parthenon, the outside of the shield of the statue of Athena Parthenos, the metopes of the Athenian treasury at Delphi, and the frieze of the temple of Hera at Bassae—all depicted the Amazonomachy. Aeschylus's trilogy, the *Oresteia*, culminated in a victory of the patriarchal, Olympian gods of sunlight and reason over the dark, bloody, maternal Erinyes (Furies); the vic-

---

[1] This article was originally published in *Arethusa* 10 (1977):7–47. The notes, except for those dealing with Freudian material, have been cut or abridged. Additional minor alterations have been made to conform with the editorial style of this volume.

tory meant the establishment of civil society and the implementation of an abstract and more humane code of justice.[2] Finally, when the struggle was transferred to the human psyche, as in the *Hippolytos* of Euripides, the destructive forces in the soul were represented as the two polarities of female types: Aphrodite or passion, versus the belligerent and sterile chastity of Artemis (patron goddess of the Amazons).

Such myths and stories as these were the stuff of which the theory of matriarchy was made. For it was assumed that these myths hid an era in the history of the human race when women had dominated society, and that the insistence upon male supremacy was a residue of the fears and anxieties attached to the struggles of this epoch.[3] Bachofen, the originator of the theory, acknowledged that the traces of this "universal cultural stage" (as he called it) were to be found "chiefly among the pre-Hellenic peoples."[4] Bachofen had mistakenly relied upon myth to present him with "the faithful picture of the oldest era" on the grounds that myth was uniquely free "from the influence of philosophical speculation." We now recognize, of course, that myth is nothing so much as a kind of first philosophy, and in addition modern anthropology and ethnography have demonstrated how insubstantial is the theory that matriarchy was a stage in human history.[5] But it is clear that Bachofen's scheme did correctly formulate an ideological model that grasped the manner in which the Greeks conceived of their own development.

In the context of such insistence upon male superiority and of such hostility to the female principle, it might seem as if we would look in vain for positive or sympathetic expressions of female consciousness. But the situation is not so hopeless. Aside from the fragments of a few female poets (Sappho, Korinna, Telesilla, Erinna, Praxilla, Moero, Anyte, Nossis, Myrtis—the nine "earthly Muses"), there are some other works of Greek literature and art that, upon analysis, reveal a peculiarly feminine sensibility.

[2] See Thomson 1972: esp. 229–77, and Thomson 1938.

[3] Under the influence of the recent feminist movement, the theory has enjoyed a revival: e.g., Davis 1971 or *Aphra: The Feminist Literary Magazine* 4.3 (Summer 1973), special issue on Matriarchy. Assessments of the theory in feminist publications like these correctly deny that the theory has any real basis but are sympathetic to its modern proponents' suspicion of male-oriented scholarship and to their efforts to discover an unbiased approach to such material.

[4] 1861 and 1967. Pembroke 1965 shows that Bachofen's evidence does not confirm his theory.

[5] Instead, what Bachofen had identified were traces of matrilineality, matrifocality or matrilocality that might and usually do exist in either a male-dominated society or in the classless and highly egalitarian band societies of hunting-gathering peoples. See further Bamberger 1974:263ff. and Sacks 1974:207ff. Leacock, on the other hand, in both her introduction to the most recent edition of Engels (1972) and 1977:13–35, emphasizes the high degree of egalitarianism characterizing certain primitive hunting-gathering societies. This evidence suggests that it may be possible to discover patterns of female dominance in primitive societies if the term itself is redefined. See further Tanner 1974:129ff.

One of these, I think, is the Homeric *Hymn to Demeter* which, as I shall show, treats the transition from "matriarchy" to "patriarchy" from the female point of view and therefore takes the form of a series of attempts to resist male domination rather than to impose it. The hymn, as I see it, could be subtitled "How to be a Mother Goddess in a Patriarchal Society," because the central problematic of the poem is Demeter's search for recognition and identity in a male-dominated cosmos. On one level Demeter's plight is therefore that of all women, who must struggle to achieve self-definition in a social and psychic world that values male attributes more highly and depreciates females. For this reason I have chosen to analyze the poem by employing the psychoanalytic model of female psycho-sexual development, which presents certain transformations in a starker, more objective and demythologized form than do the works of culture that employ them as themes and motifs.[6] The little girl's attempts to reconstitute her identity once her ear-

[6] What is known as the "Freudian theory" of female development is, in fact, Freud's contribution (in the form of three principal essays: "Some Psychological Consequences of the Anatomical Distinction between the Sexes" [1925], "Female Sexuality" [1931], and "Femininity" [1933]) to a debate on the question in the psychoanalytic movement of the time (see Fliegel 1973). According to Freud's model, the defining peculiarity in female development was the necessity for a shift in both erotogenic zone (from the clitoris to the vagina) and love object (from the mother to the father). Both of these occurred in connection with the castration complex which led in turn to the feminine Oedipus complex (love for the father, hostility toward the mother). The development is begun by the discovery of the difference between the sexes, which is interpreted by the child to mean that she has been castrated. In Freud's words, once the girl "acknowledges the fact of her castration, the consequent superiority of the male and her own inferiority, [she] . . . also rebels against these unpleasant facts" and thus may follow one of three lines of development:

1) She turns "her back on sexuality altogether. . . . She gives up phallic activity and therewith her sexuality in general and a considerable part of her masculine proclivities in other fields."

2) "She clings in obstinate self-assertion to her threatened masculinity; the hope of getting a penis . . . becomes the aim of her life, while the phantasy of really being a man . . . often dominates . . . her life." This is the so-called "masculinity complex."

3) "The girl's libido slips into a new position by means . . . of the equation 'penis child.' She gives up her wish for a penis and puts in place of it a wish for a child: and *with this purpose in view* she takes her father as a love-object. Her mother becomes the object of her jealousy." [Emphasis in the original]. This is "normal" femininity.

Few modern analysts subscribe to an unmodified version of this theory; many reject it altogether. For a presentation of several views, see two recent collections of essays: Miller, ed. 1973, esp. Thompson, Zilboorg, Sherfey, Moulton, Stoller; Jean Strouse, ed. 1974, esp. Mitchell, Person, Moulton, Stoller. Modern theory and practice recognize two components in female identity: the purely "feminine" component, which grows out of the identification of the little girl with her mother in the earliest years of life; and the "phallic" component, which manifests itself more or less as Freud described it. The primary importance is now seen to lie with the earlier, or primary sense of feminine identity, achieved before the phallic stage. The principal manifestation of the phallic stage, penis-envy, is regarded as a problem to be solved rather than as a necessary part of female identity. The "constitutional inferiority" of the female

liest fantasies have been challenged in the phallic phase of development, have an internal logic and coherence. The parallel with Demeter's adventures in the Homeric *Hymn* will help to demonstrate the unity of the poem, and the analogy of many of Demeter's paths of action with the use of the classic defense mechanisms will clarify some of the dynamics of the poem's narrative movement.

Myth, Ritual and Literature

The Homeric *Hymn to Demeter* relates the story of the rape of Demeter's daughter Persephone by the god of the underworld (Hades or Aidoneus), her mother's sorrow and anger, attempts to recover her, and the final resolution whereby Hades and Demeter share Persephone, she for two-thirds, he for one-third of the year. An additional complication in the critical assessment of this poem arises from the association of these goddesses and their myth with the Eleusinian Mysteries, a regular and important part of the religious life of Athens in the classical period, and one of several Greek festivals that increased in popularity and spread abroad in the Hellenistic era. Some sections of the poem (the wandering with torches, drinking of the *kykeôn*, the *aischrologia* [see below], and the fire ceremony) appear to have an aitiological coloring, because they portray acts that were a part of the ritual. Indeed, most of the earlier editors of the *Hymn* treated it as a religious, rather than literary, document: "Great as is the poetical value of the hymn, perhaps its chief interest lies in the fact that it is the most ancient and the most complete document bearing on the Eleusinian Mysteries."[7] Partly because the final stage of initiation into the Mysteries was kept secret (several laws insisted upon this, and some myths related the disastrous end of violators of this taboo), research into this area has taken on the character of an attempt to penetrate into the dark secrets of antiquity and thus has exercised an irresistible attraction for scholars.

Another line of investigation has been that of comparative anthropology,

---

has been discarded as a theoretical premise, and where strong signs of penis-envy appear they are interpreted as tokens of a disturbance in early relations with the parent figures. Our poem presents us with such a disturbance as a fait accompli: the bond between mother and daughter is broken and the two principal male figures are (in the opening of the poem) symbols of brutality and cruelty. In the following analysis, I have therefore employed a revised version of the model for the phallic stage (see above) and one that emphasizes the need for the girl to recover her lost identification with her mother. Indeed, one of the most important discoveries of modern psychoanalytic theory is that this identification runs like a leitmotif through the girl's orchestration of her ideas and feelings into an independent self. As we shall see, the *Hymn to Demeter* makes a similar point through its thematic and structural organization.

[7] Allen, Halliday, and Sikes 1936.

which has focused on the parallels between the Demeter-Korê (Persephone) myth and the similar Near-Eastern myths having to do with the disappearance and rebirth of a fertility deity. The story of the Hittite fertility god Telepinu offers the most exact parallel:[8] it includes the motifs of the God's rage, withdrawal from divine society, disappearance of nature's growth, attempts on the part of the other gods to persuade him to return, and eventual reconciliation. However, as the recent work of G. S. Kirk has made clear, it is important to separate myth and ritual. Kirk criticizes the old view, inherited from nineteenth-century anthropology, that ritual generated myth, or that ritual was the "dramatization" of the myth, and insists that the relation between myth and ritual "is not a simple matter of cause and effect in either direction."[9] Accordingly, in my analysis of the hymn I shall disregard, for the most part, echoes (or foreshadowings) of ritual practice and concentrate on the narrative itself. Because the Homeric *Hymn* is first and foremost a literary document, thematic analysis is the method of approach intrinsically likely to yield the most beneficial results. I have therefore introduced a further distinction than that between myth and ritual which I have already discussed—that between myth or ritual, and the literary employment of a myth. It is a truism that in classical tragedy the myth behind the drama is a vehicle for the more elaborate thoughts and ideas of the poet. But it is only recently that the Homeric Hymns have entered the domain of literature and have begun to be assessed as literary rather than religious documents.[10] Once they are treated in this way, much that has seemed irrelevant from the point of view of the story, or conversely, the otherwise unaccountable omission of well-known aspects of the divinity's characterization, can be understood as the conscious artistry of the poet.

The Homeric *Hymn to Demeter*

The *Hymn* opens with a statement of strife, in which the principal antagonists confront each other in a stark but elegant chiasmus:[11]

[8] See Pritchard, ed. 1955:126ff.

[9] 1970 and 1974. Conveniently, Kirk substantiates this point by discussing the differences between the Homeric myth of Demeter and the Eleusinian Mysteries:

> The potentially complex relations between the two overlapping forms of social behaviour (the telling of significant tales, the performing of significant acts) could hardly be better expressed than by this mysterious, manifold and in every way salutary affair of Demeter and her lost daughter. Yet the fact also remains that on *all the evidence the great majority of Greek myths were developed without any special attention to ritual*. [Emphasis in the original]

[10] See Segal 1974, Lord 1967, and Notopoulos 1962 and 1964.

[11] For the following discussion I have used the text and commentary of Richardson 1974; passages from the *Hymn* are quoted in the translation of Boer 1970.

And now let me sing
Demeter,
that awesome goddess,
with her beautiful hair,
her
and her daughter
with slender feet,
whom Aidoneus
carried away,
and Zeus,
who sees far,
in his deep voice,
allowing it,
far away from Demeter
and her gold sword,
her good harvests. . . .

The poem moves from the opposition between male and female in these first lines to the harmony between them achieved by its eventual transcendence. Before a final resolution of this major conflict can be achieved, the poet must resolve several polarities:

Male-Female
Olympian-Titan
Divine-Human
Immortal-Mortal
Young-Old
Marriage-Virginity
(Sexuality)
Joy-Sorrow

The left-hand column of polarities together stand for the patriarchal order in this poem; no unitary idea links the right-hand set of categories. Instead, they operate as modes of resistance to male domination, and only in that sense do they have any ultimate similarity to one another.

The polarity appears in the first lines of the poem as a statement of domination by the male, Olympian order over the female world. This domination finds expression as the invasion by the male—Zeus and Hades—shatters the beauty and unity of a purely female world: Persephone was playing (*paizousan*) in a lush meadow with the daughters of Ocean.

The constellation of the world-order in terms of these simple polarities parallels the situation of the infant in the beginning stages of life. The child begins life in a "symbiotic state": "that state of undifferentiation, of fusion with mother, in which the 'I' is not yet differentiated from the 'not-I,' and in which inside and outside are only gradually coming to be sensed as different."[12] In the course of development, the child slowly and gradually "separates" from the mother and "individuates" into his or her own self. The process is lifelong:

> The entire life-cycle constitutes a more or less successful process of distancing from and introjection of the lost symbiotic mother, an eternal longing for the actual or fantasied "ideal state of self," with the latter standing for a symbiotic fusion with the "all good" symbiotic mother, who was at one time part of the self in a blissful state of well being.[13]

In our poem, the lovely world of the women alone in a beautiful natural setting is like the realization of the fantasy of the symbiotic stage. One of the early mechanisms for dealing with the frustrations attendant on the disappointment of this fantasy is the projection of hostile feelings onto the mother and the subsequent displacement of these feelings onto the figure of the father. The first scenes of our poem present us with a similarly simplistically polarized world. As we might have expected, the negative, hostile, male figures of this world are shadowy, half-drawn characters, in contrast to the more pictorially complete personalities of the female realm: Hades appears only to grab Persephone; Zeus was "sitting far away / from the gods / in a temple." The world of the women, on the other hand, is richly drawn. It is a young, innocent, and childlike existence. When, for example, Persephone is entrapped, her own naiveté defeats her, for she reaches out for the narcissus as for a lovely toy (*kalon athyrma*). The association of virginity with a state of childlike innocence and bliss was a common theme in Greek literature, facilitated by the young age at which it was traditional for women to marry (as early as fourteen). Many fragments of poetry from the archaic, classical, and Hellenistic periods lament the loss of virginity as the passing of the carefree existence of childhood.[14] In Theokritos's Idyll 18 the young maidens of Sparta address a marriage-song to Helen, who has been taken away from their company and from her mother's side and can therefore no longer join them in play in the grassy meadow:

> Beautiful, graceful maiden, you're a housewife now, but we will
> go out early to the running-place and grass-fields, gathering
> bunches of sweet flowers, thinking of you still, Helena, as
> young lambs long for the teats of their mother.

> (tr. B. Mills)

[12] Mahler 1968.
[13] Mahler 1973.
[14] See esp. Sophocles frag. 524 Nauck. On death as marriage to the bridegroom of the underworld, see Meleager (*Palatine Anthology* XII.182)

Other versions of Persephone's rape emphasize virginity itself rather than childish innocence, by including the goddesses Artemis and Athena among Persephone's companions (see Homeric *Hymn to Demeter* 424ff). In Euripides (*Helen* 1315–16), the Orphic Hymn (Kern fr. 49, 40–41), and Claudian (*de raptu Proserpinae* 2), these goddesses appear, and in Euripides and Claudian they defend the young girl:

stimulat communis in arma
virginitas crimenque feri raptoris acerbat.

[Their shared virginity goaded them to arms,
And the crime of the brutal rapist stung them.]

Claudian (2.207–8)

The situation is very different in our *Hymn*. Not only is Persephone without defenders, but other details emphasize the helplessness of all the women in the first section of the poem. Demeter wanders the earth in anguish over the loss of her daughter, unable to discover what has happened, and the one goddess from whom she solicits information is unable to provide it. In Claudian (3.55ff.) Zeus expressly prohibits the giving of this information, and in other versions the role of informant is variously distributed.[15] Demeter's unsuccessful appeal to Hekate is unique to the Homeric version and, in addition, its function is not immediately apparent. The Sun, Moon, and Stars are commonly approached for information in mythology and folktale, but Hekate's association with the moon is Hellenistic. The key to the meaning of this episode lies in Hekate's Titan heritage. She, like Helios, was one of the generation who opposed Zeus's dominion and was eventually defeated. Hekate was subsequently honored by Zeus with unique and far-reaching privileges (*Theogony* 409ff.). But in this section of the hymn, she only heard and did not see; the role of knowledgeable informer must thus pass to Helios, another Titan deity. Hekate had volunteered her skimpy information to Demeter in a spontaneous gesture of concern; Helios must be supplicated for his knowledge. Hekate's relative impotence thus parallels Demeter's (and Persephone's) own and contrasts with her portrayal in the *Theogony*. Helios's superior position parallels the role of Zeus, for whom he acts as apologist:

> But goddess,
> stop
> your own great weeping.
> It does not fit you,

[15] It is the Argive woman Chrysanthis in Pausanias (1.14.2); Eubouleus and Triptolemos in a rival story; the sun in Ovid *Fosti* IV.583ff.; the people of Hermion in Apollodoros (1.5.1); the spring Arethusa in Ovid *Metamorphoses* V.504ff.; the people of Eleusis in the most common form of the legend.

> this anger that's
> so vain
> and insatiate.
> He is not unworthy as son-in-law
> among the gods,
> Aidoneus,
> The Ruler of Many,
> your own brother,
> your own blood.

The contrast in the roles of Hekate and Helios, then, as well as their contrasting associations with darkness and light (see lines 25 and 69–70), respectively, point up the central opposition between the nature and power of the female and male deities. Furthermore, the only goddess whose potency is affirmed in this section of the hymn, Gaia [Earth], cooperates in the scheme to assert male dominion: Persephone was seduced by the beauty of the narcissus

> which Earth
> as a trick
> grew
> for this girl,
> as a favor for Him Who Receives So Many [Hades],
> and with Zeus
> allowing it.

The opening section of the *Hymn*, then, has described the rape of Persephone and Demeter's reaction in such a way as to introduce a contrast between two kinds of existence for women. The first, the innocent virginal state, is a romantic paradise of carefree joy. It is like the symbiotic state of being in that the young girl exists in a condition of near-fusion with her mother and/or other women. The second, the patriarchal order controlled by men, carelessly and brutally disregards women's feelings and imposes helplessness upon them. The analogy on the psychic level is the experience of the anxiety and frustration of the move toward differentiation which culminates in the phallic phase. The blow to the little girl's self-love generated by the discoveries of this stage, and the assumption of the superiority of the male organ, are as harsh a proclamation of male supremacy as Hades' rape of Persephone and Zeus's complicity in our poem. In psychic life the events of the phallic stage impel the little girl toward a new, more realistic and more secure definition of her identity. The rape of Persephone in the *Hymn* plays the same function for Demeter.

In psycho-sexual development the young girl follows a tripartite line of development once she has entered the phallic stage.

1. She withdraws and renounces her own sexuality.

2. She manifests penis-envy in the form of a desire to acquire the male organ or in the persistence of the fantasy that she is endowed with it.

3. She identifies successfully with her mother and takes her father as a love-object; she substitutes for the penis-wish a desire for coitus with the father and for a baby from him.

Demeter's path is a similar one:[16] she first withdraws altogether from the company of the gods and renounces her own divinity; she then attempts a compensation for her deprivation; finally, she returns to Olympus, rejoins the company of the gods, and accommodates herself to the patriarchal order. In the following pages, I want to show how Demeter's various attempts to deal with the blow that Zeus and the patriarchal order have dealt her constitute the narrative core of the hymn; as such, all of the events of the poem will be seen as internally interrelated.

The first stage in Demeter's withdrawal is her initial reaction of grief to the loss of Persephone: she tears off her veil and cloak and rushes madly over land and sea. During her nine-day search,

> not once did she taste
> ambrosia,
> or that sweet brew,
> nectar,
> for she was grieving.
> Nor did she once
> plunge her body
> in bath.

Once she discovers the truth, "sharper pain, / more savage even, / struck her heart," and her attitude of mourning intensifies:

> she withdrew
> from the company of the gods
> and from Great Olympus,
> she went to the cities of men
> and their grasslands,

[16] The attempt to reestablish the mother-child unity is related in the *Hymn* from the mother's point of view. This should not deter us from making the analogy with the child in the psychoanalytic scheme, because the roles of mother and daughter are structurally interchangeable. See Klein and Rivière, 1964: "There are many threads which link the relationship of the mother to her child with that of her own relation to her mother in babyhood" (76). Cf. also Deutsch 1944: "In relation to her own child, woman repeats her own mother-child history"; and Benedek 1959:389ff. In this connection it is of interest to note that, in at least one version, Demeter herself was the object of a rape (Pausanias 8.25.5–6), and in her lying tale in this hymn (see below) Demeter presents herself as a woman whom men have brutalized.

> disguising her beauty
> for a long time.

When she finally assumes the guise of an old woman and sits down by the Virgin's Well (the Parthenion), the renunciation of all her proper attributes is complete:[17] she has transformed herself from a young, Olympian, immortal goddess of joy and beauty into an old, gnarled, mortal woman of sorrow;

> who was beyond
> child-bearing,
> beyond the gifts
> of Aphrodite—
> the lover of garlands.

In other versions (e.g., Ovid [*Metamorphoses* and *Fasti*], the Orphic hymn) Demeter's wanderings among mortals are motivated by her search for her daughter. But in this hymn, the conjunction of that theme with the traditional motif of the divinity's withdrawal from heaven in anger (cf. the story of Telepinu, above) serves the purpose of complicating the withdrawal theme and of helping to transform it into the central motif of the poem. The entire struggle has been "displaced"[18] from the divine to the human realm. Demeter attempts to cope with the threat to her identity as a mother and power as a goddess which the rape of Persephone has posed, by translating the battle onto the human plane, where her natural superiority as a goddess

[17] Berry 1975 correctly identifies Demeter's state as a "classic" depression:

Within this depression we can see many classically psychiatric attributes: she ceases to bathe, ceases to eat, disguises her beauty, denies the future (her possibilities of rejuvenation and productivity), regresses to menial tasks beneath her ability (or sees her tasks as menial), becomes narcissistic and self-concerned, sees (and actually engenders) worldwide catastrophe, and incessantly weeps.

Clearly, the richness as well as the meaning of the narrative is reduced by subsuming the whole panorama of Demeter's actions under the label of a symptom-formation. Persephone, according to this account, is "raped into consciousness," while the rapist Hades is "constellated in response to [the woman's] too narrow virginity, and his purpose [is] to escort her physically into that deeper body which lies beneath all surfaces, the psychic realm." Such an interpretation of the two major actions of the poem (Persephone's rape and Demeter's withdrawal/anger), aside from being intrinsically offensive, seems to me to bear very little relation to either the narrative realities or the structural dynamics of the poem.

[18] Displacement is a common defense against frustration or anxiety: in dreams it allows the impulse that seeks for expression to escape censorship (Freud 1935, Lecture 9: "The Dream-Censorship"). The anxiety-filled desire for sexual gratification may, for example, appear in a dream as the harmless and admissible wish to go swimming (only the dreamer's associations would be able to reveal the exact nature of the hidden wish). In symptom-formation, displacement may "allow the ego to prevent any further development of anxiety" (Freud 1936:61); in the famous case of "little Hans," for example, the boy substituted the more easily controlled fear of horses (he had only to avoid them) for terror of his father (whom he could less easily avoid, and about whom his feelings were of course ambivalent).

protects her. In order to achieve this, however, she must renounce all of the aspects of her divine character that especially distinguish her. In the course of the poem Demeter gradually, or sometimes, temporarily resumes individual facets of her lost identity. But because she does not reacquire all of her lost qualities together (i.e., her total identity) until the end of the poem, all of these intermediate measures take on the character of compromise-formations. In describing the psychology of "errors" such as slips of the tongue, Freud explained that a compromise-formation "[expresses] part-success and part-failure for each of the two intentions [to restrain an impulse and to gratify it]; the threatened intention is neither entirely suppressed nor . . . does it force itself through intact."[19] Demeter's partial manifestation of the various features of her identity in the next section of the poem is just such a phenomenon—midway between a bold proclamation of herself and demand for her rights, and the self-abnegation inherent in the assumed identity of an old woman.

The identity of the characters who receive Demeter on earth varies greatly from version to version: in the Orphic hymn it was Dysaules and Baubo (fr. 52 Kern); in Ovid (*Fasti* 4.507ff.) Keleos is a poor farmer; according to Pausanias in the Argive legend, one family rejected Demeter and was punished, the other received her and was rewarded (2.35.4); in the Sicyonian version (Pausanias 2.5.8), Demeter disguised as a strangerwoman nursed the king's only surviving son; in Ovid's *Metamorphoses* (5.446ff.) Demeter passes by a straw-roofed cottage where an old woman received her kindly; a little boy who made fun of her she turned into a lizard. It is clear that a wide choice of characters and situations was available for the account of Demeter's reception. But our version seems in many significant respects to have been modeled on the reception of Odysseus by Nausikää in *Odyssey* 6.[20] The epic parallel is a meaningful one in several ways. First, the introduction of young girls enables their youthful and light-hearted spirit to contrast with the mood and character of Demeter (see esp. 174ff.). Second, the daughters of Keleos like their epic prototype Nausikää, are virgins; but, in contrast to the mood associated with virginity and its loss in the beginning of our poem, they look forward anxiously to the time of their marriage. Nausikää had gone down to the sea to wash the clothing in preparation for her wedding feast (*Odyssey* 6. 25ff.), and in the Demeter hymn the name of the well "may . . . indicate that girls drew water from it at their marriage."[21] In any case, the task of fetching water was a woman's duty, and the well was often the scene of abduction (see Richardson 1974 on lines 98ff.); vase-

---

[19] Freud 1935:70.

[20] See the discussion of parallels in situation and language by Richardson 1974:Appendix III and on lines 99ff.

[21] Richardson 1974 on lines 99ff.

paintings on many *hydriai* testify to both these facts. Demeter's wishes for the girls clearly echo their own (see also *Odyssey* 6.180ff.):

> But may the gods
> who live on Olympus
> grant you
> young husbands,
> and may they let you
> bear the children
> their parents want.

Demeter has therefore entered a patriarchal world, but one in which women hold an honored place. Although, as the girls explain to her, men rule Eleusis and they "all have wives / to take care of the house," we are introduced only to the female dimension of life in Eleusis until after Demeter reveals herself. Similarly, in the *Odyssey* Nausikäa tells Odysseus that Alkinoös "holds the power and lordship here" (6.197; see also 7.66ff.) but advises him to supplicate the queen Arete, Nausikäa's mother.[22] Another sign of the patriarchal character of Eleusis is the high valuation of the male child,

> who was born
> late,
> long-desired
> and much-loved.

Demeter adapts herself readily to *this* patriarchal world (as opposed to the Olympian one):

> Dear children,
> whose house can I go to,
> what man
> or woman's
> where I might work
> graciously
> for them,
> the sort of work
> that is proper for
> an elderly woman?
> Gladly
> I would hold
> a new-born child
> in my arms
> and nurse him,

---

[22] See further Arthur 1973:esp. 18ff.

> and I would take care of
> the house,
> and make the beds
> in the master's sturdy rooms,
> and oversee the women's work.

Her accommodation to a male-dominated society is facilitated by the high status of women within it (see above, and note that Metaneira makes the decision on Demeter's hiring [171ff.]), and by Demeter's actual superiority, by virtue of her divinity, to the whole human realm.

There are two points, then, in this section of the poem, where Demeter partially recovers some of the aspects of the world she has rejected. First, she once again enters a social world and it is, like the existence of which she has been deprived, a world of women and, initially, of young virgins. But this woman's world is not hostile to or opposed to the male realm; it is instead incorporated within it. Second, Demeter accommodates herself to this world by taking on the role of nurse in Keleos's household; but she retains her divine status, which is emphasized by the girls' recognition of her noble bearing (157ff.), Kallidikê's statement of the platitude (ironic in its context) about the necessity of putting up with the gifts of the gods (147ff.), and Demeter's epiphany on the threshold of the *megaron* (188f.). Demeter does not renounce her sorrow or her disguise, and her lying tale reminds us of her real situation. Like the similar tales of Odysseus (*Odyssey* 14.334ff.) the falsity is only superficial, for the message of the tale is true. Demeter tells of enforced submission to men and enslavement to their desires: "for pirates took me / against my will / with force and violence." Doso/Demeter expressed her *sorrow* and *anger* at being captured by refusing food *and* by eventually running away from her "arrogant masters." She was particularly outraged by their intention to sell her, when they had paid no price for her in the first place. The addition of the last detail suggests that a "price" of some kind, some compensation, would have mitigated her anger and outrage. This detail foreshadows the end of the poem, where reconciliation to the patriarchal world is achieved, but only with payment to Demeter of the "price" that she demands.

As Demeter enters the *megaron* of the home of Metaneira, she precedes her entrance with a manifestation of her divinity (a warding off, as it were, of the implications of the menial status she is about to assume; see below) and resumes her sorrow with a new intensity:

> Then the goddess sat down
> and drew down her veil
> with her hands.
> And for a long time
> she sat on this chair

grieving
and silent,
without embracing anyone
with a word
or an act.
Without smiling,
without eating
food
or drink,
she sat there,
wasting away with longing
for her daughter
in her low dress. . . .

This section of the poem, especially, has an aitiological coloring. Richardson 1974 (on lines 192–211) details the parallels with Eleusinian ritual: 1) preliminary purification (where Demeter is seated on the ram's fleece, veils her head, and is silent); 2) fasting and abstention from wine; *3) aischrologia* (ritual jesting); and 4) the drinking of the *kykeôn* (a mixture of grain and liquid seasoned with herbs, sometimes employed medicinally[23]). But in the *Hymn* all of these actions are internally motivated and function within the established thematic structure of the poem (even though at points the poet directs our attention to the practices of the ritual: 205, 211). Thus Demeter's silence and veiling of her head, and her refusal to eat, may be seen as a renewal of her sorrow and a retarding of her return to her proper status. In psychoanalytic terms it would be interpreted as the reactivation of a symptom formation (depression) under the pressure of the anxiety generated by this first step into the world of heterosexual human relations.[24]

In the Orphic hymn, Baubo is Demeter's hostess who, as Clement reports the event (*Protreptikos* 2.20.1 = Kern fr. 52), "was unhappy [when Demeter would not drink the *kykeôn*] because [her hospitality] was disdained, uncovered her genitals and displayed them to the goddess; Demeter was pleased by the sight and finally took the drink, in her pleasure at the display." A

---

[23] See Richardson 1974:Appendix IV.

[24] This reactivation of the symptom is one of the forms that resistance takes and is aided by what is known as the "secondary gain of illness" in neurosis (or the epinosic gain). The symptom itself, as Freud describes it, gradually "becomes intertwined more and more intimately with the ego, becoming ever more indispensable to the latter" (1936:27). For Demeter the adoption of the persona of the old woman functions similarly. The goddess is able to alleviate some of her anxieties and acquire some of her desires (see below), the more she immerses herself in the false identity. Her mourning attitude is an essential component of her assumed identity, but the reverse is not true. In the following sections of the poem, each time that the goddess reverts to the mourning attitude, she renounces some of the other attributes that are part of her disguise. Her "resistance" is thus broken down little by little, and she finally gives up mourning altogether.

further association of Baubo with Iambe (the eponym of the iambic meter, used in raillery and scurrilous attack) and with Demeter was the combined worship of Baubo with Demeter on the island of Paros. The island was the home both of an important Demeter cult and of the poet Archilochos, the first to write in the iambic meter and the author of a hymn to Demeter (*scholia* to Aristophanes *Birds* 1764). One dedicatory inscription (*Inscriptiones Graecae* 12.5.227) links their names "to Demeter Thesmophoros and Korê and Zeus Eubouleus and Babo (Baubo)."

All of our testimony having to do with cult practices in Greece mentions ritual jesting rather than exposure. But the latter custom was not uncommon and was attested in antiquity from as widely varying regions as Egypt (the story of Hathor; the festival of Artemis at Bubastis) and Japan.[25] The Baubo figurines from Priene in Asia Minor (fifth century B.C.E.) provide further evidence of the explicitly sexual content of the humor associated with Baubo. The figurines are "personifications" of the female genital organs: arms, facial features, and hair molded to look like clothes drawn up, are added to the lower abdomen and legs.[26]

Aischrologia, or ritual jesting, was a common part of all the festivals of Demeter, including the Eleusinian celebration, and of women's festivals (like the Stenia) in general. Apollodoros explains that women indulge in jesting at the Thesmophoria in memory of the time when "a certain old woman named Iambe made the goddess laugh with her raillery" (1.5.1). Diodorus Siculus (5.4.7) adds that ritual jesting at this festival derived from the time when "it made Demeter laugh when she was grieving over the rape of Korê."

One theory about the ritual jest provides a plausible connection between indecent exposure and laughter: S. Reinach[27] discusses several myths in which the deity's laugh creates or restores life, and the importance attached to the infant's first smile on the fourteenth day of life: "c'est comme une prise de possession formelle de la vie." The laughter, in Reinach's view, is a symbol of rebirth, whose force, when it is laughter at an obscene act, is increased because it violates a taboo. The account of Iambe and her joking in the

---

[25] For a more complete account, see Richardson 1974:213–17; Mylonas 1961, Nilsson 1941:623, and others insist that ritual jesting, rather than obscene display, must have been the practice in the Athenian ritual.

[26] Freud 1916 discusses these figurines in connection with an obsession of a male patient (the word *father-arse*, which Freud found was "a jocular Teutonizing of the honourable title 'patriarch,' " and a mental picture in which the whole person of the father was represented by the lower part only. The most complete discussion of Baubo and of the Baubo-figurines is to be found in Guthrie 1935:135 ff. See also Neumann 1974:132, 138, and pl. 48. Recently, Ruck 1976:239 and n.6, following Marie Delcourt 1951 (1956), has suggested that "the Baubo figurines . . . could be interpreted as phalloi which have been decorated as females by the addition of a face and genitalia beneath the glans. In her [Baubo] therefore, the opposition of male and female are mediated."

[27] Reinach 1912 was Freud's source.

hymn, therefore, probably conceals a reference to the grosser and more explicitly sexual aspects of Demeter's fertility powers. The associations of the ritual jest with obscenity are so clear that we can safely infer that the sexual content of Iambe's "jokes and clowning around" in the Homeric poem would have been understood. The inference is supported by the fact that Aphrodite plays the analogous role of comforting the goddess, and of being the first to induce her to abandon her sorrow, in the hymn to the Great Mother in Euripides' *Helen* (lines 1349ff.).

In the Homeric *Hymn*, however, the interest of the scene lies in the effect on Demeter of Iambe's humor, rather than in its content:

> [she] forced
> this sacred lady
> to smile,
> to laugh,
> and to
> cheer up her spirits.

Demeter then drinks the *kykeôn* that she has instructed Metaneira to prepare. In the *Hymn*, then, Demeter's laughter is an abrupt and momentary abandonment of her sorrow. But it is also a further movement toward the recreation of her identity. Because the object of her laughter is a display of sexuality in some form or other, Demeter's laughter signifies an acceptance, although an ambivalent one,[28] of female sexuality. In terms of the economics of psychic energy, laughter is a reverse expenditure of the energy used for inhibition.[29] By her laughter, therefore, Demeter momentarily abandons both her sorrow and her rejection of sexuality and achieves a temporary return to her joyous, life-sustaining true self.

In the next section of the poem, Demeter goes further in recovering her lost identity. The episode in which Demeter cares for the child Demophoön and attempts to immortalize him is highly complex. On one level, it is Demeter's first approach toward and acceptance of the male—but in a form, as a child and human, in which the male is not threatening or potent. Demophoön is also a substitute for the lost Persephone, and Demeter

---

[28] Laughter is commonly interpreted as the result of a compromise whose function is to defend against anxiety. See Kris 1952:215, and Freud 1963. From a psychoanalytic point of view, the exposure of female genitals may have further import. For the comparative inaccessibility of the female sexual organs may delay, or inhibit, the formation of a realistic "body-image" in early development (see, among others, Greenacre 1952). Exposure, in either word or deed, to this area of the female body would then be an important aid to Demeter's reestablishment of her female identity. I owe this suggestion to Eleanor Schuker. The hermaphroditic aspects of Baubo, and Ruck's suggestion (1976) that they make her a mediative figure, would add point to my argument that the Iambe episode in the hymn is one of several points where Demeter wavers between two mutually incompatible forms of female identity (an excessively "masculine" and an excessively "feminine" one).

[29] See Freud 1963:section IV, and Kris 1952:Part III.

lavishes upon him the affection that later characterizes her reunion with her daughter:

> Demeter
> anointed him
> with ambrosia,
> as if
> he were born from a god,
> she breathed on him
> sweetly
> as she held him
> in her lap.

As the above passage indicates, Demeter's attempt to make the child immortal is an effort to assimilate him to her own realm, to make him her own. The attempted immortalization is therefore a highly ambivalent gesture. On the one hand, her desire to adopt the child represents an attempt to restore the ruptured symbiotic unity with Persephone. Demeter therefore nurtures the child with the characteristic selfless devotion of a mother. But there is also an important hostile component to her actions. Although the poet of the hymn has largely suppressed any direct manifestation of this hostility, Demeter's anger at being discovered and her reaction, in which she throws the child to the floor, serve to express the negative feelings. In some important variants of the myth, the child dies in the fire. Both the Orphic hymn (Kern fr. 49.100) and Apollodoros (1.5.1) preserve this variant. In neither case was the death deliberate, but another version (that of the Second Vatican Mythographer, 97[30]) has Demeter kill the child in her rage.

The mechanism of this ambivalence has the same character as the child's pregenital eroticism (especially oral eroticism): the active-aggressive desire to incorporate alternates with the passive-submissive desire to be incorporated. The mother characteristically repeats this pattern (in a more sophisticated and less dangerous form, of course) when she cares for her child.[31] But there is another factor in Demeter's attitude toward Demophoön. Because he is a male and not a female child, Demeter's ambivalent feelings are more easily elicited. For it is the male world that has been so hostile and threatening to her. Demeter's actions can thus also be interpreted as a manifestation of penis-envy.[32] This analogy makes it easier to understand the reasons for Demeter's ambivalence and for her anger (stressed by the poet: see 251,

---

[30] In Bode 1834:1.94–95.

[31] Several psychoanalytic discussions of the mother-child relationship point out that "not only does the helpless infant need the mother and feed on her, but the mother also needs and—emotionally—even feeds on the child" (Jacobson 1964:56). The mother's nurturance of the child extends to the point of allowing him/her to "borrow" her ego for the fulfillment of its own needs (Ibid.:58). See also the references cited in note 16.

[32] The equation penis = child is common in psychic symbolism.

254). At this point in the poem, Demeter has adopted a course of action similar to the second line of development followed by the little girl in the phallic stage (see above). Penis-envy, as modern psychoanalytic writers on the subject have made clear, springs from an overvaluation of the male organ and its endowment with magical powers. Its necessary correlate is always, therefore, the little girl's imperfect realization of and acceptance of her own sexual identity. Demeter in the *Hymn* is in an analogous situation: she attempts to reestablish the ruptured primal unity while at the same time maintaining her fictitious identity as an asexual, old, mortal serving-woman—a being, in other words, inferior to the goddess that she is. At the same time, her assumption of a menial role was the means for her to acquire the child. The two actions—self-denial and acquisition of the child—are therefore linked.

In psychic life the overvaluation of the male organ also produces a reaction of hostility and contempt for the characteristic that holds the woman in thraldom. An analogous mechanism may be observed in Demeter's anger and ambivalent attitude toward Demophoön in the poem. We should remark here too that in other myths and religious rituals the worship of a young male god-child in conjunction with a mother-goddess often entails the devaluation of the latter.[33] Bachofen described this phenomenon eloquently in his account of the Dionysian stage (as he called it) of matriarchal development. It is a call on the god's part for "recognition of the glorious superiority of his own male-phallic nature." The gloomy sternness of the Amazonian form of the matriarchy (in Bachofen's view; see note 4) prepared for this stage: the extremism of its own severity invited the Dionysian sensualization of existence and the development of the male principle at the expense of womanhood. The parallels with the girl's overvaluation of the penis and renunciation of her own sexuality, and with Demeter's similar renunciation and fervent desire for the male child, are obvious.

The pivotal point in the narrative and thematic development of the poem is Metaneira's thwarting of Demeter's plan. It inaugurates the actions that

[33] The worship of the divine son or of a young boy as part of the Eleusinian Mysteries is well known; the child is variously identified: he is Ploutos, Demophoön, Eleusis, Triptolemos, or sometimes Dionysos in his Iacchos character. See Richardson 1974:27. The interpretation of this figure in the ritual by Jung and Neumann points up the implied subordination of the female principle; e.g., "The luminous male principle is experienced by woman in two forms, as fire and as higher light. In this connection the fire that is everywhere tended by woman is lower fire, earth fire and fire contained in the woman, which the male need only 'drill' out of her." (Neumann 1974:310). This idea is similar to Berry's postulation of a need for the woman to be "raped into consciousness" (1975. See above, note 17). The Jungian interpretation of this myth (which, in any case, usually attends more closely to the ritual), while focusing on the two stages of the female's confrontation with the male (the first in which he overpowers her; the second in which he fulfills her), does not identify the mechanics of the transformation from the first to the second stage. The final reconciliation therefore tends to take the form of the female's submission to (rather than overcoming of) her idealization of the male.

culminate in Demeter's return to Olympus and to her true identity. There are several implications of the shift of action at this point in the poem which are important. First, Metaneira's intrusion and her fears for her baby act for Demeter like the impingement of reality on the child's fantasies in the phallic stage. Demeter is suddenly forced to realize and to adjust to the values of the wholly human realm into which she has come, even though she dismissed the humans contemptuously as "stupid people, / brainless." Second, Demeter's anger, which we discussed above, was certainly directed as much at Metaneira as at Demophoön ("Demeter . . . was furious with her [Metaneira]"). The two women are, in effect, competing for possession of the child. Metaneira's maternal feeling for her child is expressed in her outburst of concern:

> Baby Demophoön,
> the stranger
> hides you in all that fire
> and makes me weep
> and brings me bitter pain.

The description of the child inserted into the next lines repeats a theme expressed earlier, which had made clear how highly valued the baby was: "this child / whose mother bore it / in the palace long after / a child had ceased to be hoped for." Demeter, for her part, grants to the child "undying honor" in remembrance of the nurturing she gave him:

> because of the fact that
> he climbed on my knees,
> and slept in my arms.

The theme of hostile competition with a woman appears only here in the poem and is analogous to the girl's hostile feelings for her mother in the phallic stage. Its resolution, we recall (see above), and the substitution for it of an identification with the mother, was a critical move in the girl's positive realization of her own sexual identity. The same, as we shall see, is true for Demeter, in the section of the poem where she is united with Persephone, Hekate, and her mother Rheia.

Demeter's hostile rejection of Metaneira, of her baby, and of her world, is coupled with her first true manifestation of her divinity, and the proclamation of her true identity:

> I am the honorable Demeter,
> producer of
> the greatest blessing,
> the greatest joy,
> for man
> and god alike. . . .

The goddess
said this
and changed
her size
and shape,
throwing away
her agedness,
and beauty
drifted
all around her
and a lovely fragrance
from her perfumed veils
spread about
and a brightness
from the immortal flesh
of the goddess
shone far away
and her blond hair
fell
to her shoulders
and the sturdy house
was filled with light
like lightning.

At this point in the poem, then, Demeter recovers many of her characteristics of femininity and partially resumes her divine status. For by giving the orders for building her temple, Demeter establishes herself as divine in relation to the whole human community at Eleusis. She still holds herself apart from the Olympian realm, however. For this new phase of withdrawal is accompanied by a renewal of mourning:

Then the blond Demeter
installed herself there [in the temple],
far away from
all the happy gods,
she stayed there,
wasting away
with longing
for her daughter
in her low dress.

Now Demeter's antipathy towards the gods expresses itself as a reversal of her potentiality. She is properly, as she told Metaneira just before bringing on the famine, "producer of / the greatest blessing, / the greatest joy, / for man / and god / alike." But although she has ceased to deny her divinity,

Demeter withholds complete affirmation of herself as a goddess of joy both by staying in her temple on earth and by refusing to actualize her divine powers. Instead, she manifests her divinity in a perversion (or inversion) of these powers:

> And she made this
> the most terrible year
> on this earth
> that feeds so many,
> and the most cruel.

The all-night vigil in which the women attempt to propitiate the goddess has been identified as a type of *pannychis*, or all-night festival, which seems to have been associated more or less exclusively with women's festivals and certainly formed part of the celebration of the Eleusinian Mysteries. This section of the rite was celebrated by the women alone (or at least by the women segregated from the men) and consisted in dancing around the well (called Kallichoron: the well of beautiful dances [see Pausanias 1.38.6]) and perhaps *aischrologia*. This well still survives today (it was constructed in the second half of the sixth century but certainly had predecessors). It is outside the sanctuary, which accords with Demeter's instructions in the hymn to build her temple "above the Kallichoron on the protruding hill."

The episode in the poem in which the women attempt a fearful and tentative alliance with Demeter and which occurs before Keleos is informed of the events in the house, is a first step in trying to recreate the broken solidarity among the women. The older commentators on the *Hymn* attribute a similar importance to the *pannychis* itself: "In the very earliest period the worship of Demeter Thesmophoros at Eleusis, as elsewhere, was confined to women . . . and the hymn clearly shows the important part played by the women, even in a later stage of the Eleusinian religion." (Allen and Sikes, 1904 on line 292).

In the next section of the poem, the focus of action shifts from the interior of the home, the female realm, to the male world of the assembly, where Keleos had called the people together to build Demeter's temple. This shift of interest in Eleusis foreshadows the widening of the compass of the poem to include the larger, patriarchally governed world-order.

Zeus, the divine counterpart to Keleos, reenters the poem at this point. He, like Keleos, attempts to propitiate Demeter. In this section of the poem, both Zeus and Hades (on Zeus's instructions) employ persuasion rather than force in their approaches to the two goddesses. Zeus sends first Iris, and then "every one of the blessed gods":

> But no one
> was able to persuade
> her mind and heart

> because she was furious
> inside,
> and she rejected
> their words
> cold.

The reason for this is clear. Iris had appealed to the goddess to submit simply to Zeus's will ("Come on, / don't let / the word of Zeus / go unfulfilled.") But Demeter demands satisfaction:

> For she said
> she would not ever again
> set foot on
> fragant Olympus,
> she would not
> let the fruit of the earth
> come up
> until she saw with her eyes
> her daughter's
> beautiful face.

Zeus agrees to Demeter's terms and sends Hermes to fetch Persephone. He, too, must use "soft words" in his exhortation of Hades. For this section of the poem everywhere emphasizes reconciliation through persuasion and the avoidance of infringement of the rights and feelings of any of the gods. The mood is similar to that in the final sections of the *Theogony*, where Zeus distributes rights and privileges (881 ff.) and thus secures his position as king and consolidates his rule.

When Hermes meets Persephone and Hades in their domain, it is clear that Persephone is by no means totally reconciled to her marriage:

> [Persephone] was very reluctant[34]
> because of a longing
> for her mother.

Before he releases Persephone, Hades attempts to persuade her to agree willingly to be his wife. The opening lines of his appeal repeat the consolatory speech that Helios had offered Demeter in the first part of the poem (see above), but to no avail. Now, however, Hades adds that Persephone will be honored and revered, and this is clearly crucial to winning her over:

> When you're here
> you will reign
> over everyone who lives
> and moves,

[34] Boer's (1970) translation of this (*aekazomenê* – "unwilling") is rather too mild.

and you will have
the greatest honors
among the gods. . . .

In addition, Hades gives Persephone the pomegranate to eat. The addition of the adverb *lathrêi* (= "secretly") may indicate that Hades did not wish Hermes to observe him (so Richardson 1974 on line 373). Although Persephone later insists to Demeter that Hades "forced me, / unwillingly, / violently, / to eat it [the pomegranate seed]," this does not accord with the original account. In other versions of the myth Persephone herself picked the fruit and ate it (e.g., Ovid *Metamorphoses* 5.534ff.), and in an interesting variant reported by Apollodoros (1.5.3) Persephone punishes the tattletale Askalaphos, who informed on her.

The pomegranate itself, according to the most plausible interpretation, symbolized both blood and death, both fertility and marriage. It was a taboo food in the celebrations of Demeter. Kerényi, in one of the most interesting sections of his book on the cult,[35] defines two groups of plants, one associated with the male divinity (pomegranate, apple, fig, vine) and the other with the female fertility goddesses (pomegranate, almond, date palm). The association of the pomegranate with both the male and female fertility deities makes it an ideal symbol for the union of Persephone and Hades in this poem. As a symbol it was both male and female: the womblike shape and bloodlike liquid that flowed from it associated it with the female; its seeds were a male feature.

Persephone's youthful naiveté enables the male to win her over more easily than Demeter. Her acceptance of the pomegranate recalls her original fascination with the narcissus (similarly associated with both death and fertility). Persephone's easy seduction by these symbols indicates her greater susceptibility to the dangers and pleasures of sexuality with the male.

When Persephone returns to Demeter, the accounting that her mother demands from her emphasizes her unwillingness and Hades' employment of force in both the original rape and in the eating of the pomegranate (see above). The focus on the male's intrusion into the female world, which Persephone's recapitulation and expansion of the story of the rape and of her exploits in the underworld provide, introduces a renewal of the theme of female solidarity:

They spent
the whole of that day
with hearts united,
and they warmed
each other's hearts

[35] 1967a:134.

> with many gestures
> of affection,
> and her heart stopped
> grieving.
> They gave
> and received
> joy
> from each other.

Hekate then joins them and shares in their delight. Finally, Zeus sends Rheia to them, and with her arrival all of the principal female deities in the poem are joined together. Their reunion expresses a female solidarity discovered in the context of a patriarchal world. Our fragment of the Hymn by Philikos (Page *GLP* #90, end of the third century B.C.E.) by contrast, collapses into one event the three discreet episodes in our poem of female bonding (the joking of Iambe, the *pannychis*, and the reunion of the goddesses). In that hymn, which is clearly based on the Homeric one, the Nymphs, Graces, and mortal women attempt unsuccessfully to console Demeter until Iambe arrives with an assurance that she can discover a remedy for the goddess's sorrow (the fragment breaks off here).

In the Homeric hymn, Rheia's arrival marks both Demeter's return to her true, feminine, divine nature and her incorporation into the patriarchally ruled world of Olympus. She does not capitulate, however. On the contrary, she has her special privileges affirmed. As Rheia puts it to Demeter:

> Come here
> my child,
> Zeus
> with his deep voice
> who sees far,
> calls you to come up
> with the race of the gods,
> and he offers to give you
> whatever honors you want
> among the gods.

Persephone is permanently restored to Demeter, but in a form that necessitates recognition of the bond that each of them has with the male. However, in contrast to other versions (Ovid, Apollodoros), Persephone is restored to Demeter for two-thirds (rather than for one-half) of the year.

In this context the unity of the female goddesses, which is such a striking aspect of the last sections of the poem, takes on a different character than the symbiotic unity that we discussed in connection with the female world of the first part of the *Hymn*. For this later form of female solidarity expresses a bond whose basis is the special and particular comfort, affection, and general gratification that women are able to offer one another by virtue simply of their appreciation of and identification with one another. This contrasts with the false (or naive) unity produced by their mutual antipathy toward the male and encasement in an enchanted world of virginity (the symbiotic phase of the first stage of the poem). In this connection, it is significant that Rheia, Demeter's mother, is the agent of her daughter's final reconciliation with the Olympian realm, and the instrument of her return to Olympus and activation of her positive divine powers:

> She [Rheia] said this,
> and Demeter,
> in her beautiful crown,
> was not inattentive.
> Immediately
> she brought in a harvest
> from fertile lands.

As with the little girl's final successful transition to "normal" femininity in the third stage of her development (see above), the critical factor is the achievement of a successful identification with the mother. What for the little girl would be the constitution of a self-reliant ego, is for Demeter the return to her rightful place on Olympus as a divine goddess of youthfulness, joy, and beauty:

> And when the divine goddesses
> had accomplished everything,
> they went up
> to Olympus
> to join the company
> of the other gods.
> That's where they live,
> these sacred
> and venerable goddesses,
> near to Zeus
> who enjoys the lightning.

The final section of the poem raises once more issues having to do with ritual practice and religious significance. As part of her return to her true state, Demeter gives the two gifts with which she was identified in later Attic tradition, agriculture and the religious rite:

[Demeter] gave us these two gifts, which are the greatest gifts there are—the grain, which enables us to live other than like animals, and the rite, whose initiates have sweeter hopes regarding both the end of life and the whole of existence.

Isokrates, *Panegyrikos* IV.28

The hymn similarly divides Demeter's gifts:

> Immediately
> she brought
> in a harvest
> from fertile lands. . . .
> And she went
> and taught the kings
> who administer law, . . .
> she taught them
> the ministry of her rites,
> and she revealed to them
> her beautiful mysteries.

The initiate is "happy" (*olbios* = "blessed"), unlike the person who has not participated in the rites and thus "does not share / the same fate, / when he dies / and is down in / the squalid darkness." While he or she lives, if the goddesses "graciously / decide to love [him]," wealth (*Ploutos*) and happiness come to his house.

Pindar (fr. 212 Bowra), Sophocles (*Triptolemos* fr. 753 Nauck) and the Hellenistic poet Krinagoras of Lesbos (*Palatine Anthology* 11.42) all describe the blessedness of the initiate in similar terms. The religious issues here are very complicated ones, having to do with the nature of the final vision in the celebration of the Mysteries, and with the precise meaning of "blessedness" in early Greek thought. Whole books (e.g., Deichgräber, *Eleusinische Frömmigkeit*) have been written on the subject,[36] which obviously does not admit of summary treatment. In any case, it is unnecessary for our purposes. From the point of view of thematic and narrative structure, this ending serves two purposes. First, the promise of happiness to humankind through participation in the rites dissolves the alienation of the human from the divine realm. This had been an important subsidiary theme of the poem. As the daughters of Keleos had explained to Demeter earlier (see above):

> We who are human
> have to endure
> gifts from the gods,
> though hard,
> for they are stronger
> than we are
> by far.

[36] See further Richardson 1974:304ff.

The irony of the situation is purposeful, of course: "In the Hymn, the gulf between men and gods . . . is emphasized exactly at the points where an encounter between the two takes place, and again at the point of Demeter's departure."[37] The attempted immortalization of Demophoön resumes the theme, and Demeter's rebuke to Metaneira once again makes the point of the helplessness of mortals in the face of the gods:

> Stupid people,
> brainless,
> you don't even know
> when fate
> is bringing you something good,
> or something bad.

The gift of the Mysteries partially resolves this opposition; it brings humans closer to gods and the gods closer to humans. Although immortality is impossible, the Mysteries free humans from the fear of death.

The final section of the poem, then, portrays the gift of the rite as a dissolution of the hostility between humans and gods. Second, the gift of agriculture and the institution of the rites is associated in the narrative with the ascension of Demeter and Persephone to Olympus and their incorporation into "the company of the other gods."

The end of the poem thus describes the arrival of the new world-order and defines its nature. We are reminded, through the description of Zeus as "[he] who enjoys the lightning" (*terpikeraunos*), that this world-order is organized under male dominion, for Zeus's control of the lightning was always the symbol of his power and kingship. But Zeus's power is underplayed in the *Hymn*. The construction of the lines is such that *terpikeraunoi* at the end of one line is followed by two adjectives at the beginning of the next line—*semnai t'aidoiai te* ("sacred and venerable")—that focus on the awesome character of the two goddesses. The end of the poem thus shows us a stable world coming into being under male dominion; but the female element is incorporated into it and occupies an honored and respected place. The female element, moreover, through its association with agriculture and with the Mysteries, is the agency that transforms mortal dependence on the gods and helplessness before them into a more genuinely reciprocal relationship.[38] The relationship between the female and male deities thus parallels that between the human and divine worlds. And so the

---

[37] Richardson 1974:on lines 147ff.

[38] The gods' relationship with humans at the beginning of the poem was one of simple dominance, even exploitation; there was no indication of concern on the gods' part for human welfare. When Demeter imposes the famine, the gods' somewhat comical reaction is concern over losing their sacrificial offerings(!)

poem ends with a suggestion that Demeter, as the one who can be propitiated, symbolizes all hope, all possibility of transcendence, all promise of renewal:

> "The mysteries remain,
> I keep the same
> cycle of seed-time
> and of sun and rain;
> Demeter in the grass
> I multiply,
> renew and bless
> Iacchus in the vine;
> I hold the law,
> I keep the mysteries true,
> the first of these
> to name the living, dead;
> I am red wine and bread.

> *I keep the law,*
> *I hold the mysteries true,*
> *I am the vine,*
> *the branches, you*
> *and you."*

H.D. ("The Mysteries" VI [from *Red Roses for Bronze*]).[39]

[39] I would like to express my thanks for their helpful suggestions to the participants in the symposium Applications of Modern Critical Theory to Classical Literature, and especially to Bennett Simon, M.D., and to the members of the Columbia University Seminar on Women and Society (where I first presented the revised version of this paper), and especially to Eleanor Shucker, M.D.

FAMILY STRUCTURE AND FEMININE

PERSONALITY

Nancy Chodorow

I PROPOSE HERE[1,2] a model to account for the reproduction within each generation of certain general and nearly universal differences that characterize masculine and feminine personality and roles. My perspective is largely psychoanalytic. Cross-cultural and social-psychological evidence suggests that an argument drawn solely from the universality of biological sex differences is unconvincing.[3] At the same time, explanations based on patterns of deliberate socialization (the most prevalent kind of anthropological, sociological, and social-psychological explanation) are in themselves insufficient to account for the extent to which psychological and value commitments to sex differences are so emotionally laden and tenaciously maintained, for the way gender identity and expectations about sex roles and gender consistency are so deeply central to a person's consistent sense of self.

This paper suggests that a crucial differentiating experience in male and female development arises out of the fact that women, universally, are largely responsible for early child care and for (at least) later female socialization. This points to the central importance of the mother-daughter relationship for women, and to a focus on the conscious and unconscious effects of early involvement with a female for children of both sexes. The fact that males and females experience this social environment differently as they grow up accounts for the development of basic sex differences in personality. In particular, certain features of the mother-daughter relationship are internalized universally as basic elements of feminine ego structure (although not necessarily what we normally mean by "femininity").

[1] This essay was originally published in *Women, Culture and Society*, ed. M. Rosaldo and L. Lamphere (Stanford 1974) 43–66. Some of the notes have been abridged, indicated by ellipsis points where the notes now conclude. Additional minor alterations have been made to conform to the editorial style of this volume.

[2] My understanding of mother-daughter relationships and their effect on feminine psychology grows out of my participation beginning in 1971 in a women's group that discusses mother-daughter relationships in particular and family relationships in general. All the women in this group have contributed to this understanding. An excellent dissertation by Marcia Millman (1972) first suggested to me the importance of boundary issues for women and became a major organizational focus for my subsequent work. . . .

Specifically, I shall propose that, in any given society, feminine personality comes to define itself in relation and connection to other people more than masculine personality does. (In psychoanalytic terms, women are less individuated than men; they have more flexible ego boundaries.[4]) Moreover, issues of dependency are handled and experienced differently by men and women. For boys and men, both individuation and dependency issues become tied up with the sense of masculinity, or masculine identity. For girls and women, by contrast, issues of femininity, or feminine identity, are not problematic in the same way. The structural situation of child rearing, reinforced by female and male role training, produces these differences, which are replicated and reproduced in the sexual sociology of adult life.

The paper is also a beginning attempt to rectify certain gaps in the social-scientific literature, and a contribution to the reformulation of psychological anthropology. Most traditional accounts of family and socialization tend to emphasize only role training, and not unconscious features of personality. Those few that rely on Freudian theory have abstracted a behaviorist methodology from this theory, concentrating on isolated "significant" behaviors like weaning and toilet training. The paper advocates instead a focus on the ongoing interpersonal relationships in which these various behaviors are given meaning.[5]

More empirically, most social-scientific accounts of socialization, child development, and the mother-child relationship refer implicitly or explicitly only to the development and socialization of boys, and to the mother-son relationship. There is a striking lack of systematic description about the mother-daughter relationship, and a basic theoretical discontinuity between, on the one hand, theories about female development, which tend to stress the development of "feminine" qualities in relation to and comparison with men, and on the other hand, theories about women's ultimate mother-

---

[3] Margaret Mead provides the most widely read and earliest argument for this viewpoint (cf., e.g., 1935 and 1949); see also Chodorow 1971 for another discussion of the same issue.

[4] Unfortunately, the language that describes personality structure is itself embedded with value judgment. The implication in most studies is that it is always better to have firmer ego boundaries, that "ego strength" depends on the degree of individuation. Gutmann, who recognizes the linguistic problem, even suggests that "so-called ego pathology may have adaptive implications for women" (1965:231). The argument can be made that extremes in either direction are harmful. Complete lack of ego boundaries is clearly pathological, but so also, as critics of contemporary Western men point out (cf., e.g., Bakan 1966 and Slater 1970), is individuation gone wild, what Bakan calls "agency unmitigated by communion," which he takes to characterize, among other things, both capitalism based on the Protestant ethic and aggressive masculinity. With some explicit exceptions that I will specify in context, I am using the concepts solely in the descriptive sense.

[5] Slater 1968 provides one example of such an investigation. LeVine's recent work on psychoanalytic anthropology (1971a,b) proposes a methodology that will enable social scientists to study personality development in this way.

ing role. This final lack is particularly crucial, because women's motherhood and mothering role seem to be the most important features in accounting for the universal secondary status of women.[6] The present paper describes the development of psychological qualities in women that are central to the perpetuation of this role.

In a formulation of this preliminary nature, there is not a great body of consistent evidence to draw upon. Available evidence is presented that illuminates aspects of the theory—for the most part psychoanalytic and social-psychological accounts based almost entirely on highly industrialized Western society. Because aspects of family structure are discussed that are universal, however, I think it is worth considering the theory as a general model. In any case, this is in some sense a programmatic appeal to people doing research. It points to certain issues that might be especially important in investigations of child development and family relationships and suggests that researchers look explicitly at female versus male development, and that they consider seriously mother-daughter relationships even if these are not of obvious "structural importance" in a traditional anthropological view of that society.

The Development of Gender Personality

According to psychoanalytic theory,[7] personality is a result of a boy's or girl's social-relational experiences from earliest infancy. Personality development is not the result of conscious parental intention. The nature and quality of the social relationships that the child experiences are appropriated, internalized, and organized by her/him and come to constitute her/his personality. What is internalized from an ongoing relationship continues independent of that original relationship and is generalized and set up as a permanent feature of the personality. The conscious self is usually not aware of many of the features of personality, or of its total structural organization. At the same time, these are important determinants of any person's behavior, both that which is culturally expected and that which is idiosyncratic or unique to the individual. The conscious aspects of personality, like a person's general self-concept and, importantly, her/his gender identity, require and depend upon the consistency and stability of its unconscious organization. In what follows I shall describe how contrasting male and female experiences lead to differences in the way that the developing masculine or feminine psyche resolves certain relational issues.

[6] Chodorow 1971; Ortner 1974 and Rosaldo 1974.

[7] Particularly as interpreted by object-relations theorists (e.g., Fairbairn 1952 and Guntrip 1961) and, with some similarity, by Parsons 1964 and Parsons and Bales 1955.

Separation and Individuation (Preoedipal Development)

All children begin life in a state of "infantile dependence"[8] upon an adult or adults, in most cases their mother. This state consists first in the persistence of primary identification with the mother: the child does not differentiate herself/himself from her/his mother but experiences a sense of oneness with her. (It is important to distinguish this from later forms of identification, from "secondary identification," which presuppose at least some degree of experienced separateness by the person who identifies.) Second, it includes an oral-incorporative mode of relationship to the world, leading, because of the infant's total helplessness, to a strong attachment to and dependence upon whoever nurses and carries her/him.

Both aspects of this state are continuous with the child's prenatal experience of being emotionally and physically part of the mother's body and of the exchange of body material through the placenta. That this relationship continues with the natural mother in most societies stems from the fact that women lactate. For convenience, and not because of biological necessity, this has usually meant that mothers, and females in general, tend to take all care of babies. It is probable that the mother's continuing to have major responsibility for the feeding and care of the child (so that the child interacts almost entirely with her) extends and intensifies her/his period of primary identification with her more than if, for instance, someone else were to take major or total care of the child. A child's earliest experience, then, is usually of identity with and attachment to a single mother, and always with women.

For both boys and girls, the first few years are preoccupied with issues of separation and individuation. This includes breaking or attenuating the primary identification with the mother and beginning to develop an individuated sense of self, and mitigating the totally dependent oral attitude and attachment to the mother. I would suggest that, contrary to the traditional psychoanalytic model, the preoedipal experience is likely to differ for boys and girls. Specifically, the experience of mothering for a woman involves a double identification.[9] A woman identifies with her own mother and, through identification with her child, she (re)experiences herself as a cared-for child. The particular nature of this double identification for the individual mother is closely bound up with her relationship to her own mother. As Deutsch expresses it, "In relation to her own child, woman repeats her own mother-child history."[10] Given that she was a female child, and that identification with her mother and mothering are so bound up with her being a woman, we might expect that a woman's identification with a girl child might be stronger; that a mother, who is, after all, a person who is a woman

[8] Fairbairn 1952.
[9] Klein and Rivière 1937.
[10] Deutsch 1944:205.

mothers relate more to their girls than to boys

and not simply the performer of a formally defined role, would tend to treat infants of different sexes in different ways.

There is some suggestive sociological evidence that this is the case. Mothers in a women's group in Cambridge, Massachusetts (see note 2), say that they identified more with their girl children than with their boy children. The perception and treatment of girl vs. boy children in high-caste, extremely patriarchal, patrilocal communities in India are in the same vein. Families express preference for boy children and celebrate when sons are born. At the same time, Rajput mothers in North India are "as likely as not"[11] to like girl babies better than boy babies once they are born, and they and Havik Brahmins in South India[12] treat their daughters with greater affection and leniency than they do their sons. People in both groups say that this is out of sympathy for the future plight of their daughters, who will have to leave their natal family for a strange and usually oppressive postmarital household. From the time of their daughters' birth, then, mothers in these communities identify anticipatorily, by reexperiencing their own past, with the experiences of separation that their daughters will go through. They develop a particular attachment to their daughters because of this and by imposing their own reaction to the issue of separation on this new external situation.

It seems, then, that a mother is more likely to identify with a daughter than with a son, to experience her daughter (or parts of her daughter's life) as herself. Fliess's description (1961) of his neurotic patients who were the children of ambulatory psychotic mothers presents the problem in its psychopathological extreme. The example is interesting, because, although Fliess claims to be writing about people defined only by the fact that their problems were tied to a particular kind of relationship to their mothers, an overwhelmingly large proportion of the cases he presents are women. It seems, then, that this sort of disturbed mother inflicts her pathology predominantly on daughters. The mothers Fliess describes did not allow their daughters to perceive themselves as separate people but simply acted as if their daughters were narcissistic extensions or doubles of themselves, extensions to whom were attributed the mothers' bodily feelings and who became physical vehicles for their mothers' achievement of autoerotic gratification. The daughters were bound into a mutually dependent "hypersymbiotic" relationship. These mothers, then, perpetuate a mutual relationship with their daughters of both primary identification and infantile dependence.

A son's case is different. Cultural evidence suggests that insofar as a mother treats her son differently, it is usually by emphasizing his masculinity in opposition to herself and by pushing him to assume, or acquiescing in his assumption of, a sexually toned male-role relation to her. Whiting (1959)

[11] Minturn and Hitchcock 1963.
[12] Harper 1969.

and Whiting et al. (1958) suggest that mothers in societies with mother-child sleeping arrangements and postpartum sex taboos may be seductive toward infant sons. Slater (1968) describes the socialization of precarious masculinity in Greek males of the classical period through their mothers' alternation of sexual praise and seductive behavior with hostile deflation and ridicule. This kind of behavior contributes to the son's differentiation from his mother and to the formation of ego boundaries (I will later discuss certain problems that result from this).

Neither form of attitude or treatment is what we would call "good mothering." However, evidence of differentiation of a pathological nature in the mother's behavior toward girls and boys does highlight tendencies in "normal" behavior. It seems likely that from their children's earliest childhood, mothers and women tend to identify more with daughters and to help them to differentiate less, and that processes of separation and individuation are made more difficult for girls. On the other hand, a mother tends to identify less with her son, and to push him toward differentiation and the taking on of a male role unsuitable to his age, and undesirable at any age in his relationship to her.

For boys and girls, the quality of the preoedipal relationship to the mother differs. This, as well as differences in development during the oedipal period, accounts for the persisting importance of preoedipal issues in female development and personality that many psychoanalytic writers describe.[13] Even before the establishment of gender identity, gender personality differentiation begins.

Gender Identity (Oedipal Crisis and Resolution)

There is only a slight suggestion in the psychological and sociological literature that preoedipal development differs for boys and girls. The pattern becomes explicit at the next developmental level. All theoretical and empirical accounts agree that after about age three (the beginning of the "oedipal" period, which focuses on the attainment of a stable gender identity) male and female development becomes radically different. It is at this stage that the father, and men in general, begin to become important in the child's primary object world. It is, of course, particularly difficult to generalize about the attainment of gender identity and sex-role assumption, because there is such wide variety in the sexual sociology of different societies. However, to the extent that in all societies women's life tends to be more private and domestic, and men's more public and social,[14] we can make general statements about this kind of development.

[13] Cf., e.g., Brunswick 1940; Deutsch 1932, 1944; Fliess 1948; Freud 1931; Jones 1927; and Lampl-de Groot 1928.

[14] Rosaldo 1974.

In what follows, I shall be talking about the development of gender personality and gender identity in the tradition of psychoanalytic theory. Cognitive psychologists have established that by the age of three boys and girls have an irreversible conception of what their gender is.[15] I do not dispute these findings. It remains true that children (and adults) may know definitely that they are boys (men) or girls (women), and at the same time experience conflicts or uncertainty about "masculinity" or "femininity," about what these identities require in behavioral or emotional terms, etc. I am discussing the development of "gender identity" in this latter sense.

A boy's masculine gender identification must come to replace his early primary identification with his mother. This masculine identification is usually based on identification with a boy's father or other salient adult males. However, a boy's father is relatively more remote than his mother. He rarely plays a major caretaking role even at this period in his son's life. In most societies, his work and social life take place farther from the home than do those of his wife. He is, then, often relatively inaccessible to his son and performs his male role activities away from where the son spends most of his life. As a result, a boy's male gender identification often becomes a "positional" identification, with aspects of his father's clearly or not-so-clearly defined male role, rather than a more generalized "personal" identification— a diffuse identification with his father's personality, values, and behavioral traits—that could grow out of a real relationship to his father.[16]

Mitscherlich (1963), in his discussion of Western advanced capitalist society, provides a useful insight into the problem of male development. The father, because his work takes him outside of the home most of the time, and because his active presence in the family has progressively decreased, has become an "invisible father." For the boy, the tie between affective relations and masculine gender identification and role learning (between libidinal and ego development) is relatively attenuated. He identifies with a fantasied masculine role, because the reality constraint that contact with his father would provide is missing. In all societies characterized by some sex segregation (even those in which a son will eventually lead the same sort of life that his father does), much of a boy's masculine identification must be of this sort, that is, with aspects of his father's role, or what he fantasies to be a male role, rather than with his father as a person involved in a relationship to him.

There is another important aspect to this situation, which explains the psychological dynamics of the universal social and cultural devaluation and subordination of women.[17] A boy, in his attempt to gain an elusive mas-

[15] Cf. Kohlberg 1966.

[16] The important distinction between "positional" and "personal" identification comes from Slater 1961 and Winch 1962.

[17] For more extensive argument concerning this, cf., e.g., Burton and Whiting 1961, Chodorow 1971, and Slater 1968.

culine identification, often comes to define this masculinity largely in negative terms, as that which is not feminine or involved with women. There is an internal and external aspect to this. Internally, the boy tries to reject his mother and deny his attachment to her and the strong dependence upon her that he still feels. He also tries to deny the deep personal identification with her that has developed during his early years. He does this by repressing whatever he takes to be feminine inside himself, and, importantly, by denigrating and devaluing whatever he considers to be feminine in the outside world. As a societal member, he also appropriates to himself and defines as superior particular social activities and cultural (moral, religious, and creative) spheres—possibly, in fact, "society"[18] and "culture"[19] themselves.

Freud's description of the boy's oedipal crisis speaks to the issues of rejection of the feminine and identification with the father. As his early attachment to his mother takes on phallic-sexual overtones, and his father enters the picture as an obvious rival (who, in the son's fantasy, has apparent power to kill or castrate his son), the boy must radically deny and repress his attachment to his mother and replace it with an identification with his loved and admired, but also potentially punitive, therefore feared, father. He internalizes a superego.[20]

To summarize, four components of the attainment of masculine gender identity are important. First, masculinity becomes and remains a problematic issue for a boy. Second, it involves denial of attachment or relationship, particularly of what the boy takes to be dependence or need for another, and differentiation of himself from another. Third, it involves the repression and devaluation of femininity on both psychological and cultural levels. Finally, identification with his father does not usually develop in the context of a satisfactory affective relationship but consists in the attempt to internalize and learn components of a not immediately apprehensible role.

The development of a girl's gender identity contrasts with that of a boy. Most important, femininity and female role activities are immediately apprehensible in the world of her daily life. Her final role identification is with her mother and women, that is, with the person or people with whom she also has her earliest relationship of infantile dependence. The development of her gender identity does not involve a rejection of this early identification, however. Rather, her later identification with her mother is embedded in and influenced by their ongoing relationship of both primary identification and preoedipal attachment. Because her mother is around, and she has had a genuine relationship to her as a person, a girl's gender and gender role identification are mediated by and depend upon real affective relations.

[18] Rosaldo 1974. . . .

[19] Ortner 1974.

[20] The question of the universality of the oedipus complex as Freud describes it is beyond the scope of this paper. . . .

Women are continuos to childhood identificati

Identification with her mother is not positional—the narrow learning of particular role behaviors—but rather a personal identification with her mother's general traits of character and values. Feminine identification is based not on fantasied or externally defined characteristics and negative identification, but on the gradual learning of a way of being familiar in everyday life, and exemplified by the person (or kind of people—women) with whom she has been most involved. It is continuous with her early childhood identifications and attachments.

The major discontinuity in the development of a girl's sense of gender identity, and one that has led Freud and other early psychoanalysts to see female development as exceedingly difficult and tortuous, is that at some point she must transfer her primary sexual object choice from her mother and females to her father and males, if she is to attain her expected heterosexual adulthood. Briefly, Freud considers that all children feel that mothers give some cause for complaint and unhappiness: they give too little milk; they have a second child; they arouse and then forbid their child's sexual gratification in the process of caring for her/him. A girl receives a final blow, however: her discovery that she lacks a penis. She blames this lack on her mother, rejects her mother, and turns to her father in reaction.

Problems in this account have been discussed extensively in the general literature that has grown out of the women's movement, and within the psychoanalytic tradition itself. These concern Freud's misogyny and his obvious assumption that males possess physiological superiority, and that a woman's personality is inevitably determined by her lack of a penis.[21] The psychoanalytic account is not completely unsatisfactory, however. A more detailed consideration of several theorists[22] reveals important features of female development, especially about the mother-daughter relationship, and at the same time contradicts or mitigates the absoluteness of the more general Freudian outline.

[21] These views are most extreme and explicit in two papers (Freud 1925, 1933) and warrant the criticism that has been directed at them. Although the issue of penis-envy in women is not central to this paper, it is central to Freud's theory of female development. Therefore I think it worthwhile to mention three accounts that avoid Freud's ideological mistakes while allowing that his clinical observations of penis-envy might be correct.

Thompson 1943 suggests that penis-envy is a symbolic expression of women's culturally devalued and underprivileged position in our patriarchal society: that possession of a penis symbolizes the possession of power and privilege. Bettelheim 1954 suggests that members of either sex envy the sexual functions of the other, and that women are more likely to express this envy overtly, because, in that men are culturally superior, such envy is considered "natural." Balint 1954 does not rely on the fact of men's cultural superiority but suggests that a little girl develops penis-envy when she realizes that her mother loves people with penises, i.e., her father, and thinks that possession of a penis will help her in her rivalry for her mother's attentions.

[22] See, e.g., Brunswick 1940; Deutsch 1925, 1930, 1932, 1944; Freedman 1961; Freud 1931; Jones 1927.

These psychoanalysts emphasize how, in contrast to males, the female oedipal crisis is not resolved in the same absolute way. A girl cannot and does not completely reject her mother in favor of men but continues her relationship of dependence upon and attachment to her. In addition, the strength and quality of her relationship to her father is completely dependent upon the strength and quality of her relationship to her mother. Deutsch suggests that a girl wavers in a "bisexual triangle" throughout her childhood and into puberty, normally making a very tentative resolution in favor of her father, but in such a way that issues of separation from and attachment to her mother remain important throughout a woman's life:[23]

> It is erroneous to say that the little girl gives up her first mother relation in favor of the father. She only gradually draws him into the alliance, develops from the mother-child exclusiveness toward the triangular parent-child relationship and continues the latter, just as she does the former, although in a weaker and less elemental form, all her life. Only the principal part changes: now the mother, now the father plays it. The ineradicability of affective constellations manifests itself in later repetitions.

We might suggest from this that a girl's internalized and external object-relations become and remain more complex, and at the same time more defining of her, than do those of a boy. Psychoanalytic preoccupation with constitutionally based libidinal development, and with a normative male model of development, has obscured this fact. Most women are genitally heterosexual. At the same time, their lives always involve other sorts of equally deep and primary relationships, especially with their children, and importantly, with other women. In these spheres also, even more than in the area of heterosexual relations, a girl imposes the sort of object-relations she has internalized in her preoedipal and later relationship to her mother.

Men are also for the most part genitally heterosexual. This grows directly out of their early primary attachment to their mother. We know, however, that in many societies their heterosexual relationships are not embedded in close personal relationship but simply in relations of dominance and power. Furthermore, they do not have the extended personal relations women have. They are not so connected to children, and their relationships with other men tend to be based not on particularistic connection or affective ties, but rather on abstract, universalistic role expectations.

Building on the psychoanalytic assumption that unique individual experiences contribute to the formation of individual personality, culture and personality theory has held that early experiences common to members of a particular society contribute to the formation of "typical" personalities organized around and preoccupied with certain issues: "Prevailing patterns of

---

[23] Deutsch 1944:205.

child-rearing must result in similar internalized situations in the unconscious of the majority of individuals in a culture, and these will be externalized back into the culture again to perpetuate it from generation to generation."[24] In a similar vein, I have tried to show that to the extent males and females, respectively, experience similar interpersonal environments as they grow up, masculine and feminine personality develop differently.

I have relied on a theory that suggests that features of adult personality and behavior are determined but that is not biologically determinist. Culturally expected personality and behavior are not simply "taught," however. Rather, certain features of social structure, supported by cultural beliefs, values, and perceptions, are internalized through the family and the child's early social object-relationships. This largely unconscious organization is the context in which role training and purposive socialization take place.

Sex-Role Learning and Its Social Context

Sex-role training and social interaction in childhood build upon and reinforce the largely unconscious development I have described. In most societies (ours is a complicated exception) a girl is usually with her mother and other female relatives in an interpersonal situation that facilitates continuous and early role learning and emphasizes the mother-daughter identification and particularistic, diffuse, affective relationships between women. A boy, to a greater or lesser extent, is also with women for a large part of his childhood, which prevents continuous or easy masculine role identification. His development is characterized by discontinuity.

Ariès, in his discussion of the changing concept of childhood in modern capitalist society,[25] makes a distinction that seems to have more general applicability. Boys, he suggests, became "children" while girls remained "little women."

> The idea of childhood profited the boys first of all, while the girls persisted much longer in the traditional way of life which confused them with the adults: we shall have cause to notice more than once this delay on the part of the women in adopting the visible forms of the essentially masculine civilization of modern times.

This took place first in the middle classes, as a situation developed in which boys needed special schooling in order to prepare for their future work and could not begin to do this kind of work in childhood. Girls (and working-class boys) could still learn work more directly from their parents and could

[24] Guntrip 1961:378.
[25] 1962:61.

begin to participate in the adult economy at an earlier age. Rapid economic change and development have exacerbated the lack of male generational role continuity. Few fathers now have either the opportunity or the ability to pass on a profession or skill to their sons.

Sex-role development of girls in modern society is more complex. On the one hand, they go to school to prepare for life in a technologically and socially complex society. On the other, there is a sense in which this schooling is a pseudo-training. It is not meant to interfere with the much more important training to be "feminine" and a wife and mother, which is embedded in the girl's unconscious development and which her mother teaches her in a family context where she is clearly the salient parent.

This dichotomy is not unique to modern industrial society. Even if special, segregated schooling is not necessary for adult male work (and many male initiation rites remain a form of segregated role training), boys still participate in more activities that characterize them as a category apart from adult life. Their activities grow out of the boy's need to fill time until he can begin to take on an adult male role. Boys may withdraw into isolation and self-involved play or join together in a group that remains more or less unconnected with either the adult world of work and activity or the familial world.

Jay (1969) describes this sort of situation in rural Modjokuto, Java. Girls, after the age of five or so, begin gradually to help their mothers in their work and spend time with their mothers. Boys at this early age begin to form bands of age-mates who roam and play about the city, relating neither to adult men nor to their mothers and sisters. Boys, then, enter a temporary group based on universalistic membership criteria, while girls continue to participate in particularistic role relations in a group characterized by continuity and relative permanence.

The content of boys' and girls' role training tends in the same direction as the context of this training and its results. Barry, Bacon, and Child, in their well-known study (1957), demonstrate that the socialization of boys tends to be oriented toward achievement and self-reliance and that of girls toward nurturance and responsibility. Girls are thus pressured to be involved with and connected to others, boys to deny this involvement and connection.

Adult Gender Personality and Sex Role

A variety of conceptualizations of female and male personality all focus on distinctions around the same issue and provide alternative confirmation of the developmental model I have proposed. Bakan[26] claims that male person-

---

[26] 1966:15.

ality is preoccupied with the "agentic," and female personality with the "communal." His expanded definition of the two concepts is illuminating:

> I have adopted the terms "agency" and "communion" to characterize two fundamental modalities in the existence of living forms, agency for the existence of an organism as an individual and communion for the participation of the individual in some larger organism of which the individual is a part. Agency manifests itself in self-protection, self-assertion, and self-expansion; communion manifests itself in the sense of being at one with other organisms. Agency manifests itself in the formation of separations; communion in the lack of separations. Agency manifests itself in isolation, alienation, and aloneness; communion in contact, openness, and union. Agency manifests itself in the urge to master; communion in noncontractual cooperation. Agency manifests itself in the repression of thought, feeling, and impulse; communion in the lack and removal of repression.

Gutmann (1965) contrasts the socialization of male personalities in "allocentric" milieux (milieux in which the individual is part of a larger social organization and system of social bonds) with that of female personalities in "autocentric" milieux (in which the individual herself/ himself is a focus of events and ties).[27] Gutmann suggests that this leads to a number of systematic differences in ego functioning. Female ego qualities, growing out of participation in autocentric milieux, include more flexible ego boundaries (i.e., less insistent self-other distinctions), present orientation rather than future orientation, and relatively greater subjectivity and less detached objectivity.

Carlson confirms both characterizations. Her tests of Gutmann's claims lead her to conclude that "males represent experiences of self, others, space, and time in individualistic, objective, and distant ways, while females represent experiences in relatively interpersonal, subjective, immediate ways."[28] With reference to Bakan, she claims that men's descriptions of affective experience tend to be in agentic terms and women's in terms of communion, and that an examination of abstracts of a large number of social-psychological articles on sex differences yields an overwhelming confirmation of the agency/communion hypothesis.

Cohen (1969) contrasts the development of "analytic" and "relational" cognitive style, the former characterized by a stimulus-centered, parts-specific orientation to reality, the latter centered on the self and responding to the global characteristics of a stimulus in reference to its total context.

[27] Following Cohen 1969, I would suggest that the external structural features of these settings (in the family or in school, for instance) are often similar or the same for boys and girls. The different kind and amount of adult male and female participation in these settings accounts for their being experienced by children of different sexes as different sorts of milieux.

[28] 1971:270.

Although focusing primarily on class differences in cognitive style, she also points out that girls are more likely to mix the two types of functioning (and also to exhibit internal conflict about this). Especially, they are likely to exhibit at the same time both high field dependence and highly developed analytic skills in other areas. She suggests that boys and girls participate in different sorts of interactional subgroups in their families: boys experience their family more as a formally organized primary group; girls experience theirs as a group characterized by shared and less clearly delineated functions. She concludes,

> Since embedded responses covered the gamut from abstract categories, through language behaviors, to expressions of embeddedness in their social environments, it is possible that embeddedness may be a distinctive characteristic of female sex-role learning in this society regardless of social class, native ability, ethnic differences, and the cognitive impact of the school.[29]

Preliminary consideration suggests a correspondence between the production of feminine personalities organized around "communal" and "autocentric" issues and characterized by flexible ego boundaries, less detached objectivity, and relational cognitive style, on the one hand, and important aspects of feminine as opposed to masculine social roles, on the other.

Most generally, I would suggest that a quality of embeddedness in social interaction and personal relationships characterizes women's life relative to men's. From childhood, daughters are likely to participate in an intergenerational world with their mother, and often with their aunts and grandmother, whereas boys are on their own or participate in a single-generation world of age mates. In adult life, women's interaction with other women in most societies is kin-based and cuts across generational lines. Their roles tend to be particularistic and to involve diffuse relationships and responsibilities rather than specific ones. Women in most societies are *defined* relationally (as someone's wife, mother, daughter, daughter-in-law; even a nun becomes the Bride of Christ). Men's association (although it too may be kin-based and intergenerational) is much more likely than women's to cut across kinship units, to be restricted to a single generation, and to be recruited according to universalistic criteria and involve relationships and responsibilities defined by their specificity.

Ego Boundaries and the Mother-Daughter Relationship

The care and socialization of girls by women ensures the production of feminine personalities founded on relation and connection, with flexible

[29] 1969:836.

rather than rigid ego boundaries, and with a comparatively secure sense of gender identity. This is one explanation for how women's relative embeddedness is reproduced from generation to generation, and why it exists within almost every society. More specific investigation of different social contexts suggests, however, that there are variations in the kind of relationship that can exist between women's role performance and feminine personality.

Various kinds of evidence suggest that separation from the mother, the breaking of dependence, and the establishment and maintenance of a consistently individuated sense of self remain difficult psychological issues for Western middle-class women (i.e., the women who become subjects of psychoanalytic and clinical reports and social-psychological studies). Deutsch (1944, 1945) in particular provides extensive clinical documentation of these difficulties and of the way they affect women's relationships to men and children and, because of their nature, are reproduced in the next generation of women. Mothers and daughters in the women's group mentioned above describe their experiences of boundary confusion or equation of self and other, for example, guilt and self-blame for the other's unhappiness; shame and embarrassment at the other's actions; daughters' "discovery" that they are "really" living out their mothers' lives in their choice of career; mothers' not completely conscious reactions to their daughters' bodies as their own (overidentification and therefore often unnecessary concern with supposed weight or skin problems, which the mother is really worried about in herself); and so on.

A kind of guilt that Western women express seems to grow out of and to reflect lack of adequate self/other distinctions and a sense of inescapable embeddedness in relationships to others. Tax describes this well (italics mine):

> Since our awareness of others is considered our duty, the price we pay when things go wrong is guilt and self-hatred. And things always go wrong. We respond with apologies; we continue to apologize long after the event is forgotten—and *even if it had no causal relation to anything we did to begin with*. If the rain spoils someone's picnic, we apologize. We apologize for taking up space in a room, for living.[30]

As if the woman does not differentiate herself clearly from the rest of the world, she feels a sense of guilt and responsibility for situations that did not come about through her actions and without relation to her actual ability to determine the course of events. This happens, in the most familiar instance, in a sense of diffuse responsibility for everything connected to the welfare of her family and the happiness and success of her children. This loss of self in

---

[30] 1970:2.

overwhelming responsibility for and connection to others is described particularly acutely by women writers (in the work, for instance, of Simone de Beauvoir, Kate Chopin, Doris Lessing, Tillie Olsen, Christina Stead, Virginia Woolf).

Slater (1961) points to several studies supporting the contention that Western daughters have particular problems about differentiation from their mother. These studies show that though most forms of personal parental identification correlate with psychological adjustment (i.e., freedom from neurosis or psychosis, *not* social acceptability), personal identification of a daughter with her mother does not. The reason is that the mother-daughter relation is the one form of personal identification that, because it results so easily from the normal situation of child development, is liable to be excessive in the direction of allowing no room for separation or difference between mother and daughter.

The situation reinforces itself in circular fashion. A mother, on the one hand, grows up without establishing adequate ego boundaries or a firm sense of self. She tends to experience boundary confusion with her daughter and does not provide experiences of differentiating ego development for her daughter or encourage the breaking of her daughter's dependence. The daughter, for her part, makes a rather unsatisfactory and artificial attempt to establish boundaries: she projects what she defines as bad within her onto her mother and tries to take what is good into herself. (This, I think, is the best way to understand the girl's oedipal "rejection" of her mother.) Such an arbitrary mechanism cannot break the underlying psychological unity, however. Projection is never more than a temporary solution to ambivalence or boundary confusion.

The implication is that, contrary to Gutmann's suggestion (see note 4), "so-called ego pathology" may not be "adaptive" for women. Women's biosexual experiences (menstruation, coitus, pregnancy, childbirth, lactation) all involve some challenge to the boundaries of her body ego ("me"/"not-me" in relation to her blood or milk, to a man who penetrates her, to a child once part of her body). These are important and fundamental human experiences that are probably intrinsically meaningful and at the same time complicated for women everywhere. However, a Western woman's tenuous sense of individuation and of the firmness of her ego boundaries increases the likelihood that experiences challenging these boundaries will be difficult for her and conflictive.

Nor is it clear that this personality structure is "functional" for society as a whole. The evidence presented in this paper suggests that satisfactory mothering, which does not reproduce particular psychological problems in boys and girls, comes from a person with a firm sense of self and of her own value, whose care is a freely chosen activity rather than a reflection of a conscious and unconscious sense of inescapable connection to and responsibility for her children.

Social Structure and the Mother-Daughter Relationship

Clinical and self-analytic descriptions of women and of the psychological component of mother-daughter relationships are not available from societies and subcultures outside of the Western middle class. However, accounts that are primarily sociological about women in other societies enable us to infer certain aspects of their psychological situation. In what follows, I am not claiming to make any kind of general statement about what constitutes a "healthy society," but only to examine and isolate specific features of social life that seem to contribute to the psychological strength of some members of a society. Consideration of three groups with matrifocal tendencies in their family structure (see Tanner 1974) highlights several dimensions of importance in the developmental situation of the girl.

Young and Willmott (1957) describe the daily visiting and mutual aid of working-class mothers and daughters in East London. In a situation where household structure is usually nuclear, like the Western middle class, grown daughters look to their mothers for advice, for aid in childbirth and child care, for friendship and companionship, and for financial help. Their mother's house is the ultimate center of the family world. Husbands are in many ways peripheral to family relationships, possibly because of their failure to provide sufficiently for their families as men are expected to do. This becomes apparent if they demand their wife's disloyalty toward or separation from her mother: "The great triangle of childhood is mother-father-child; in Bethnal Green the great triangle of adult life is Mum-wife-husband."[31]

Geertz (1961) and Jay (1969) describe Javanese nuclear families in which women are often the more powerful spouse and have primary influence upon how kin relations are expressed and to whom (although these families are formally centered upon a highly valued conjugal relationship based on equality of spouses). Financial and decision-making control in the family often rests largely in the hands of its women. Women are potentially independent of men in a way that men are not independent of women. Geertz points to a woman's ability to participate in most occupations and to own farmland and supervise its cultivation, which contrasts with a man's inability, even if he is financially independent, to do his own household work and cooking.

[31] 1957:64.

Women's kin role in Java is important. Their parental role and rights are greater than those of men; children always belong to the woman in case of divorce. When extra members join a nuclear family to constitute an extended family household, they are much more likely to be the wife's relatives than those of the husband. Formal and distant relations between men in a family, and between a man and his children (especially his son), contrast with the informal and close relations between women, and between a woman and her children. Jay and Geertz both emphasize the continuing closeness of the mother-daughter relationship as a daughter is growing up and throughout her married life. Jay suggests that there is a certain amount of ambivalence in the mother-daughter relationship, particularly as a girl grows toward adulthood and before she is married, but points out that at the same time the mother remains a girl's "primary figure of confidence and emotional support."[32]

Siegel (1969) describes Atjehnese families in Indonesia in which women stay on the homestead of their parents after marriage and are in total control of the household. Women tolerate men in the household only as long as they provide money and even then treat them as someone between a child and a guest. Women's stated preference would be to eliminate even this necessary dependence on men:

> Women, for instance, envision paradise as the place where they are reunited with their children and their mothers; husbands and fathers are absent, and yet there is an abundance all the same. Quarrels over money reflect the women's idea that men are basically adjuncts who exist only to give their families whatever they can earn.[33]

A woman in this society does not get into conflicts in which she has to choose between her mother and her husband, as happens in the Western working class (see above; also Komarovsky 1962), where the reigning ideology supports the nuclear family.

In these three settings, the mother-daughter tie and other female kin relations remain important from a woman's childhood through her old age. Daughters stay closer to home in both childhood and adulthood and remain involved in particularistic role relations. Sons and men are more likely to feel uncomfortable at home and to spend work and play time away from the house. Male activities and spheres emphasize universalistic, distancing qualities: men in Java are the bearers and transmitters of high culture and formal relationships; men in East London spend much of their time in alienated work settings; Atjehnese boys spend their time in school, and their fathers trade in distant places.

[32] 1969:103.
[33] 1969:177.

Mother-daughter ties in these three societies, described as extremely close, seem to be composed of companionship and mutual cooperation and to be positively valued by both mother and daughter. The ethnographies do not imply that women are weighed down by the burden of their relationships or by overwhelming guilt and responsibility. On the contrary, they seem to have developed a strong sense of self and self-worth, which continues to grow as they get older and take on their maternal role. The implication is that "ego strength" is not completely dependent on the firmness of the ego's boundaries.

Guntrip's distinction between "immature" and "mature" dependence clarifies the difference between mother-daughter relationships and women's psyche in the Western middle class and in the matrifocal societies described. Women in the Western middle class are caught up to some extent in issues of infantile dependence, while the women in matrifocal societies remain in definite connection with others, but in relationships characterized by mature dependence. As Guntrip describes it,

> *Mature dependence* is characterized by full differentiation of ego and object (emergence from primary identification) and therewith a capacity for valuing the object for its own sake and for giving as well as receiving; a condition which should be described not as independence but as mature dependence.[34]

This kind of mature dependence is also to be distinguished from the kind of forced independence and denial of need for relationship that I have suggested characterizes masculine personality and that reflects continuing conflict about infantile dependence:

> Maturity is not equated with independence though it includes a certain capacity for independence. . . . The independence of the mature person is simply that he does not collapse when he has to stand alone. It is not an independence of needs for other persons with whom to have relationship: *that would not be desired by the mature.*[35]

Depending on its social setting, women's sense of relation and connection and their embeddedness in social life provide them with a kind of security that men lack. The quality of a mother's relationship to her children and maternal self-esteem, on the one hand, and the nature of a daughter's developing identification with her mother, on the other, make crucial differences in female development.

Women's kin role, and in particular the mother role, is central and positively valued in Atjeh, Java, and East London. Women gain status and

[34] 1961:291.
[35] Ibid.:293; my italics.

prestige as they get older; their major role is not fulfilled in early motherhood. At the same time, women may be important contributors to the family's economic support, as in Java and East London, and in all three societies they have control over real economic resources. All these factors give women a sense of self-esteem independent of their relationship to their children. Finally, strong relationships exist between women in these societies, expressed in mutual cooperation and frequent contact. A mother, then, when her children are young, is likely to spend much of her time in the company of other women, not simply isolated with her children.

These social facts have important positive effects on female psychological development. (It must be emphasized that all the ethnographies indicate that these same social facts make male development difficult and contribute to psychological insecurity and lack of ease in interpersonal relationships in men.) A mother is not invested in keeping her daughter from individuating and becoming less dependent. She has other ongoing contacts and relationships that help fulfill her psychological and social needs. In addition, the people surrounding a mother while a child is growing up become mediators between mother and daughter, by providing a daughter with alternative models for personal identification and objects of attachment, which contribute to her differentiation from her mother. Finally, a daughter's identification with her mother in this kind of setting is with a strong woman with clear control over important spheres of life, whose sense of self-esteem can reflect this. Acceptance of her gender identity involves positive valuation of herself, and not an admission of inferiority. In psychoanalytic terms, we might say it involves identification with a preoedipal, active, caring mother. Bibring points to clinical findings supporting this interpretation: "We find in the analysis of the women who grew up in this 'matriarchal' setting the rejection of the feminine role less frequently than among female patients coming from the patriarchal family culture"[36]

There is another important aspect of the situation in these societies. The continuing structural and practical importance of the mother-daughter tie not only ensures that a daughter develops a positive personal and role identification with her mother but also requires that the close psychological tie between mother and daughter become firmly grounded in real role expectations. These provide a certain constraint and limitation upon the relationship, as well as an avenue for its expression through common spheres of interest based in the external social world.

All these societal features contrast with the situation of the Western middle-class woman. Kinship relations in the middle class are less important. Kin are not likely to live near each other, and, insofar as husbands are able to provide adequate financial support for their families, there is no need

[36] 1953:281.

for a network of mutual aid among related wives. As the middle-class woman gets older and becomes a grandmother, she cannot look forward to increased status and prestige in her new role.

The Western middle-class housewife does not have an important economic role in her family. The work she does and the responsibilities that go with it (household management, cooking, entertaining, etc.) do not seem to be really necessary to the economic support of her family (they are crucial contributions to the maintenance and reproduction of her family's class position, but this is not generally recognized as important either by the woman herself or by the society's ideology). If she works outside the home, neither she nor the rest of society is apt to consider this work to be important to her self-definition in the way that her housewife role is.

Child care, on the other hand, is considered to be her crucially important responsibility. Our post-Freudian society in fact assigns to parents (and especially to the mother[37]) nearly total responsibility for how children turn out. A middle-class mother's daily life is not centrally involved in relations with other women. She is isolated with her children for most of her workday. It is not surprising, then, that she is likely to invest a lot of anxious energy and guilt in her concern for her children and to look to them for her own self-affirmation, or that her self-esteem, dependent on the lives of others than herself, is shaky. Her life situation leads her to an overinvolvement in her children's lives.

A mother in this situation keeps her daughter from differentiation and from lessening her infantile dependence. (She also perpetuates her son's dependence, but in this case society and his father are more likely to interfere in order to assure that, behaviorally, at least, he doesn't *act* dependent.) And there are not other people around to mediate in the mother-daughter relationship. Insofar as the father is actively involved in a relationship with his daughter and his daughter develops some identification with him, this helps her individuation, but the formation of ego autonomy through identification with and idealization of her father may be at the expense of her positive sense of feminine self. Unlike the situation in matrifocal families, the continuing closeness of the mother-daughter relationship is expressed only on a psychological, interpersonal level. External role expectations do not ground or limit it.

It is difficult, then, for daughters in a Western middle-class family to develop self-esteem. Most psychoanalytic and social theorists[38] claim that the mother inevitably represents to her daughter (and son) regression, passivity, dependence, and lack of orientation to reality, whereas the father

[37] See Slater 1970 for an extended discussion of the implications of this. . . .

[38] See, e.g., Deutsch 1944, passim; Erikson 1964:162; Klein and Rivière 1937:18; Parsons 1960, passim; Parsons and Bales 1955, passim. . . .

represents progression, activity, independence, and reality orientation.[39] Given the value implications of this dichotomy, there are advantages for the son in giving up his mother and identifying with his father. For the daughter, feminine gender identification means identification with a devalued, passive mother, and personal maternal identification is with a mother whose own self-esteem is low. Conscious rejection of her oedipal maternal identification, however, remains an unconscious rejection and devaluation of herself, because of her continuing preoedipal identification and boundary confusion with her mother.

Cultural devaluation is not the central issue, however. Even in patrilineal, patrilocal societies in which women's status is very low, women do not necessarily translate this cultural devaluation into low self-esteem, nor do girls have to develop difficult boundary problems with their mother. In the Moslem Moroccan family, for example,[40] a large amount of sex segregation and sex antagonism gives women a separate (domestic) sphere in which they have a real productive role and control, and also a life situation in which any young mother is in the company of other women. Women do not need to invest all their psychic energy in their children, and their self-esteem is not dependent on their relationship to their children. In this and other patrilineal, patrilocal societies, what resentment women do have at their oppressive situation is more often expressed toward their sons, whereas daughters are seen as allies against oppression. Conversely, a daughter develops relationships of attachment to and identification with other adult women. Loosening her tie to her mother therefore does not entail the rejection of all women. The close tie that remains between mother and daughter is based not simply on mutual overinvolvement but often on mutual understanding of their oppression.

Conclusion

Women's universal mothering role has effects both on the development of masculine and feminine personality and on the relative status of the sexes. This paper has described the development of relational personality in women and of personalities preoccupied with the denial of relation in men. In its comparison of different societies, it has suggested that men, while

---

[39] Their argument derives from the universal fact that a child must outgrow her/ his primary identification with and total dependence upon the mother. The present paper argues that the value implications of this dichotomy grow out of the particular circumstances of our society and its devaluation of relational qualities. Allied to this is the suggestion that it does not need to be, and often is not, relationship to the father that breaks the early maternal relationship.

[40] Personal communication from Fatima Memissi, based on her experience growing up in Morocco and her recent sociological fieldwork there.

guaranteeing to themselves sociocultural superiority over women, always remain psychologically defensive and insecure. Women, by contrast, although always of secondary social and cultural status, may in favorable circumstances gain psychological security and a firm sense of worth and importance in spite of this.

Social and psychological oppression, then, is perpetuated in the structure of personality. The paper enables us to suggest what social arrangements contribute (and could contribute) to social equality between men and women and their relative freedom from certain sorts of psychological conflict. Daughters and sons must be able to develop a personal identification with more than one adult, and preferably one embedded in a role relationship that gives it a social context of expression and provides some limitation upon it. Most important, boys need to grow up around men who take a major role in child care, and girls around women who, in addition to their child-care responsibilities, have a valued role and recognized spheres of legitimate control. These arrangements could help to ensure that children of both sexes develop a sufficiently individuated and strong sense of self, as well as a positively valued and secure gender identity, that does not bog down either in ego-boundary confusion, low self-esteem, and overwhelming relatedness to others, or in compulsive denial of any connection to others or dependence upon them.

BIBLIOGRAPHY

NOTE: An asterisk before an entry indicates that the work is reprinted in this volume. All abbreviations are listed under the name of the author (e.g., for Page *GLP*, see Page), with the following exception:
IG2² = *Inscriptiones Graecae*. Vol. ii and iii. 1916–35. Ed. J. Kirchner.

Alderink, L. J. 1982. "Mythological and Cosmological Structure in the Homeric *Hymn to Demeter.*" *Numen* 29:1–16.
Aleshire, J. 1987. "Persephone." *Quarterly Review of Literature. Poetry Series VIII.* 27:33.
Alexiou, M. 1974. *The Ritual Lament in Greek Tradition.* Cambridge.
Alexiou, M., and P. Dronke. 1971. "The Lament of Jephta's Daughter: Themes, Tradition, Originality." *Studi Medievali* 12.2:819–63.
Allen, D. and G. Butterick, eds. 1982. *The Postmodern: The New American Poetry Revised.* New York.
Allen, T. W., ed. 1912. *Homeri Opera*, vol. 5. Oxford.
Allen, T. W, W. R. Halliday, and E. E. Sikes, eds. 1936. *The Homeric Hymns.* Oxford.
Allen, T. W., and E. E. Sikes, eds. 1904. *The Homeric Hymns.* London.
Arend. W. 1933. *Die typischen Scenen bei Homer.* Problemata, Heft 7. Berlin.
Ariès, P. 1962. *Centuries of Childhood: A Social History of Family Life.* New York.
Arthur, M. 1973. "Early Greece: The Origins of the Western Attitude Towards Women." *Arethusa* 6:7–58.
*———. 1977. "Politics and Pomegranates: An Interpretation of the Homeric *Hymn to Demeter.*" *Arethusa* 10:7–47.
———. 1982. "Cultural Strategies in Hesiod's *Theogony*: Law, Family and Society." *Arethusa* 15:63–82.
Athanassakis, A. N. 1976. *The Homeric Hymns.* Baltimore and London.
———. 1977. *The Orphic Hymns.* Missoula, Montana.
Atwood, M. E. 1961. *Double Persephone.* Toronto.
Bachofen, J. J. 1861. *Das Mutterrect.* Stuttgart.
———. 1967. *Myth, Religion and Mother Right.* Tr. R. Manheim. Princeton.
Bakan, D. 1966. *The Duality of Human Existence: Isolation and Communion in Western Man.* Chicago.
Balint, A. 1954. *The Early Years of Life: A Psychoanalytic Study.* New York.
Bamberger, J. 1974. "The Myth of Matriarchy: Why Men Rule in Primitive Society." In *Women, Culture, and Society.* Ed. M. Z. Rosaldo and L. Lamphere. 263–80. Stanford, California.
Barry, H., M. K. Bacon, and I. L. Child. 1957. "A Cross-Cultural Survey of Some Sex Differences in Socialization." *Journal of Abnormal and Social Psychology* 55:327–32.
Bartlett, P. B. 1978. *The Poems of George Meredith* I. New Haven and London.
Benedek, T. 1959. "Parenthood as a Developmental Phase," *Journal of the American Psychoanalytic Association* 7:389–417.

Benét, W. R. 1933. *Starry Harness*. New York.

Berg, W. 1974. "Eleusinian and Harvest Myths." *Fabula* 25:202–11.

Bernikow, L., ed. 1974. *The World Split Open: Four Centuries of Women Poets in England and America, 1552–1950*. New York.

Berry, P. 1975. "The Rape of Demeter/Persephone and Neurosis." *Spring* 1975:186–98.

Bettelheim, B. 1954. *Symbolic Wounds: Puberty Rites and the Envious Male*. New York.

Betz, H. D. 1991. "Magic and Mystery in the Greek Magical Papyri." In *Magika Hiera. Ancient Greek Magic and Religion*. Ed. C. A. Faraone and D. Obbink. 244–59. New York and Oxford.

Bianchi, U. 1964. "Sagezza olimpica e mistica eleusina nell' inno omerico Demetra." *Studi e Materiali di Storia delle Religione* 35:161–93.

Bibring, G. 1953. "On the 'Passing of the Oedipus Complex' in a Matriarchal Family Setting." In *Drives, Affects and Behavior: Essays in Honor of Marie Bonaparte*. Ed. R. M. Lowenstein. 278–84. New York.

Bishop, J. P. 1948. *The Collected Poems of John Peale Bishop*. New York.

Boardman, J. 1975. "Herakles, Peisistratos and Eleusis." *Journal of Hellenic Studies* 95:1–12.

Bode, G. H. 1834. *Scriptores rerum mythicarum Latini* I–II. Celle (Germany).

Boer, C. 1970. *The Homeric Hymns*. Chicago.

Böhme, R. 1983. *Peisistratos und sein Homerischer Dichter*. Bern and Munich.

Bolen, J. S. 1984. *The Goddess in Every Woman: A New Psychology of Women*. San Francisco.

Bonner, C. 1939. "Hades and the Pomegranate Seed (*Hymn to Demeter* 372–74)." *Classical Review* 53:3–4.

Bottrall, R. 1949. *The Palisades of Fear*. London.

———. 1961. *The Collected Poems of Ronald Bottrall*. London.

Bourdieu, P. 1977. *Outline of a Theory of Practice*. Cambridge.

Boyancé, P. "Sur les mystères d'Eleusis." *Revue des Etudes Grecques* 75(1962):460–82.

Brelich, A. 1969. *Paides e Parthenoi* I. Incunabula Graeca 36. Rome.

———. 1972. *Problemi di Mitologia I: Un corso universitario*. In "Religione e civiltà," I (1972) = *Studi e materiali di storia delle religione* 41 (1970–72), n.s. I (1972):331–525.

Bremer, J. M. 1981. "Greek Hymns." In *Faith, Hope and Worship*. Ed. H. S. Versnel. 193–215. Leiden.

Bremmer, J. N. 1983. "The Importance of the Maternal Uncle and Grandfather." *Zeitschrift für Papyrologie und Epigraphik* 50:173–86.

Bridges, R. 1912. *The Poetical Works of Robert Bridges Excluding the Eight Dramas*. Oxford.

Broumas, O. 1977. *Beginning With O*. New Haven.

Brumfield, A. C. 1981. *The Attic Festivals of Demeter and Their Relation to the Agricultural Year*. New York.

Brunswick, R. M. 1940. "The Preoedipal Phase of the Libido Development." In R. Fliess, ed. 231–53.

Burkert, W. 1977. Review of Richardson 1974. *Gnomon* 99:440–46.

———. 1979. *Structure and History in Greek Mythology and Ritual*. Berkeley.

———. 1983. *Homo Necans*. Trans. P. Bing. Cambridge, Mass. (Originally published in Berlin 1972).

———. 1985. *Greek Religion*. Trans. J. Raffan. Cambridge, Mass. (Originally published in Berlin 1977).

———. 1987. *Ancient Mystery Cults*. Cambridge, Mass.

Burton, R. V., and J.W.M. Whiting. 1961. "The Absent Father and Cross-Sex Identity." *Merrill-Palmer Quarterly of Behavior and Development* 7.2:85–95.

Bush, D. 1968. *Pagan Myth and Christian Tradition in English Poetry*. Philadelphia.

———. 1969 (1937) *Mythology and the Romantic Tradition in English Poetry*. New York.

Bynum, C. W. 1986. *Holy Feast and Holy Fast: The Religious Significance of Food to Medieval Women*. Berkeley.

———. 1991. " '. . . And Woman His Humanity': Female Imagery in the Religious Writing of the Later Middle Ages." In C. Bynum, *Fragmentation and Redemption*. 151–79. New York.

Calame, C. 1977. *Les Choeurs de jeunes filles en Grèce archaïque*. 2 Vols. Rome.

———. 1990. *Thésée et l'imaginaire athénien*. Lausanne.

Campbell, D. A. 1982. *Greek Lyric I*. Cambridge, Mass.

Caraveli, A. 1986. "The Bitter Wounding: The Lament as Social Protest in Rural Greece." In *Gender and Power in Rural Greece*. Ed. J. Dubisch. Princeton. 169–94.

Caraveli-Chavez, A. 1980. "Bridge Between Worlds: The Women's Ritual Lament as Communicative Event." *Journal of American Folklore* 93:129–57.

Carlson, R. 1971. "Sex Differences in Ego Functioning: Exploratory Studies of Agency and Communion." *Journal of Consulting and Clinical Psychology* 37:267–77.

Cassolà, F., ed. 1975. *Inni omerici*. Milan.

Chesler, P. 1972. *Women and Madness*. New York.

Chirassi, I. 1968. *Elementi di culture precereali nei miti e riti greci*. Rome.

Chirassi-Columbo, I. 1975. "I doni di Demeter: Mito e ideologia nella Grecia arcaia." In *Studi Triestini di antichità in onore di L. Stella*. Trieste. 183–213.

Chodorow, N. 1971. "Being and Doing. A Cross-Cultural Examination of the Socialization of Males and Females." In *Woman in Sexist Society: Studies in Power and Powerlessness*. Ed. V. Gornick and B. K. Moran. New York.

*———. 1974. "Family Structure and Feminine Personality." In *Woman, Culture and Society*. Ed. M. Z. Rosaldo and L. Lamphere. 43–66. Stanford, California.

———. 1978. *The Reproduction of Mothering: Psychoanalysis and the Sociology of Gender*. Berkeley and Los Angeles.

Chodorow, N., and S. Contratto. 1982. "The Fantasy of the Perfect Mother." In *Rethinking the Family*. Ed. B. Thorne and M. Yalom. New York.

Christ, C. 1987. *The Laughter of Aphrodite: Reflections on a Journey to the Goddess*. San Francisco.

Clarke, A. K. 1925. Persephone. In *Three One-Act Plays*. The British Drama League Library of Modern British Drama No. 12. Stratford-upon-Avon.

Clay, J. S. 1984. "The Hecate of the *Theogony*." *Greek, Roman and Byzantine Studies* 25.1:27–38.

———. 1989. *The Politics of Olympus*. Princeton.

Clinton, K. 1974. *The Sacred Officials of the Eleusinian Mysteries.* Philadelphia.

———. 1986. "The Author of the Homeric *Hymn to Demeter.*" *Opuscula Atheniensia* 16:43–49.

Codrescu, A., ed. 1989. *American Poetry Since 1970: Up Late.* 2d ed. New York.

Cohen, R. A. 1969. "Conceptual Styles, Culture Conflict, and Nonverbal Tests of Intelligence," *American Anthropologist* 71:828–56.

Connor, W. R. 1990. "City Dionysia and Athenian Democracy." In *Aspects of Athenian Democracy.* Classica et Mediaevalia Dissertationes XI. 7–32. Copenhagen.

Cornford, F. M. 1913. *Essays and Studies Presented to William Ridgeway.* Cambridge.

Crane, G. 1988. *Calypso: Backgrounds and Conventions in the Odyssey.* Frankfurt am Main.

Creeley, R. 1982. *The Collected Poems of Robert Creeley 1945–1975.* Berkeley and Los Angeles.

Dalley, S. 1989. *Myths from Mesopotamia.* Oxford.

Daly, M. 1978. "Prelude to the First Passage." *Feminist Studies* 4.3:81–86.

Dame, E. 1992. *Anything You Don't See.* Albuquerque, New Mexico.

Danforth, L. M. 1982. *The Death Rituals of Rural Greece.* Princeton.

Darcque, P. 1981. "Les Vestiges mycéniens découverts sous le Télestérion d'Eleusis." *Bulletin de Correspondance Hellénique* 105:593–605.

Davenport, G. 1981. *The Geography of the Imagination. Forty Essays by Guy Davenport.* New York and San Francisco.

Davis, E. G. 1971. *The First Sex.* Harmondsworth, U.K.

Deichgräber, K. 1950. "Eleusinische Frömmigkeit und homerische Vorstellungswelt im homerischen Demeterhymnus." *Akademie der Wissenschaften und der Literatur in Mainz, Geistes- und Sozialwissenschaftlichen Klasse* 6:503–37.

Delatte, A. 1955. *Le Cycéon: Breuvage rituel des mystères d'Eleusis.* Paris.

Delcourt, M. 1961 (1956). *Hermaphrodite.* London.

De Polignac, F. 1984. *La Naissance de la cité grecque.* Paris.

Detienne, M. 1968. "La Phalange: Problèmes et controverses." In *Problèmes de la guerre en Grèce ancienne.* Ed. J.-P. Vernant. 119–42. Paris.

———. 1989. "The Violence of Well-Born Ladies: Women in the Thesmophoria." In *The Cuisine of Sacrifice Among the Greeks.* Ed. M. Detienne and J.-P. Vernant. 129–47. Chicago. (Originally published Paris 1979).

Deutsch, H. 1925. "The Psychology of Woman in Relation to the Functions of Reproduction." In R. Fliess, ed. 165–79.

———. 1930. "The Significance of Masochism in the Mental Life of Women." In R. Fliess, ed. 195–207.

———. 1932. "On Female Homosexuality" In R. Fliess, ed. 208–30.

———. 1944, 1945. *Psychology of Women,* vols. 1, 2. New York.

Donovan, J. 1989. *After the Fall. The Demeter-Persephone Myth in Wharton, Cather, and Glasgow.* University Park and London.

H.D. (Hilda Doolittle). 1925. *Collected Poems of H.D.* New York.

———. 1983. *The Collected Poems of H.D. 1912–1944.* Ed. L. Martz. New York.

Dove, R. 1992. "Persephone Abducted." *Ms.* 3.1 July/August:22.

Dowden, K. 1989. *Death and the Maiden: Girls' Initiation Rites in Greek Mythology.* London and New York.

Drinkwater, J. 1926. *Persephone.* New York.

Duncan, R. 1966. *The Years as Catches. First Poems (1939–1946) by Robert Duncan.* Berkeley.

Eitrem, S. 1940. "Eleusinia—les mystères et l'agriculture." *Symbolae Osloenses* 20:33–41.

———. 1961. "Die Eleusinischen Mysterien und das Synthema der Weihe." *Symbolae Osloenses* 37:72–81.

Engels, F. 1972 (1884). *The Origin of the Family, Private Property and the State.* Trans. A. West. Ed. E. Leacock. New York.

Erdmann, W. 1934. *Die Ehe im alten Griechenland.* Munich.

Erikson, E. H. 1964. *Insight and Responsibility.* New York.

Evelyn-White, H. G., ed. 1964 (1914). *Hesiod, The Homeric Hymns and Homerica.* Cambridge, Mass.

Fairbairn, W.R.D. 1952. *An Object-Relations Theory of the Personality.* New York.

Faraone, C. A. 1990. "Aphrodite's ΚΕΣΤΟΣ and Apples for Atalanta: Aphrodisiacs in Early Greek Myth and Ritual." *Phoenix* 44:219–243.

Farnell, L. R. 1896–1909. *The Cults of the Greek City States.* 5 vols. Oxford.

Feder, L. 1971. *Ancient Myth in Modern Poetry.* Princeton.

Felman, S. 1978. "To Open the Question." *Yale French Studies* 55/56:5–10.

Ferguson, J. 1989. *Among the Gods: An Archaeological Exploration of Ancient Greek Religion.* New York.

Fliegel, Z. 1973. "Feminine Psychosexual Development in Freudian Theory." *Psychoanalytic Quarterly* 42:385–408.

Fliess, R. 1948. "Female and Preoedipal Sexuality: A Historical Survey." In R. Fliess, ed. 159–64.

———. 1961 (1971) *Ego and Body Ego: Contributions to Their Psychoanalytic Psychology.* New York.

Fliess, R. ed. 1969 (1948). *The Psychoanalytic Reader: An Anthology of Essential Papers with Critical Introductions.* New York.

Foley, H. P. 1982. "The 'Female Intruder' Reconsidered: Women in Aristophanes' *Lysistrata* and *Ecclesiazusae*." *Classical Philology* 77:1–21.

———. 1985. *Ritual Irony: Poetry and Sacrifice in Euripides.* New York.

———. 1992. "Anodos Dramas: Euripides' *Alcestis* and *Helen*." In *Innovations of Antiquity.* Ed. R. Hexter and D. Selden. 133–160. New York.

Förster, R. 1874. *Der Raub und Rückkehr der Persephone.* Stuttgart.

Foti, G., and G. Pugliese Carratelli. 1974. "Un Sepulcro di Hipponion e un Nuovo Testo Orfico." *La Parola del passato* 29, fasc. 154–55:91–126.

Foucart, P. 1914. *Les Mystères d'Eleusis.* Paris.

Frazer, J. G. 1967 (1921). "Putting Children on the Fire." In *Apollodorus, The Library* 2:311–17. Cambridge, Mass.

Freedman, D. 1961. "On Women Who Hate Their Husbands." In H. M. Ruitenbeek, ed. 221-87.

Freud, S. 1916. "A Mythological Parallel to a Visual Obsession." In *The Standard Edition of the Complete Psychological Works of Sigmund Freud.* Vol. 14. Ed. J. Strachey. 337–38. London.

———. 1925. "Some Psychological Consequences of the Anatomical Distinction Between the Sexes." In *The Standard Edition of the Complete Psychological Works of Sigmund Freud.* Vol. 19. Ed. J. Strachey. 248–58. London.

———. 1931. "Female Sexuality." *Collected Papers* 5:186–97. Also in Ruitenbeek, ed. 88–105.

———. 1933. "Femininity." in *New Introductory Lectures in Psychoanalysis. Standard Edition*, Vol. 22.: 112–35. New York.

———. 1935. *A General Introduction to Psychoanalysis*. Trans. J. Rivière. New York.

———. 1936. *The Problem of Anxiety*. New York.

———. 1963. *Jokes and Their Relation to the Unconscious*. New York.

Friedländer, P. 1966. "Das Proömium von Hesiods Theogonie." In *Hesiod*. Ed. E. Heitsch. *Wege der Forschung* 44:277–94. Darmstadt.

Friedman, S. Stanford. 1981. *Psyche Reborn. The Emergence of H. D.* Bloomington, Indiana.

———. 1990. *Penelope's Web: Gender, Modernity, H.D.'s Fiction*. Cambridge.

Furley, W. D. 1981. *Studies of the Use of Fire in Ancient Religion*. New York.

Gaisser, J. H. 1974. "Noun-Epithet Combinations in the Homeric *Hymn to Demeter*." *Transactions and Proceedings of the American Philological Association* 104:113–27.

Gallop, J. 1987. "Reading the Mother Tongue: Psychoanalytic and Feminist Criticism." *Critical Inquiry* 13:314–29.

Garvie, A. F. 1969. *Aeschylus' Supplices: Play and Trilogy*. Cambridge, England.

Gasparro, G. Sfameni. 1986. *Misteri e culti di Demetra*. Rome.

Geertz, H. 1961. *The Javanese Family: A Study of Kinship and Socialization*. New York.

Gelfant, B. H. 1991. " 'Everybody Steals': Language as Theft in Meridel Le Sueur's *The Girl*." In *Tradition and the Talents of Women*. Ed. Florence Howe. Urbana and Chicago.

Gennep, A. van. 1960. *The Rites of Passage*. Trans. M. B. Vizedom and G. L. Caffee. London (originally published in Paris 1909).

Gilligan C. 1982. *In a Different Voice: Psychological Theory and Women's Development*. Cambridge, Mass.

Gilligan, C., J. V. Ward, and J. M. Taylor. 1988. *Mapping the Moral Domain*. Cambridge, Mass.

Golden, M. 1990. *Children and Childhood in Classical Athens*. Baltimore and London.

Graf, F. 1974. *Eleusis und die orphische Dichtung Athens in vorhellenistischer Zeit*. Berlin.

———. 1991. "Prayer in Magical and Religious Ritual." In *Magika Hiera: Ancient Greek Magic and Religion*. Ed. C. A. Faraone and D. Obbink. 188–213. New York and London.

Graves, R. 1927. *Poems (1914–26)*. London.

Greenacre, P. 1952. "Early Female Sexual Development". In *Trauma, Growth and Personality*. 149–64. New York.

Gubar, S. 1979. "Mother, Maiden and the Marriage of Death: Women Writers and an Ancient Myth." *Women's Studies* 6.3:301–15.

Guntrip, H. 1961. *Personality Structure and Human Interaction: The Developing Synthesis of Psycho-Dynamic Theory*. New York.

Guthrie, W.K.C. 1935. *Orpheus and Greek Religion*. London.

Gutmann, D. 1965. "Women and the Conception of Ego Strength." *Merrrill-Palmer Quarterly of Behavior and Development* 12:229–40.

Hall, N. 1980. *The Moon and the Virgin. Reflections on the Archetypal Feminine.* New York.

Hamilton, R. 1984. "Sources for the Athenian Amphidromia." *Greek, Roman and Byzantine Studies* 25:243–51.

Harper, E. B. 1969. "Fear and the Status of Women." *Southwestern Journal of Anthropology* 25:81–95.

Harrison, G., and D. Obbink. 1986. "Vergil, *Georgics* I 36–39 and the Barcelona Alcestis (P. Barc. Inv. No. 158–61) 62–65: Demeter in the Underworld." *Zeitschrift für Papyrologie und Epigraphik* 63:75–81.

Harrison, J. 1903. *Prolegomena to the Study of Greek Religion.* Cambridge.

Henrichs, A. 1981. "Human Sacrifice in Greek Religion: Three Case Studies." In *Le Sacrifice dans l'antiquité. Entretiens sur l'antiquité classique* 27. Ed. J. Rudhardt and O. Reverdin. 195–242. Geneva.

———. 1983. "Changing Dionysiac Identities." In *Jewish and Christian Self-Definition.* Ed. B. F. Meyer and E. P. Sanders. 137–60. Philadelphia.

Herman, G. 1987. *Ritualized Friendship and the Greek City.* Cambridge.

Hermann, G. 1806. *Homeri hymni et epigrammata.* Leipzig.

Hinds, S. 1987. *The Metamorphosis of Persephone.* Cambridge.

Hine, D. 1972. *The Homeric Hymns and the Battle of the Frogs and Mice.* New York.

Hirsch, M. 1989. *The Mother/Daughter Plot: Narrative, Psychoanalysis, Feminism.* Bloomington and Indianapolis.

Hope, A. D. 1986. *Select Poems.* Manchester.

Humbert, J. 1936. *Homère: Hymnes.* Paris.

Huxley, G. L. 1969. *Greek Epic Poetry from Eumelos to Panyassis.* Cambridge, Mass.

Irigaray, L. 1981. "And one doesn't stir without the other." *Signs* 7.1:60–67.

———. 1985. *Speculum of the Other Woman.* Paris.

———. 1986. "Women, the sacred and money." *Paragraph* 8:6–18.

———. 1991. *Marine Lover of Friedrich Nietzsche.* Trans. G. C. Gill. New York.

Jackson, H. 1892. *Poems by Helen Jackson.* Boston.

Jacobson, E. 1964. *The Self and the Object World.* New York.

Jacoby, F. 1957–. *Die Fragmente der griechischen Historiker.* Leiden.

Jameson, M. 1969. "The Mysteries of Eleusis." *Bulletin of the Philadelphia Association for Psychoanalysis.* 19.3:114–32.

———. 1976. "The Homeric *Hymn to Demeter.*" *Athenaeum* 54:441–46.

———. 1979. Review of Wasson et al. 1978. *Classical World* 73:197–98.

Janko, R. 1981. "The Structure of the Homeric Hymns: A Study in Genre." *Hermes* 109:9–24.

———. 1982. *Homer, Hesiod and the Hymns: Diachronic Development in Epic Diction.* Cambridge.

Janssens, E. 1962. "Poésie et espérances eschatologiques dans l'Hymne homérique à Déméter." In *Religions de Salut, Annales du Centre d'Etude des Religions* 2:38–57. Brussels.

Jay, R. R. 1969. *Javanese Villagers: Social Relations in Rural Modjokuto.* Cambridge, Mass.

Jeanmaire, H. 1939. *Couroi et courètes: Essai sur l'éducation spartiate et sur les rites d'adolescence dans l'antiquité hellénique*. Lille.

Jenkyns, I. 1983. "Is There Life After Marriage? A Study of the Abduction Motif in Vase Paintings of the Athenian Wedding Ceremony." *Bulletin of the Institute of Classical Studies of the University of London* 30:137–45.

Jones, E. 1927. "The Early Development of Female Sexuality." In Ruitenbeek, ed. 21–35.

Joseph, J. 1985. *Persephone*. Newcastle upon Tyne.

Jung, C. G. 1967. "The Psychological Aspects of the Kore." In *Essays on a Science of Mythology: The Myth of the Divine Child*. By C. G. Jung and K. Kerényi. 156–77. Princeton.

Kahane, C. 1988. "Questioning the Maternal Voice." *Genders* 3:82–91.

Kelly, R. 1978. *The Book of Persephone*. New Paltz, New York.

———. 1981. *The Alchemist to Mercury*. Collected and Edited by J. Rasula. Richmond, California.

Kerényi, K. 1967a *Eleusis: The Archetypical Image of Mother and Daughter*. Trans. R. Manheim. Princeton.

———. 1967b. "Korê." In *Essays on a Science of Mythology: The Myth of the Divine Child*. By C. G. Jung and K. Kerényi. 101–55. Princeton.

Kern, O., ed. 1922. *Orphicorum Fragmenta*. Berlin.

Kirk, G. S. 1970. *Myth, Its Meaning and Functions in Ancient and Other Cultures*. Berkeley and Los Angeles.

———. 1974. *The Nature of Greek Myths*. Harmondsworth, U.K.

Kittay, E. F., and D. T. Meyers. 1987. *Women and Moral Theory*. Lanham, Maryland.

Kizer, C. 1961. *The Ungrateful Gardens*. Bloomington, Indiana.

Klein, M., and J. Rivière. 1937 (1964). *Love, Hate and Reparation*. New York.

Kohlberg, L. 1966. "A Cognitive-Developmental Analysis of Children's Sex-Role Concepts and Attitudes." In *The Development of Sex Differences*. Ed. E. E. Maccoby. 82–173. Stanford, California.

Kolb, F. 1977. "Die Bau-, Religions- und Kulturpolitik der Peisistratiden." *Jahrbuch des deutschen Archäologischen Instituts* 92:88–138.

Komarovsky, M. 1962 (1967). *Blue-Collar Marriage*. New York.

Kris, E. 1952. "Ego Development and the Comic." In *Psychoanalytic Explorations in Art*. New York.

Kunitz, S. 1979. *The Poems of Stanley Kunitz*. Boston.

Kurke, L. 1991. *The Traffic in Praise*. Ithaca, N.Y., and London.

Lacey, W. K. 1966. "Homeric HEΔNA and Penelope's KΥΡΙΟΣ." *Journal of Hellenic Studies* 86:55–68.

Lampl-de Groot, J. 1928. "The Evolution of the Oedipus Complex in Women." In R. Fliess, ed. 180–94, and in Ruitenbeek, ed. 36–50.

Latacz, J. 1977. *Kampfparänase, Kampfdarstellung und Kampfwirklichkeit in der Ilias, bei Kallinos und Tyrtaios*. Zetemata 66. Munich.

Leacock, E. 1977. "The Dawn of Woman: Prehistoric Times." In *Becoming Visible: Women in European History*. Ed. R. Bridenthal and C. Koonz. 13–35. Boston.

Leduc, C. 1992. "Marriage in Ancient Greece." In *The History of Women*. Ed. P. Schmitt-Pantel. 233–94. Cambridge, Mass.

Lenz, L. 1975. *Der homerische Aphroditehymnus und die Aristie des Aineias in der Ilias*. Bonn.

Le Sueur, M. 1978. *The Girl*. Minneapolis.

——. 1982. *Ripening. Selected Work, 1927–80. Meridel le Sueur*. Ed. E. Hedges. New York.

LeVine, R. A. 1971a. "The Psychoanalytic Study of Lives in Natural Social Settings." *Human Development* 14:100–109.

——. 1971b. "Re-thinking Psychoanalytic Anthropology." Paper presented at the Institute on Psychoanalytic Anthropology, 70th Annual Meeting of the American Anthropological Association. New York.

Levy, G. R. 1953. *The Sword from the Rock*. London.

Lincoln, B. 1979. "The Rape of Persephone: A Greek Scenario of Women's Initiation." *Harvard Theological Review* 72:223–35.

Linder, R. 1984. *Der Raub der Persephone in der antiken Kunst*. Würzburg.

Lloyd-Jones, H. 1983. "Artemis and Iphigeneia." *Journal of Hellenic Studies* 103:87–102.

Lloyd-Jones, H. and Parsons, P. 1983. *Supplementum Hellenisticum*. Berlin.

Loraux, N. 1978. "Sur la race des femmes at quelques-unes de ses tribus." *Arethusa* 11:43–87.

——. 1990. *Les Mères en deuil*. Paris.

Lord, A. B. 1960. *The Singer of Tales*. Cambridge, Massachusetts.

*Lord, M. L. 1967. "Withdrawal and Return: An Epic Story Pattern in the Homeric *Hymn to Demeter*." *Classical Journal* 62:241–48.

Low, N. 1982. "The Relationship of Adult Daughters to Their Mothers." *Parent Counseling Association of New England* 2:108–35.

——. 1984. "Mother-Daughter Relationships: The Lasting Ties." *Radcliffe Quarterly*. December:1–4.

Lowell, R. 1951 (1946). *The Mills of the Kavanaughs*. New York.

Luppe, W. 1985. "Hekate als 'Amme' der Persephone." *Zeitschrift für Papyrologie und Epigraphik* 58:34.

Mahler, M. 1968. *On Human Symbiosis and the Vicissitudes of Individuation*. New York.

——. 1973. "On the First Three Phases of the Separation-Individuation Process." *Journal of the American Psychoanalytic Association* 21:135–54.

Malten, L. 1909. "Altorphische Demetersage." *Archiv für Religionswissenschaft* 12:417–46.

Manning, F. 1910. *Poems*. London.

Martin, L. H. 1986. "Those Elusive Eleusinian Mystery Shows." *Helios* 13.1:17–32.

Martin, P. 1970. *Voice Unaccompanied*. Canberra.

Masters, E. L. 1935. *Invisible Landscapes*. New York.

May, R. 1980. *Sex and Fantasy*. New York and London.

Mayerson, P. 1971. *Classical Mythology in Literature, Art, and Music*. Waltham, Massachusetts.

McClelland, D. C. 1975. *Power: The Inner Experience*. New York.

Mead, M. 1935 (1963). *Sex and Temperament in Three Primitive Societies*. New York.

———. 1949 (1967). *Male and Female: A Study of Sexes in a Changing World*. New York.

Méautis, G. 1959. *Les Dieux de la Grèce et les Mystères d'Eleusis*. Paris.

Millay, E. St. Vincent. 1956. *Collected Poems*. New York.

Miller, A. M. 1985. *From Delos to Delphi: A Literary Study of the Homeric Hymn to Apollo*. Leiden.

Miller, J. B., ed. 1973. *Psychoanalysis and Women*. Baltimore.

Millman, M. 1972. "Tragedy and Exchange: Metaphoric Understandings of Interpersonal Relationships." Diss. Brandeis University.

Minton, W. W. 1970. "The Proem-Hymn of Hesiod's *Theogony*." *Transactions and Proceedings of the American Philological Association* 101:357–77.

Minturn, L., and J. T. Hitchcock. 1963. "The Rajputs of Khalapur, India," In *Six Cultures: Studies in Child Rearing*. Ed. B. B. Whiting. New York.

Mitscherlich, A. 1963 (1970). *Society Without the Father*. New York.

Monro, D. B., and T. W. Allen, eds. 1912–20. *Homeri Opera*. 5 vols. Oxford.

Morris, I. 1986. "The Use and Abuse of Homer." *Classical Antiquity* 5:81–138.

———. 1987. *Burial and Ancient Society*. Cambridge.

Mylonas, G. 1942. *The Hymn to Demeter and Her Sanctuary at Eleusis*. Washington University Studies n.s. Language and Literature Studies. St. Louis.

———. 1972 (1961). *Eleusis and the Eleusinian Mysteries*. Princeton.

Myres, J. L. 1938. "Persephone and the Pomegranate (*H. Dem.* 372–74)." *Classical Review* 53:51–52.

Nagler, M. 1974. *Spontaneity and Tradition*. Berkeley and Los Angeles.

Nagy, G. 1979. *The Best of the Achaeans*. Baltimore.

———. 1982. "Hesiod." In *Ancient Writers*. Ed. T. J. Luce. 43–78. New York.

———. 1990a. *Greek Mythology and Poetics*. Ithaca, N.Y.

———. 1990b. *Pindar's Homer*. Baltimore and London.

Nauck, A. 1964. *Tragicorum Graecorum Fragmenta*. Supplement by B. Snell. Hildesheim.

Neumann, E. 1956. *Amor and Psyche: The Psychic Development of the Feminine, A Commentary on a Tale by Apuleius*. Trans. R. Manheim. Princeton.

———. 1974 *The Great Mother: An Analysis of the Archetype*. Trans. R. Manheim. Princeton. (Originally published in German 1963)

Newman, F., ed. 1978. *Cameos: 12 Small Press Women Poets*. Trumansburg, New York.

Nilsson, M. P. 1935. "Die eleusinischen Gottheiten." *Archiv für Religionswissenschaft* 32:79–141.

———. 1941. *Geschichte der Griechischen Religion*. Vol. I. Munich.

———. 1951–52. *Opuscula Selecta*. 2 vols. Lund.

Nock, A. D. 1933. *Conversion*. Oxford.

Notopoulos, J. A. 1962. "The Homeric Hymns as Oral Poetry." *American Journal of Philology* 83:337–68.

———. 1964. "Studies in Early Greek Oral Poetry." *Harvard Studies in Classical Philology* 68:1–77.

O'Brien, A., C. Rasmussen, and C. Costello, eds. 1981. *Womanblood: Portraits of Women in Poetry and Prose*. San Anselmo, California.

Olender, M. 1989. "Aspects of Baubo: Ancient Texts and Contexts." Trans. R. Lamberton. In *Before Sexuality: The Construction of Erotic Experience in the Ancient Greek World*. Ed. D. M. Halperin, J. J. Winkler, and F. I. Zeitlin. 83–113. Princeton. (Originally published in French, 1985)

Ortner, S. B. 1974. "Is Female to Male as Nature Is to Culture?" In *Women, Culture, and Society*. Ed. M. Z. Rosaldo and L. Lamphere. 67–88. Stanford, California.

Osborne, R. G. 1985. *Demos: The Discovery of Classical Attika*. Cambridge.

———. 1989. "A Crisis in Archaeological History? The Seventh Century in Attica." *Annual of the British School at Athens* 84:297–322.

———. 1991. "Archaeology, the Salaminioi and the Politics of Sacred Space in Archaic Attica." Paper delivered at the 1991 Archaeological Institute of America Meetings, Chicago.

Ostriker, A. S. 1986. *Stealing the Language: The Emergence of Women's Poetry in America*. Boston.

Padgug, R. 1972. "Eleusis and the Union of Attika." *Greek, Roman and Byzantine Studies* 13:135–50.

Page, D. 1955 (rep. 1975). *Sappho and Alcaeus*. Oxford.

———. 1962. *Poetae melici graeci*. Oxford. = PMG

———. 1970 (1941). *Select Papyri*. Vol. 3. Cambridge, Mass. = GLP

Parke, H. W. 1977. *Festivals of the Athenians*. Ithaca, N.Y.

Parker, R. 1983. *Miasma*. Oxford.

———. 1988. "Demeter, Dionysus and the Spartan Pantheon." In *Early Greek Cult Practice*. Ed. R. Hägg, N. Marinatos, and G. C. Nordquist. 99–104. Stockholm.

———. 1989. "Dionysus at Agrai." *Liverpool Classical Monthly* 14.10:154–55.

———. 1991. "The *Hymn to Demeter* and the Homeric Hymns." *Greece and Rome* 38:1–17.

Parsons, T. 1964. *Social Structure and Personality*. New York.

Parsons, T. and R. F. Bales. 1955. *Family, Socialization and Interaction Process*. New York.

Pater, W. 1911. *Greek Studies*. London.

Peek, W. 1955. *Griechische Vers-Inschriften*. Berlin.

Pembroke, S. 1965. "Last of the Matriarchs: A Study in the Inscriptions of Lycia." *Journal of the Economic and Social History of the Orient* 8.3:217–47.

Peradotto, J. 1977. Introduction to *Arethusa. Special Issue on Classical Literature and Contemporary Literary Theory* 10.1:5–6.

Peschlow-Bindokat, A. 1972. "Demeter und Persephone in der attischen Kunst des 6. bis 4 Jahrhunderts v. Chr. Mit 54 Abbildungen." *Jahrbuch des deutschen Archäologischen Instituts* 87:60–157.

Pfeiffer, R. 1949–53. *Callimachus*. Oxford.

Piccaluga, G. 1966. "*Ta Pherephattês anthologia*." *Maia* 18:232–53.

Plath, S. 1960 (rep. 1981). *The Collected Poems: Sylvia Plath*. Ed. Ted Hughes. New York.

Pound, E. 1938 (rep. 1968). *Guide to Kulchur*. New York.

Pritchard, J. B. 1950. 3d ed. 1969. *Ancient Near Eastern Texts Relating to the Old Testament*. Princeton.

Pritchett, W. K. 1985. *The Greek State at War*. Part 5. Berkeley.

Prückner, H. 1968. *Die lokrischen Tonreliefs*. Mainz.

Rabe, H. 1906 (rep. Stuttgart 1971). *Scholia in Lucianum*. Leipzig.

Race, W. H. 1982. "Aspects of Rhetoric and Form in Greek Hymns." *Greek, Roman and Byzantine Studies* 23:5–14.

Radt, S. 1977. *Tragicorum Graecorum Fragmenta*. Vol. 4. Göttingen.

Raine, K. 1956. *Collected Poems*. New York.

Ramnoux, C. 1959. *Mythologie ou la famille olympienne*. Paris.

Redfield, J. 1982. "Notes on the Greek Wedding." *Arethusa* 15. 1–2:181–202.

Reinach, S. 1912. "Le rire ritual." In his *Cultes, mythes et religions*, vol. 4:109–29. Paris.

Reitzenstein, R. 1927. *Die hellenistischen Mysterienreligionen nach ihren Grundegedanken und Wirkungen*. Leipzig and Berlin. Rep. Darmstadt 1956.

Rich, A. 1976. *Of Woman Born: Motherhood as Experience and Institution*. New York.

Richardson, N. J. 1974. *The Homeric Hymn to Demeter*. Oxford.

———. 1978. Review of Scarpi 1976. *Numen* 25. Fasc. 2:187–89.

Ricks, C. 1969. *The Poems of Tennyson*. New York.

Roberts, M. 1986. *The Mirror of the Mother*. London.

Rohde, E. 1898. *Psyche: Seelencult und Unsterblichkeitsglaube der Griechen*. 2d edition. Freiburg.

———. 1925. *Psyche*. Trans. W. B. Hillis. London.

Rosaldo, M. Z. 1974. "Woman, Culture, and Society, a Theoretical Overview." In *Women, Culture, and Society*. Ed. M. Z. Rosaldo and L. Lamphere. 17–42. Stanford, California.

Roscher, W. H., ed. 1884–1937. *Ausführliches Lexikon der griechischen und römischen mythologie*. 6 vols. Leipzig.

Rose, G. 1967. "The Quest of Telemachus." *Transactions and Proceedings of the American Philological Association* 98:391–98.

Rose, H. J. 1959. *A Handbook of Greek Mythology*. New York.

Roussel, P. 1930. "L'Initiation prélable et le symbole éleusininien." *Bulletin de Correspondance Hellénique* 54:51–74.

Rubin, G. 1975. "The Traffic in Women: Notes on the 'Political Economy' of Sex." In *Towards an Anthropology of Women*. Ed. R. R. Reiter. 157–210. New York and London.

*Rubin, N., and H. Deal. 1980. "Some Functions of the Demophon Episode in the Homeric *Hymn to Demeter*." *Quaderni Urbinati di Cultura Classica* 34:7–21.

Ruck, C. 1976. "On the Sacred Names of Iamos and Ion." *Classical Journal* 71:235–52.

Rudhardt, J. 1958. *Notions fondamentales de la pensée religieuse et actes constitutifs du culte dans la Grèce classique*. Geneva.

———. 1970. "Les Mythes grecs relatifs à l'instauration du sacrifice: Les Roles corrélatifs de Prométhée et de son fils Deucalion." *Museum Helveticum* 27:1–15.

*———. 1978. Trans. Lavinia Lorch and Helene Foley. "A propos de l'hymne homérique à Déméter." *Museum Helveticum* 35, Fasc. 1:1–17.

Ruitenbeek, H. M., ed. 1966. *Psychoanalysis and Female Sexuality*. New Haven.

Rumens, C. 1988. *The Greening of the Snow Beach*. Newcastle upon Tyne.

Sabbatucci, D. 1965. *Saggio sul misticismo greco*. Rome.

Sacks, K. 1974. "Engels Revisited: Women, the Organization of Production, and

Private Property." In *Women, Culture, and Society*. Ed. M. Z. Rosaldo and L. Lamphere. 207–22. Stanford, California.

Saintillan, D. 1986. "Fécondité, mort et mariage: A propòs des mythes d'Ouranos et Déméter." In *Mort et fécondité dans les mythologies*. Ed. F. Jouan. Actes du colloque de Potiers, 13–14 mai. 51–70.

Sale, W. 1975. "The Temple Legends of the Arkteia." *Rheinisches Museum* 118:265–84.

Sargent, T. 1973. *The Homeric Hymns*. New York.

Scarborough, J. 1991. "The Pharmacology of Sacred Plants, Herbs and Roots." In *Magika Hiera: Ancient Greek Magic and Religion*. Ed. C. A. Faraone and D. Obbink. 138–74. New York and Oxford.

Scarpi, P. 1976. *Letture sulla religione classica: L'inno omerico a Demeter*. Florence.

Schmid, W., and O. Stählin. 1929. *Geschichte der griechischen Literatur*. Volume 1, part 1, by W. Schmid. Munich.

Schober, A. 1988. "Philodemi *De Pietate* pars prior." *Cronache Ercolanesi*:67–125.

Schwabl, H. 1970. "Hesiodos" (*Paulys Real-Encyclopädie der classischen Altertumswissenschaft*) Suppl. 12:434–86. Stuttgart.

Schwartz, G. 1987. *Triptolemus. Grazer Beiträge*, Supp. II.

Seaford. R. 1987. "The Tragic Wedding." *Journal of Hellenic Studies* 107:106–30.

———. 1988. "The Eleventh Ode of Bacchylides: Hera, Artemis and the Absence of Dionysus." *Journal of Hellenic Studies* 108:118–36.

———. 1990. "The Imprisonment of Women in Greek Tragedy." *Journal of Hellenic Studies* 110:76–90.

Segal, C. 1974. "The Homeric Hymn to Aphrodite: A Structuralist Approach." *Classical World* 67:205–12.

———. 1981. "Orality, Repetition and Formulaic Artistry in the Homeric 'Hymn to Demeter.'" In *I poemi epici non omerici e la tradizione orale*. Ed. C. Brillante, M. Cantilena, and C. O. Pavese. 107–60. Padua.

Shapiro, H. A. 1989. *Art and Cult Under the Tyrants in Athens*. Mainz am Rhein.

Sheppard, J. T. 1922. *The Pattern of the Iliad*. London.

Siegel, J. T. 1969. *The Rope of God*. Berkeley.

Slater, P. E. 1961. "Toward a Dualistic Theory of Identification." *Merrill-Palmer Quarterly of Behavior and Development* 7:113–26.

———. 1968. *The Glory of Hera: Greek Mythology and the Greek Family*. Boston.

———. 1970. *The Pursuit of Loneliness: American Culture at the Breaking Point*. Boston.

Slatkin, L. 1986. "The Wrath of Thetis." *Transactions and Proceedings of the American Philological Association* 116:1–24.

———. 1991. *The Power of Thetis: Allusion and Interpretation in the Iliad*. Berkeley and Los Angeles.

Smith, P. M. *Nursling of Mortality: A Study of the Homeric Hymn to Aphrodite. Studien zur klassischen Philologie* 3. Frankfurt.

Snell, B. 1934. *Bacchylides*. Teubner. Leipzig.

———. 1964. *Pindari Carmina cum fragmentis*. 2 vols. Teubner. Leipzig.

Snyder, J. 1989. *The Woman and the Lyre: Women Writers in Greece and Rome*. Carbondale, Illinois.

Sokolowski, F., ed. 1962. *Lois sacrées des cités grecques, supplément*. Paris.

―――. 1969. *Lois sacrées des cités grecques*. Paris.

Sourvinou-Inwood, C. 1988. *Studies in Girls' Transitions*. Athens.

―――. 1991. *'Reading' Greek Culture: Texts and Images, Rituals and Myths*. Oxford.

Sowa, C. A. 1984. *Traditional Themes and the Homeric Hymns*. Chicago.

Spitz, E. H. 1989. "Psychoanalysis and the Legacies of Antiquity." In *Freud and Art: His Personal Collection of Antiquities*. Ed. L. Gamwell and R. Wells. 153–71. New York.

―――. 1990. "Mothers and Daughters: Ancient and Modern Myths." *The Journal of Aesthetics and Art Criticism* 48:411–20.

Spretnak, C. 1978. *Lost Goddesses of Early Greece*. Boston.

Starhawk. 1989. *The Spiral Dance*. San Francisco.

Stedman, E. C. 1900. *An American Anthology 1787–1900*. Cambridge, Mass.

Stern, G. B. 1928. *Debonair. The Story of Persephone*. New York.

Stratford, W., ed. 1988. *Many Voices: Many Lands. Anthology of Poetry I and II*. Orinda, Ca.

Strouse, J., ed. 1974. *Women and Analysis*. 1974.

Suter, A. 1991. "*Homophrona thumon echousai*: Mothers and Daughters in the *Homeric Hymn to Demeter*." *New England Classical Newsletter and Journal* 19.2:13–15.

Sutton, R. 1981. *The Interaction Between Men and Women Portrayed on Attic Red-Figure Pottery*. Diss. University of North Carolina, Chapel Hill.

Swinburne, A. C. 1924–27. *Swinburne's Collected Poetical Works*. Vol I. New York and London.

Szepes, E. 1975. "Trinities in the Homeric Demeter-Hymn." *Annales Universitatis Budapestinensis de Rolando Eötvös nominatae, sectio classica* 3:23–38.

Tanner, N. 1974. "Matrifocality in Indonesia and Africa and Among Black Americans." In *Women, Culture, and Society*. Ed. M. Z. Rosaldo and L. Lamphere. 129–56. Stanford, California.

Tarn, N. 1964. *Old Savage/Young City*. London

―――. 1974. *The Persephones*. Santa Barbara, California.

Tax, M. 1970. *Woman and Her Mind: The Story of Daily Life*. Boston.

Thalmann, W. G. 1984. *Conventions of Form and Thought in Early Greek Epic Poetry*. Baltimore.

Thompson, C. 1943. " 'Penis Envy' in Women." In Ruitenbeek, ed. 246–51.

Thomson, G. 1938. *The Oresteia*. 2 vols. Cambridge (includes work of W. G. Headlam).

―――. 1972. *Aeschylus and Athens*. New York.

Tod, M. N. 1933–48. *A Selection of Greek Historical Inscriptions*. 2 vols. Oxford.

Tullos, R., D. Keller, and A. Ostriker. 1980. *US1: An Anthology. The Contemporary Writing from New Jersey*. Union City, N.J.

Turner, J. 1983. *Hiereiai: Acquisition of Feminine Priesthoods in Ancient Greece*. Diss. University of Santa Barbara.

Turner, V. 1969. *The Ritual Process*. London.

Van Nortwick, T. "The Artifice of Eternity: A Literary Study of the Major Homeric Hymns." Unpublished ms., Oberlin College.

Vernant, J.-P., ed. 1968. *Problèmes de la guerre en Grèce ancienne*. Paris.

————. 1980. *Myth and Society in Ancient Greece*. Atlantic Highlands, N.J. (Originally published in Paris 1974)

Vian, F. 1987. *Les Argonautiques orphiques*. Paris.

Walton, F. 1952. "Athens, Eleusis and the Homeric *Hymn to Demeter*." *Harvard Theological Review* 45:105–14.

Wasson, G. R., A. Hoffmann, and C.A.P. Ruck. 1978. *The Road to Eleusis. Unveiling the Secret of the Mysteries*. New York and London.

Watkins, C. 1977. "On *Menis*." *Indo-European Studies* 1:694–95.

Wehrli, F. 1934. "Die Mysterien von Eleusis." *Archiv für Religionswissenschaft* 31:77–104.

Weiss, T. and R. Weiss, eds. 1987. *Quarterly Review of Literature. Poetry Series VIII*. Princeton.

Wellesley, D. 1955. *Early Light. Collected Poems of Dorothy Wellesley*. London.

West, M. L. 1966. *Hesiod Theogony*. Oxford.

————. 1975. "Zum neuen Goldplättchen aus Hipponion." *Zeitschrift für Papyrologie* 18:229–36.

————. 1983. *The Orphic Poems*. Oxford.

White, R. 1975. *The Interpretation of Dreams by Artemidorus*. Park Ridge, N.J.

Whiting, J.W.M. 1959 (1967). "Sorcery, Sin, and the Superego: A Cross-Cultural Study of Some Mechanisms of Social Control." In *Cross-Cultural Approaches: Readings in Comparative Research*. Ed. C. S. Ford. New Haven. 147–68.

Whiting, J.W.M., R. Kluckhohn, and A. Anthony. 1958. "The Function of Male Initiation Rites at Puberty." In *Readings in Social Psychology*. Ed. E. E. Maccoby, T. M. Newcomb, and E. L. Hartley. New York.

Whitman, C. H. 1958. *Homer and the Heroic Tradition*. Cambridge, Mass.

Willard, N. 1974. *Carpenter of the Sun*. New York.

Williams, W. C. 1967 (1921). *Kora in Hell. Improvisations*. San Francisco.

Willing, Mrs. C. 1881. *Persephone and Other Poems*. Philadelphia.

Winch, R. F. 1962. *Identification and Its Familial Determinants*. New York.

Winkler, J. 1990. *The Constraints of Desire*. New York and London.

Wolff, H. J. 1944. "Marriage Law and Family Organization in Ancient Athens." *Traditio* 2:43–95.

Woolger, J. B. and R. J. Woolger. 1987. *The Goddess Within: A Guide to the Eternal Myths That Shape Women's Lives*. New York.

Young, M., and P. Willmott. 1957 (1966). *Family and Kinship in East London*. London.

Yount, N.J.S. 1978. "America: Song We Sang Without Knowing—Meridel Le Sueur's America." Diss. University of Minnesota. University Microfilms, Ann Arbor 1983.

Zeitlin, F. I. 1978. "The Dynamics of Misogyny: Myth and Mythmaking in the *Oresteia*." *Arethusa* 11:149–84.

————. 1982. "Cultic Models of the Female: Rites of Dionysus and Demeter." *Arethusa* 15.1–2:129–57.

Zuntz, G. 1971. *Persephone: Three Essays on Religion and Thought in Magna Graecia*. Oxford.

BIBLIOGRAPHICAL ADDENDUM

NOTE: The following entries are some additional nineteenth- and twentieth-century poetry and drama in English influenced by the Demeter/Persephone myth.

Abbott, K. 1989. "Persephone." In *American Poetry Since 1970: Up Late*, 2nd edition. Ed. A. Codrescu. New York.

Atwood, M. E. 1987. "Letter to Persephone." In *Selected Poems II: Poems Selected and New 1976–1986*. Boston.

Baring, M. 1925. "Proserpine: A Masque." In *Collected Poems*. London.

Binyon, R. L. 1890. *Persephone*. Oxford.

Carpenter, E. 1873. "Persephone." In *Narcissus and Other Poems*. London.

Cawein, J. M. 1887. "Demeter" and "Persephone." In *Poems of Mystery and of Myth and Romance*. Boston.

———. 1894. "Demeter" and "Persephone." In *Blooms of the Berry*. Louisville, Kentucky.

———. 1894. "Eleusinian." In *Intimations of the Beautiful*. New York.

de Tabley, Lord J. 1860. "Proserpine at Enna." In *Ballads and Metrical Sketches*. London.

———. 1901. "An Eleusinian Chant." In *Orpheus in Thrace and Other Poems*. London.

De Vere, A. T. 1884. "The Search After Persephone." In *Poetical Works*. London.

Dove, R. 1991. "Persephone, Falling" and "Persephone Underground." In *New American Poets of the 90's*. Ed. J. Myers and R. Weingarten. Boston.

———. 1995. *Mother Love: Poems*. New York.

Erskine, J. 1917. "The Sons of Metaneira." In *The Shadowed Hour*. New York.

Farley, J. 1970. "Kore to Co-ed." In *Figure and Field*. Durham, N.C.

Ficke, A. D. 1907. "Demeter." In *From the Isles. A Series of Songs Out of Greece*. Norwich, England.

Fields, A. A. 1877. *The Return of Persephone, a Dramatic Sketch*. Privately printed, Cambridge, Mass.

Getty, S. 1996. "A Winter's Tale." In *The Land of Milk and Honey*. Columbia, S.C.

Gunn, T. 1994. "The Goddess." In *Collected Poems*. New York.

Guthrie, W. N. 1900. "The Vision of Demeter." In *Songs of American Destiny: A Vision of New Hellas*. Cincinnati.

Hill, E. D. 1918. "Demeter." In *Demeter and Other Poems*. Oxford.

Ingelow, J. 1867. "Persephone." In *Poems*. Boston.

Lattimore, R. 1972. "Demeter in the Fields." In *Three Decades*. New York.

Ledoux, L. V. 1914. "Persephone: A Masque." In *Shadow of Aetna*. New York and London.

———. 1916. *The Story of Eleusis: A Lyrical Drama*. New York.

Ledwidge, F. 1919. "The Departure of Persephone." In *The Complete Poems of Francis Ledwidge*. London.

Manning, F. 1910. "Demeter Mourning." In *Eidola*. London.

Ollier, E. 1867. "Eleusinia" and "Proserpina in the Shades." In *Poems from Greek Mythology*. London.

Palmer, M. 1984. "Documentation." In *Nineteen New American Poets of the Golden Gate*. Ed. P. Dow. New York.

Perkins, W. R. 1890. *Eleusis: A Narrative Poem*. Privately printed, Chicago.

Pitter, R. 1931. *Persephone in Hades*. Privately printed, New York.

Procter, B. W. ("Barry Cornwall") 1822. "The Rape of Proserpine." In *The Poetical Works of Barry Cornwall*. London.

Rossetti, D. G. 1903. "Proserpina." In *Complete Poetical Works*. Ed. W. M. Rossetti. Boston.

Scheck, L. 1990. "Persephone to Demeter" and "Persephone." In *Io at Night*. New York.

Stoddard, R. H. 1857. "The Search for Persephone." In *Songs of Summer*. Boston.

———. 1880. "The Search for Persephone. Book II." In *The Poems of Richard Henry Stoddard*. New York.

Stringer, A.J.A. 1903. "Persephone at Enna." In *Hephaestus and Other Poems*. Toronto.

Thomas, E. M. 1885. "Demeter's Search" and "Persephone." In *A New Year's Masque*. New York.

Whitman, S. H. 1879. "Proserpine to Pluto in Hades." In *Poems*. Boston.

Woodbury, G. W. 1914. "Demeter" and "Persephone." In *Flight and Other Poems*. New York.

INDEX LOCORUM

GENERAL INDEX